Also from Georgetown University Press

The Image of the Enemy:
Intelligence Analysis of Adversaries since 1945
Paul Maddrell, editor

Intelligence Elsewhere:
Spies and Espionage outside the Anglosphere
Philip H. J. Davies and Kristian C. Gustafson, editors

Soviet Leaders and Intelligence:
Assessing the American Adversary during the Cold War
Raymond L. Garthoff

SPY CHIEFS

Volume 2

INTELLIGENCE LEADERS
in Europe, the Middle East, and Asia

PAUL MADDRELL

CHRISTOPHER MORAN

IOANNA IORDANOU

MARK STOUT

Editors

Foreword by
SIR RICHARD DEARLOVE,
former chief of the
Secret Intelligence Service
of the United Kingdom

GEORGETOWN UNIVERSITY PRESS / WASHINGTON, DC

Library of Congress Cataloging-in-Publication Data
Names: Moran, Christopher R., editor. | Stout, Mark, 1964– editor. | Iordanou, Ioanna, editor. | Maddrell, Paul, editor.
Title: Spy chiefs / Christopher Moran, Mark Stout, Ioanna Iordanou and Paul Maddrell, editors.
Description: Washington, DC : Georgetown University Press, 2018. | Includes bibliographical references and index. | This book grew out of two academic meetings. The first was a panel, organized by Paul Maddrell, on Intelligence Leaders in International Relations at the 55th annual convention of the International Studies Association in Toronto, Canada, in March 2014. This led to a second, a conference entitled Spy Chiefs: Intelligence Leaders in History, Culture and International Relations, which was organized by Christopher Moran and his colleagues at Warwick University and held at the Palazzo Pesaro Papafava in Venice, Italy, in May of that year. The purpose of these meetings was to discuss the leadership of intelligence and security agencies; what good leadership of such agencies is and what impact it has had on the performance of the agencies concerned — Preface to volume 1. | Description based on print version record and CIP data provided by publisher; resource not viewed.
Identifiers: LCCN 2017008735 (print) | LCCN 2017012716 (ebook) | ISBN 9781626165182 (volume 1 : hc : alk. paper) | ISBN 9781626165199 (volume 1 : pb : alk. paper) | ISBN 9781626165205 (volume 1 : eb) | ISBN 9781626165212 (volume 2 : hc : alk. paper) | ISBN 9781626165229 (volume 2 : pb : alk. paper) | ISBN 9781626165236 (volume 2 : eb)
Subjects: LCSH: Intelligence service—Congresses. | Intelligence service—History—Congresses. | Espionage—Congresses. | Espionage—History—Congresses. | International relations—Congresses. | Leadership—Case studies—Congresses.
Classification: LCC JF1525.I6 (ebook) | LCC JF1525.I6 S635 2018 (print) | DDC 327.12092/2—dc23
LC record available at https://lccn.loc.gov/2017008735

This book is dedicated to the memory of one of its contributors,

Dr. Chikara Hashimoto (1975–2016),

a dedicated scholar with a passion for the study of intelligence

and a good and delightful man.

May he rest in peace.

CONTENTS

FOREWORD

The characteristics of leadership are elusive, but we seem to know instinctively when we see it done well or badly. Explaining leadership is always difficult. Great leadership is a complex mix of personality, innate capability, favorable circumstances, and the right opportunities. Great historical leaders largely defy categorization. They are "one-offs" who find themselves in the right place at the right time, and they have probably sown as much tragedy in the world as they have brought about beneficial outcomes. At a more prosaic level we are all thoroughly familiar with good and bad leadership in most aspects of our lives that depend on the performance of a team or group, but explaining the chemistry of the group or how the individuals that make up the group interact and allow themselves to be led often defies logical analysis.

The leadership of intelligence and security is a particularly esoteric and challenging area of study, and equally elusive. This is because the services themselves vary enormously in role and function between different countries and the place that they occupy in government. It is therefore essential to make a fundamental distinction between the leadership of these services in democratic states that are fully accountable politically and legally, and in authoritarian states or dictatorships where they are usually an intimate part of the structure of power and repression, and operate without any of the legal and political controls that we take for granted in most Western liberal democracies. Any direct comparison, therefore, between the responsibilities and performance of, for example, the director of the CIA and his Russian opposite number, the director of the SVR, would be invidious. Perhaps a small amount of common ground might be found in how successful each service is in collecting intelligence on major requirements, but the cultural gulf between them is in reality too wide to be bridged. The essays in this collection do bring out this key difference.

I will therefore outline the special problems, not well understood outside the intelligence community, that pertain to leadership of an intelligence service in Western liberal democracies in the twenty-first century. This, I hope, will provide scholars with a template for making more informed judgments about this area of research.

Complete intelligence services (that is, services that collect and analyze intelligence and have a full range of operational capabilities) are always highly compartmentalized with strict need-to-know procedures. The existence of successful operations, especially the identity of sources, will be carefully hidden except from those staff who really do need to know about them. Even very senior officers will not know about them; only at the very top will there be a complete picture of the service's activities. The leadership cannot, therefore, build a narrative around the organization's current success. This means that a key ingredient is necessarily lacking when it comes to building a team, motivating its members, and promoting its performance. This situation is probably unique to intelligence services and underlines the day-to-day challenge of running an organization whose currency is its ability to keep its biggest successes completely secret for as long as they remain valuable. Imagine leading a business that could not use its success to promote itself and where anything that goes wrong risks attracting an excessive amount of media attention. Failures are widely broadcast and endlessly discussed, successes are very seldom even heard about. The leadership must therefore build a cohesive and positive service culture using other means—for example, by emphasizing a sense of specialness and exclusivity through pride in belonging to an elite organization, through judicious use of service history (that is, past casework that can be discussed), and insistence on the very highest professional standards.

The leader therefore most likely to be able to build esprit de corps will need to have high levels of professional credibility with his or her staff, especially those who are on or close to the front lines of intelligence collection. Someone whom staff respect because they know he or she has done the same job successfully is likely to be able to achieve this rather better than someone who is seen as being without direct experience of intelligence work. Unfortunately, it is not uncommon for the heads of some Western services to be appointed politically from outside the intelligence community. Their deficit of professional experience puts them at a severe disadvantage and means that while they enjoy excellent political links, they simply run their services without providing professional leadership. The burden to provide this, therefore, probably falls on their professional deputies. This is a workable arrangement, but the head of service becomes a rather detached figure whose role is to represent the service's interest at the political level; Italy, Spain, and France have all at times followed this type of arrangement, and the performance of their services has been mediocre when they have done so.

Herein lies the dilemma for those who lead intelligence and security services in today's complicated threat environment. How do you balance the problems of running an operational service with the head of service's need to connect his organization effectively to the government machine at the highest level, especially during times of crisis? Professional heads of service will have spent a whole career preparing to lead the service like a general in the military with many years of active service. However, operating on the political stage is probably not within their orbit of experience and something for which they have had no training and little preparation. Personally, I found the step up from the deputy slot and to being the chief of the Secret Intelligence Service an enormous one. Few of my immediate colleagues had any real concept of what operating at the very top level was like, particularly in the febrile political atmosphere that followed the terrorist attacks of September 11, 2001, on New York and Washington, DC. There was also the added difficulty that the then prime minister, Tony Blair, wanted his intelligence chief at his side (for example, during extensive overseas travel and meetings with foreign leaders), while the chief also had a service to run at a time when the pressure on the service to produce intelligence on the crisis and its aftermath was immense. There is, of course, no ideal answer to the question of how best to combine these very different but equally important aspects to the position, but successful leadership of a modern intelligence service would imply the ability to meet both the political expectations and the demands of providing clear and decisive operational leadership as well. This is the measure against which successful leadership should best be judged. Many heads of service were good at one or the other. Few have demonstrated equal success at both.

My final point is to pose the question of why nonprofessional heads of service now should ever be appointed to the position. It would never occur to any government to appoint a nonmilitary person to command its army, and the parallel with intelligence and security services is today entirely valid. Their work has become central in meeting the terrorist and other contemporary threats; indeed, in many countries the intelligence and security budget is growing at the expense of defense spending, and their operations have become immensely more complicated because they combine human and technical intelligence resources and because of the necessity to work cooperatively across a range of national and international partnerships. Leading this type of effort effectively requires years of careful preparation. However, the intelligence profession remains a relatively narrow one; the choice of candidates for leadership is often limited, and the top individuals are often not known outside their specialized roles. It is therefore inevitable that politicians will sometimes want to impose their trusted nominees, especially if they have anxieties about political control of the services and they identify the leadership they inherit as being more attached to their opponents. Therefore, we will continue to see unqualified heads of service appointed to control those services rather than to lead them, though this is more likely to happen in countries that have weak constitutional arrangements for accommodating their intelligence and security organization within the government.

However, the intelligence services that have a strong professional ethos and are well established within their governments will continue to be the best-performing ones because they will continue to be led largely by seasoned professionals who can inspire their staff and who have also learned how to represent their services effectively in the high-level political environment in which any head of service must also be able to move with ease and confidence.

Sir Richard Dearlove, KCMG, OBE
Chief of the Secret Intelligence Service of the United Kingdom, 1999–2004
Seal Harbor, Maine, August 2016

ABBREVIATIONS

APN/IWF   Aussenpolitischer Nachrichtendienst/Institut für Wirtschaftswissen-
          schaftliche Forschung (Foreign Political Intelligence Service of East
          Germany
ÁVH   Államvédelmi Hatóság (State Protection Authority, of Hungary)
BfV   Bundesamt für Verfassungsschutz (Federal Office for the Protection
          of the Constitution, of West Germany)
BND   Bundesnachrichtendienst (Federal Intelligence Service, of West Ger-
          many)
CDU   Christlich Demokratische Union (Christian Democratic Union, of
          West Germany)
CEO   chief executive officer
Cheka   Extraordinary Commission for Combating Counter-Revolution and
          Sabotage (of the Communist regime in Russia, 1917–1922)
CIA   Central Intelligence Agency (of the United States)
CID   Criminal Investigation Department (of India, Iraq, and Jordan)
CSU   Christlich-Soziale Union (Christian Social Union, of West Germany)
DCI   US director of Central Intelligence (of the US intelligence commu-
          nity)
DIB   director of the Intelligence Bureau (of India)
FBI   Federal Bureau of Investigation (of the United States)
FDP   Freie Demokratische Partei (Free Democratic Party, of West Ger-
          many)
FSB   Federalna Sluzhba Bezopasnosti (Federal Security Service of Russia)
GDR   German Democratic Republic
GID   General Investigations Directorate (of Egypt). In 1971, it was renamed
          the General Department of State Security Investigations; its name
          was later changed again, to the State Security Investigations Service.
GIS   General Intelligence Service (of Egypt)
GPU   Gosudarstvennoye Politicheskoye Upravleniye (State Political
          Administration, of the Soviet Union, 1922–23)
GRU   Glavnoye Razveditvatelnoye Upravleniye (Main Intelligence Direc-
          torate, of the Soviet Union's armed forces)

HVA	Hauptverwaltung Aufklärung (Main Intelligence Directorate of the Ministry of State Security of the German Democratic Republic)
IB	Intelligence Bureau (of India)
JIC	Joint Intelligence Committee (of India; also of the United Kingdom)
KGB	Komitet Gosudarstvennoi Bezopasnosti (Committee for State Security, of the Soviet Union)
MI5	commonly used name for the Security Service of the United Kingdom
NATO	North Atlantic Treaty Organization
NKVD	Narodnyi Komissariat Vnutrennikh Del' (People's Commissariat of Internal Affairs, of the Soviet Union)
NSA	National Security Agency (of the United States)
OGPU	Obyedinyonnoye Gosudarstvennoye Politicheskoye Upravleniye (United State Political Administration, 1923–34)
PBI	Presidential Bureau of Information (of Egypt)
PGU	Pervoye Glavnoye Upravleniye (First Chief Directorate, of the KGB)
R&AW	Research and Analysis Wing (India's foreign intelligence service)
SED	Sozialistische Einheitspartei Deutschlands (Socialist Unity Party of Germany, the ruling Communist Party of the GDR)
SIS	Secret Intelligence Service (of the United Kingdom)
SMERSH	"Death to Spies," the Soviet Union's military counterintelligence agency in the Second World War
SPD	Sozialdemokratische Partei Deutschlands (Social Democratic Party of [West] Germany)
SSNP	Syrian Social Nationalist Party
Stasi/MfS	Ministerium für Staatssicherheit (Ministry of State Security of the German Democratic Republic)
SVR	Sluzhba Vneshnei Razvedki (Foreign Intelligence Service, of the Russian Federation)
S&TI	scientific and technological intelligence
VA/NVA	Verwaltung Aufklärung / Nationale Volksarmee (Intelligence Directorate, National People's Army, of the GDR)

Introduction

Leading in Secret

Paul Maddrell

This book grew out of two academic meetings. The first was a panel, Intelligence Leaders in International Relations, organized by Paul Maddrell at the Fifty-Fifth Annual Convention of the International Studies Association in Toronto, Canada, in March 2014. This led to a second, a conference titled Spy Chiefs: Intelligence Leaders in History, Culture, and International Relations, which was organized by Christopher Moran and his colleagues at Warwick University and held at the Palazzo Pesaro Papafava in Venice, Italy, in May of that year. The purpose of these meetings was to discuss the leadership of intelligence and security agencies—what good leadership of such agencies is and what impact it has had on the performance of the agencies concerned. These discussions have yielded a book in two volumes, both edited by scholars currently researching intelligence leadership. The first is *Spy Chiefs*, volume 1: *Intelligence Leaders in the United States and United Kingdom*; the second is this book, *Spy Chiefs*, volume 2: *Intelligence Leaders in Europe, the Middle East, and Asia*.

Although there is a large academic literature on leadership, the literature on the leadership of intelligence agencies is tiny. This second volume of *Spy Chiefs* seeks, like the first, to identify what intelligence leadership is and how it can be improved for the benefit of intelligence and security agencies and thus to increase national security. It addresses broadly the same questions as the first volume: How have intelligence leaders operated in different national, institutional, and historical contexts; What role have they played in the conduct of domestic affairs and international relations; How has their role differed according to the political character of the regime they have served; How much power have they possessed; How have they led their agencies; What qualities make an effective intelligence leader; and How valuable is good leadership to an intelligence agency's success? While the first volume examined the traditions of leadership that developed in the twentieth century in the United

States and Great Britain, the purpose of this book is to offer a broader perspective. It studies intelligence leadership from the sixteenth century to the very recent past and analyzes the three principal traditions observable across the world in the last century and this one: the Western, the Communist, and the dictatorial. The case studies contained in the book have been chosen because they shed light on these traditions. The editors hope that further research will be undertaken into the leadership of intelligence and security agencies worldwide that will deepen scholarly understanding of it and increase the number of leaders whose role in history is understood.

The three traditions are analyzed and compared in the opening chapter of the book. Then the book turns to examine the Western tradition of intelligence, whereby two parallel systems of intelligence collection grew up. The first involved intelligence collection by government agencies, these being the diplomatic service, the armed forces, and the police. The second involved intelligence collection by merchants, traders, and commercial middlemen as part of the expansion of trade. Light is shed on this tradition by Ioanna Iordanou's chapter on Venice's Council of Ten and Emrah Safa Gürkan's on the "baili" of early modern Venice as well as by Bodo Hechelhammer's later chapter on the Federal Republic of Germany's first foreign intelligence chief, Gen. Reinhard Gehlen.

The book also studies the Communist tradition, which saw the collection of intelligence by security services controlled by Communist parties with totalitarian aspirations. Iain Lauchlan's chapter on Feliks Dzerzhinsky, Paul Maddrell's on Erich Mielke, and Kristie Macrakis's on Markus Wolf shed light on this development path.[1] The book also explores a third strand of development: that of intelligence agencies established by states that have achieved independence from European colonial domination. Paul McGarr's chapter shows that because India has remained a democracy since 1947, its model of intelligence leadership has remained within the Western tradition. Chikara Hashimoto shows in his chapter that Emir Farid Chehab, the chief in the 1950s of Lebanon's security service, the Sûreté Générale, tried to follow the example of the service's French parent and make it the reliable security arm of the Lebanese government. He was frustrated, however, by the sectarian divisions that racked Lebanese society and his own service; these divisions finally caused the country, in the 1970s, to descend into civil war. As Dina Rezk shows in her chapter, because Egypt has been a military dictatorship for almost the entire period since 1952, its intelligence chiefs have been the underlings of military rulers. This is a third model of intelligence leadership: the dictatorial. It is different from the other two and is very common in the developing world. These three models of leadership will be analyzed in the next chapter.

The first volume of *Spy Chiefs* argued that leading intelligence and security agencies was a form of organizational leadership, reasoning that a leader guides the process by which an organization solves problems it faces. The director is an essential part of the process by which an organization overcomes uncertainty. A leader asks the questions that guide the organization toward an appropriate course of action and motivates subordinates to take corresponding action. That volume considered a model example of leadership to be President Kennedy's role in the US government during the Cuban Missile Crisis: the president asked questions about appropriate responses to the Soviet Union's deployment of intermediate- and medium-range nuclear missiles in Cuba that required his administration to reflect carefully before taking action. That action, when it came, was moderate, placing pressure on the Soviet leadership to withdraw the missiles without being so aggressive that the result was war. This volume makes the same argument, though it maintains that the intelligence leader's authority and ability to solve problems—and thus exercise leadership—arise from, and are affected by, the very different political and organizational contexts and cultures to be found within the Western, Communist, and dictatorial traditions.

In the first volume, leadership was defined variously as holding a particular position, having particular gifts, achieving particular results, or conducting particular processes. This volume takes exactly the same approach, though leadership in this context must come chiefly from holding the job of intelligence chief since that is what gives the leader authority to solve problems. The gifts possessed, the results achieved, and the activities engaged in are all secondary to that.[2]

Therefore, both the authority and ability to exercise leadership depend on the political and organizational context and culture in which the intelligence chief and the agency act. The next chapter analyzes the three principal models of political and organizational culture.

Notes

1. The two traditions are also compared in an interesting book on the spy chiefs during the Cold War of the two German states, the Federal Republic of Germany and the German Democratic Republic: see Dieter Krüger and Armin Wagner, eds., *Konspiration als Beruf: Deutsche Geheimdienstchefs im Kalten Krieg* [Secrecy as an occupation: German secret service chiefs in the Cold War] (Berlin: Christoph Links Verlag, 2003).

2. Christopher Moran, Mark Stout, and Ioanna Iordanou, introduction to *Spy Chiefs*, ed. Christopher Moran, Mark Stout, Ioanna Iordanou, and Paul Maddrell, vol. 1, *Intelligence Leaders in the United States and United Kingdom* (Washington, DC: Georgetown University Press, 2018).

1 What Is Intelligence Leadership?

Three Historical Trends

Paul Maddrell

Let us start with the Western model of leadership. The best way to analyze the leadership of an intelligence agency is first to explain what it is not.

The "Great Man" view of leadership, so beloved of Thomas Carlyle, does not apply, because it relies too much on individual genius; the individual displaces any organization that might have been working for him.[1]

Nor does Max Weber's model of "charismatic" leadership apply. The Weberian "charismatic" leader was a child of the mass politics of the democratic era: such a leader made a moral—indeed, quasi-religious—appeal to the masses. Some writers claim that there have been instances of charismatic leadership in business; Steve Jobs, the late, long-serving chief executive officer (CEO) of Apple Corporation, and Lee Iacocca, the chief executive officer of Chrysler Corporation in the 1980s, are given as examples. However, both men greatly increased the stock market value of their companies; in the language of modern leadership (see below) they were principally "transactional" leaders. It is questionable whether the idea of charismatic leadership can apply in a business context, in which a leader is judged first and foremost on how much money he earns for others.[2] Those who argue that the business leader performs a charismatic role generally mean only that he or she needs to motivate and empower subordinates to ensure the organization's success. They also stress that this charismatic role is only one part of the business leader's job: the other part is the "instrumental" role of managing the organization and the people who work in it.[3]

Quite clearly, an intelligence chief cannot be a "charismatic" leader. Weber's "charismatic" individual is a person endowed with extraordinary powers. This type of leadership is an exceptional one, arising in times of crisis. An intelligence chief belongs to a different, much more stable type identified by Weber: the rational-legal. Intelligence agencies are firmly established parts of government; they derive their purpose and such legitimacy as they have

5

from the nation-state—an international legal norm.[4] The authority of intelligence chiefs is derived entirely from their position, not from the possession of exceptional gifts. Their personal appeal, however great it may be, does not extend beyond their agency and the government it serves; they very much lead an organization—that is to say, a team, not the mass of the people. He or she is not in the same position as a political leader but is more similar to the CEO of a corporation listed on the stock exchange. There are considerable similarities between the two types of leadership: both leaders are, in practice, appointed to the position; both depend for their success on maintaining good relations with two sets of people—stockholders and employees in the business leader's case; consumers of intelligence and subordinates in the intelligence leader's case.

Business leadership is the principal model of leadership for intelligence chiefs today. George Tenet, the director of Central Intelligence (DCI) under Presidents Clinton and George W. Bush, is a good example of a recent intelligence chief who regarded himself as, in effect, the CEO of a corporation. As DCI, he stressed the need for a long-term strategy focusing on core missions, strict financial management, good management of people, energetic recruitment of the best possible college graduates (offering salaries that competed with those available in business), unified training across the Central Intelligence Agency (CIA), systematic encouragement of racial diversity among employees, development and exploitation of the most modern information technology, and performance-related pay. All these initiatives are staples of modern business management. Tenet even compares himself with Jack Welch, the former CEO of General Electric. Modestly, he does so unfavorably.[5]

However, there are differences as well. The business leader has more autonomy than an intelligence counterpart: the former is responsible for determining the corporation's mission; the latter's mission is determined by its consumers (all the intelligence leader does is determine how the mission will be accomplished). The intelligence leader contends with enemies or, at the very least, threats; any failure on his or her part may cause the country to suffer very serious harm. The business leader contends only with competitors and so has only commercial failure to fear. The business leader's success can be measured in financial terms; for the most part, the intelligence leader's success cannot. Perhaps most significantly, as Sir Richard Dearlove stresses in his foreword to this book, the intelligence chief cannot motivate his subordinates by pointing to the agency's successes, which have to be kept secret. Much follows from the fact that the intelligence leader's organization is a secretive part of government. The leader has a more distant relationship with staff members than the modern business leader. The maxim of business leadership, "Be visible all the time," does not apply well.[6] Until recent times, the intelligence chief neither met nor addressed most subordinates. Even the modern director of Central Intelligence, who can address thousands of subordinates at one time by closed-circuit television, needs to shun publicity in order to do the job properly. A director of the CIA also spends a great deal of time briefing the president, liaising with the Congress, and meeting representatives of foreign intelligence agencies.[7]

Distance, rather than visibility and accessibility, has been a device used by intelligence chiefs to motivate their subordinates. According to his biographer, Dick White, the director ("C") of Britain's Secret Intelligence Service (SIS) from 1956 to 1968, "rarely ventured beyond the fourth floor to the remainder of the Broadway offices. . . . apart from the most senior officers, no one in the service knew C, who deliberately isolated himself from the majority of his staff."[8] He maintained a distance even from his senior officers. His predecessor but one, Sir Stewart Menzies, had been even more distant from his staff. White explained his aloof style of leadership to his biographer: "Secret service organizations don't have reputations, but mystique, and the chief needs to adopt a similar pose."[9]

Since the intelligence chief is appointed to the position of leader, not elected to it, James MacGregor Burns's concepts of the "transforming" and "transactional" leader do not apply. In his important book *Leadership*, Burns was trying to identify types of political leader. His two types of leader are people trying both to win the support and satisfy the needs and wishes of followers.[10] "Transactional" leadership involves an exchange of favors between leader and follower; it is based on self-interest. The classic example is that of the electoral candidate who is voted into political office and then gives those who voted for him or her what they demanded.

"Transforming" leadership is an engagement between leader and follower in which each lifts the other up to "higher levels of motivation and morality."[11] It is leadership with a strong moral element; the leader tries to inspire followers to nobler conduct by invoking high ideals such as freedom, justice, equality, or peace. It is a very similar concept to "charismatic" leadership but is open to the obvious objection that such a style may be to a considerable extent transactional.

Neither type of leadership applies to the directors of intelligence and security agencies. They are not trying to satisfy the wishes of those under them but rather are trying to meet the information and security needs of a third party— the government that appointed them and that they serve. They concern themselves with the needs and wishes of their subordinates only to achieve this end. They are much more concerned with their subordinates' abilities and responsibilities. They do not make great moral appeals. They are very much bureaucratic leaders (a type of leadership that Burns distinguished from "transforming" leadership). That said, Burns rightly stresses that the purpose of leadership is to help followers achieve their goals. However, intelligence chiefs have two sets of followers: the employees they lead and the government officials they serve. For that reason, they have two main tasks: to manage an organization capably and to win the confidence of the consumers of their intelligence reports.

A distinction is often made between management and leadership; these are regarded as different, though overlapping, tasks. Leadership is the guiding of people and involves motivating subordinates and providing the organization with a vision and concrete goals. Management is treated as more bureaucratic in nature; it involves organizing the agency's work, implementing its procedures, and preparing budgets. Essentially, the term "management" is used to describe the more mundane tasks of leadership; "leadership" is used to describe the more motivational and inspirational part of the leadership spectrum. As Gary Yukl, a scholar of business management, puts it, "The essential distinction appears to be that leaders influence commitment, whereas managers merely carry out position responsibilities and exercise authority."[12] Since both roles involve managing people and persuading them, the distinction cannot be strictly maintained. It has little relevance to the work of intelligence chiefs, who are both leaders and managers: they lead people and agencies, though they also manage the agencies' business. The two words "leader" and "manager" can be used interchangeably and will be so used here.

This book argues in favor of using business leadership as a model for the leadership of intelligence agencies. This is a particular application of the scientific management model of leadership that became influential in the 1920s, especially in the United States, owing to modern industrial management techniques. An intelligence chief is a leader and manager, though one working in a political context.[13] Gary Yukl considers leadership "a complex, multifaceted phenomenon" that can be defined as including "influencing task objectives and strategies, influencing commitment and compliance in task behavior to achieve these objectives, influencing group maintenance and identification, and influencing the culture of an organization."[14] Intelligence leadership is a form of organizational leadership; the leader-manager guides the people, goals, and culture of the agency (while the mundane aspects of organizational administration can be called "management," that distinction will not be made here).

The core of organizational leadership is cultural leadership: a good chief of an intelligence and security agency is one who, in addition to developing well-judged intelligence operations and procedures, nurtures an organizational culture that promotes success and also maintains the confidence of political masters.

Many writers on business management have questioned whether the leader is important to the success of the organization; in their view, success is the result of many factors, ones both external to the organization and internal to it. In the view of Gary Yukl, "An accurate conception of leadership importance lies between the two extremes of heroic leader and impotent figurehead. How an organization performs is determined by a variety of external and internal factors. The internal factors include leadership processes at all levels, not just the competence and actions of the CEO."[15]

Key Aspects of Leadership

The record of business leadership illustrates the challenges that face intelligence leaders as directors of organizations: creating a culture that enables the abilities of all staff to be applied to the organization's tasks; guiding their colleagues toward the achievement of the agency's goals; asserting their own abilities without overshadowing their colleagues; managing resources, procedures, and structures as well as people; and representing the organization capably before the consumers of its intelligence and the general public. The last task does not come easily to many intelligence officials, who have spent their entire careers working in secret.

Culture

Because leadership involves managing people, it is embedded in culture. Leadership is above all a cultural activity: a leader's main task is to create a culture for the organization and those who work in it. A culture is a code of values, attitudes, and behavior that governs how subordinates interact with their superiors and one another, what goals they pursue and how they pursue them. It is made up of the organization's mentality, rules, values, procedures, and the state of its morale. It has a decisive influence on the organization's identity and is taught to new recruits.[16] Management of people, procedures, plans, and budgets is inseparable from this. The anthropologist Clifford Geertz describes culture as "the fabric of meaning in terms of which human beings interpret their experience and guide their action."[17] Directors of organizations, whether public or private, guide their subordinates, to a considerable extent, by managing their culture.

Since intelligence chiefs, like the CEOs of corporations or the directors of any other institutions (public or private), wield authority delegated to them, they are both the products of a culture and the managers of one. Their importance as leaders should not be overestimated: they are appointed to the position of director because they conform to the prevailing culture of the government concerned. They are appointed in part to pass this culture on. This is truer of intelligence and security chiefs than it is of any other leaders in either public or private life, save only for leaders of the armed forces themselves. Intelligence and security chiefs, like the senior officers of the army, navy, air force, and police from whom so many of them are drawn, are expected to be utterly loyal to the state. In his book *The Lessons of History*, Michael Howard noted that since they draw their strength from the entire resources of society, "armies are microcosms of their society; often indeed their core."[18] A variant of this dictum applies to intelligence and security agencies: they are the very core of the governments whose security they seek to maintain. This is above all true of the intelligence and security services of Communist regimes, which depended on these services' spying and coercion to stay in power. The similarity between the armed forces and intelligence services is attitudinal as well as organizational; intelligence agencies, like the armed forces, regard themselves as engaged in actual or potential combat with hostile powers.[19] All the intelligence chiefs and organizations studied in this book were distinctive products of a political culture.

Ideas of leadership derive from complex social interactions; consequently, different societies have different understandings of it. The leadership style of directors of government agencies is strongly influenced not only by social attitudes but also by the culture of the governments they serve. In American culture, thanks to such institutions as the US presidency and state governorships, there is an individualistic understanding of leadership: a leader is seen as being a strong individual (historically a man, though this is changing) with authority over others, who can make decisions that they will not like. This understanding of leadership is very influential within the US intelligence community;[20] it was the perception that the director of Central Intelligence was providing ineffectual leadership to the community that led to the creation of the position of director of National Intelligence (DNI) in 2005.[21] By contrast, in Scandinavian culture, society understands leadership less as being that of an individual than of someone working in a team. British intelligence chiefs, schooled as they are in Whitehall's committee culture, have rarely been forceful enough to stand up to the Foreign Office.[22]

An appropriate culture should embrace all abilities (and many disabilities). The literature on business management shows that successful managers do display particular qualities such as self-confidence, ability to show initiative, ability to remain calm under pressure, and dedication to one's work. Analytical ability, a good memory, and skill in dealing with others are, naturally, valuable. Ambition can also be valuable, so long as one's ambition for the organization is greater than one's ambition for oneself; one has to be willing to delegate to others. This socialized form of ambition is essential to successful intelligence leadership. Competitiveness is not necessarily harmful, so long as it does not lead to too much independence of the team or a desire to undermine colleagues. It is essential to be able to balance character traits. For example, it is very important to be ambitious without losing regard for others and their need for success and to be energetic in promoting change without losing patience with those less supportive of it. A good way of achieving such a balance is in a leadership team—leadership skills are the attributes of a group, not an individual. Successful managers also make use of particular management styles, such as praising and rewarding subordinates and delegating authority to them and empowering them.[23]

Abilities and Qualities

The abilities scholars of business administration have identified in leaders are possessed by their intelligence counterparts. Leaders' abilities matter because the abilities of every member of a team are one of the factors that affect the team's performance. The other five factors are the effort made by each member of the team, how well the work is organized, how well the team works together, whether the resources the team needs are available, and how well the team coordinates its work with other parts of the organization.[24] Allen Dulles's time as DCI shows the importance of the last factor. He led the agency with conviction because he had the strong support of President Eisenhower; both men believed that the CIA had to go on to the attack and obtain aggressively the intelligence needed to inform Cold War policy toward the Soviet Union. Dulles also placed much emphasis on high standards of intelligence analysis. As a result, he was, in the words of one of his principal analysts, both "the 'Great White Case Officer' for all of CIA, spending at least three-fourths of his time and energy . . . on clandestine collection and covert action tasks" and the man who succeeded "in creating a dynamic, productive central intelligence system that really did enrich the policymaking process."[25] Dulles finally went too far and had to resign over the misconceived invasion of Cuba by exiles at the Bay of Pigs.

Leaders are able people who, in the words of Professor Manfred Kets de Vries, are "much better than other people at *managing cognitive complexity*. They are good at searching out and structuring the kind of information they need; their strength lies in making sense of an increasingly complex environment and then in using the data obtained in problem solving. This talent manifests itself in their knack for simplification, of making highly complex issues very palatable" (italics in original).[26]

John McCone, director of Central Intelligence under Presidents Kennedy and Johnson (1961–65), had this ability to a high degree, which is why he was a successful DCI. An engineer by training, McCone had been a highly successful industrialist before joining the public service. The man he appointed head of the CIA's Directorate of Intelligence, Ray Cline, wrote of McCone that "he absorbed more from complex briefings than any senior official I have worked with."[27] McCone's principal interest was in intelligence analysis, and under his leadership, the agency put more emphasis on this and less on the covert action that had prompted Allen Dulles's fall. Cline considers that, in consequence, in the first half of McCone's time as director, the CIA "operated at its peak performance level."[28] McCone not only reined in the CIA but also displayed an ability to focus on his own core tasks of providing the president with incisive intelligence analysis and of coordinating the intelligence-collection operations of the entire US intelligence community. He was a demanding taskmaster and an excellent delegator. McCone was capable of canny intelligence analysis himself: he realized in September 1962, as his own analysts did not, that the Soviet leader Nikita Khrushchev might be stationing offensive nuclear missiles on Cuba. Under his leadership, the Directorate of Intelligence advised the Johnson administration well about the Vietnam War, correctly arguing, in contrast to the Defense and State Departments, that aerial bombing was not weakening North Vietnam's determination to prosecute the war and that time was on North Vietnam's side since, as the Communists knew, domestic and international opposition to the United States' involvement in the war was likely to increase.[29] Markus Wolf, who also briefly studied engineering, also displayed an outstanding ability to manage cognitive complexity, which is analyzed in the conclusion to this book.

As Kets de Vries notes, other qualities frequently identified among good business leaders are "*conscientiousness* (which includes dependability, achievement orientation and perseverance), *extroversion, dominance, self-confidence, energy, agreeableness* (meaning flexibility and sense of trust), *intelligence, openness to experience* (including a lack of ethnocentrism), and *emotional stability*" (italics in original).[30]

These qualities enable effective business leaders to motivate others to work well and to build successful teams. Thus they get the best out of their subordinates. They generally set demanding work goals. Possessing all these gifts will not guarantee success. As writers on business leadership remind us, "effective leadership strongly depends on a complex pattern of interaction among leader, follower, and situation."[31]

Many intelligence leaders have not only displayed these qualities but used them to give successful leadership to their agencies. Remarkably conscientious men abound in the history of both the British and the US intelligence communities. The job of director of an American intelligence agency today is so onerous that only a very conscientious person can do it. George Tenet, DCI from 1997 to 2004, has observed, "The work matters enormously, and it's never over."[32] Though proud to have held the position, Tenet was glad to give it up. Vice Admiral Bobby Ray Inman, director of the National Security Agency from 1977 to 1981, worked a ten- to twelve-hour day, six days a week (and a further half-day on Sunday); he was usually in his office at Fort Meade by six o'clock in the morning.[33] Even in more relaxed ages, many intelligence chiefs have worked punishing days. Mansfield Smith-Cumming, the founder-chief of Britain's Secret Intelligence Service, worked a twelve-hour day most days of the week. The charm he used to lead SIS derived from a mixture of amiability and eccentricity.

Walter Bedell Smith, often regarded as the best DCI, succeeded because the US intelligence community was then so disorganized that it needed someone of his abrasiveness to give it leadership.[34] He was the archetypal dominant leader: thanks to his forceful personality, he was able to dominate the intelligence community; incorporate the government's covert action agency, the Office of Policy Coordination, into the agency; and ensure that analysts from all agencies worked together to prepare agreed interagency estimates. The result was a central intelligence system that began to function as it was meant to.[35]

By contrast, William Odom, considered by one historian of the NSA to have been one of the worst directors of that agency, was too abrasive and autocratic to get on well with many of his staff at the NSA; his aggressive style prompted resignations, and he served only three years in the position.[36] J. Edgar Hoover's self-confidence was the basis of his success as director of the Federal Bureau of Investigation (FBI). He knew what he wanted to achieve and set out to achieve it with great determination.

One type of chief who automatically raises morale is a professional intelligence officer; by choosing such a candidate, the government demonstrates to the staff of an intelligence agency that it values their skills. In his foreword to this book, Sir Richard Dearlove, the former chief of the United Kingdom's Secret Intelligence Service, has argued that appointing an intelligence professional is so important to achieving good performance that it is a mistake to appoint a nonprofessional. The leaders of Britain's foreign intelligence service (SIS), domestic security service (MI5), and communications intelligence agency (Government Communications Headquarters, GCHQ) have usually been veterans of those agencies. With one exception (Sir John Rennie), every chief of SIS since the appointment of Dick White in 1956 has been a professional intelligence officer; indeed, he has usually been a veteran of SIS itself. The morale of SIS staff was high during Maurice Oldfield's five years as "C" (1973–78) because he was the outstanding intelligence officer of his generation; officers who worked with him have spoken of "his very high, almost phenomenal professional competence."[37] The government clearly held the same opinion of him: he was the first chief of SIS ever to be awarded the Grand Cross of the Order of St. Michael and St. George, a very high decoration. Old-field was a highly intelligent man with a legendary memory. A devout Christian, he further improved morale by insisting that the service's operations be morally defensible; he disapproved of any participation in assassination or any other violent disruptive action (as did McCone).[38] However, he lacked balance; he lived for his work. He made conscientiousness a failing by taking on too much work—work that he might have delegated to others. His intelligence was another reason he did not delegate as much as he might have done: he reckoned that he could do a job faster than some of his subordinates.[39]

By contrast, the United States' director of Central Intelligence in the years between the creation of the position in 1947 and its subordination to the DNI in 2005 was usually a high-ranking officer in the armed forces or an important civilian official who enjoyed the administration's confidence. Professional intelligence officers rarely achieved the position of DCI. Both Allen Dulles and Richard Helms might lay claim to having been the first professional intelligence officer to become director of Central Intelligence (while intelligence was Helms's principal career and he worked his way up the agency, Dulles oscillated between careers in law and intelligence).[40] As with all SIS chiefs since 1973, the success of both men as DCI was based on their record of loyal, successful service beforehand. Dulles drew on his intelligence experience and President Eisenhower's support to commit the agency to its Cold War missions: energetic intelligence collection, by human sources and by technical means, and aggressive covert propaganda and paramilitary operations. In Ray Cline's view, "No other man left such a mark on the Agency."[41]

Management of Culture

The most successful leaders of intelligence agencies have been those who have created a working culture that has yielded good results—by which I mean strict security and effective collection of valuable intelligence. It involves management of skills, resources, people, and the organization itself. The leader must identify problems and challenges and guide his or her subordinates toward finding solutions. The task has both charismatic and instrumental parts: the charismatic part is to motivate and empower others to achieve as much as they can, and the instrumental is to build appropriate teams, establish suitable organizational structures, allocate the necessary resources, and evaluate performance (Manfred Kets de Vries describes it as "organizational design, control and reward"[42]). They must also devise appropriate operations or commission others to do so, changing operational techniques as the situation requires.

Those best able to create such a culture have been leaders who either founded the intelligence agency they led or who led them early on, when their culture and organization were most susceptible to influence. So it comes as no surprise that, as with other types of organization, prominent among those lauded for their leadership skills are founding or early spy chiefs such as Mansfield Smith-Cumming (SIS), Feliks Dzerzhinsky (of the Bolsheviks' Cheka), J. Edgar Hoover (FBI), Markus Wolf (of the East German Stasi's Hauptverwaltung Aufklärung, or HVA), and Walter Bedell Smith (CIA). Cumming's biographer, Alan Judd (himself a former SIS officer), considers the original "C's" main achievement to have been to give his service a culture, one that expressed British national culture itself:

> He personified and embodied his creation to a degree unusual even in that arcane branch of human bureaucracy, unmatched in this respect by any except perhaps Feliks Dzerzhinsky, founder of the Russian Cheka. This was probably all they had in common, for their differences were fundamental, being those of national character and national political personality. For good and ill, expression of these qualities is often found in purest form in national Secret Service.
>
> For all the many and major differences between now and then, the service inherited by Cumming's successors still bears his imprint. Apart from the hallowed gimmicks, such as the use of the chiefly green ink and the letter C, as well as his title (CSS, Chief of the Secret Service), there are inherited organizational structures and, more importantly, attitudes. Prominent among the latter are the insistence on putting the work first and the easy informality of working relationships.[43]

While Cumming evidently played a significant role in transmitting these attributes to SIS's forerunner, the Secret Service Bureau, they were characteristics of the organizations he in turn served. The Royal Navy, from which he was transferred to lead the bureau, had a centuries-old tradition of dedicated service to Britain's national defense. Informality and collegiality were very much characteristics of the British government as a whole at that time. Within the Secret Service Bureau (known from the 1920s as the Secret Intelligence Service[44]), they were also very much encouraged by the recruitment of officers from a narrow circle of people.[45] That said, Cumming clearly did inspire his colleagues to follow his example. He was a workaholic with a good sense of humor and a liking for inventiveness, and he transmitted these qualities to his service. To this very day, the Secret Intelligence Service has a high reputation among intelligence agencies worldwide for its inventive use of technology to collect intelligence.[46] His kindness aside, it was because Cumming dedicated himself to his job, working a very long day, that he was so highly regarded by his agents and colleagues.[47]

It is not necessary to be a founder-director to have a profound impact on an intelligence agency. Major reorganizations are a staple of modern organizational management and are, of course, designed to change culture as well as structure, procedures, levels of performance, recruitment, or financing. J. Edgar Hoover, who became the director of the Bureau of Investigation of the United States' Department of Justice in 1924, was in fact the bureau's fifth chief. He made great efforts to shape the bureau's culture, making it more professional and turning it into a bastion of American social conservatism: he drove out female special agents (for forty-four of his forty-eight years as director the bureau had no female agents at all); the men he appointed as special agents were Protestant middle-class law graduates, often from the southern states; he issued a code of conduct to his agents that required they remain faithful to their wives and consume no alcohol; and to ensure that his agents were well trained, in 1935 the FBI established its National Police Academy. Throughout his career Hoover showed great flair for manipulating the press, radio, and television, which consistently gave him and the bureau flattering publicity. While Hoover sought thereby to glorify both the bureau and himself, his efforts in the 1930s to ensure that the press gave his "G-men" ("government men") favorable publicity had a legitimate law enforcement objective: to end Hollywood's glamorization of gangsters and replace it with respect for the police, law, and order. In doing so he decisively improved the morale of his agents.[48]

The history of the US intelligence community offers many other examples of major reorganizations intended to transform the culture of the agencies concerned. To consider only recent history, in the 1980s and 1990s American intelligence agencies made strenuous efforts to recruit and promote more women and people from ethnic minority backgrounds. The termination in 1993 of the FBI's ban on the employment of homosexuals also initiated a profound change in the bureau's culture.[49] And for the last twenty years intelligence agencies throughout the Western world have been conducting extensive reorganizations so as to keep pace with the revolution in electronic communication.

Management of People

In any organization people need to be managed well; the leader needs to motivate them to achieve the highest level of performance of which they are capable. This is essential to maintaining (and raising) the levels of skill within an organization. Empathy with colleagues and the ability to show and inspire trust in them are important to the success of any leader because these traits enable him or her to get the best out of the organization.[50] In the intelligence context, people need to be attracted to the agency, immersed in its culture, taught the importance of security, trained in essential skills, and guided to collect the intelligence needed. Ambitious people need to be chosen for work teams, set demanding yet appropriate goals, and given feedback and praise. Their work needs to be evaluated fairly and accurately. The morale of the agency's staff needs to be kept high, in part by achieving success but also by persuading the staff of the importance of the work and of the need for change, and integrating changes into the agency's culture. Intelligence agencies find it easier than corporations do to achieve high morale since national security depends on them. However, they are vulnerable to devastating blows to morale, such as when a traitor is found in their ranks—the treason of Aldrich Ames and Harold Nicholson did severe damage to morale at the CIA in the 1990s, for example.[51] Necessary changes need to be made, and to persuade his or her workforce to support them, the intelligence chief must present them as consistent with the existing culture.[52]

Good Organization

An intelligence chief needs to devise appropriate organizational structures, ones that integrate the agency firmly into the government it serves so that it receives clear guidance about the government's information needs. Intelligence-collection agencies need to understand clearly what information they are meant to collect, and the collection requirements imposed on them must be clear, precise, and important. If they are not, then it is less likely that the agency will collect good, usable information. Britain's Secret Intelligence Service learned this as soon as it was founded. A key step in its development was the attachment of officials from the Foreign Office, War Office, and Admiralty—the government departments that received SIS's product—to the sections in the service that collected the intelligence.[53] At the same time, the service needs to maintain its independence so that it works equally for all its customers, not just for one, and develops its own esprit de corps.

Winning the Confidence of Consumers

Some secret services have maintained their secrecy so well that little is known about how successful they really were; more is known about how successful they were considered to be by the governments they served. An example is Britain's Secret Intelligence Service. Dick White was considered to be a successful director: when he retired as "C," the government appointed him coordinator of intelligence at the Cabinet Office.[54] Half of Whitehall attended the memorial service for him when he died in 1993. Yet there is no evidence indicating that under his leadership SIS was, on balance, particularly successful.

While there were successes, such as the recruitment of Oleg Penkovsky in 1961, there were serious reverses as well. One was the uncovering in the service of the penetration agent of the Soviet KGB (*Komitet Gosudarstvennoi Bezopasnosti*: Committee for State Security), George Blake, which devastated its operations against the Soviet Bloc and forced a complete reorganization of SIS. Another setback was SIS's failure to warn the government of Rhodesia's Unilateral Declaration of Independence in 1965.[55] During White's twelve years as chief, SIS became even more a junior partner of the CIA; its main value to the agency lay in its ability to supply intelligence from places where the CIA found it hard to operate, such as North Vietnam and Cuba, since the United States had no diplomatic relations with those countries.

White's one undoubted success was to win the confidence of Whitehall in his service (which is why it thought so well of him). He was unfailingly pleasant, constructive, and honest in his dealings with his customers. The task suited his abilities well: he was intelligent, pleasant, good-natured, and modest, even deferential. He had a natural listener's gift of appearing to defer to other people: "He [was] so good at getting on with people," said one of his principal supporters, the Foreign Office official Sir Patrick Dean, "very honest, straightforward and never conceited."[56] His senior officers thought that he did not stand up enough for the service when it wanted to mount operations to which the Foreign Office was opposed, because he tended to give way to the diplomats' objections.[57] White's biography is titled *The Perfect English Spy*, but a better title would be *The Perfect English Civil Servant*. His success in building a relationship of confidence with his superiors stands in sharp contrast to the inability of some DCIs to persuade the president of the United States to listen to them. John McCone and James Woolsey (DCI, 1993–95) are examples. That said, the position of DCI has been held by men with an outstanding ability to get on well with others; George H. W. Bush, DCI from 1976 to 1977 and later president of the United States, is a case in point. Indeed, most DCIs were not career agency officials and achieved that position because the administration had confidence in them.

Since the age of modern legislative oversight dawned in the mid-1970s, intelligence chiefs in the Western world have had to win the confidence of legislative overseers as well; his ability to do so was one reason why George Tenet, a former staff director of the Senate Select Committee on Intelligence, was appointed DCI in 1997.[58] As Tenet's nomination and confirmation by the Senate show, winning the confidence of consumers is so important that there is an argument for appointing people from the policy-making community— John Rennie, a Foreign Office official who was appointed director-general of SIS in 1968, is the British counterpart to Bush and Tenet. Bobby Ray Inman, a highly intelligent director of the NSA, is considered to have represented the

agency outstandingly well before the House and Senate intelligence committees.[59]

Communist foreign intelligence chiefs had much more distant relations
with the regimes they served. One reason is practical: they were directors of
foreign intelligence departments of large state security ministries and were
subordinates of state security ministers much more important than they
were. Consequently, they had far fewer dealings with their leaders, whom
they tended not to advise directly. More important, Communist foreign
intelligence chiefs had a more distant relationship with their political masters because the latter were skeptical of the information they were provided.
Communist political leaders had an ideologically distorted view of world
events, which they frequently regarded unjustifiably as developing in their
favor. Much information they would not like was not forwarded to them. For
example, when Leonid Brezhnev was Soviet leader (from 1964 to 1982), information that conflicted with his thinking was kept from him by the General
Department of the Central Committee so as not to "upset" him.[60]

Political Influence

The security chief collects intelligence on domestic politics and is therefore
well placed to wield political influence. This is so even in democratic countries, J. Edgar Hoover being the prime example. Hoover collected so much
discreditable information on American politicians, including presidents, that
he was, in effect, able to intimidate them into keeping him in office. As the
Democratic Party's nominee for the US presidency, John F. Kennedy reas-
sured Hoover publicly that he would not replace him as director of the FBI. He
knew that Hoover still had tape recordings of him having sexual intercourse
during the Second World War with a suspected German spy, Inga Arvad. His
brother, Robert F. Kennedy, whom the president appointed attorney general (and thus Hoover's immediate superior), was as unfaithful to his wife as
John F. Kennedy was to his. Hoover used to show Robert Kennedy who was
boss by regularly sending him information on allegations about himself or
people Kennedy knew. President Lyndon Johnson, who, as a rising politician,
had been much involved in electoral corruption in his home state of Texas,
feared Hoover so much that he exempted him from the compulsory retirement age for federal officials.[61]

Hoover cultivated the presidents he served skillfully. He did so both to stay
in office and to wield influence over national policy. Strongly anti-Communist
and racist, Hoover had a conservative influence on policy. He supplied presidents from Herbert Hoover in the 1920s to Richard Nixon in the 1970s with

information on their political rivals. He went too far in cultivating presidents; although he did win influence, he put his own ambitions before the interests of the bureau. In practice, he turned the FBI into an arm of the presidency. He encouraged the US Congress and several presidents to exaggerate the Communist menace within the United States. As far as presidents are concerned, he had most success with President Johnson. Johnson enjoyed information on other men's failings, and Hoover supplied him with a lot (particularly on his political rivals). On Johnson's instructions, FBI officers even examined televised hearings of the Senate Foreign Relations Committee for similarities between its discussions and Communist policy.

While Johnson gave instructions to Hoover, Hoover also wielded influence over Johnson. In particular, he encouraged Johnson to believe that the popular movement within the United States against American involvement in the Vietnam War was Communist-inspired.[62] He had less success in his efforts to persuade Johnson that the civil rights movement (and particularly its leader, the Reverend Martin Luther King) were under Communist influence. However, Johnson was entertained by tape recordings he received from Hoover of King having extramarital sexual intercourse in hotel bedrooms.[63] Hoover himself subjected King to a campaign of degrading harassment, which included sending him anonymous letters calling on him to commit suicide.[64] In his forty-eight year career as director of the FBI (1924–72), Hoover exercised too much influence over both the bureau and American politics. Consequently, the FBI director's term of service since 1976 has been limited by law to a single term of no more than ten years.[65]

The foreign intelligence chief, by contrast, is usually under the thumb of the foreign minister, defense minister, or head of government for whom he or she works. For the most part, histories of the CIA or NSA do not show that the directors of these agencies had any particular influence on foreign policy. An exception is William Casey, President Reagan's first DCI (1981–87). This example shows how deep-rooted the culture of professionalism was in the CIA by the 1980s: not only the agency but also the policy makers it served knew that CIA analysts were expected to be objective in preparing intelligence reports and briefing policy makers. These policy makers complained bitterly when they felt that the CIA, rather than being objective, was trying to manipulate them. Casey was as conservative as Reagan himself and had very strong views on foreign policy. Not only did he encourage Reagan to go too far in undertaking covert action to fight nonexistent Soviet expansion; worse, his own briefings on intelligence were influenced by his foreign policy views. During Casey's time as DCI, the State Department felt that it received from the CIA carefully selected reports designed to influence policy on several parts of the world, most importantly the Soviet Union, Iran, and Afghanistan.[66] George

Shultz, Reagan's secretary of state, considered the CIA at that time to be "an alternative State Department with its own strong policy views." Allowing policy biases to influence intelligence analysis, as Casey did, led to erroneous intelligence advice that Shultz dismissed as "bum dope."[67] Casey's influence was all the greater since President Reagan appointed him to the cabinet—he is the only DCI ever to sit in it. However, Casey's influence was limited to the president's first term; in his second term, Reagan was guided by Secretary of State Shultz to embrace détente with the Soviet Union.[68]

The Tradition of Communist Dictatorship

How good was the leadership of the security and intelligence agencies of the Communist Bloc? This section analyzes the leadership and managerial culture of the Soviet security service. This service was known by several names between its foundation in 1917 and breakup in 1991; here, the term "KGB" will most frequently be used because that was its last and most long-lasting name (the security service was so called from 1954 to 1991). Can the successes this notorious service achieved be attributed to the way it was led? The position of chief of a Communist security agency was one of great political sensitivity— even greater than in the democratic case—and the men appointed were therefore expected to serve the political purposes of the state's leader or leadership. Only in particular cases did the security chief enhance his service's effectiveness. Since they were appointed to maintain a Marxist-Leninist regime and impose Marxism-Leninism on their subordinates, their outlook was severely distorted by ideology. Indeed, as Iain Lauchlan shows in chapter 4 of this volume, their intelligence reporting was alarmist and increased the paranoia of their political masters. Since their job was to impose the viciously repressive policies of their regime, they lacked the charm and finer human qualities of their democratic counterparts.

Throughout the seventy-four-year history of the Soviet Communist Party's domination of Russia and the countries it conquered, the leadership of the political police displayed consistent characteristics that reflected its subordination to the Communist Party. It was an obedient—indeed, servile— instrument of the party; it was led by people who were, on any reasonable view, criminals and were willing to act criminally; its political thinking was very much that of the party; and like the party bureaucracy, it was corrupt. These characteristics lowered the quality of its leadership.

There were, of course, developments over that time. In the post-Stalin era, party leaders made great efforts to ensure that the leaders of the political police posed no threat to them. They were often drawn from the party itself and were political clients of the leader. Loyalty to the leader and the party tended to prevail over any other criterion of selection. Whatever the quality of the security services' performance, their leadership tended to be mediocre or even bad.

The Soviet Political Police in the Period 1917–53

The Soviet political police was born in the throes of a popular socialist revolution in Russia, when the new Communist regime deliberately stirred up popular hatred of "the bourgeoisie" so as to stay in power. Then known as the Cheka, the political police contained many criminals and drug addicts. The Cheka's character was criminal. Its mentality was one of vengeance and destruction and naturally attracted criminals. The local political police units were, in practice, free of any judicial control or moral restraint; they could do as they wished and became vicious and tyrannical murderers and torturers.[69] Their complete power over their victims made some of them sadists. Many drank heavily or resorted to drugs to make the task of killing easier to bear.

Since the political police's task was to uncover disloyalty, it attracted suspicious and devious people and encouraged these failings in them. As the Communist Viktor Serge put it, "The only temperaments that devoted themselves willingly and tenaciously to this task of 'internal defence' were those characterized by suspicion, embitterment, harshness and sadism. . . . The Chekas inevitably consisted of perverted men tending to see conspiracy everywhere and to live in the midst of perpetual conspiracy themselves."[70]

This was criminality married to ideas: the brutal ideology of Marxism-Leninism justified the Cheka's cruelty. Its first leader was an outstanding revolutionary: Feliks Dzerzhinsky, a Polish Communist utterly dedicated to the Bolshevik Party and the triumph of the revolution. Dzerzhinsky is the subject of Iain Lauchlan's chapter in this book and will be discussed only briefly here. Suffice it to say that his outstanding characteristic was fanaticism: he was a devout Catholic as a child, and in adulthood Marxism-Leninism became his faith. He believed that class oppression—and the class oppressors—had to be destroyed and a perfect society created with the aid of violence. He had the mercilessness that Marxism-Leninism required. As head of the Cheka he displayed extraordinary energy, working up to eighteen hours a day, seven days a week, and sleeping in his office. His endurance earned him the nickname "Iron Feliks." He supplied the expertise the new organization needed, showing such an aptitude for security work that he not only ran the Cheka but many of its operations as well. Until 1920, when the civil war ended, he ran not only the entire agency but also its important Special Department, responsible for the loyalty of the Red Army. He proved so industrious an administrator that he was given other important ministerial posts as well (from

1919, the position of People's Commissar for Internal Affairs; from 1921, the job of People's Commissar for Communications). These distracted him from the task of leading the Cheka, which he increasingly had to delegate to others.[71]

The political police was part of the party-state bureaucracy and quickly took on two of its main characteristics: servility to the top leadership and corruption. Viacheslav Menzhinsky, who succeeded Dzerzhinsky, his fellow Pole, when the latter died in office in 1926, did not have the strength of character to stand up to Stalin, who by the late 1920s was the Communist Party's undisputed leader. His malleability is the likely reason why Stalin allowed Menzhinsky to remain in office until his death in 1934. Menzhinsky's successor, Genrikh Yagoda, who led the NKVD (as it now was) from 1934 to 1936, was both servile and corrupt. He turned his ministry from being the party's instrument to being Stalin's. He may even have organized the murders of some of Stalin's opponents, such as Sergei Kirov and Maksim Gorki. In August 1936 he organized the first show trial of Stalin's party opponents Lev Kamenev and Grigori Zinoviev and supervised their execution.[72] He also embezzled state funds and used them to build himself a magnificent dacha. Among his possessions at the time of his arrest in 1936 were 3,904 pornographic pictures and eleven pornographic films.[73]

This process of "negative evolution" reached its apogee in the period of High Stalinism, from the early 1930s to the early 1950s, when the leaders of Soviet state security were morally utterly degraded people. The murder and terrorism in which the regime engaged were so extreme that its own security officials were either incapable of thinking for themselves or too scared to do so. The guiding maxim of the political police, including its leaders, became "Sniff out, suck up, survive."

An outstanding example of these degraded people is Yagoda's successor, Nikolai Yezhov. Nicknamed the "poison dwarf," Yezhov was a psychological inadequate. Whereas Dzerzhinsky had been devoted to the party, Yezhov was devoted to Stalin. He was appointed to kill Stalin's enemies (his biography is, appropriately, titled *Stalin's Loyal Executioner*). Yezhov's principal psychological traits were how easily he could be dominated by others and a tendency to take everything he did to an extreme. In performing any task, he never knew when to stop. He suffered from a severe inferiority complex, resulting from his small stature (he was five feet tall) and his very limited education (he attended primary school for only a year[74]). The psychologist Viktor Topolianskii has argued that Yezhov's inferiority complex made him a natural sadist because it prompted him to torment others (psychologists call this "infantilism").[75] Certainly, under the influence of Stalin's paranoid and malevolent personality Yezhov became a vicious sadist. After the executions of such party grandees as Kamenev and Zinoviev, Yezhov gathered up and saved in a drawer the bullets that had killed them.[76] As NKVD chief he personally participated in beatings to procure confessions.[77] He was considered insignificant by those who met him; the later Politburo member, Dmitri Shepilov, called him "a little cultured and in theoretical respects totally ignorant man."[78] He was crude and immature: when drunk, he and a friend used to take their trousers off and competed at blowing cigarette ash off a penny by farting. Yezhov later had the friend, Lev Mar'iasin, the president of the USSR's State Bank, viciously tortured and shot.[79] Indeed, in 1936–38 he personally ordered the arrest and execution of many of his former friends and colleagues (even his mistress); this demonstrates his principal psychological characteristic: his extreme zeal in performing any task. He had no political gifts; his career was made by Stalin, who gave him all the positions he held.

Yezhov became a vicious killer for intellectual as well as for psychological reasons: as a Bolshevik he genuinely believed in a huge oppositionist-fascist conspiracy against the Soviet government. He followed the Bolshevik reasoning by which any group that stood in their way, whatever it subjectively thought of itself, was objectively opposed to revolution and thus to the cause of humanity. So he saw his actions as good. Those who were not with them were against them.[80]

From the late 1920s, when he was appointed deputy people's commissar for agriculture, he consistently held jobs that required more ability than he had, and from that time on he depended heavily on alcohol. He was so shaken by the vicious work he had to perform as general commissar of state security that he was an alcoholic and constantly drunk throughout his time at the NKVD.[81] His alcoholism was one of the reasons why Stalin fired him in November 1938. Throughout his career his work caused him stress, which brought on illnesses such as neurasthenia. It is questionable whether he was up to the job of NKVD chief; he himself wrote in November 1938, just after his dismissal, in an unsent letter to Stalin that his two years' work as NKVD chief had put his nervous system under great strain.[82] He was executed in February 1940. He was such a coward that he was dragged screaming to his execution.[83]

As NKVD chief Yezhov had little in the way of ability. All he brought to the job was his extremism in carrying out his duties and his experience of cadre selection (he had worked in this field from 1924).[84] There is some evidence that he was efficient, hard-working, and a good organizer, but among his early work evaluations were negative assessments of him; it is likely that his abilities were, at best, very ordinary.[85] Anyway, they were so impaired by alcoholism, stress, and ill health during his tenure as NKVD chief that it is unlikely that he was capable of much good organization. Throughout his time as chief he drank heavily on every single day and never started work before four or five in the afternoon. In practice, as Yezhov himself told his principal subordinates at the NKVD, the ministry was run by Stalin (his words were "Comrade Stalin is the first Chekist"). Stalin was the director-general of the "Great Terror"; Yezhov was merely his instrument. There is no evidence that he ever exceeded Stalin's instructions. He was fired when Stalin wanted to get rid of him. He was dismissed because he had served Stalin's purposes.[86] In the three great Moscow show trials Stalin decided who was to receive the death sentence. The lie that his party rivals had forged an alliance with hostile intelligence services was invented by Stalin to damn his enemies.[87] Stalin monitored the NKVD's investigations into his enemies carefully; Yezhov had to send investigation records relating to important prisoners to the Kremlin without delay.[88] Yezhov's instructions to his officers seem even to have repeated phrases he had heard Stalin say (for instance, "If during this operation an extra thousand people will be shot, that is not such a big deal.")[89]

Yezhov's successors were as vile as he was. He was replaced by Lavrenti Beria, a Georgian. An able and efficient administrator, Beria was also a degenerate—a serial rapist whose bodyguards procured women for him and who neglected his wife and child.[90] Stalin certainly knew of his depravity but took no action because Beria was too useful to him. Beria's ability made him unusual at the top of the NKVD in the late 1930s and 1940s. He had joined the Georgian secret police when it was formed in 1921. Stalin, whom he met in the mid-1920s, transferred him to Moscow in July 1938, initially as Yezhov's deputy. He was given Yezhov's job four months later. In his rise Beria displayed the skills necessary to survive in the Stalinist bureaucracy: cruelty, brutality, duplicity, cunning. Realizing the absolute power that Stalin had over the regime, his behavior toward his boss was utterly sycophantic. He proved a skillful courtier, flattering Stalin incessantly and fueling his suspicions of others.[91] He cultivated the ruling elite with equal cunning and became a member very quickly; according to the Russian historian Anton Antonov-Ovseenko, "Beria felt himself at home right away. He was clinking wine glasses with the crafty Mikoian, being photographed arm-in-arm with the simple-minded Voroshilov, listening attentively to the slow-witted Molotov. He amazingly quickly and naturally joined the entourage of this inner circle."[92] Although he groveled before Stalin and ingratiated himself with his retinue, Beria was domineering and abusive in his dealings with subordinates. He was dismissive of their views. This mixture of sycophancy toward superiors and bullying of subordinates was typical of Communist security chiefs.[93]

His cruelty grew and grew. In 1937–38, as Georgian party chief, he took part in the interrogation and beating of prisoners.[94] He continued to participate in the torture of victims as NKVD chief, deriving sadistic pleasure from it.[95] He reserved his particular cruelty for people he knew well. He had a feud with Nestor Lakoba, a leading Georgian Communist politician. Lakoba died in December 1936 in suspicious circumstances—many people have suggested that he was poisoned by Beria. In 1937, when Stalin's terror was at its height, Beria destroyed the rest of the Lakoba family: Nestor's brother Mikhail was shot after a trial in which he was convicted on false charges of treason and terrorism, Mikhail's wife died under torture, and his teenage son was shot. Almost all of Nestor Lakoba's family were shot or imprisoned.[96]

Beria's ruthlessness and organizational ability were the keys to his effectiveness. During the war he supervised the forcible deportations of the minority nationalities of the Soviet Union—the Volga Germans, Chechens, Ingush, Kalmyks, Crimean Tartars, and others—which the regime regarded as disloyal. These deportations of millions of people caused the death by dehydration, malnutrition, exhaustion, or disease of tens of thousands, chiefly elderly people, women, and children. While this was a crime against humanity, Beria accomplished what Stalin wanted.[97]

He also had responsibility for the Soviet atomic bomb project, and under his direction Soviet physicists and engineers made a bomb in a remarkably short time (four years).[98] Some of the scientists who worked for him considered him an excellent, determined administrator. Others resented his authoritarian, abusive management style. One of them, A. P. Aleksandrov, called Beria "a terrifying man, vile."[99]

Beria had the intelligence not to treat everyone badly. He deliberately built up his own "tail" of supporters in the Georgia Cheka: Georgians like Vladimir Dekanozov, Avksentii Rapava, and Nikolai Rukhadze; Armenians like Vsevolod Merkulov and Bogdan Kobulov; and Azerbaijanis like M. D. Bagirov. (A "tail," in Soviet parlance, was a group of supporters whom a leading figure appointed to positions below him.) Beria transferred them to Moscow when he became NKVD chief in 1938. They were so closely identified with him that Beria's enemies made a point of executing them in the wake of his own execution in December 1953.[100] He was the first NKVD chief to have a strong power base of supporters in the ministry and the Georgian Communist Party apparatus (the result of his service first as state security chief and then as party chief in Georgia). His predecessors as NKVD chief in Moscow had either been professional policemen (Yagoda) or party officials without a personal following (Dzerzhinsky, Menzhinsky, Yezhov).[101] This had made them easy to dismiss. Stalin only allowed Beria to create such a strong position for himself at the NKVD because by that time so many security officials had been killed by Yezhov that expertise was badly lacking. Beria's own competence as an administrator was valuable in a huge organization gravely weakened by the execution of much of its staff in 1937–38.

The state security chiefs of the late Stalin period were Vsevolod Merkulov, Viktor Abakumov, and Semyon Ignat'ev. Merkulov was appointed state security minister in 1943, when the security service was separated from the Interior Ministry and given its own minister. Stalin may have done this simply to reduce Beria's power. Alternatively, the combined State Security and Internal Affairs Ministry was gigantic and may have become too big to be run efficiently. Whichever explanation is true, Merkulov added little to the position of minister. He had the cruelty and servility the job demanded. Though an intelligent man who wrote plays and screenplays, Merkulov lacked initiative. He knew the dangers of having a mind of one's own. Before the German invasion of the Soviet Union in June 1941, he refused to sign and pass on to Stalin a report by his foreign intelligence chief, Pavel Fitin, which concluded that intelligence reports warning of an impending attack were reliable. Merkulov's reason was that he knew that Stalin considered the reports to be false. Fitin later said that Merkulov told him, "Up there at the top, they [Stalin] know how to analyze it [intelligence] better than we do."[102] Markus Wolf, the long-serving Stasi foreign intelligence chief who is the subject of a chapter in this volume, also encouraged his political masters' delusions by not standing up for the intelligence his service had collected.

Merkulov was succeeded in 1946 by Viktor Abakumov, the former head of the wartime military counterintelligence service SMERSH (an acronym for "Death to Spies"). Stalin probably appointed Abakumov to reduce Beria's influence over the security service. He failed because Abakumov knew that political allies were essential in order to stay alive. According to Khrushchev, Abakumov was "Beria's man; he never reported to anyone, not even to Stalin, without checking first with Beria."[103] He was a brute who personally tortured some of his victims, which is all he brought to the position of state security minister. He was as fond of expensive foreign luxuries as Yagoda had been before him (corruption was one of the reasons for his execution). In 1951 Stalin replaced Abakumov with Ignat'ev, a Central Committee official, and had him thrown into prison. Merkulov and other rivals of Abakumov had denounced him to Stalin, whose suspiciousness had by now turned into paranoia.[104] Stalin was then moving against Beria and used Ignat'ev to fabricate the "doctors' plot," which was intended to serve as his excuse for a blood purge. Beria replaced Ignat'ev as minister for state security as soon as Stalin died.[105]

From the start the Bolshevik regime relied for its existence on the NKVD. So repressive was the regime in the last twenty years of Stalin's dictatorship that this dependence became even greater, which enabled Beria to make a bid for supreme power when Stalin died. He was one of only two security chiefs to do so. His bid failed, but that of Yuri Andropov, thirty years later, succeeded. Beria had the intelligence to see the crisis of the Soviet system in the early

1950s; this prompted him to propose a reform policy that antagonized his colleagues and led to his own arrest and execution.[106] The triumvirate that succeeded Stalin—Malenkov, Molotov, and Khrushchev—appointed Sergei Kruglov as a stopgap head of the security police. Kruglov had a pitiless reputation; during the war he had been responsible for the loyalty of the Soviet army and had ordered numerous executions of demoralized soldiers. He had also participated in the deportations of the minority peoples. An obscure figure, brutality seems to have been his only professional asset. The security police was not his calling; a party official, he was transferred to it in 1938 only because so many of the NKVD's staff had been shot. Khrushchev had him expelled from the Communist Party in 1960. He died in 1977, in poverty, when he fell under a train.[107]

As soon as Khrushchev had established himself as the principal figure in the regime in 1954, he replaced Kruglov with his own creature, the long-serving Chekist Ivan Serov. Dmitri Shepilov, who served in the Politburo and was briefly foreign minister in the mid-1950s, described Serov as "an utterly amoral and ignorant figure, directly and personally involved in many of the security agencies' past crimes." Serov had been heavily involved in the brutal deportations from the Baltic states in 1939–40 and of the minority peoples of the USSR in 1943–44.[108] His cruelty was his only professional skill. He was utterly servile in his obedience to Khrushchev, the party leader. Shepilov comments that he "was ready with a serf's zealousness to carry out any of his [Khrushchev's] lawless instructions and personal whims."[109]

All these vile personalities reflected the tyranny the Bolsheviks had established. Vicious criminality and murderousness had been necessary to establish this tyranny; gross psychological inadequacies and depravity were tolerated—indeed, encouraged—because they were the price Stalin and his acolytes had to pay to get the killers they needed. They were the apparatchiks of a regime that sought complete power over society.

The Stalin era brought about another important change in the character of the political police's top leadership. Before Yezhov became chief in 1936, the political police had been led by non-Russians. Dzerzhinsky and Menzhinsky were Poles. Yagoda, though raised in Russia, was probably born in Poland as well; he was also Jewish. Poles, Latvians, Jews, and members of other minority nationalities featured prominently among the Cheka's senior staff.[110] After 1936 the political police was more often than not led by Russians. The exceptions were Beria, who was Georgian; Merkulov, who was Armenian; and Semichastny and Fedorchuk, who were Ukrainians. The political police became the most xenophobic and anti-Semitic element of the regime. Russians dominated its senior staff.[111] Poles and Jews were, of course, particular victims of the "Great Terror."[112]

Communist State Security Chiefs in the Post-Stalin Era

With Stalin dead, the Communist regimes of the Soviet Union and Eastern Europe declined into semi-totalitarian systems. Corruption was tolerated because it was an essential feature of all these regimes, but gross depravity became rarer. The office culture of the Soviet security service remained very mistrustful, uncollegial, and unpleasant. The KGB was a hierarchical organization that produced bullies wedded to a conspiracy theory that exaggerated the scale of dissent and blamed it all on the West; its officers acted obsequiously toward their superiors and oppressed their subordinates. It and its sister services were production lines churning out paranoid bullies. Nevertheless, their leaders had more self-discipline than the likes of Yezhov, Beria, and Abakumov. The perfect representative of this type was the East German state security minister, Erich Mielke, who is also the subject of a chapter in this book. Examples within the KGB in the late Cold War were Semyon Tsvigun, first deputy chairman under Yuri Andropov, and the Leningrad KGB chief in the 1980s, Daniil Nozyrev.[113]

Top appointments were made for political reasons at the expense of operational effectiveness. The KGB chairmen of the post-Stalin era lacked political stature. They were either party functionaries or professional policemen. For twenty-four years after 1958 they came from the party bureaucracy because the party insisted on control of the political police after the horrors perpetrated against it by Stalin. Some KGB chairmen were able; others were not. None save Yuri Andropov and Aleksandr Shelepin had enough ability to become a considerable figure in the regime. They were closely tied to leading figures in the party, and many were supporters of the leader himself. Khrushchev and Brezhnev both put their supporters in leading positions in the "power ministries," including the KGB.[114] There was a perennial tendency for the Communist Party's disease of clientelism to spread to the KGB: senior officers built up their "tails" of loyal clients among the officers below them by tolerating mediocrity and overlooking security lapses and blunders. Thus they strengthened their position, but at the expense of the service. Vladimir Kryuchkov, the KGB's foreign intelligence chief from 1974 to 1988, is a good example. Their failings reflected those of the political leaders they served, who were "pompous mediocrities."[115] The senior staff of the KGB in the post-Stalin period were, like their chairmen, either career policemen or men transferred from the party bureaucracy or Communist Youth League (Komsomol). The army was also a significant source of recruits. The chairmen tended to serve for relatively long periods because they formed part of an oligarchy whose members disliked instability at the top. Yuri Andropov set the record for longevity of tenure (fifteen years). Abakumov, executed in 1954, was the last state security minister to die in this way. The KGB's staff as a whole enjoyed excellent job security because stability within the organization was essential to the stability of the regime. This job security, combined with the Chekist tradition, their close identification with the party, and their considerable prestige in Soviet society, gave KGB officers some esprit de corps.[116]

Khrushchev appointed three KGB chairmen. The first was Serov, whom Khrushchev appointed because the two had worked closely together in Ukraine when Khrushchev was party secretary there. When, in 1958, he wanted to reform the KGB and improve its public image, Khrushchev replaced Serov with Aleksandr Shelepin. Shelepin came from the Communist Party's youth wing, the Komsomol, whose chairman he had been from 1952 to 1958. His loyalty to the party was clear. Only forty at the time of his appointment, he lacked political authority and did not undermine that of Khrushchev. The party's authority over the KGB was enhanced by the infusion of Komsomol personnel into it. An able man, Shelepin's most striking characteristic as KGB chairman was ambition. He was ambitious both for himself (he wanted to become party leader) and for the Communist cause. Nevertheless, he does not seem to have added anything significant to Soviet policy. He did indeed propose to Khrushchev in June 1961 an aggressive "active measures" strategy designed to exploit Western decolonization and stir up national liberation movements in the developing world, thus forcing the United States on the back foot in the Cold War. However, to make common cause with such movements was already Soviet policy.[117] From his time KGB officers became better educated. Shelepin may have had a hand in this policy.

Shelepin's ability made him no less criminal than his predecessors: during his tenure the KGB continued to assassinate troublesome dissidents abroad (the Ukrainian nationalist Stepan Bandera was murdered on Shelepin's orders in 1959). Shelepin's understanding of the outside world was just as primitive and distorted by Marxist-Leninist conspiracy theory as his predecessors': it was he who in June 1960 passed on to Khrushchev very flawed intelligence obtained within NATO that the United States was considering a first strike on the USSR. His association with the KGB harmed his later rise because his Politburo colleagues did not want a former KGB chief to lead the Communist Party.[118]

Khrushchev replaced Shelepin in 1961 with Vladimir Semichastnyi, Shelepin's protégé. A Ukrainian, he was known to Khrushchev because he had become first secretary of the Ukrainian Komsomol in 1947, when Khrushchev was party first secretary there. He became head of the entire Soviet Komsomol in 1958, replacing Shelepin, and was transferred to the KGB chairmanship from a senior position in the Azerbaijani Communist Party. Aged only thirty-seven at the time of his appointment to lead the KGB, he was given the job because he lacked political weight; Khrushchev put a crony in the job so as to secure the political loyalty of the KGB. Semichastnyi was so ignorant of intelligence that he had not wanted to accept the job and did so only because Khrushchev insisted.[119] He does not seem to have been an effective chairman, but this was not the reason he was fired. He was dismissed in May 1967 because he was too close to Shelepin, who was a political rival of the new party first secretary, Leonid Brezhnev. Brezhnev had by this time got the better of Shelepin in the Politburo and wanted to weaken his political position further.

Yuri Andropov succeeded Semichastnyi as KGB chairman. He was an intelligent, reflective, impressive, and civil man, so as a matter of character he was different from the KGB officials who served him. Politically, however, he was identical to them: a devout Communist wedded to conspiracy theories about the West. He stands out among KGB chairmen because he was, unusually, a considerable political figure at the time of his appointment; indeed, the job was a step down from his exalted position as secretary of the Communist Party's Central Committee and head of its department for liaison with socialist countries. He was compensated by being elected a candidate member of the party's Politburo the month after his appointment. Since he was not a member of any of the factions in the party leadership, he was probably chosen for the KGB chairmanship because he was a neutral figure and acceptable to all. He was acceptable to the KGB because his central committee job overseeing the USSR's relations with the satellite states had made him very familiar with its work (these relations were, to a significant degree, handled by the KGB). He was also a proven hard-liner, having played a key role in the reimposition of Soviet control on Hungary after the 1956 uprising.[120]

Andropov was not a crony of Brezhnev. Brezhnev was not strong enough to put his own man in as KGB chairman; his Politburo colleagues would not allow it.[121] However, Brezhnev made sure that many of his cronies were among Andropov's senior officials. Andropov's first deputy chairman, Semyon Tsvigun, was Brezhnev's brother-in-law (he had married a sister of Brezhnev's wife). He was a career political policeman, having served in the security police since 1939. Another deputy chairman, Viktor Chebrikov, was a Communist Party official who belonged to Brezhnev's "Dnepropetrovsk mafia" (he had served in Ukraine, had had ties to Brezhnev there, and had attended the same institute of higher education as Brezhnev, Dnepropetrovsk Metallurgical Institute). Yet another deputy chairman, Georgi Tsinyev, had known Brezhnev in the Ukrainian Communist Party, had then moved to head up Soviet military counterintelligence in the GDR, and had then transferred to the KGB. All three men were elected to the Communist Party's Central Committee. In the late 1970s another Brezhnev associate in the KGB was Gen. Viktor Alidin, the head of the large and powerful Moscow branch.[122] Tsvigun and Tsinyev received particularly high honors clearly intended to increase their standing in the KGB and thus Brezhnev's influence over it. Tsvigun also had a high public profile intended to strengthen his position in the KGB.

More sophisticated than other leading Communists—he liked jazz and wrote poetry—Andropov won the reputation among Western observers of being a liberal. This was unjustified: he was a Communist hard-liner. In the words of Oleg Kalugin, his foreign counterintelligence chief in the 1970s, Andropov "possessed one of the more virulent anti-Western streaks among the Soviet leadership"[123] and "genuinely believed that the United States and the West were working day and night to destroy the Soviet Union."[124] These "orthodox communist views often blinded him to a steadily changing reality." When Western European Communist parties started to seek independence from the Soviet Communist Party, Andropov viewed the trend not as a natural historical development but as "the dastardly work of Western intelligence services." His orthodox Communism meant that he was unable to understand why the USSR was in difficulties in the 1970s. Kalugin's assessment is that "Andropov himself was so devout a communist that, on the domestic Soviet scene, he couldn't see the forest for the trees. As our economy slid steadily downward in the late 1970s, he attributed the decline in production to poor worker discipline and disorder at factories. All that was needed, he said, was to boost worker productivity by tightening control over the economy and the workplace."[125] This shows how deluded the Politburo was.

Andropov's Communist orthodoxy was evident from his fierce repression of dissidence. Under his leadership, the KGB's persecution of dissidents was intense: they were committed to psychiatric hospitals; a very strict policy on state secrets was pursued; border protection was stepped up; Soviet citizens were not allowed to meet alone with foreigners; anyone whose behavior was out of the ordinary was viewed as a potential spy. Andropov's position was clear from his dictum, "No sane individual will oppose a regime that wants so badly to make the lives of its people better."[126] He was a leading hawk in the Politburo pressing for repression; under his influence, the KGB's intelligence reports to the party leadership encouraged the leaders in their belief that dissidents were in the pay of the Western intelligence services.[127]

As a rule the KGB under Andropov persecuted and intimidated dissidents by more discreet means than high-profile trials that attracted damaging publicity and turned the accused into heroes of the international media. Famous dissidents like Aleksandr Solzhenitsyn were expelled from the USSR; Jews and Volga Germans were allowed to emigrate; some dissidents were blackmailed or bullied into silence; others were incarcerated in psychiatric hospitals; yet more were dismissed from their jobs, expelled from the Communist Party, denied university places, conscripted into the army, or prosecuted for nonpolitical crimes that tarnished their reputation. How much of a hand Andropov had in this change of approach is hard to say, but it is consistent with his intelligent and civil personality.[128]

Andropov left the KGB in May 1982 to return to the Central Committee Secretariat (in practice, as the senior secretary since Brezhnev was very ill and close to death). His successor at the head of the KGB, Vitaly Fedorchuk (chairman from May to December 1982), was the first career political policeman to lead the KGB since 1958. He had no close ties to Andropov: by appointing him Brezhnev and those around him may have wanted to reduce Andropov's influence over the KGB. Andropov's influence had increased a few months earlier, in January 1982, when Semyon Tsvigun had committed suicide, apparently because he feared prosecution owing to a corruption investigation initiated by the KGB, at Andropov's order, into friends of Brezhnev's daughter Galina and her husband, Yuri Churbanov, the deputy minister of internal affairs.[129]

Fedorchuk had previously been the chairman of the KGB in Ukraine, where he had persecuted dissidents viciously. Oleg Kalugin describes him as "a Brezhnev hack. . . . He was a rude, conceited bonecrusher, bent on smashing internal dissent in our society and tightening discipline within the KGB. He peppered KGB offices at home and abroad with ridiculous warnings of impending Western aggression, imperialist plots, and CIA efforts to destroy the Soviet economy."[130]

Fedorchuk was promoted to minister of internal affairs at the end of 1982, as Andropov extended the KGB's influence over other parts of the government. Fedorchuk's successor, Viktor Chebrikov, had served in the KGB for fifteen years prior to becoming its chairman (he served until 1988). Before that he had been a party apparatchik. Kalugin describes him as "an absolute nonentity, a weak and indecisive man who was a pale reflection of Andropov" and "an obedient communist party servant. He was a pleasant man, but like so many party bureaucrats, terribly cautious and afraid to move without approval from his superiors. He was a prime example of our leaders during the depths of the 'stagnation' period before Gorbachev—servile, sickly, and indecisive."[131]

Gifted politician though he was, Mikhail Gorbachev had one severe failing for a politician: naivety, which often made him a poor judge of people. His predecessors had insisted that they have a considerable measure of control over the KGB. Gorbachev did not. He did not appoint his supporters to leading positions within the KGB; there was no Gorbachev faction within it during his time as general secretary. This was a fatal weakness; it enabled the KGB chairman in 1991 to organize a conspiracy against him and overthrow him without Gorbachev receiving any warning of the plot. Indeed, the KGB chairman concerned, Vladimir Kryuchkov, was his own appointee. In 1988 Gorbachev replaced Chebrikov with Kryuchkov, considering him more sophisticated than the other KGB officers. One influence on him was that Kryuchkov, like Gorbachev himself, was a protégé of Andropov. Looks deceived him: Kryuchkov was a typical KGB hard-liner who was bound to oppose Gorbachev's reform policy.

Kryuchkov was not just a political foe. According to Kalugin, who worked with him, he was a typical product of a KGB culture that encouraged sycophancy, political infighting, and bullying at the expense of operational effectiveness. Kalugin's assessment of Kryuchkov was that he was "the classic assistant, the consummate bureaucrat": obsequious and skilled at bureaucratic infighting and getting the better of rivals but cautious, indecisive, fainthearted, physically cowardly, and jealous of his colleagues' successes. He had "a serious intellectual inferiority complex" and was "a real bastard."[132] Kalugin maintains that, as chief of the KGB's foreign intelligence service, Kryuchkov got rid of people willing to argue with him and replaced them with sycophants and Communist Party apparatchiks. This diminished the service's aggression in its struggle with the CIA in the late 1970s and 1980s, while the number of KGB defectors soared. The culture of the foreign intelligence service became one of sycophantic back-scratching; office politics became more important than the fight against the CIA.[133]

Kalugin is a biased source on the KGB's culture since he lost his struggle to preserve his career to the sycophantic bullies he condemns. However, he is not the only veteran of the KGB's foreign intelligence service, the PGU (Pervoye Glavnoye Upravleniye: First Chief Directorate), to claim that it was badly led. Others have called its last head, Leonid Shebarshin, "the first genuinely competent head of the First Chief Directorate in decades."[134] Moreover, Kalugin's portrayal of the PGU as so racked by internal politics and poor leadership that its operational effectiveness suffered is supported by its record at the time. It was unsuccessful then in identifying and recruiting good agents. It certainly had outstandingly valuable agents in the United States' intelligence agencies—Aldrich Ames at the CIA and Robert Hanssen at the FBI—but they volunteered their services (they were "walk-ins," in intelligence terminology). The number of agents in the USSR's security and intelligence agencies whom Ames and Hanssen were able to betray confirms Kalugin's point that morale gravely declined in the last ten or fifteen years of the Soviet Union's existence. They betrayed at least twenty Western agents in the Soviet Union, most of them reporting to American intelligence agencies. Most of them were officers in either the KGB or the GRU (Glavnoye Razvedivatelnoye Upravleniye: Main Intelligence Directorate), the Soviet military intelligence service. The most senior KGB officer betrayed was Oleg Gordievsky, then the KGB's resident-designate in London, who was a spy of Britain's Secret Intelligence Service.[135]

The Soviet security service took on the flaws of the regime it served. The Soviet Communist system tended to produce a strong leader: the man who dominated the Central Committee dominated the party and thus the entire regime. Consequently, their state security chiefs were, of necessity, personalities who subordinated themselves to party leaders and implemented their orders. Able men, committed Communists, and party loyalists like Dzerzhinsky increasingly gave way to ignorant, uneducated, brutal creatures of the leader like Yezhov and Serov and intelligent degenerates like Beria. After Stalin died, the party leaders agreed that none of them should control the political police and that no KGB chairman should become party leader. Appointment to the top job in the KGB was consistently a political decision: relatively unimportant party officials and colorless political policemen without any political following were usually chosen. As a rule, they did not have either the ability or the other personal qualities of their democratic counterparts. Unlike those Westerners, most seem to have contributed nothing to the effectiveness of their agencies. Indeed, some of them—Yezhov is the outstanding example—gravely impaired it.

All the USSR's security chiefs, being brutal men, enhanced their service's ability to act brutally. This contribution aside, Soviet security chiefs who improved the performance of their agencies are the exception rather than the rule. Dzerzhinsky's dedication to the task of repressing White opposition and peasant and worker uprisings enabled the Bolshevik Party to hang on to power in the turbulent period of the civil war. Beria supplied valuable professional experience when the political police was being reconstructed after the "Great Terror." He also marshaled the resources of the Soviet political police and labor camp system behind the USSR's atomic bomb project. Some of the ferocity with which the KGB persecuted dissidents in the 1970s is attributable to Andropov personally. The organization's political influence grew during his leadership. He also played a role in refashioning political police methods in the late 1960s and 1970s, ensuring that the KGB made more use of manipulation and less of coercion and terror, and improved his staff's professional skills.[136]

As a rule, whatever operational successes the Soviet security service achieved had nothing to do with the quality of their leadership. Political considerations prevailed over operational ones. The job was too sensitive, in the Soviet Union as in its satellite states, for the choice of chairman or minister to be decided on operational grounds. The KGB and its predecessors were successful because security service work is not rocket science and people of ordinary abilities, armed with all the powers of a ruthlessly repressive state,

Table 1.1 The Leadership of the Soviet Security Service, 1917–91

Period	Security chief
1917–26	Feliks Dzerzhinsky (Pole)
1926–34	Viacheslav Menzhinsky (Pole)
1934–36	Genrikh Yagoda (Jewish; probably Polish by birth)
1936–38	Nikolai Yezhov (Russian)
1938–41	Lavrenti Beria (Georgian of Mingrelian ethnicity)
1941 (February–July)	Vsevolod Merkulov (Armenian)
1941–43	Lavrenti Beria
1943–46	Vsevolod Merkulov
1946–51	Viktor Abakumov (Russian)
1951–53	Semyon Ignat'ev (Russian)
1953 (March–June)	Lavrenti Beria
1953–54	Sergei Kruglov (Russian)
1954–58	Ivan Serov (Russian)
1958–61	Aleksandr Shelepin (Russian)
1961–67	Vladimir Semichastnyi (Ukrainian)
1967–82	Yuri Andropov (Russian)
1982 (May–December)	Vitaly Fedorchuk (Ukrainian)
1982–88	Viktor Chebrikov (Russian)
1988–91	Vladimir Kryuchkov (Russian)
1991	Vadim Bakatin (Russian)

could master it. The millions of people they murdered, arrested, deported, imprisoned, exiled, and starved to death were defenseless before it.

The Dictatorial Tradition

The end of European imperialism gave rise to a variety of political systems in the newly independent former colonies. Some, India being the principal example, successfully established a democratic form of government. As Paul McGarr shows in his chapter in this book, the leadership its intelligence agencies have had has remained within the Western tradition. By contrast, as Chikara Hashimoto demonstrates, owing to the sectarian politics of postindependence Lebanon, its security chiefs have been more concerned with regime security than state security. Many former colonies became dictatorships—Egypt, the subject of Dina Rezk's chapter, is an example. The twentieth-century tradition of intelligence leadership within dictatorships is similar to the Communist, although the ideological element is less prominent because the ideology is less totalitarian. The range of dictatorships is wide, extending from the royal and nationalist-socialist dictatorships of the Arab Middle East to the military dictatorships of Burma and Pakistan and to Russia's contemporary authoritarian, security service–led pseudo-democracy. In such a dictatorship, the security service's task is to provide security to the regime and its leader. It is answerable only to them. They must be protected from a popular revolt, terrorist violence, the spying and subversion of foreign powers, and even plots within the regime itself. This task has been aptly described as "coup-proofing."[137] "Coup-proofing" is a difficult task since the regime must be protected against both a popular uprising and plotters within the regime. Dictators who fear a coup on the part of officers of their own security services or armed forces more than they fear an uprising will tend to create multiple security agencies, led by men unquestionably loyal to them, and set them to keep watch on one another. By contrast, dictators who fear a popular uprising more than a coup will, like Communist leaders, tend to prefer a single security service that prioritizes the collection of intelligence on the populace.[138]

The security agencies of dictatorships are vicious and above the law. The most notorious examples are the security services of the dictatorial regimes of the Arab states, which make much use of torture in order to frighten their peoples into obedience. The word in Arabic for "security service" is *al-mukhabarat*. Since the Russian regime no longer relies on either democratic legitimacy or an official ideology to justify its hold on power, the successor agency to the KGB, the Federal Security Service (Federalnaya Sluzhba Bezopasnosti, FSB) has become a Russian *mukhabarat*.[139]

The Western tradition, then, has tended to produce leaders who have reflected national and bureaucratic culture, have regarded themselves as people managers, are increasingly drawn to the model of a corporate chief executive officer, and are judged by the quality of the information they provide. It has been rare for them to have political influence; J. Edgar Hoover and William Casey are examples of ones who did. They increasingly have to cope with the tension between leading their agencies and representing them before the policy makers and legislative bodies to which they are accountable. The Communist tradition produced sycophantic "bonecrushers" willing to engage in the mass repression essential to Communist rule. Many of these men were creatures of the party leaders they served. However, such was the importance of their service to the regime that Soviet security chiefs could be powerful political figures—Dzerzhinsky, Beria, Andropov, and Kryuchkov are the leading examples. The same tendency for security chiefs to be both creatures of the state leader and powerful political figures is visible in the dictatorial tradition. Intelligence and security chiefs who exemplify these traditions are analyzed in the chapters that follow.

Notes

1. For an introduction to types of leadership, see Bernard M. Bass, with Ruth Bass, *The Bass Handbook of Leadership: Theory, Research, and Managerial Applications*, 4th ed. (New York: Free Press, 2008), chaps. 2 and 3.

2. Mats Alvesson, "Leadership and Organizational Culture," in *The SAGE Handbook of Leadership*, ed. Alan Bryman, David Collinson, Keith Grint, Brad Jackson, and Mary Uhl-Bien, (Los Angeles, CA: SAGE Publications, 2011), 157.

3. Manfred F. R. Kets de Vries, "The Leadership Mystique," *Academy of Management Executive* 8, no. 3 (1994): 73–74.

4. Jay A. Conger, "Charismatic Leadership," in *SAGE Handbook of Leadership*, 86.

5. George Tenet, *At the Center of the Storm: My Years at the CIA* (London: HarperCollins, 2007), 16–27.

6. Mats Alvesson, *Management of Knowledge-Intensive Companies* (Berlin: de Gruyter, 1995), 180.

7. Tenet, *At the Center of the Storm*, 19–20, 30–35.

8. Tom Bower, *The Perfect English Spy: Sir Dick White and the Secret War, 1935–1990* (London: William Heinemann, 1995), 168.

9. Ibid.

10. James MacGregor Burns, *Leadership* (New York: Harper and Row, 1978), 4–5, 18–28. A similar, though more sophisticated, typology of political leadership is to be found in Archie Brown, *The Myth of the Strong Leader: Political Leadership in the Modern Age* (London: Bodley Head, 2014). Since this typology is so focused on political leadership, it does not apply to the organizational leader.

11. Burns, *Leadership*, 20.

12. Gary Yukl, "Managerial Leadership: A Review of Theory and Research," *Journal of Management* 15, no. 2 (1989): 253.

13. There is strong support among veteran intelligence officers for this view: see Michael Herman, *Intelligence Power in Peace and War* (Cambridge: Cambridge University Press/Royal Institute of International Affairs, 1996), chaps. 17 and 18. For the influence of the governmental context on styles of intelligence reporting, see Paul Maddrell, ed., *The Image of the Enemy: Intelligence Analysis of Adversaries since 1945* (Washington, DC: Georgetown University Press, 2015), introduction.

14. Yukl, "Managerial Leadership: A Review of Theory and Research," 253.

15. Ibid., 277.

16. Alvesson, "Leadership and Organizational Culture," 155–63.

17. Clifford Geertz, *The Interpretation of Cultures* (London: Hutchinson, 1975), 145.

18. Michael Howard, *The Lessons of History* (New Haven, CT: Yale University Press, 1991), 41.

19. See William Odom, *Fixing Intelligence: For a More Secure America* (New Haven, CT: Yale University Press, 2003).

20. See Tenet, *At the Center of the Storm*, 16.

21. On the Office of the Director of National Intelligence, see https://www.dni.gov /index.php.

22. On the influence of the presidential model on the US intelligence community and of Whitehall's committee system on British intelligence, see Herman, *Intelligence Power in Peace and War*, chap. 15.

23. Yukl, "Managerial Leadership: A Review of Theory and Research," 258–61.

24. Ibid., 268–69.

25. Ray S. Cline, *Secrets, Spies and Scholars* (Washington, DC: Acropolis Books, 1976), 151–54, 183–91. On Allen Dulles, see Peter Grose, *Gentleman Spy: The Life of Allen Dulles* (Boston, MA: Houghton Mifflin, 1994); and James Srodes, *Allen Dulles: Master of Spies* (Washington, DC: Regnery Publishing, 1999).

26. Kets de Vries, "Leadership Mystique," 74.

27. Cline, *Secrets, Spies and Scholars*, 193.

28. Ibid., 191.

29. Christopher Andrew, *For the President's Eyes Only: Secret Intelligence and the American Presidency from Washington to Bush* (London: HarperCollins, 1995), 271, 284, 291, 314–16, 318–22.

30. Kets de Vries, "Leadership Mystique," 76.

31. Ibid., 73.

32. Tenet, *At the Center of the Storm*, 477.

33. Matthew M. Aid, *The Secret Sentry: The Untold History of the National Security Agency* (New York: Bloomsbury Press, 2010), 160–61.

34. Andrew, *For the President's Eyes Only*, 187–93.

35. Cline, *Secrets, Spies and Scholars*, 109–15.

36. Aid, *Secret Sentry*, 182.

37. Richard Deacon, *"C": A Biography of Sir Maurice Oldfield* (London: Futura, 1985), 209, 260.

38. Ibid., 166–68, 174.

39. Ibid., 164.

40. Thomas Powers, *The Man Who Kept the Secrets: Richard Helms and the CIA* (London: Weidenfeld and Nicolson, 1980), 171.

41. Cline, *Secrets, Spies and Scholars*, 112.

42. Kets de Vries, "Leadership Mystique," 76.

43. Alan Judd, *The Quest for C: Sir Mansfield Cumming and the Founding of the British Secret Service* (London: HarperCollins Publishers, 1999), 469–70.

44. Keith Jeffery, *MI6: The History of the Secret Intelligence Service, 1909–1949* (London: Bloomsbury, 2010), 209.

45. Philip H. J. Davies, *MI6 and the Machinery of Spying* (London: Frank Cass, 2004), 8–9, 255–56.

46. See, for example, Deacon, *"C"*, 196; and Anthony Glees, *The Stasi Files* (London: Free Press, 2003).

47. Judd, *Quest for C*, 10–11, 58–59, 206, 253–54; and Jeffery, *MI6*, 729–30.

48. Rhodri Jeffreys-Jones, *The FBI: A History* (New Haven, CT: Yale University Press, 2007), 85–86, 215–16.

49. Ibid., 216–18.

50. Kets de Vries, "Leadership Mystique," 76.

51. Tenet, *At the Center of the Storm*, 15–17.

52. Alvesson, "Leadership and Organizational Culture," 158.

53. Bower, *Perfect English Spy*, 376, 383–85.

54. Ibid., 359–61.

55. Ibid., 262–71; and Davies, *MI6 and the Machinery of Spying*, 278–79.

56. Bower, *Perfect English Spy*, 201.

57. Ibid., 174–77, 341, 353.

58. Tenet, *At the Center of the Storm*, 3, 7.

59. Aid, *Secret Sentry*, 162.

60. Raymond L. Garthoff, "Soviet Leaders, Soviet Intelligence, and Changing Views of the United States, 1965–91," in *Image of the Enemy*, 37; and Paul Maddrell, "The Stasi's Reporting on the Federal Republic of Germany," in ibid., 83–84.

61. Andrew, *For the President's Eyes Only*, 276–78, 310.

62. Ibid., 310–14, 322–23, 336.

63. Ibid., 311, 364.

64. Athan Theoharis and John Stuart Cox, *The Boss: J. Edgar Hoover and the Great American Inquisition* (London: Harrap, 1989), 349–60.

65. Exceptionally, Congress in 2011 passed a law enabling Robert S. Mueller III, the then director of the FBI, to serve a further two years in the position. In all, he served for twelve years (from 2001 to 2013).

66. George P. Shultz, *Turmoil and Triumph: My Years as Secretary of State* (New York: Charles Scribner's Sons, 1993), 691, 851, 864–67.

67. Ibid., 865–66.

68. Andrew, *For the President's Eyes Only*, 478.

69. Stéphane Courtois, Nicolas Werth, Jean-Louis Panné, Andrzej Paczkowski, Karel Bartosek, and Jean-Louis Margolin, *The Black Book of Communism: Crimes, Terror, Repression* (Cambridge, MA: Harvard University Press, 1999), 103–4.

70. Quoted in George Leggett, *The Cheka: Lenin's Political Police* (Oxford: Clarendon Press, 1981), 189.

71. Ibid., 250–56.

72. Leggett, *Cheka*, 275, 461.

73. J. Arch Getty and Oleg V. Naumov, *Yezhov: The Rise of Stalin's "Iron Fist"* (New Haven, CT: Yale University Press, 2008), 215–16.

74. Ibid., 18.

75. Marc Jansen and Nikita Petrov, *Stalin's Loyal Executioner: People's Commissar Nikolai Ezhov, 1895–1940* (Stanford, CA: Hoover Institution, 2002), 202–3.

76. Ibid., 182.

77. Ibid., 110.

78. Quoted in ibid., 198.

79. Ibid., 19–20, 201.

80. Getty and Naumov, *Yezhov*, 222–24.

81. Jansen and Petrov, *Stalin's Loyal Executioner*, 123–24.

82. Ibid., 15, 179.

83. Ibid., 186–89.

84. Getty and Naumov, *Yezhov*, 112–14, 120–21, 219–20.

85. Ibid., 23, 55–56, 103–4.

86. Jansen and Petrov, *Stalin's Loyal Executioner*, 203–11.

87. Ibid., 58–59.

88. Ibid., 62.

89. Ibid., 84–85.

90. Amy Knight, *Beria, Stalin's First Lieutenant* (Princeton, NJ: Princeton University Press, 1993), 97–98; and Dmitrii Shepilov, *The Kremlin's Scholar: A Memoir of Soviet Politics under Stalin and Khrushchev* (New Haven, CT: Yale University Press), 272–73.

91. Knight, *Beria, Stalin's First Lieutenant*, 7.

92. Quoted in ibid., 95–96.

93. Quoted in ibid., 131.

94. Jansen and Petrov, *Stalin's Loyal Executioner*, 152.

95. Knight, *Beria, Stalin's First Lieutenant*, 99–101.

96. Ibid., 72, 81, 83. Beria was head of the Georgian GPU from 1926 to 1931; first secretary of the Georgian Communist Party from 1931 to 1938; deputy chief of the NKVD from August to November 1938; and NKVD chief from November 1938 to 1941.

97. Courtois et al., *Black Book of Communism*; and Knight, *Beria, Stalin's First Lieutenant*, 126–27.

98. See David Holloway, *Stalin and the Bomb: The Soviet Union and Atomic Energy, 1939–1956* (New Haven, CT: Yale University Press, 1994).

99. Quoted in Knight, *Beria, Stalin's First Lieutenant*, 137.

100. Ibid., 30, 223.

101. Ibid., 91.

102. Christopher Andrew and Oleg Gordievsky, *KGB: The Inside Story of Its Foreign Operations from Lenin to Gorbachev* (London: Hodder and Stoughton, 1990), 208–9.

103. Quoted in ibid., 279–80.

104. Knight, *Beria, Stalin's First Lieutenant*, 115, 158.

105. Entry on Ignat'ev in *Lexikon der Geheimdienste im 20. Jahrhundert* [Encyclopedia of secret services in the 20th century], ed. Helmut Roewer, Stefan Schäfer, and Matthias Uhl (Munich: Herbig Verlag, 2003), 214.

106. Knight, *Beria, Stalin's First Lieutenant*, 9, 184–94.

107. Entry on Kruglov in Roewer, Schäfer, and Uhl, *Lexikon der Geheimdienste im 20. Jahrhundert*, 253.

108. Knight, *Police and Politics in the Soviet Union*, 51.

109. Shepilov, *Kremlin's Scholar*, 276.

110. Leggett, *Cheka*, 256–76.

111. Amy Knight, *KGB: Police and Politics in the Soviet Union* (London: Allen and Unwin, 1988), 158–60; and Paul Maddrell, "Cooperation between the HVA and KGB, 1951–1989," in *Bulletin of the German Historical Institute*, suppl. 9, *The Stasi at Home and Abroad, Domestic Order and Foreign Intelligence* (2014), ed. Uwe Spiekermann, 189–90.

112. Jansen and Petrov, *Stalin's Loyal Executioner*, 42.

113. Oleg Kalugin, *Spymaster: My Thirty-Two Years in Intelligence and Espionage against the West* (London: Smith Gryphon, 1994), 289.

114. Shepilov, *Kremlin's Scholar*, 306.

115. Kalugin, *Spymaster*, 306.

116. Knight, *KGB: Police and Politics in the Soviet Union*, 154–78.

117. Jonathan Haslam, *Russia's Cold War: From the October Revolution to the Fall of the Wall* (New Haven, CT: Yale University Press, 2011), chap. 5.

118. Christopher Andrew and Vasili Mitrokhin, *The Mitrokhin Archive: The KGB in Europe and the West* (London: Allen Lane/Penguin Press, 1999), 5–6, 235–39, 471.

119. Knight, *KGB: Police and Politics in the Soviet Union*, 64–65, 68–69.

120. Ibid., 80–86.

121. Zhores Medvedev, *Andropov* (Oxford: Basil Blackwell, 1983), 60.

122. Kalugin, *Spymaster*, 268–69.

123. Ibid., 253.

124. Ibid., 256.

125. Ibid., 259–60.

126. Ibid., 262.

127. Andrew and Mitrokhin, *Mitrokhin Archive*, 427.

128. Knight, *Police and Politics in the Soviet Union*, 190–91, 197–203; and Medvedev, *Andropov*, 75–87.

129. Knight, *KGB: Police and Politics in the Soviet Union*, 188; and Medvedev, *Andropov*, 95–96.

130. Kalugin, *Spymaster*, 303; and Knight, *KGB: Police and Politics in the Soviet Union*, 89–90.

131. Kalugin, *Spymaster*, 259, 305.

132. Ibid., 242–44.

133. Ibid., 248–52.

134. Entry on Shebarshin in Roewer, Schäfer, and Uhl, eds., *Lexikon der Geheimdienste im 20. Jahrhundert*, 398.

135. Andrew and Mitrokhin, *Mitrokhin Archive*, 287.

136. Knight, *KGB: Police and Politics in the Soviet Union*, 308, 310–11.

137. See James T. Quinlivan, "Coup-Proofing: Its Practice and Consequences in the Middle East," *International Security* 24, no. 2 (Fall 1999): 131–65.

138. See Sheena Chestnut Greitens, *Dictators and Their Secret Police: Coercive Institutions and State Violence* (Cambridge: Cambridge University Press, 2016).

139. Andrei Soldatov and Irina Borogan, *The New Nobility: The Restoration of Russia's Security State and the Enduring Legacy of the KGB* (New York: PublicAffairs, 2010), 5–6.

2 The Spy Chiefs of Renaissance Venice

Intelligence Leadership in the Early
Modern World

Ioanna Iordanou

Intelligence and espionage have been the subject of fascination for a long time. As a result, official and unofficial narratives of covert missions, undercover agents, and secret services have claimed substantial shelf space in libraries and bookshops, while the ever-appealing genre of spy fiction has featured prominently in book pages and on cinema screens. Historians have not escaped the charms of this constantly evolving scholarly domain and have ceaselessly striven to reveal the past's secrets and their keepers. This past, however, spans largely from the eve of the Great War to the Edward Snowden era, while more distant periods still remain largely unexplored.[1] This is not to say that scholars have not made worthwhile attempts to explore and reduce this gap. Indeed, some excellent work has been done on the diplomatic and, by extension, intelligence operations of early modern states like England (and later Britain),[2] France,[3] the Dutch Republic,[4] the Ottoman and Austrian Habsburg Empires,[5] Portugal,[6] Spain,[7] and the dominant Italian states.[8]

While in most of these states intelligence operations were organized by powerful individuals for the purpose of consolidating political power and control, Venice, as this chapter will show, organized an intelligence service that was centrally administered by the government. Indeed, in an exemplary display of political maturity, Venice created and systematized one of the world's earliest centrally organized state intelligence services. This was responsible for the methodical organization of bureaucracy, diplomacy, and centralized intelligence that supported the city's commercial and maritime supremacy.[9] At the helm of this process was the Council of Ten—Venice's spy chiefs— who, through an elaborate system of managerial delegation, masterminded and oversaw the clandestine activities of a great variety of professional and amateur spies and intelligencers.

Utilizing freshly discovered material from the Venetian State Archives and the Vatican Secret Archives, this chapter will shed light on how the Council

of Ten pulled the strings of Venice's centrally controlled intelligence operations. A long-overdue analysis of the council's centralized administration and
corporate-like leadership practices will demonstrate the effective organization and the masterful system of rigid managerial delegation they employed
in their efforts to administer Venice's intelligence operations. Subsequently,
the chapter will focus on the Ten's remarkable ability to engage politically
excluded commoners in politically significant clandestine missions, often with
no financial benefit to them. In doing so, it will reveal a hitherto unknown
facet of Venice's popular classes. Finally, the last section of the chapter will
offer an evaluation of the Ten's leadership abilities as Venice's spy chiefs.

Overall, drawing on sociological theorizations of secrecy and discussions of
the amorphous "Myth of Venice"—the contemporaneous view that the common good triumphed over private interests in the Venetian Republic—this
chapter will contend that the Ten's efficacy as spy chiefs was due to their effective construction of an exclusive community of followers sharing a collective
identity that was premised on secrecy and, by extension, the principles of
reciprocal confidence and trust. To incentivize participation, the Ten tapped
into the commercial predisposition of Venetians, turning intelligence into a
mutually beneficial transaction between rulers and ruled. Ultimately, to legitimize their actions, they made a public virtue of active contribution to the
public good. In consequence, this chapter will show how the Ten's leadership
practices, which resulted from the heavy institutionalization and growing
bureaucratization that pervaded the politics of Venice in the early modern
period, bore a remarkable resemblance to both the "transactional" and "transformational" styles of contemporary leadership practices.

The Spy Chiefs of Renaissance Venice

"Once did she hold the gorgeous east in fee," wrote the great Romantic William Wordsworth about Venice.[10] This is because by the mid-sixteenth century
the Republic of Venice had built a maritime empire with hegemony over the
most strategic trade routes between the Levant and the Mediterranean world.
This supremacy enabled Venice to control the market in luxury commodities like spices and silk from India and Egypt, which she defended zealously.[11]
As a result, and owing to its strategic geographic position midway between
Habsburg Spain and the Ottoman Levant, Venice gradually metamorphosed
into a bustling emporium of traders, goods, and news.[12] In fact, Venice, had
already turned news into a commodity by the mid-sixteenth century, with the
circulation of one of the world's earliest newspapers, the *gazeta della novita*.[13]
This was a monthly news publication targeted at merchants, informing them

Photo 2.1 The "Giovedì Grasso" Festival in front of the Ducal Palace in Venice, 1765/1766, by Canaletto. (*Wolfgang Ratjen Collection, Paul Mellon Fund, National Gallery of Art*)

of political events that could interfere with their business pursuits.[14] It is not accidental, therefore, that the most famed line from Shakespeare's *The Merchant of Venice*, "What news on the Rialto?" sparks the report of the commercial debacle of an alleged shipwreck.

It is within this commercially charged political setting that Venice's spy chiefs constructed its centrally organized state intelligence service. Established in 1310 under Doge Piero Gradenigo, the Council of Ten was the exclusive committee responsible for state security. Within its jurisdiction were secret affairs, public order, and domestic and foreign policy. The council was actually made up of seventeen men, who included ten ordinary members, six ducal councilors, and in the chair, the Doge. Every month three members took turns at heading the Ten's operations. They were called *Capi*, the heads of the Ten.[15]

Initially, the Ten were tasked with protecting the government from overthrow or corruption. Progressively, however, their powers extended to such a degree that, by the mid-fifteenth century, they encompassed Venice's diplomatic and intelligence operations, military affairs, and other legal matters of state security. Such weighty responsibilities, so central to the city's governance, merited a prominent place in the city's topography. The Ten, therefore, were housed in one of the most impressive state intelligence headquarters of the early modern (and even the modern) world, the Ducal Palace, overlooking the Venetian lagoon in Saint Mark's Square. There the Ten organized and administered the world's earliest state intelligence service. In a way, this resembled a kind of proto-modern public sector organization that operated with remarkable maturity. Its organization comprised several departments, including operations, science and technology, and analysis.[16] This service was also supported by several other state departments, including the Senate, the *Collegio* (an executive branch of the government), and the office of state attorneys (*Avogaria di Comun*).

Gradually, the Ten, together with the *Collegio*, assumed almost complete control of the government.[17] This, inexorably, gave them the bad name of being authoritarian. Indeed, the autocratic way in which the Ten wielded their power tarnished their reputation. Their infamous eruptions were committed to ink by several contemporaneous chroniclers, such as the inveterate diarist Marino Sanudo. "This Council imposes banishment and exile upon nobles, and has others burned or hanged if they deserve it, and has authority to dismiss the Prince, even to do other things to him if he so deserves," he once wrote in his account of Venice's quotidian existence.[18] The Ten's alleged authoritarianism stemmed out of respect for two fundamental Venetian values: order that was achieved by secrecy, and maturity that was guaranteed by gerontocracy. Both these virtues were deemed paramount for state security.[19] It is not a coincidence, therefore, that the Ten's stringent regulations did not exclude the council's members. As the responsible body for state security, if they failed to act speedily on issues that imperiled it, they became liable to a 1,000-ducat fine.[20]

In a way, the Ten seemed to espouse Machiavelli's maxim that a prince "must not worry if he incurs reproach for his cruelty, so long as he keeps his subjects united and loyal. By making an example or two, he will prove more compassionate than those who, being too compassionate, allow disorders which lead to murder and rapine."[21] Yet their authoritarian tendencies were not left uncontrolled. The extraordinarily mature Venetian political system endeavored to contain any potential autocracy, at least in principle. The institution of the *zonta* (the Venetian linguistic variation of *aggiunta* or *addizione*, meaning "addition") was the mechanism put in place for that purpose. The *zonta* was an adjunct commission of fifteen men participating in all important assemblies of the Council of Ten. Either elected or co-opted, they played the role of an arbitrary referee whose duty was to recognize and combat instances of nepotism and cronyism. It was usually made up of patricians who had not secured election to the other exclusive governing bodies. The *zonta*, therefore, was a "constitutional shortcut" for those noblemen who wished to actively participate in Venetian oligarchy but had not accumulated the necessary backing.[22]

By the beginning of the sixteenth century several significant state affairs, like the ongoing war with the Ottomans and the specter of the new Portuguese spice route, rendered the protection of state secrets a matter of urgency. As a result, in 1539 the Council of Ten, with the blessing of the Senate and the Great Council (the assembly of the Venetian aristocracy), decided to establish a counterintelligence authority. This took shape in the institution of the Inquisitors of the State.[23] Initially titled "Inquisitors against the Disclosures of Secrets," the State Inquisitors were a special magistracy made up of three men, two from the ranks of the Ten and one ducal councilor.[24] While they were primarily responsible for counterintelligence and the protection of state secrets, gradually their activity encompassed all aspects of state security, including conspiracies, betrayals, public order, and espionage.[25] All of these were expected to be concealed under a thick mantle of secrecy.

Secrecy, a State Virtue

Secrecy was one of the most important virtues demanded by the Ten. This is because, to them, it epitomized harmony and civic concord.[26] In a miniature island of 150,000 inhabitants,[27] rumors and fabrications, especially those exposing conflict and dispute, were precarious for domestic security. Thus they ought to be concealed at all costs.[28] As such, Venetian patricians who sat on government councils were forbidden by law to reveal any disputes or debates arising during assemblies. Disobedience was punishable by death and the subsequent confiscation of all personal possessions.[29] This stringent legislation made up for the lack of a royal court, where sensitive information could be confined and safeguarded. In practice, however, secrecy was far from achieved in Venice. In a city so obsessed with news, chatter circulated through the maze of Venice's canals and labyrinth of streets at great speed.

Ironically, while the Venetian ruling class was ordered to keep quiet, the Venetian ruled were urged to speak up. In consequence, gathering and divulging information that pertained to state security was considered an act of good citizenship. If citizens became aware of potential threats to the stability of the state, they were urged to inform the authorities through formal denunciations. These were to be left in any public place, including churches, the stairs of state buildings, even the doorsteps of government officials. These denunciations were treated with utmost solemnity by the Ten.

To facilitate this process of state control, by the late sixteenth century the authorities had invented the premodern version of surveillance cameras, the infamous *bocche di leone*.[30] Sculpted in the shape of lions' mouths—as their name indicates—and resembling carved carnival masks, these were postboxes into whose orifice denizens were invited to deposit denunciations on any issue of public order and security. Venetians took to this "I spy with my little eye" pastime with great zeal and even paid for the services of professional scribes, as the documents' immaculate penmanship reveals.[31] This had tragicomic implications, as the inveterate informers could not see a distinction between major and minor threats. As a result, a blizzard of worthless reports flooded the Ducal Palace on a daily basis. To contain their frequency, in 1542 the government passed a law whereby, to be valid, all anonymous denunciations had to be signed by three witnesses.[32]

This impediment did not have the intended effect, and the craze for this tell-tale game assumed gigantic proportions and lasted until the fall of the Venetian Republic in 1797. This is because the authorities were eager to reward worthy revelations.[33] As a result, the city turned into what can be regarded as a "Big Brother" studio, where nothing escaped the ears and eyes of the numerous self-appointed spooks.[34] These denouncers penetrated all social circles and reported on anyone and anything that could pose a threat, from gamblers and suspicious foreigners to potential heretics and foreign ambassadors.[35] A well-known victim of denunciation was the infamous Venetian womanizer Giacomo Casanova. In 1755, aged thirty, Casanova was sentenced to five years' imprisonment in the Ducal Palace's *piombe*, the terrifying cells reserved for political criminals. His conviction was a result of several denunciations by aggrieved husbands, religious devotees, and righteous city dwellers.[36] His crimes can be summed up as insatiable promiscuity, sensationalist religious sophistries, and a libertine lifestyle, all of which were deemed threatening to state security. Ironically, Casanova's mischievous disposition—that led to his spectacular prison escape just over a year after his arrest—not only set him on the path to stardom but also to the Venetian authorities' payroll as a professional secret agent.[37] The interested reader can find enthralling details of this story in his oft-reprinted *Histoire de ma fuite* (*Story of My Flight*).[38]

Central Intelligence Administration and Corporate-like Leadership

So, how did the Council of Ten and its subordinate body, the Inquisitors of the State, manage to collect the intelligence necessary for the Venetian state's domestic and foreign security? This became possible through the spies and informants they employed. Before getting acquainted with these information procurers, it is important to contextualize intelligence in the early modern period. What exactly was intelligence at that time? Was it a state affair or a private initiative? A professional service or a civic duty? An act of institutional loyalty or financial need? In early modern Venice, intelligence was all of the above. For Venetians, the word *intelligentia* meant "communication" or "understanding." Within the context of state security, it indicated any kind of information of a political, economic, social, or cultural nature that was worthy of evaluation and potential action by the government. But how did information arrive at the Venetian intelligence headquarters?

The Council of Ten was responsible for the central administration of intelligence-gathering and espionage in Venice. To this end, the Ten masterminded and oversaw a network of professional and amateur informers that branched out into three key communication channels: the *professional* channel, composed of the official diplomats and state servants; the *mercantile* channel, made up of Venetian merchants located in commercial hubs of strategic significance, like the territories of the Levant;[39] and the *amateur* channel, whereby individuals at all levels of society, either anonymously or disclosing their identity, for a fee or gratis, gathered and disclosed information relevant to the security of the state. To be sure, disentangling hard facts from rumors and fabrications was not an easy task. Yet the existence of these channels enabled the systematic evaluation of information through a process of comparing and contrasting.[40] Depending on the channel, a plethora of formal or informal spies and informers were recruited for intelligence purposes.

The Professional Communication Channel

"An ambassador," once wrote Henry Wotton, "is an honest man, sent abroad to lie for the good of his country."[41] The Venetian ambassador, as the official formal representative, was the most obvious professional informant. The gradual systematization of bureaucratic and administrative processes in the early modern period owes much to the organized information networks of embassies. Venetian ambassadors were instrumental in this process.[42] Tasked with three primary responsibilities—representation, negotiation, and the collection of information—they had mastered the art of covert communication from early on.[43] Indeed, Venice was one of the first Italian states to establish resident embassies abroad.[44] By the sixteenth century Venice had managed to secure permanent representation in all leading states of early modern Europe, and its ambassadors professionalized the act of clandestine information-gathering and reportage. They did so through their meticulous composition and dispatch of detailed intelligence reports that were often written in cipher to ensure secrecy.

Ambassadors acted as the heads of intelligence operations within the territory of their jurisdiction. To successfully fulfill their responsibilities, they employed and managed their own spies and informers. These were paid for by a discrete budget granted to them for "secret expenses."[45] In 1586, for instance, the Venetian ambassador in Spain reported to the State Inquisitors that he had "recruited" a blue-blooded spy from within the royal Spanish entourage. The new recruit's compensation was in kind, particularly in fine muscat wines, as his status precluded monetary bribes.[46] High-class informers from the Spanish court were quite eclectic in their choice of compensation. In 1576, the Venetian ambassador in Madrid communicated to the Ten the desire of Antonio Pérez, Philip II's secretary of state (who was just about to fall from grace by being accused of treason) to acquire a "good old" painting of Titian's in exchange for "great benefits" for Venice. The council unanimously agreed to disburse 200 ducats for this purpose.[47] The gift must have born fruit, as two years later the Ten decided to increase their spending on Titian's art to 500 ducats in order to keep the secretary gratified.[48] Could any of these rewards be Titian's *The Fall of Man*, now at the Prado?[49]

The *professional* communication channel of Venice's intelligence service was not solely restricted to formal exchanges between ambassadors and the ruler, as was the case with the other Italian states.[50] This channel was so meticulously organized that its highly sophisticated diplomatic network branched out to officially appointed representatives in the Venetian-dominated regions of the Balkans and the Mediterranean (the *Provveditori*); the Venetian cities of the Italian mainland (the *rettori*); and other Mediterranean regions where there was a notable Venetian merchant presence (the *consoli*) but no formal diplomatic representation. Intelligence-gathering and espionage were considered part of these envoys' responsibilities. Accordingly, they were expected to recruit and manage their individual spies and informants.

In July 1533, for instance, while the war with the Ottomans was imminent, the governor of Zante received direct orders from the Ten to send a "practical and faithful" messenger to Admiral Andrea Doria, the legendary Genoese mercenary commander (*condottiere*). During the first half of the sixteenth century, Doria had been the nemesis of the Ottomans in the Levant, patrolling the Mediterranean and launching several naval expeditions against the Turks and other Barbary corsairs.[51] It was obvious that the Ten had a top-secret message to convey to Doria, as the governor was ordered to refrain from written communication with the messenger, most probably for secrecy purposes. In consequence, he was advised to find an informant who spoke Turkish or any other language that Doria spoke, in order to forgo the need for an interpreter. If the latter was unavoidable, the governor was instructed not to use a well-known Genoese translator who was also in the Ottomans' employ. The Ten expected reports on the progress of the mission in cipher.[52]

On a similar note, in July 1574 the Ten requested from the rector of the Venetian city of Brescia the whereabouts of a certain Giulio Sala. Sala was suspected of treasonous dealings with the Spanish and was believed to have involved his cronies in his machinations. The Brescian authorities were asked to locate him and ship him off to the prisons of the Ten while keeping a close eye on his relatives and acquaintances. They were also ordered to change all the guards on the city's gates, most probably suspecting that Sala could have bribed them in order to escape.[53] Ordering the alternation of the guards' shifts, so that they were constantly placed at different places on the city's walls and forts, was a common tactic employed by the Ten to prevent the guards' collaboration with potential traitors.[54]

Venetian governors were given even more daring clandestine missions. In July 1570, as the Papal representative in Venice reported to Rome, it was learned that the Ottomans were engineering the seizure of Spalato, a Venetian colony in Dalmatia.[55] A secret missive was dispatched to the local governor, containing eight bottles of poison. The lethal liquid was intended for the contamination of the water supply of the advancing Ottomans. The governor was instructed to be extremely careful in carrying out his mission so that the quality of the water of the Christian population living there, and thus its safety, was not affected.[56] Indeed, sanitation was one of the Ten's top domestic security priorities.

Even the Venetian consuls who were stationed in cities with no permanent diplomatic representation were tasked with the provision of vital intelligence.[57] Consuls were not formal diplomats but acted as intermediaries between Venetian envoys abroad and the intelligence headquarters in the Ducal Palace. Thus, on several occasions they oversaw the safe exchange of letters between the Ten and the designated Venetian diplomat in the region.[58] Their responsibilities could also extend to intelligence missions if this was considered necessary by the Ducal Palace. At the close of the sixteenth century, for example, the consul of Aleppo in Syria received direct instructions to gather information on Turkish affairs (and a large reward).[59]

All these instances demonstrate that the *professional* channel of information-gathering and reportage that the Council of Ten had devised was complex. Yet the Ten managed it through a meticulous system of delegation. The Venetian spy chiefs did not micromanage their underlings. They delegated and expected detailed reports on execution—more often than not in cipher—trusting that their appointees would successfully carry out the job. As the central executive committee, they also oversaw the effective communication of information about significant developments to all their delegates who could benefit from it, not just the ones directly involved in the events concerned.

When a major diplomatic scandal nearly broke in 1574, for instance, because the French ambassador refused to surrender a Venetian turncoat who revealed state secrets to the French, communication was sent not only to the Venetian ambassador in France, but also to the *bailo* (the Venetian ambassador in the Ottoman capital) in Constantinople. The former was instructed to appeal to the king of France for a "more dexterous" ambassador; the latter was charged with communicating the events to the sultan, who was always interested in French affairs.[60]

Finally, in a good example of modern-day business leadership, the Venetian spy chiefs were generous in acknowledging their trust in their underlings. "We are convinced of your utmost prudence in assigning this undertaking to a person of trust, as befits such a mission," they informed the governor of Zante when they asked him to find a messenger for Doria.[61] "We applaud the manner in which you 'bought off the soul' of Feridun Agà, as a person who can advance our interests in that Porte. And we approve of the manner in which you presented the affair. You are granted permission to render him your informant," they wrote to the bailo.[62] This system of delegation of duties, infused with qualities of trust, acknowledgment, even reward, set the Venetian apparatus apart from those of other Italian states' intelligence operations. Those were restricted to direct communication between rulers and their ambassadors, without the systematized contribution of other formally appointed intermediaries.[63]

The Mercantile Communication Channel

The intelligence network that the Venetian spy chiefs created with such refinement was not confined to the diplomatic and political sphere. In a less formal yet equally meaningful manner, Venetian merchants and businessmen who were frequent travelers in the Mediterranean and the Levant made up the *mercantile* channel of intelligence-gathering and reportage. As adroit dealers in goods and news, Venetian merchants were aware of the value of good (and at times covert) intelligence for competitive advantage.[64] They thus made perfect undercover spies for the Venetian authorities. In 1496, for instance, at a time of diplomatic turbulence between the Ottoman Empire and Venice, the young merchant and future Doge of Venice Andrea Gritti was residing in Constantinople. In the absence of a bailo, who had been expelled a few years earlier when he was discovered to spy for the Spanish,[65] Gritti took the reins of diplomatic negotiations. In 1497 he convinced the sultan to overturn the embargo on grain export that the Ottomans had imposed on Italian merchants in Constantinople.[66] In 1503 he successfully negotiated the final details of the peace treaty between Venice and the Ottoman Empire.[67] His diplomatic missives to the motherland were overflowing with intelligence on the size and moves of the Ottoman fleet. To divert suspicion he coded his dispatches in commercial jargon and presented them as business communications instead. Once, he sent a letter informing the authorities that commercial goods were arriving in Venice from sea and land. The actual meaning of this report was that the Ottomans were preparing to attack with their fleet and army.[68]

Constantinople was a strategic hub of both economic and political significance for Venice. It was not surprising, therefore, that Venetian merchants living in the city doubled as covert informants or spies for the Republic. Leonin Servo, a Venetian subject of Cretan origins, was a merchant residing in the Ottoman capital. With an impressive network of connections and knowledge of current affairs, he acted as an informer to the bailo and the Ten throughout his residence in that city.[69] In July 1566 he notified the bailo that Ibrahim Granatin, a favorite of Sokollu Mehmet Pasha and a foe of Venice, was en route to the city. The news had already reached Venice a month earlier and had caused uproar among the Ten,[70] who ordered Granatin's assassination as a top-secret priority.[71] So dexterous was Servo in smuggling covert communications to Venice that he allegedly hid letters of the bailo Barbaro in hollow canes and transported them on board his ship.[72] Often even when not on official covert missions, Venetian merchants considered it their duty to pass on news of any suspicious maneuvers of enemy ships, especially from areas of the Middle East where they were stationed.[73]

The Amateur Communication Channel

In the early modern period, Venice was a maritime and commercial empire. Unlike other European states, its ruling class—the patricians—were first and foremost merchants who made their living through trade. The citizens, the "secondary elite" of Venice,[74] followed in their footsteps.[75] And of course, in a city of craftsmen and traders, the popular masses had been spoon-fed a steady diet of capitalist ideals. Within this context, the business shrewdness of Venice's spy chiefs devised several ways to benefit from the personal intelligence-gathering pursuits of all layers of Venetian society.[76] These even included individuals of different ethnicities and religions.

Jews made perfect undercover agents for the Ten, owing to their disenfranchisement as people at the margins of society and their much sought-after professional expertise, especially in medicine and commerce. In the next chapter, Emrah Safa Gürkan shows how the Jewish physician Solomon Ashkenazi smuggled the letters of bailo Barbaro in his shoes and shipped them off to Venice when the bailo was under house arrest.[77] At around the same time, in the 1570s, the Jewish merchant Hayyim Saruk from Thessaloniki was appointed to spy on "the affairs, designs and military equipment of the Turks" in Constantinople. For this purpose he even produced a self-made merchant-style cipher, in which he coded the Ottomans as "drugs," people as "money," and dispatches as "purchases." His compensation reached the staggering sum of 500 ducats at a time when the starting salary of a Venetian cryptanalyst was 50 ducats annually.[78]

Intelligence concerned more than the city's foreign affairs. Domestic security was of the utmost importance to the authorities, and this domain was overseen by the State Inquisitors. For this purpose, they maintained contact with distinguished individuals and well-connected professionals, whom they put on the formal payroll at times. Lawyers and notaries, who had direct access to their clients' private affairs, formed part of this group. In 1616, for instance, a lawyer boastfully told the Inquisitors that "lawyers have the occasion of hearing many of their clients' private affairs and, when a gentleman hears something concerning the interest of the state, he must at all costs let your Excellencies know about it."[79] Of course, when the opportunity arose to fill their pockets, some of these gentlemen did not hesitate to leak information to the Spanish and French ambassadors, whose purse strings always became loose at the prospect of valuable information.[80] At times, the services of these specialist agents extended to duties more daring than the supply of information. In 1574, for instance, the professor of botany at the University of Padua was entrusted with the production of a deadly poison that was intended for a villainous Ottoman spy. When he botched the job, the Ten appointed a physician to carry out the task.[81]

More impressively, commoners of various backgrounds and occupations were directly or indirectly urged to take part in the Republic's clandestine missions. Residents in Venetian subject territories were among the most sought-after informants owing to their local knowledge. In November 1570, on the eve of the war with the Turks, the mission of the Cypriot Manoli Soriano involved attacking the Ottoman settlements in the town of Skradin (situated in modern Croatia) and setting fire to the Ottoman fleet stationed in the eastern Adriatic.[82] The authorities rewarded brazen acts in a variety of ways. Banished criminals, for example, were granted the revocation of their sentence in exchange for taking part in intelligence operations. To successfully carry out his daring mission, Soriano requested a squadron of three hundred men. As several of them were expected to be exiled convicts, the condition set was that, upon completion of the operation, their banishment would be revoked.[83]

As this *commodification* of intelligence gradually put down roots in Venice, it became more common for banished felons to become secret agents in return for their freedom.[84] A striking example, in a later era, is, once again, the serial seducer Giacomo Casanova. Owing to his spectacular escape from the ducal penitentiary and the countless connections his dissolute lifestyle had yielded, Casanova managed to get headhunted by the State Inquisitors. In consequence, for nearly twenty years after his daring escape from the city that subsequently banished him, when in need of cash Casanova offered his services to the Republic as a "secret agent," hoping for a revocation of his expulsion.[85] For this purpose, he kept his eyes on anyone or anything that could be considered mildly suspicious. It took him quite some time to find a target until, in 1770, he exposed and halted the illegal operation of an Armenian printing house in Trieste that was competing with its Venetian counterpart. This was his golden ticket back to Venice.[86]

Leadership, Identity, and the "Myth of Venice"

It is evident that Venice created an extremely efficient state intelligence apparatus that operated like a public sector organization. Notable for evolving processes of institutionalization and bureaucratization, this organization was steered by the Council of Ten, who acted as the chief executives. As mentioned previously, the highly developed management processes and central administration of the Venetian intelligence service rendered it unique among contemporaneous Italian and European states. Other states largely confined themselves to communication between the ruler and his ambassadors, in the case of the former,[87] or were organized by prominent individuals for personal advancement, in the case of the latter.[88] In a striking demonstration of organizational maturity, the Ten created a seamless system of managerial delegation that branched out into three communication channels, the *professional*, the *mercantile*, and the *amateur*. While it is easier to understand how the Ten managed the formally appointed delegates who made up the *professional* channel of communication—the ambassadors, the governors, and other state officials—what is striking is their ability to recruit and direct a large number of informally appointed spies and intelligencers from the ranks of Venice's mercantile community and the wider public. A key question arises in this connection: How did the Ten get the public to cooperate in their state security pursuits, even when financial benefits were not guaranteed?

One definition of leadership implies persuading the collective to take responsibility for complex collective problems.[89] This accomplishment presupposes that the collective has accepted its position as the followers and is receptive to being led by the leader. Leaders, thus, cannot exist in isolation from a group of followers. In other words, a leader's authority is sanctioned by the followers' identification and self-acceptance as followers. According to this definition, leadership is premised on two prerequisites: the creation of a group that followers can feel part of and wittingly situate themselves in,[90] and the mobilization of that group to proceed to certain actions that the leader deems necessary.[91] In effect, leadership presupposes the social construction of the context that legitimizes a particular action by a group at a specific point in time.[92] Using this definition, how can we evaluate the Ten's leadership?

Let us start with the first prerequisite, the creation of a group of followers. The foundation of any collective is rooted in a socially constructed, shared identity. Identity is not a rigid entity but "a social, contingent, discursive and dynamic phenomenon."[93] It is predicated on the creation of a *me* or *us* and a *them*,[94] which, by extension, erects social and cognitive boundaries between insiders and outsiders.[95] It is the responsibility of the leader to construct an identity that potential followers can share so as to become part of the intended group.[96] This is because only through creating a shared identity can a leader construct the group of followers that will advance intended strategies.[97] Were the Venetian spy chiefs successful in creating such a group?

Intelligence, as a social process, presupposes secrecy, one of the Ten's most revered virtues. Secrecy, as per its sociological theorizations, is instrumental in identity construction.[98] This is because it enables the creation of the boundary between two separate entities, *those in the know* and the *ignorant others*. The exclusivity of being *in the know*, compared to the *ignorant others*, can boost the sense of distinctive inclusiveness in a group and, by extension, cement one's identification with it.[99] Additionally, the social aspect of secrecy that requires and promotes the conscious awareness of the group owing to the intention of concealment and boundary construction can enhance the process of group identity creation.[100] The sense of belonging that ensues can potentially augment the need to protect and perpetuate secrecy so as to maintain the group. Secrecy, therefore, creates a dynamic and ongoing relationship between its agents and becomes both the condition and the consequence of the formation of group identity.[101] By actively inviting ordinary Venetians to take part in clandestine communication of information even in informal ways, the Ten created an exclusive group of people whose common identity was premised on secrecy and, by extension, the principles of reciprocal confidence and trust.[102]

This interpretation of the Ten's leadership challenges the conventional appreciation of early modern commoners as either devoid of political consciousness or rebellious against the state, owing to their exclusion from political participation.[103] In Venice a whole body of contemporaneous celebratory literature attributed the city's unique internal stability to the political exclusion of the commoners.[104] Even the guilds and their representatives were offered no political representation and were closely monitored by the authorities.[105] Still, are not anonymous denunciations and voluntary or even casual salaried intelligence missions politicized (if not political) acts? What made people who were excluded from politics engage willingly—and more often than not without payment—in such pursuits, even at their own expense at times? In other words, how did the Venetian spy chiefs legitimize the necessary actions—the second prerequisite of leadership—required to advance their strategies?

"Identity," claims one of the most eminent leadership literati, "is constructed out of the amorphous baggage of myth and the contested resources of history."[106] Thus, to successfully instigate the construction of an identity that followers can share, the leader's job is to create a shared vision for the present and the future and the sociopolitical conditions that necessitate and legitimize the followers' action so as to achieve the intended vision. The Ten's exhortations to the people, that still survive en masse in the Venetian State Archives, expressed the state's consistent preoccupation with prioritizing the *servizio publico*, the public good, that was the mainstay of Venice's security and serenity. Their bombastic pronouncements on this subject, that is evident in nearly every document they produced, from secret reports to public proclamations, proclaimed everyone's obligation, prevailing over any private profit, to support the state's efforts to uphold that vision of public good. Remarkably, the commoners' denunciations and reports also expressed this belief in "the obligation of my loyalty" to the state.[107]

This happy image of communal serenity triumphing over private interests and discrepancies was the essence of the famous "Myth of Venice."[108] Although historiographical debates over the validity of the "Myth of Venice" are beyond the scope of this chapter, Venetian history abounds with instances of "community spirit" instigating action for the "common good."[109] Empowering followers to pursue the leader's intended vision through the creation of a collective sense of identity is the essence of "transformational" leadership.[110] In effect, transformational leaders have the ability to inspire and motivate their followers to act for a shared vision. The Ten were adept at this style of leadership. But how did they manage to persuade Venetians to contribute to the collective good through their formal or informal involvement in clandestine undertakings?

To incentivize cooperation, the authorities mobilized the quintessential Venetian activity: trade. In a state where political and diplomatic activities influenced successful commercial transactions and vice versa, intelligence was turned into a trade of information for benefits. Espionage became a transaction between followers and leaders whereby the former expected some kind of benefit in return for services rendered, while the latter advanced strategic objectives by obtaining information. Enshrined in this *commodification* of intelligence, ordinary Venetians, who were excluded from political participation, developed a political purpose within the state, one that was masked in the form of business.[111] The Ten employed what in contemporary leadership parlance would be called a "transactional" leadership style whereby the leader exchanges favors and tangible rewards for services rendered by the followers.[112]

Had all this taken place in a later era, the commercial character of early modern Venice could easily have made Benjamin Franklin snub it as "no longer a Nation, but a great Shop."[113] Adam Smith could have fallen into the trap of misperceiving it as a state of shopkeepers or, more precisely, a state "whose government is influenced by shopkeepers."[114] Yet Venetians were not devoid of sensitivity to state security, nor were they enticed solely by the lure of rewards. As recent scholarship has shown, ordinary Venetians saw it as incumbent on themselves to contribute to the common good. This predisposition stemmed from their communal sense of pride that was partly rooted in their professional identity.[115] The thorough organization of the Venetian workforce into guilds facilitated this process.[116] In fact, the government was notorious for inducing certain professional groups to perform particular tasks by presenting them as the privilege of service to the state.[117] In the same way, the Ten presented the need for intelligence as the privilege of contributing to the security and posterity of the Serenissima, "the most serene of states." Accordingly, reporting on anything that could pose a threat to the state, including the minutiae of daily life, became the discharge of one's duty of contributing to the community. Indeed, a Venetian subject was made to feel obliged "to dedicate his everything, even his life" to the Republic.[118] This was the "Myth of Venice" in full flower.

While the "Myth of Venice" was merely a compelling narrative intended to legitimize the Venetians' cooperation in clandestine activities, it also reflects the Ten's achievement in smoothly wielding two different styles of leadership: the transformational style by which they inspired their followers to take action, and the transactional style whereby they offered favors and tangible benefits in exchange for public service. In essence, the Ten's followers were made to feel themselves to be an indispensable part of a state apparatus that operated for the public benefit—the preservation of the glorious Venice of the past and the future, a bustling emporium of commodities, prospering by its people working for its people.

This idealized portrayal of the Ten's leadership is by no means the whole picture. It is doubtful that they or their delegates thought of any myth when going about their daily business. Their intention was not to construct a myth but to create what generated it, a community spirit that guided people's actions toward the common good. If this intention developed into a myth, this is a different story. Even so, the discussion of Venice's myth is unavoidable, as "inevitably, whoever writes the history of Venice seems condemned to write the history of its myths."[119] In a way, the myth is to the historian of Venice what the *bocca di leone* is to the visitor to this remarkable city: an indispensable prop in the phantasmagoria of Venice through the centuries.

Notes

A version of this chapter was presented at the Social History Society Conference, Lancaster, March 2016. I would like to thank the conference delegates, especially Matthew Pawelski, for their insightful comments, remarks, and suggestions. I am particularly grateful to Filippo De Vivo, Jola Pellumbi, Anna Gialdini, Emrah Safa Gürkan, and Paul Maddrell for their constructive criticism and feedback.

1. The bibliography on this topic is vast. For an overview, see Philip Knightley, *The Second Oldest Profession: Spies and Spying in the Twentieth Century* (London: Deutsch, 1987). Especially for Britain, see Christopher R. Moran, "The Pursuit of Intelligence History: Methods, Sources, and Trajectories in the United Kingdom," *Studies in Intelligence* 55 (2011): 33–55.

2. Mildred G. Richings, *The Story of the Secret Service of the English Crown* (London: Hutchinson, 1935); Peter Fraser, *The Intelligence of the Secretaries of State and Their Monopoly of Licensed News* (Cambridge: Cambridge University Press, 1956); Richard Deacon, *A History of the British Secret Service* (London: Panther Books, 1990), 16–22; Alan Marshall, *Intelligence and Espionage in the Reign of Charles II, 1660–1685* (Cambridge: Cambridge University Press, 1994); Paul S. Fritz, "The Anti-Jacobite Intelligence System of the English Ministers, 1715–1745," *Historical Journal* 16 (1973): 265–89; and Roger Kaplan, "The Hidden War: British Intelligence Operations during the American Revolution," *William and Mary Quarterly*, 3rd ser., 47 (1990): 115–38.

3. Lucien Bély, *Espions et Ambassadeurs au Temps de Louis XIV* [Spies and ambassadors at the times of Louis XIV] (Paris: Fayard, 1990).

4. Karl De Leeuw, "The Black Chamber in the Dutch Republic during the War of the Spanish Succession and Its Aftermath, 1707–1715," *Historical Journal* 42 (1999): 133–56.

5. Emrah Safa Gürkan, "Espionage in the 16th Century Mediterranean: Secrecy, Diplomacy, Mediterranean Go-betweens and the Ottoman Habsburg Rivalry" (PhD diss., Georgetown University, 2012).

6. Fernando Cortés Cortés, *Espionagem e Contra-Espionagem numa Guerra Peninsular, 1640–1668* [Espionage and counterespionage in a peninsular war, 1640–1668] (Lisbon: Livros Horizonte, 1989).

7. Carlos J. Carnicer Garcia and Javier Marcos Rivas, *Espias de Felipe II: Los Servicios Secretos del Imperio Español* [Philip II's spies: The secret services of the Spanish Empire] (Madrid: La esfera de los libros, 2005); and Geoffrey Parker, *The Grand Strategy of Philip II* (New Haven, CT: Yale University Press, 1998). For an overview of the literature, see Christopher Storrs, "Intelligence and the Formulation of Policy and Strategy in Early Modern Europe: The Spanish Monarchy in the Reign of Charles II (1665–1700)," *Intelligence and National Security* 21, no. 4 (2006): 493–519.

8. On Venice, see Paolo Preto, *I Servizi Segreti di Venezia: Spionaggio e Controspionaggio ai Tempi della Serenissima* [The secret services of Venice: Espionage and counterespionage in the time of the most serene republic] (Milan: Il Saggiatore, 1994); Ioanna Iordanou, "What News on the Rialto? The Trade of Information and the Early Modern Venice's Centralised Intelligence Organisation," *Intelligence and National Security* 31, no. 3 (2016): 305–26. On Venice and Genoa, see Romano Canosa, *Alle Origini delle Polizie Politiche: Gli Inquisitori di Stato a Venezia e a Genova* [On the origins of political police: The state inquisitors in Venice and Genoa] (Milano: Sugarco, 1989). On Savoy, see Christopher Storrs, *War, Diplomacy and the Rise of Savoy, 1690–1720* (Cambridge: Cambridge University Press, 1999). On Milan, see Francesco Senatore, *"Uno Mundo de Carta": Forme e Strutture della Diplomazia Sforzesca* ["A world of paper": Forms and structures of the Sforza diplomacy] (Naples: Liguori, 1998). On the Italian states in general, see the relevant essays in Daniela Frigo, ed., *Politics and Diplomacy in Early Modern Italy: The Structure of Diplomatic Practice, 1450–1800* (Cambridge: Cambridge University Press, 2000).

9. Iordanou, "What News on the Rialto?"

10. William Wordsworth, "On the Extinction of the Venetian Republic," in *The Poetical Works of William Wordsworth* (London: Edward Moxon, 1836), 3:180. On the economy of sixteenth-century Venice, see Gino Luzzatto, *Storia Economica di Venezia dall'XI al XVI Secolo* [Economic history of Venice from the 11th to the 16th century] (Venice: Centro Internazionale delle Arti e del Costume, 1961); Frederic C. Lane, *Venice, a Maritime Republic* (Baltimore, MD: Johns Hopkins University Press, 1973); and Paola Lanaro, ed., *At the Centre of the Old World: Trade and Manufacturing in Venice and on the Venetian Mainland (1400–1800)* (Toronto: Centre for Reformation and Renaissance Studies, 2006).

11. Lane, *Venice*.

12. On news in Venice, see Pierre Sardella, *Nouvelles et Spéculations à Venise au Début du XVIe Siècle* [News and speculations in Venice at the beginning of the 16th century] (Paris: Colin, 1947). On Venice as a center of news, see Peter Burke, "Early Modern Venice as a Center of Information and Communication," in *Venice Reconsidered: The History and Civilization of an Italian City-State, 1297–1797*, ed. John Martin and Dennis Romano (Baltimore, MD: Johns Hopkins University Press, 2002), 389–419.

13. See Mario Infelise, *Prima dei Giornali. Alle origini della pubblica informazione (secoli XVI e XVII)* [Before the newspapers: On the origins of public information (16th and 17th centuries)] (Bari: Laterza, 2005).

14. Brian Winston, *Messages: Free Expression, Media and the West from Gutenberg to Google* (London: Routledge, 2005), 31.

15. On the Council of Ten, see Robert Finlay, *Politics in Renaissance Venice* (London: Ernst Benn, 1980).

16. Iordanou, "What News on the Rialto?"

17. Finlay, *Politics*, 189.

18. David Chambers and Brian Pullan, eds., *Venice: A Documentary History* (London: University of Toronto Press, 1992), 55.

19. Finlay, *Politics*, 189.

20. Samuele Romanin, *Storia Documentata di Venezia* [A documentary history of Venice] (Venice: Pietro Naratovich, 1857–61), 4:523–33.

21. Niccolò Macchiavelli, *The Prince*, trans. George Bull (London: Penguin, 1999), 53.

22. Finlay, *Politics*, 187, 189. On the *zonta*, see ibid., 185–90.

23. Samuele Romanin, *Gli Inquisitori di Stato di Venezia* [The state inquisitors of Venice] (Venice: Pietro Naratovich, 1858), 4.

24. Ibid., 16.

25. For a balanced analysis of the Inquisitors of the State, especially in the seventeenth century, see Simone Lonardi, "L'anima dei governi. Politica, spionaggio e segreto di Stato a Venezia nel secondo Seicento (1645–1699)" [The soul of governments. Politics, espionage and state secrets in Venice in the second half of the seventeenth century] (PhD diss., University of Padua, 2016).

26. Filippo De Vivo, *Information and Communication in Venice: Rethinking Early Modern Politics* (Oxford: Oxford University Press, 2007), 43.

27. On the population of Venice, see Andrea Zannini, "Un Censimento del Primo Seicento e la Crisi Demografica ed Economica di Venezia" [An early seventeenth-century census and Venice's demographic and economic crisis], *Studi Veneziani* [Venetian studies] 26 (1993): 87–116.

28. De Vivo, *Information*, 43.

29. Romanin, *Storia Documentata di Venezia*, 138; see also Archivio di Stato di Venezia (hereafter ASV), Consiglio dei Dieci (hereafter CX), *Parti Secrete*, Registro (hereafter Reg.), 3, cc. 2 recto/verso (hereafter r./v.) (March 3, 1529).

30. See, for instance, ASV, CX, *Parti Secrete*, Reg. 19, c.115v. (March 30, 1644). On the *bocche*, see Paolo Preto, *Persona Per Ora Secreta: Accusa e Relazione nella Repubblica di Venezia* [Someone who shall remain secret: Accusation and account in the Venetian Republic] (Milan: Il Saggiatore, 2003).

31. See, for instance, ASV, Capi del Consiglio dei Dieci (hereafter CCX), *Lettere Secrete*, Filza (hereafter f.) 10 (July 3, 1583).

32. ASV, CX, *Parti Comuni*, Reg. 15, c.54v. (August 30, 1542).

33. Iordanou, "What News on the Rialto?"

34. Paolo Preto, "Giacomo Casanova and the Venetian Inquisitors: A Domestic Espionage System in Eighteenth-Century Europe," in *The Dangerous Trade: Spies, Spymasters and the Making of Europe*, ed. Daniel Szechi (Dundee: Dundee University Press, 2010), 142.

35. Ibid., 144–45.

36. Ibid., 146–47.

37. See ibid.

38. Casanova first published his *Histoire de ma fuite des prisons de la République de Venise qu'on appele les Plombs* [The story of my escape from the prisons of the Venetian Republic called the Piombe] in 1788 in Prague, according to Charles Klopp, *Sentences: The Memoirs and Letters of Italian Political Prisoners from Benvenuto Cellini to Aldo Moro* (Toronto: University of Toronto Press, 1999), 29.

39. On the challenges of identifying and examining this body of documentation, see

Richard Mackenney, "Letters from the Venetian Archive," *Bulletin of the John Rylands Library* 72 (1999): 133–44.

40. Gürkan, "Espionage," 39–40.

41. Logan Pearsall Smith, *Life and Letters of Sir Henry Wotton* (Oxford: Clarendon Press, 1904), 1:47.

42. Béatrice Perez, ed., *Ambassadeurs, Apprentis Espions et Maîtres Comploteurs: Les Systèmes de Renseignement en Espagne à l'époque Moderne* [Ambassadors, apprentice spies and master conspirators: Intelligence systems in Spain in modern times] (Paris: PU Paris-Sorbonne, 2010).

43. Isabella Lazzarini, "Renaissance Diplomacy," in *The Italian Renaissance State*, ed. Andrea Gamberini and Isabella Lazzarini (Cambridge: Cambridge University Press, 2012), 425–43.

44. Garrett Mattingly, "The First Resident Embassies: Medieval Italian Origins of Modern Diplomacy," *Speculum* XII (1937): 423–39; Mattingly, *Renaissance Diplomacy* (London: Jonathan Cape, 1955); and Donald E. Queller, *Early Venetian Legislation on Ambassadors* (Geneva: Droz, 1966). For a recent review of Italian diplomacy in the Renaissance, see Isabella Lazzarini, *Communication and Conflict: Italian Diplomacy in the Early Renaissance, 1350–1520* (Oxford: Oxford University Press, 2015).

45. See, for instance, ASV, CX, *Parti Secrete*, Reg. 14, cc. 1v., 22r., 25v. (March 22, 1596; September 5, and December 16, 1597).

46. ASV, *Inquisitori di Stato* (hereafter *IS*), busta (hereafter b.) 483 (September 1, 1586).

47. ASV, CX, *Parti Secrete*, Reg. 11, cc. 83r./v. (February 14, 1575, *more veneto*, hereafter m.v. Nb. The expression "more veneto" indicates that the Venetian calendar started on March 1st. All dates in this article follow that pattern).

48. Ibid., cc. 155v. (April 4, 1578).

49. It is not certain how this painting became part of Pérez's impressive collection. See Angela Delaforce, "The Collection of Antonio Pérez, Secretary of State to Philip II," *Burlington Magazine* 124 (1982): 746.

50. Senatore, *"Uno Mundo de Carta"*; and Frigo, "'Small States' and Diplomacy: Mantua and Modena," in *Politics and Diplomacy in Early Modern Italy: The Structure of Diplomatic Practice, 1450–1800*, ed. Daniela Frigo (Cambridge: Cambridge University Press, 2000), 147–75.

51. On Doria, see Francesco D. Guerrazzi, *Vita di Andrea Doria* [The life of Andrea Doria], 2 vols. (Milan: Guigoni, 1864).

52. ASV, CX, *Parti Secrete*, Reg. 4, cc. 14r./v. (July 21, 1533).

53. Ibid., Reg. 11, cc. 17r./v. (July 1, 1574).

54. Ibid., Reg. 14, c. 10r. (December 29, 1596).

55. Archivio Segreto Vaticano (ASVat), *Nunziatura Venezia*, in Microfilmotecca Fondazine Giorgio Cini, Dispacci del Nunzio a Venezia alla Segreteria di Stato, Filza 8, c. 12r. (July 15, 1570).

56. ASV, CCX, *Lettere Secrete*, f. 7 (August 21, 1570).

57. Preto, *I Servizi Segreti*, 208.

58. ASV, CCX, *Lettere Secrete*, f. 10 (March 27, 1579).

59. ASV, CCX, *Lettere di Rettori et di Altre Carriche*, b. 255 (January 3, 1584, m.v.)

60. ASV, CX, *Parti Secrete*, Reg. 5, cc.73r.–75r. (August 22, 1542).

61. Ibid., Reg. 4, cc. 14r./v. (July 21, 1533).

62. Ibid., Reg. 11, c. 45r./v. (January 26, 1574, m.v.).

63. Senatore, *"Uno Mundo de Carta"*; and Frigo, "Small States."

64. Andrea Barbarigo, for instance, the famous fifteenth-century Venetian merchant, went so far as to create a cipher for his confidential communications with his agent in the Levant. This can be found in ASV, *Archivio Grimani-Barbarigo*, b. 41, Reg. 1, c.158r. On Barbarigo, see Frederic C. Lane, *Andrea Barbarigo: Merchant of Venice, 1418–1449* (Baltimore, MD: Johns Hopkins University Press, 1944).

65. James C. Davis, "Shipping and Spying in the Early Career of a Venetian Doge, 1496–1502," *Studi Veneziani* [Venetian studies] 16 (1974): 97–108.

66. Marino Sanudo, *I Diarii* [The diaries], ed. Rinaldo Fulin, Federico Stefani, Nicolò Barozzi, Guglielmo Berchet, and Marco Allegri (Venice: F. Visentini, 1879–1903), 1:508.

67. Lane, *Venice*.

68. Davis, "Shipping," 101–2.

69. On Servo, see Christos Apostolopoulous, "Λεονίνος Σέρβος: Ένας Πολυπράγμων Χανιώτης Έμπορος του 16ου Αιώνα στην Κωνσταντινούπολη [Leonino Servo: Mercante Faccendiere Caniota a Costantinopoli Cinquecentesca] [Leonino Servo: A resourceful Cretan merchant in sixteenth-century Constantinople], *Ανθή Χαρίτων* 18 (1998): 9–27.

70. The bailo had written on June 21st. ASV, CX, *Parti Secrete*, Reg. 8, cc.63r./v. (July 13, 1566).

71. Ibid., c.64v (July 23, 1566).

72. Apostolopoulos, "Λεονίνος Σέρβος," 19.

73. Preto, *I Servizi Segreti*, 248–50.

74. Chambers and Pullan, *Venice*, 261.

75. On Venetian patricians and citizens, see Dennis Romano, *Patricians and Popolani: The Social Foundations of the Venetian Renaissance State* (Baltimore, MD: Johns Hopkins University Press, 1987).

76. Hans J. Kissling, "Venezia come centro di informazione sui Turchi" [Venice as an information center on the Turks], in *Venezia Centro di Mediazione fra Oriente e Occidente (sec. XV-XVI): Aspetti e Problemi* [Venice mediation center between East and West (15th–16th centuries): Aspects and problems], ed. Hans G. Beck, Manoussos Manoussakas, and Agostino Pertusi (Florence: L. S. Olschki, 1977): 1:97–109.

77. Benjamin Arbel, *Trading Nations: Jews and Venetians in the Early Modern Eastern Mediterranean* (New York: Brill, 1995), 77.

78. ASV, CX, *Parti Secrete*, f. 15 (November 23; December 30, 1571); ibid., Reg. 19, cc. 18r./v. (July 14, 1636). On Saruk, see Arbel, *Trading Nations*, especially chaps. 6 and 7.

79. Quoted in De Vivo, *Information*, 78.

80. Ibid.

81. ASV, CX, *Parti Secrete*, Reg. 11, cc. 32v.–33r.; 35v. (October 6, 10, and 24, 1574).

82. ASV, CCX, *Lettere Secrete*, f. 7 (November 25, 1570).

83. Ibid.

84. On the *commodification* of intelligence in early modern Venice, see Iordanou, "What News on the Rialto?"

85. His reports to the State Inquisitors can be found in ASV, IS, b. 565.

86. Preto, "Giacomo Casanova," 149.

87. Senatore, *"Uno Mundo de Carta"*; and Frigo, "Small States."

88. See, for instance, James Cooper, *The Queen's Agent: Francis Walsingham at the Court of Elizabeth I* (London: Faber and Faber, 2011); Alan Haynes, *Walsingham: Elizabethan Spymaster and Statesman* (Stroud: Gloucestershire: Sutton, 2004); and Jacob Soll, *The Information Master: Jean-Baptiste Colbert's Secret State Intelligence System* (Ann Arbor: University of Michigan Press, 2009).

89. Keith Grint, "The Cuckoo Clock Syndrome: Addicted to Command, Allergic to Leadership," *European Management Journal* 28 (2010): 307.

90. Keith Grint, *The Arts of Leadership* (Oxford: Oxford University Press, 2000), 6–7.

91. Keith Grint, "Problems, Problems, Problems: The Social Construction of Leadership," *Human Relations* 58 (2005): 1469.

92. Ibid., 1470–71.

93. Jana Costas and Christopher Grey, "Bringing Secrecy into the Open: Towards a Theorization of the Social Processes of Organizational Secrecy," *Organization Studies* 35, no. 10 (2014): 26.

94. Ibid., 27.

95. Harold Behr, "Special Section: Secrecy and Confidentiality in Groups," *Group Analysis* 39 (2006): 356–65.

96. Idem, *The Arts*, 7.

97. Richard Jenkins, *Social Identities* (London: Routledge, 1996), 25.

98. Georg Simmel, "The Secret and the Secret Society," in *The Sociology of Georg Simmel*, ed. and trans. Kurt H. Wolff (1906; repr., Chicago: Free Press, 1950).

99. See Simmel, "The Secret," 497; and Blake E. Ashforth and Fred Mael, "Social Identity Theory and the Organization," *Academy of Management Review* 14, no. 1 (1989): 20–39.

100. Mats Alvesson, Karen L. Ashcraft, and Robyn Thomas, "Identity Matters: Reflections on the Constructions of Identity Scholarship in Organization Studies," *Organization* 15, no. 1 (2008): 5–28; and Sierk Ybema, Tom Keenoy, Cliff Oswick, and Armin Beverungen, "Articulating Identities," *Human Relations* 62, no. 3 (2009): 299–322.

101. Costas and Grey, "Bringing Secrecy," 3.

102. Sissela Bok, *Secrets: On the Ethics of Concealment and Revelation* (New York: Vantage Books, 1989), 121.

103. See Romano, *Patricians and Popolani*.

104. De Vivo, *Information*, 44.

105. On the guilds of Venice, see Richard Mackenney, *Tradesmen and Traders: The World of the Guilds in Venice and Europe, c. 1250–c. 1650* (London: Croom Helm, 1987); Mackenney, "Guilds and Guildsmen in Sixteenth-Century Venice," *Bulletin of the Society for Renaissance Studies* 2, no. 2 (1984): 7–12; Francesca Trivellato, "Guilds, Technology, and Economic Change in Early Modern Venice," in *Guilds, Innovation and the European Economy, 1500–1800*, ed. Stephan R. Epstein and Maarten Prak (Cambridge: Cambridge University Press, 2008), 199–231.

106. Ibid., 27.

107. ASV, CCX, *Lettere Secrete*, f. 11 (March 1597).

108. On the "Myth of Venice," see James S. Grubb, "When Myths Lose Power: Four Decades of Venetian Historiography," *Journal of Modern History* 58 (1986): 43–94; Elizabeth Crouzet-Pavan, "Towards an Ecological Understanding of the Myth of Venice," in *Venice Reconsidered: The History and Civilization of an Italian City-State, 1297–1797*, ed. John Martin and Dennis Romano (Baltimore, MD: Johns Hopkins University Press, 2000), 39–64.

109. Crouzet-Pavan, "An Ecological Understanding," 57.

110. On a general overview of transformational leadership, see the classic by James MacGregor Burns, *Leadership* (New York: Harper and Row, 1978), esp. part 3 (Burns uses the term "transforming" leadership). On the link between transformational leadership and identity construction, see Bernard M. Bass, "From Transactional to Transformational Leadership: Learning to Share the Vision," *Organizational Dynamics* 18, no. 3 (1990): 19–31.

111. Iordanou, "What News on the Rialto?"

112. On an introduction to the term of "transactional leadership," see Burns, *Leadership*, esp. part 4.

113. Benjamin Franklin to Charles-Guillaume-Frédéric Dumas, August 6, 1781, in *The Papers of Benjamin Franklin*, ed. Leonard W. Labaree et al., 41 vols. (New Haven, CT: Yale University Press, 1959–2014), 35:341.

114. Adam Smith, *An Inquiry into the Nature and Causes of the Wealth of Nations*, ed. Edwin Cannan (Chicago: University of Chicago Press, 1977), 2:129.

115. Ioanna Iordanou, "Pestilence, Poverty, and Provision: Re-evaluating the Role of the *Popolani* in Early Modern Venice," *Economic History Review* 69, no. 3 (2016): 801–22.

116. See Mackenney, *Tradesmen and Traders*.

117. The Venetian shipbuilders, for instance, since they were responsible for one of Venice's most significant industries, were granted the "privilege" of rowing the *Bucintoro*—the Doge's ceremonial state barge—on festive occasions, guarding St. Mark's Square during the Great Council assemblies, and patrolling the areas of Piazza San Marco and the Rialto Bridge during the evening. They were also the designated firefighters of the city. See Robert Davis, *Shipbuilders of the Venetian Arsenal: Workers and Workplace in the Preindustrial City* (Baltimore, MD: Johns Hopkins University Press, 1991).

118. "spender l'havere et la vita propria," in ASV, CCX, *Lettere Secrete*, f. 10 (July 7, 1583). The Republic of Venice was known from the Middle Ages as "La Serenissima"

(the most serene). The title "serenissima" was originally that of Venice's supreme governing body, the "Signoria," which was known as "La Serenissima Signoria" to indicate that it was a sovereign body. The Signoria was presided over by the Doge, Venice's head of government, whose title derived from the Latin word "dux" (leader).

119. Crouzet-Pavan, "Ecological Understanding," 57.

3 Laying Hands on *Arcana Imperii*

Venetian Baili as Spymasters in Sixteenth-Century Istanbul

Emrah Safa Gürkan

Historians have long lauded early modern Venice as a center of information.[1] Venice's role as a transmitter of information becomes more palpable when it comes to news regarding the Ottoman Empire. Enjoying the fruits of centuries-long connections of diplomacy and trade, the Venetians regularly attained reliable information from the eastern Mediterranean, as is evident from the detailed entries in Marino Sanudo's fifty-eight-volume compendium, *I diarii*, which recorded summaries of Venice's incoming and outgoing correspondence.[2]

The close relationship between diplomacy and information-gathering is well-known.[3] Since the emergence of modern diplomacy with the establishment of permanent embassies in the late fifteenth and early sixteenth centuries, an ambassador's job description has included gathering information on rival states' secrets. It was this quality of theirs that aroused the suspicion of the authorities and urged them to keep these resident diplomats under strict surveillance. In the early years of modern diplomacy, commercial and diplomatic relations were intertwined as resident consuls at the head of merchant communities in foreign cities gradually turned into professional diplomats representing their governments. With extensive trade connections throughout the eastern Mediterranean, the Venetians had a diplomatic presence in Istanbul long before its conquest by the Ottomans. They quickly established good relations with the city's new masters and kept there an official consul and ambassador named the *bailo* (pl. *baili*) who served the Serenissima's interests by developing good relations with key political figures of the empire for purposes of diplomacy, espionage, and trade.[4]

After the Ottoman-Venetian War of 1499–1503, it became obvious that the Venetians could not meet the Ottoman challenge on their own and defend their dispersed colonies throughout the eastern Mediterranean, which was increasingly controlled by the Ottomans, especially after their conquest of

Syria and Egypt in 1517. This meant that they had to remain on alert constantly, making full use of diplomacy and espionage. The baili's most important function, then, was to keep a vigilant eye on the Ottoman decision-making process and military preparations and feed the Venetian authorities with up-to-date information.

Yet how did a Christian diplomat from a small merchant republic gather information in a Muslim empire? Which sources of information did he have at his disposal on the other side of the religious frontier that supposedly divided the Mediterranean into two irreconcilably hostile blocs? How successful was he in penetrating jealously guarded state secrets in a foreign capital where access to information was the primary criterion of power?[5] What kind of a role did common ethnic, cultural, linguistic, and religious ties between Venetian baili and renegade Ottoman pashas play in this information exchange?

Using an extensive corpus of documentation from Venetian (Archivio di Stato di Venezia—ASV) and Spanish (Archivo General de Simancas—AGS) archives, this chapter will try to answer these questions and attempt to delineate the exceptional role baili played in Venetian information-gathering efforts in the Ottoman Empire. In the first part, it will demonstrate how these seasoned diplomats successfully gathered information by building an extensive network of spies and informants not only at every level of the Ottoman administrative and military structure (in the Arsenal, Imperial Council and its chancery, and even the very core of the Ottoman state, the palace), but also in other embassies as well as among enemy agents operating in the Ottoman capital. Having delineated the baili's sources of information in Istanbul, the second part of the chapter will show how they took advantage of the Venetian postal monopoly in order to screen every sort of letter that passed between Istanbul and the West, sometimes including the Ottomans' own correspondence.

The concluding part will concentrate on leadership skills of the baili, who were entrusted with the difficult task of managing a large intelligence network composed of spies and informants, as well as the embassy personnel, especially the dragomans and the secretaries who helped them in diplomatic and intelligence-related tasks. Apart from recruiting agents and gathering information, however, the baili were expected to function in a number of other capacities that required the experience and organizational capabilities of a seasoned diplomat and intelligence leader. They were supposed to verify, analyze, contextualize, and prioritize the received intelligence and then organize its safe and timely transmission to relevant authorities in Venice and its maritime empire, the *Stato da Mar*. Moreover, they were to use information as a diplomatic tool and share some of it with the Ottomans in order to ingratiate themselves with them. Counterintelligence was also among the baili's responsibilities; they constantly kept tabs on every move that enemy agents operating in the Ottoman capital made.

Sources of Information: Spies and Informants

Part of an ambassador's job was to curry favor among the ruling elite and establish friendly relations that would provide him with sensitive information in a foreign capital. The Venetian baili seem to have excelled in this task. While they were obliged to regularly communicate with Ottoman grand viziers, they also paid occasional visits to other officers, courtiers, and power brokers who played an important role in the formulation and implementation of Ottoman strategy.

In spite of obvious religious and cultural differences, the Ottomans and European diplomats were "similar by virtue of their status as part of the elite in the Ottoman imperial system."[6] Among the dispatches of the Venetian baili, one occasionally finds references to one-on-one conversations with the Ottoman grandees during which secret information was exchanged. It was usual that the Ottoman grand viziers tried to learn from the baili the recent political developments in Europe. In turn, they offered regular information as could be seen in Rüstem Pasha's regretful statement that at that particular moment he did not have "any news to tell you."[7] For sure, shared information was seldom detrimental to the empire itself, but it could still be valuable for other purposes. Moreover, the baili and their adroit interpreters occasionally managed to induce the Ottoman grandees to let slip things they should not have said.

Similarly, other high-ranking officers such as viziers and governors general regularly fed baili with precious information. The governor general of Tunisia and Cyprus, Cafer Pasha, for instance, wrote to the baili in Italian (he was a Calabrian renegade[8]), informing them of internal machinations, private meetings, and important developments in Istanbul.[9] Sometimes dismissed Ottoman officials became Venetian informants, lured by a combination of resentment owing to falling from favor and desire for financial remuneration (the reacquiring of a lucrative office depended on lavish gift-giving and bribery).[10] Especially those from frontier regions would have the most up-to-date information regarding the faraway provinces that remained out of the bailo's sphere of communication. Mehmed, the former governor general of Tripolitania, for instance, provided bailo Hieronimo Lippomano with important insights as to how to deal with the Berber insurrection that wreaked havoc in this troublesome Ottoman province.[11]

It was not only pashas with military and administrative responsibilities but also other influential officers, courtiers, and power brokers who spent confidential time with the baili. The most interesting encounters are perhaps the ones with the empire's religious elite, the *'ulema* (sing. *'alim*), who started to play an increasingly influential political role in the Ottoman capital in the second half of the sixteenth century. In 1590, for instance, the grand mufti (*Şeyhü'l-İslam*), Bostanzade Mehmed Efendi, freely shared with bailo Lippomano the details of Ottoman political strategy and revealed his dissatisfaction with Grand Vizier Sinan's war plans that aimed, according to Bostanzade, to serve his own interests rather than those of the empire.[12] Such face-to-face conversations between a Christian diplomat and the highest Islamic religious authority in the empire was quite usual;[13] there were also other times when the baili used intermediaries to consult with such influential religiopolitical figures. For instance, in 1585, the tutor (*hoca*) of the bailate, hired to teach Ottoman to apprentice interpreters, visited Grand Mufti Çivizade Hacı Mehmed Efendi to give him the plates that the latter had asked for from the bailo. The mufti told the hoca that he had been asked whether an attack on the Venetians was permissible according to Islamic law and that he had responded in a firm negative. The hoca quickly transmitted this important piece of information to bailo Lippomano and added his prediction that the person who asked this question was none other than the Sultan's royal tutor, the omnipotent power broker Hoca Sadeddin Efendi.[14] A final example whereby an *'alim* revealed sensitive information to a bailo is Grand Vizier Sinan Pasha's hoca. In 1590, he assured Lippomano, on alert because of the rumors of a naval expedition against Venetian Crete, that his master had no desire to pursue an aggressive policy in the Mediterranean, and added that it was rather the Grand Admiral and his allies who advocated a bellicose strategy.[15]

Needless to say, such one-on-one encounters with foreign diplomats could give rise to rumors; therefore, the baili and the Ottoman grandees needed a pretext to see each other. Most of the time, official business brought the baili and the grand viziers together; but this was not the case with other viziers and courtiers. So they met in remote places. In 1569, Marcantonio Barbaro met with one of the men of the head of the janissaries (janissary agha) in his "pleasant place by the water."[16] In 1590, Giovanni Moro met with Mehmed Pasha in a garden toward the Black Sea coasts, the north of the city in 1590. In such meetings, which took place "with the usual secrecy" and away from prying eyes, the pashas and the baili could converse freely.[17] Secrecy was of such importance that the baili went to such meetings dressed in black "according to the baili's custom in similar instances."[18]

A theoretically marginal yet politically influential figure in Ottoman politics, the Jewish power broker, on whom I have written elsewhere in more detail,[19] is omnipresent in the baili's letters. These courtiers with trans-imperial life trajectories and Mediterranean-wide connections provided a bridge between European ambassadors and the Ottoman grandees for whom they gathered information from Europe, procured luxury items, and made financial resources available. They provided Venetian diplomacy and information-gathering with all sorts of assistance. Moses Benveniste, the close confidant of Grand Vizier Siyavuş Pasha, for instance, was on the Venetian payroll and was a major source of information for the baili.[20] Even Joseph Nasi, who would soon become the Serenissima's arch-nemesis, shared information.[21] He went as far as insinuating that the next Ottoman target would be Cyprus, and he did this only three years before the actual expedition, which the Ottomans undertook with his encouragement.[22] Similarly, bailo Marcantonio Barbaro shared his physician Solomon Ashkenazi with Grand Vizier Sokollu Mehmed Pasha. Solomon proved himself useful to a wartime diplomat who was detained in his house with limited contact with the outside world. He smuggled the bailo's letters out of his residence in his shoes and then sent them with his own correspondence on a ship to Crete.[23] It was his profession that allowed Solomon to visit the imprisoned bailo freely and serve as a go-between. He also carried the bailo's messages to Sokollu, who preferred to stay in touch with the Venetian diplomat in order to bring an end to a war that he had not wanted to declare in the first place.

Being a physician was the perfect profession for an information trader. It provided regular contact with the Ottoman grandees and gave access to restricted areas such as pashas' bedrooms and even the inner court of the imperial palace, theoretically inaccessible to any male except for the pages of the Sultan.[24] Therefore, Ashkenazi was unsurprisingly not the only physician who abused the privileges of his profession and brokered information. Jewish Abramo Abensazio and David Valentino, for instance, served both the baili and the Ottoman grandees. The Cypriote noble Doctor Flangini, whose brother Osman was a high official in the imperial palace, regularly provided the baili with invaluable information, too.[25]

A key figure for the Venetian baili who wanted to keep their government abreast of Ottoman military strategy was the grand admiral, a post at times occupied by renegades of western Mediterranean origin. A good part of the information that the baili conveyed to Venice consisted of preparations in the Ottoman Arsenal[26] and the possible target of the Ottoman navy. Moreover, they regularly met with grand admirals in order to resolve diplomatic issues related to trade rights, corsair attacks,[27] illegal enslavement of Venetian subjects, runaway slaves, and all sorts of disputes. In short, the baili had both a good reason and the means to keep a close eye on Ottoman grand admirals.[28]

Sometimes the Venetian diplomat found a compatriot such as Uluc Hasan Pasha (aka Hasan Veneziano)[29] who was willing to provide, in several face-to-face encounters that lasted for hours, information regarding naval preparations in the Arsenal and the Ottoman navy's possible targets should there be any expedition.[30] Even when the Ottoman fleet was out in the Mediterranean, the baili had access to the most up-to-date information. Hasan's men communicated to bailo Giovanni Moro the latest news that their master wrote to the capital regarding the actions and whereabouts of the Ottoman fleet under his command.[31] Hasan also shared information about a wide range of events such as the Ottoman army fighting with the Safavids in the East, discussions in the Imperial Council, the Sultan's opinion on war and peace, rivalries between pashas, other states' diplomatic initiatives in Istanbul, the Mahdi Rebellion in Tripolitania, and the strength and composition of the Habsburg fleet in the western Mediterranean.[32]

When they had to deal with a less friendly grand admiral, such as the cantankerous Calabrian renegade Uluc Ali, the baili then relied on men who belonged to these pashas' households. Among the numerous renegades in Uluc Ali's household, there were many who were willing to profit from their privileged access to Ottoman military plans. The baili managed to corrupt even Uluc's steward (Ott. *kahya*) Rıdvan, a Venetian renegade.[33] He was so important to bailo Lorenzo Bernardo that the latter was seriously disappointed when he heard that Uluc Ali had dismissed Rıdvan on charges of embezzlement. Bernardo felt compelled to buy a replacement in the person of Hasan Corso, the majordomo of the Arsenal (*Tersane-i Amire Ağası*).[34]

It was not always easy to corrupt officers as important as Rıdvan, Hasan Corso, or the paymaster general of the Arsenal (*Tersane Emini*), who related his conversation with Rüstem Pasha regarding the strength of the next year's fleet to the bailo's dragoman Giannettino Salvago in 1551.[35] Nevertheless, there was always somebody willing to share information in grand admirals' large households. In 1569, just before the outbreak of an Ottoman-Venetian War, Marcantonio Barbaro tried to learn the grand admiral's plans from one of his trusted men.[36] On the eve of another potential Ottoman aggression in 1590–91, bailo Lippomano regularly acquired information from one of the men of Uluc Hasan's household.[37] Sometimes, a grand admiral's social circle could also provide valuable insiders. Bernardo Navagero refers to one of his informants as "someone who eats and drinks with this Admiral."[38]

The Ottoman Arsenal was a huge complex on the right bank of the Golden Horn, and it was hard to conceal what was going on there; at times, the baili personally counted the galleys that were being prepared.[39] Still, they needed more reliable sources than plain eyesight. The impressive quality of the detailed information regarding Ottoman naval preparations is a clear testimony to their connections with Arsenal workers and sailors.[40] There were several Christians in the Ottoman Arsenal, some of whom were the Serenissima's subjects born in its possessions scattered throughout the eastern

Mediterranean.[41] Moreover, the Ottoman naval establishment was dominated by renegades of Western European provenance, fluent in Spanish or some form of Italian.

We have records from as early as 1499 of Venetian informants in the Ottoman Arsenal. The Venetian diarist Marino Sanudo records that a caulker, who had been banished by the Venetians from Candia (Crete) on charges of homicide, provided the Venetian "orator"[42] Andrea Zachani with extensive information on the condition of the Ottoman galleys and the preparations in the Arsenal.[43] Half a century later, uncomfortable about rumors of an Ottoman desire to dispatch a large fleet to the Mediterranean, bailo Navagero sent a Turkish agent, whom he called "a very good friend" (i.e., a spy) to spy on preparations in the Arsenal.[44] He also maintained a close relationship with Cafer Agha from Cattaro, formerly a favorite of the deceased Ottoman grand admiral Hayreddin Barbarossa and a man whom Navagero considered "very clever and experienced in the affairs of the world." Cafer provided him with information not only on Ottoman maritime affairs but also on strategic calculations and diplomatic priorities.[45] The baili occasionally relied on their numerous informers in the Arsenal, but unfortunately, their correspondence reveals very little on these anonymous "friends" in the heart of the Ottoman naval establishment.[46] We know, however, they were in contact with galley commanders (*reis,* pl. *rüesa*) who formed the backbone of the Ottoman fleet. In 1588, for instance, bailo Giovanni Moro inquired from the rüesa coming from Tripolis information regarding the Berber revolt in the region.[47]

Grand admirals' households were not the only targets of the baili, who also sought informants among the men of other Ottoman grandees. The documentation at our disposal refers to them as *homo dependente* [*da Sciemps Bassa*] (a servant or courtier),[48] *li suoi* (his people),[49] or *persona sua domestica* (a person in his household).[50] Leaving their identity anonymous with such vague expressions made perfect sense given that the Ottomans frequently intercepted the diplomatic dispatches.[51] Still, the documents openly name some of these informants, adding their office or position as well: the first steward of Lala Mustafa Pasha;[52] the first steward of the deceased Grand Vizier Rüstem Pasha and his wife, the Ottoman princess Mihrimah Sultan;[53] a relative of *Nişancı* (Chancellor) Muhyi Çelebi;[54] the secretary of Grand Vizier Sinan Pasha;[55] and finally the governor of Herzegovina's steward, who lost his job when his master realized he was leaking information to the bailo.[56] The fact that the baili chose to reveal the identity of their higher-ranked informants suggests that they took the risk of exposing their sources in order to add credibility to the information they communicated.

It was among the duties of the European diplomats in the Ottoman capital to keep an eye on Christian slaves in the Ottoman capital, negotiate their ransom, discourage their conversion to Islam, and more important, protest to the Ottoman authorities if they were enslaved in contravention of international treaties. Some of these slaves, especially those in pasha households, could bring valuable information. A Cypriot slave, Gioan Maria de Verona, for instance, revealed to the bailo's secretary the names of the Ottoman spies in Cyprus in 1568, only three years before the Ottoman conquest of the island.[57] In another example, an unnamed Neapolitan slave, a painter in Sokollu Mehmed Pasha's service, told Marcantonio Barbaro the things he overheard in the grand vizier's palace.[58] Finally, a Roman slave in Venetian chief white eunuch Gazanfer Agha's household served as an informant to the baili between 1574 and 1581.[59]

The baili also succeeded in penetrating the very corridors (or more literally, courtyards) of the Ottoman palace. A reliable informant and a close friend of Süleyman I's physician Amon Moses (*medico Amon Hebreo*), for instance, provided information regarding the ailing Sultan's health.[60] A year later, the *bostancıbaşı*, the palace's chief gardener, who had recently received luxurious clothes from the Venetians, told the bailate dragoman (interpreter) that there would not be a military expedition to Transylvania that year.[61] In 1568, a eunuch of the palace told the bailo's secretary what he learned from Selim II's *Hasodabaşı* (head of the privy chamber): a certain Hoca Piri who arrived from Venice was provoking the Sultan against the Venetians.[62] Similarly, the Queen Mother Safiye Sultan's influential mute freely commented in front of the bailo on the war plans discussed in the Imperial Council.[63] Finally, bailo Marco Venier even managed to arrange a secret meeting with an influential woman in the imperial harem, the most unusual feat in the extremely gender-segregated world of Ottoman high society. The unnamed woman sat hidden from view and provided the bailo, through her Jewish lady-in-waiting (*kira*), with precious information.[64]

Venetians with access to the Ottoman palace proved extremely useful for information-gathering purposes. In the last quarter of the sixteenth century, the chief white eunuch of the palace, one of the most influential men in the Ottoman court, was a Venetian renegade named Gazanfer whose family links with Venice provided a crack through which the baili could glimpse Ottoman court politics. Even though the cautious Gazanfer tried to keep his distance from his compatriots, he still helped Venetian diplomacy in many ways; he even agreed in 1594 to a secret face-to-face rendezvous with Marco Venier inside the imperial palace. The baili found a more consistent ally in Gazanfer's sister, Beatrice Michiel (aka Fatma Hatun),[65] who followed her brother to Istanbul and reneged on her religion as well as his marriage, only to walk down the aisle with an Ottoman officer who was her brother's protégé.[66] Thanks to her access to the inner palace and "through her participation in the court's female networks," Beatrice sent the baili handwritten notes that included precious information regarding Ottoman strategy, military preparations, economic problems, and factional rivalries.[67] In short, she became the baili's usual Venetian female informant.[68]

Particularly influential figures in negotiations between the Ottoman grandees and the European ambassadors were the interpreters, or the dragomans, working either in European embassies or in the Imperial Council. These linguistic brokers played a key role in daily diplomacy as they were the ones who went back and forth between the Ottoman officials and the ambassadors to deal with myriad diplomatic issues of minor importance.[69]

In the sixteenth century, the Ottomans generally chose their dragomans from among the renegades. Their linguistic and cultural proximity to European ambassadors allowed these interpreters a greater degree of sociability that facilitated information exchange; they frequently visited the baili, conversed freely, and even dined with them in the bailate.[70] Moreover, their privileged access to diplomatic negotiations and official correspondence between the Ottomans and the Europeans made them a treasure trove of information for foreign intelligence services. They leaked information of cardinal importance, especially regarding negotiations between the Ottomans and their nemeses in Europe, the Habsburgs;[71] efforts of competing city-states (Genoa, Florence, et al.) to acquire trade agreements (capitulations) from the Ottomans; and the details of the deposition of caught enemy agents in the Imperial Council.[72] Sometimes, they even shared official diplomatic letters, the translation of which the Ottomans had entrusted to them.[73] The leaking of such fresh firsthand information in detail allowed the curious baili to closely monitor other powers' diplomatic initiatives in the Ottoman capital.

Also, embassy dragomans played an intelligence role of first-rate importance. European diplomatic missions recruited their dragomans from the Latin-rite community of Galata, the celebrated *Magnifica Comunità*.[74] These dragomans met with the Ottoman dignitaries more frequently and could stroll through the city more freely, making acquaintances and establishing friendships; it was through them that the baili contacted most of their spies and informants in the city.[75] For instance, it was to dragoman Giannettino Salvago that the aforementioned *Tersane Emini* revealed classified information.[76] While he was in the Imperial Council, the same Giannettino eavesdropped on a conversation between the agent of the famous Ottoman corsair Turgud Reis and that of the governor of Delvine on the necessity of attacking the Venetians.[77] In 1568 dragoman Pasquale Navone's brother gave bailo Giacomo Soranzo some information on the naval preparations in the Arsenal, while Pasquale retrieved insider information from the grand admiral's secretary (*tezkireci*).[78] In 1581 apprentice dragoman Cristoforo Brutti acquired information regarding the war on the Persian front from the nephew of Sinan Pasha and the leading figures in the latter's household.[79] As a compatriot of the Albanian Sinan, Cristoforo was well connected to his household;[80] none other than Sinan's tutor would write a letter of recommendation for him in 1582, addressed to bailo Giovan Francesco Morosini, who responded to this letter with words of praise. The latter also urged the heads of the Council of Ten to send Cristoforo back to Istanbul as soon as possible; there he could give "useful and distinguished services" in case Sinan Pasha, then dismissed from office, assumed the post of grand vizier once again.[81] Both of Morosini's predictions—that Sinan Pasha would one day be reinstated and that Cristoforo's ties with him would be useful—would turn out to be accurate.

The baili were carefully monitoring other states' diplomatic and commercial efforts in the Ottoman capital lest these jeopardize Venetian interests. Especially disconcerting were the efforts of other Italian mercantile republics to obtain commercial privileges by means of capitulations. Every time Genoa or Florence sent an envoy to the Ottoman capital under certain pretexts, the baili tried to find out what they discussed with the Ottomans. In this endeavor, the dragomans proved quite useful and leaked information to baili. In 1579, for instance, bailo Nicolò Barbarigo acquired the copies of official documents from Ambrosio Grillo, the Tuscan ambassador's dragoman.[82]

The imperial dragomans were not the only ones with access to official correspondence; if they translated them, there were others who composed, filed, and carried them. The baili had several informants and collaborators among the scribes of the Imperial Council and the palace couriers (*ulaks* and *çavuşes*) who carried official correspondence not only between Istanbul and foreign capitals but also between the Ottoman capital and the provinces. These had no scruples in sharing the copies of official documentation with the baili, who had them translated into Italian and quickly passed on to Venice in cipher.[83] The copies as well as the originals of Ottoman correspondence with foreign rulers;[84] diplomatic treaties;[85] orders dispatched to provincial officials,[86] mostly regarding military preparations; and news sent from the army or navy in action[87] are ubiquitous in the *dispacci* (dispatches) section in the Venetian archives.

Still, it should be noted that the baili did not transmit everything that they intercepted but instead summarized its content. When Marcantonio Barbaro sent all the letters exchanged between the Ottoman sultan and "other princes" in 1569, the Venetian Council of Ten reminded him of a previous order dated March 30, 1557, that the baili should not send these letters unless their whole content was important and that they should rather summarize them in enciphered letters directly addressed to the heads of the council. Always jealous of its control of the Venetian information-gathering mechanism and fearful of a possible leakage,[88] the Ten ordered Barbaro that he should not reveal his sources in public letters, which would be read in the Senate. He should instead use vague expressions such as "from a good place."[89] These precautions suggest that those numerous letters that have survived in the archives are only the tip of the iceberg and more had in fact passed through the baili's hands.

The leakage from within the Ottoman chancery is a clear proof of the baili's efficiency as spymasters in finding informants among the Ottoman court officers. It was the very chief of the Ottoman chancery, the Nişancı himself, who furnished Giovanni Moro in 1588 with two imperial orders that were dispatched to the Ottoman officials on the Safavid frontier.[90] In 1566 bailo Giacomo Soranzo could not acquire the order sent to Grand Admiral Piyale Pasha because his informant, an imperial scribe, fell ill.[91] Fortunately, he succeeded in obtaining from a second scribe a copy of the Ottoman-Austrian treaty that had recently been renewed. Even though the second scribe was unable to locate the original text that provided the basis for the new treaty, he was still able to assure the bailo that the new treaty was a verbatim copy of the original. Unconvinced even after the Ottoman dragoman Ibrahim's confirmation, Soranzo continued to search for the original text.[92] In another example, two years later an Ottoman superintendent of finances told one of bailo Barbaro's spies that Cyprus and Corfu would share the same destiny with the island of Chios, recently conquered from the Genoese by the Ottomans.[93] The same year, when Barbaro wanted to obtain the letters and the orders sent to the governors in Dalmatia (the frontier region between the Ottomans and the Venetians), his agents in the Imperial Council could not locate them even though they checked the records in the official registers for the last three months. Their conclusion was that the orders should have been sent from the grand vizier's chancery instead of the Imperial Council.[94]

As this last example demonstrates, the pasha chanceries also produced official documentation. The baili penetrated there, too. On the eve of the Ottoman-Venetian War of 1570–73, Grand Admiral Piyale Pasha's secretary (It. *teschiregi*, Ott. *tezkireci*) revealed information of critical value; he not only gave exact numbers for the next year's fleet but also told bailo's dragoman Pasquale Navone that its target would be, as many suspected, Cyprus, a possession of Venice.[95] Around the same time, the bailo provided Venice with similar numbers that he had received from Grand Vizier Sokollu's secretary; the latter further promised to give classified documentation in a couple of days.[96]

Imperial couriers were even more prone to selling the information that they carried. The baili frequently communicated the content of the messages and the orders that the imperial *çavuşes* and *ulaks* carried between Istanbul and the provinces; they even produced the original copies of the documents.

In 1578 the Council of Ten ordered bailo Nicolò Barbarigo to send spies with the mission of befriending the couriers coming from the Persian front by eating and drinking with them and paying their bills; the council allocated 500 *zecchini* for such missions.[97] The baili's spies seemed to have excelled in this task. For instance, they gave their masters regular access to letters sent by the army commanders in the East.[98] Moreover, in 1585 Mustafa Çavuş informed Lorenzo Bernardo that Pietro, the voivode of Wallachia, fled the battlefield against the Transylvanians. He even produced the inventory of goods that were confiscated from Pietro's camp and sent to Istanbul to be presented to the sultan.[99] Mustafa and the like who brought information from the battlefield were invaluable for the baili's information-gathering efforts. In 1566 a gatekeeper brought fresh news regarding Süleyman I's last expedition,[100] while simultaneously bailo Soranzo managed to intercept the orders for the Crown Prince Selim to send sailors to Izmir and Silifke.[101]

When they were set for foreign countries, the *çavuşes* assumed diplomatic functions as well; this made the information they provided even more relevant. For instance, when bailo Soranzo learned in 1566 that the Ottomans would send Hacı Murad to negotiate a truce with Philip II of Spain, he invited the *cavuş*[102] to his house with the pretext of negotiating the release of the illegally enslaved Venetians in North Africa. He then asked him questions regarding his mission. Murad spoke with the bailo in Spanish and revealed the details of the negotiations that he had conducted with the Spanish on his visit to France a year ago. In Perpignan, he had met with the Duke of Alba and discussed with him the possibility of a truce between Madrid and Istanbul. He also revealed to Soranzo the details of his new diplomatic mission in France. He was entrusted with arranging the release of the French slaves in Algeria and delivering them to the French authorities; moreover, he was to announce Selim II's coronation to Charles IX. He was secretly ordered, however, to contact the Spanish ambassador to France, Don Francés de Aláva y Beaumont, or any Spanish subject in Algiers or Paris in order to instigate negotiations for a truce. Having acquired such crucial information, Soranzo would moreover manage to obtain a copy of the imperial letter sent to the French king.[103]

As the aforementioned law of 1557 and the Council of Ten's warnings clearly demonstrate, the baili were expected not to reveal their sources in their letters, which would be read in the Senate in front of two hundred senators. This is why they either referred to them with very vague expressions such as *amico* (a friend),[104] *persona che molto bene lo puo sapere* (a person in a very good position to know),[105] *persona intelligente* (a knowledgeable person),[106] and *per buona strada* (from a reliable source),[107] or did not refer to them at all, contenting themselves with sharing the information. They were mentioned explicitly by name only on exceptional occasions.[108] Even then, their names were sometimes erased by the vigilant Council of Ten. In 1570, for instance, the heads of the Council of Ten "silenced" Ottoman dragoman Ibrahim's name while remitting the bailo's letter to the Senate. They wanted to make sure, however, that the senators did not consider the piece of information that the bailo sent as unreliable rumor, and thus they decided to add to the letter that he heard it from an informant. The decision clearly stipulates that this was done in order to give these letters credibility in the eyes of the senators.[109]

Although the Council of Ten's censorship prevented us from learning their names, it is evident that the baili had informants and spies at every level of the Ottoman administrative and military apparatus. It should be stated, nonetheless, that the Ottoman officials were not their only source of information. Sixteenth-century Istanbul was a diplomatic center in the making, with major European states slowly setting up permanent diplomatic missions (France in 1535, Austria in 1547, England in 1580, Holland in 1612) and giving birth to a diplomatic community in Galata, the port city on the other side of the Golden Horn facing Istanbul. Ambassadors frequently met and discussed political events and diplomatic negotiations with no hesitation about exchanging information when and to the extent that doing so suited their purposes. As the head of the oldest diplomatic mission in the Ottoman capital, the Venetian baili were attentive observers of other powers' diplomatic initiatives. They hosted and visited other foreign ambassadors who occasionally shared the content of their negotiations. In the second half of the sixteenth century, for instance, the baili's most fruitful source of information among the diplomats in Istanbul were the French ambassadors.[110] In 1580 the Venetian government explicitly asked Jacques de Germigny, the French ambassador to Istanbul who was passing through the lagoon, to share information with the bailo; this was what the French king had promised to the Venetian ambassador in Paris.[111] On one occasion, Giacomo Soranzo even succeeded in corrupting one of the French ambassador's intimates in order to "penetrate this ambassador's secrets."[112] During wartime, the diplomats of friendly powers, such as, once again, the French ambassador, provided a vital link of communication between Venice and an incommunicado bailo under lock and key in Istanbul.[113]

In addition to being a political and diplomatic center, Istanbul was also a thriving commercial port city where ships flowed from all parts of Europe and the Mediterranean. Merchants brought a broad variety of goods, and one of the most precious was fresh information. It was a regular practice in Mediterranean port cities that the authorities interrogated the crews of the ships coming from the four corners of the Mare Nostrum in order to keep themselves abreast of the latest political events and military preparations. Even though they could not interrogate the incoming ships as freely as the Venetian officials could in a Venetian port, the baili still succeeded in acquiring the latest news from them, especially those coming from the Venetian colonies in the eastern Mediterranean, the *Stato da Mar*.[114]

I have elsewhere pointed out the existence of an intelligence community in sixteenth-century Istanbul, a cosmopolitan trade, diplomatic, and political center where people from every walk of life intermingled with relatively little interference. I have also demonstrated how go-betweens with trans-imperial life trajectories for whom espionage was one of the several professional hats served more than one government.[115] This meant that an efficient spymaster such as the bailo had to remain vigilant on enemy spies' activities,[116] not only lest their reports produce detrimental results for the Venetians but also because these spies could be used for Venetian intelligence purposes. For instance, the baili closely watched the actions of the Spanish information-gathering net-work in Istanbul;[117] they even facilitated the dispatch of letters and the transfer of salaries.[118] Unsurprisingly, some of the spies on the Spanish payroll were also working for the Venetians.[119] There is even a documented example in which a spy on the Safavid payroll attempted to contact the Venetian bailo.[120]

Dealing with such untrustworthy figures eager to work for several patrons was a double-edged sword, however. Bailo Lippomano expressed his strategy for walking the thin line between remaining in contact with these information brokers and frustrating the Ottoman authorities: "If he [Guillermo de Saboya, a Jewish *Marrano* on the Spanish payroll] comes here, I will deal with him the way one deals with the likes of him, which is to 'keep the business with them in a balanced manner' in order not to arouse the suspicion of the Turks 'by getting intimate with them.'"[121] No one knew how to do this better than Lip-pomano, who was himself a traitor and a mole who leaked the most sensitive state secrets to the Spanish government.[122]

The baili's efficiency in gathering information should by now be apparent. These veteran spymasters demonstrated impressive leadership skills by finding and recruiting qualified spies and informants in a wide range of government bureaus and grandee households and thus obtaining the most precious state secrets. They also did not remain passive observers but actively participated in intelligence operations. They closely supervised the spies on their payroll and coordinated their activities through the bailate dragomans and secretaries. Moreover, they sent agents to specific locations, even beyond the Ottoman capital,[123] asking them to check the veracity of rumors and gather information on specific topics.

These numerous agents constituted a network that regularly provided sensitive information to the baili, who transmitted it to other Venetian authorities in the eastern Mediterranean. Most important, changes in the office did not bring ruptures. The fact that the Senate ordered that bailo Soranzo in 1567 should stay in touch with all of his predecessors' agents testifies to the value attached to an operative network as well as the concern for continuity.[124] The network was tied to the bailate, the office, and not the bailo, the officer.

A Venetian "Cabinet Noir"

The Venetian secret service did not only target Ottoman correspondence. When it comes to intercepting other European diplomats' letters and acquiring their secrets, the Venetians were in an exceptional position. In the sixteenth century, the only regular mail service between Istanbul and Europe was provided by the Serenissima's postal couriers.[125] Letters written by European diplomats, merchants, spies, and even the Ottoman grandees were first dispatched from Istanbul to Venice and then forwarded to other cities in Europe. This postal monopoly enabled the bailate to function like a black chamber *ante litteram*, a *cabinet noir* where letters were unsealed, checked for relevant information, and then resealed. Therefore, both the baili and the Council of Ten had regular access to the most classified information, including the details of key diplomatic negotiations.[126]

This security problem did not escape the attention of other diplomats who constantly complained to their governments. The issue was not only that their letters were screened by the Venetian authorities; the Serenissima's postal monopoly also gave them the option to retain these letters in order to gain diplomatic advantage. When French ambassador Guillaume de Grandchamp, for instance, complained to bailo Soranzo in 1567 that his letters did not reach Paris on time, he was making a veiled accusation.[127] Similarly, Austrian diplomat Giovanni Maria Malvezzi clashed with Bernardo Navagero, who did not inform him that his dispatches had arrived. The Venetian diplomat preferred to keep his Austrian colleague in the dark until he himself went to Grand Vizier Rüstem Pasha in order to share the newly arrived information and discuss his government's business. Without reading the letters sent to him, Malvezzi could neither provide the Ottomans with updated information nor intervene in Navagero's negotiations. Navagero, moreover, failed to tell Malvezzi when the embassy courier was going to leave; he thus forced him to make a tough choice between losing time and spending a fortune on extraordinary couriers.[128]

In spite of all these shortcomings and contrary to their ambassadors' advice, sixteenth-century governments could do little to remedy the situation. Setting up a regularly functioning postal system between Istanbul and Europe was simply too costly for those states that were not as commercially entrenched in the Levant as Venice.[129] In spite of occasional complaints, however, the baili were generally careful not to fuel unnecessary diplomatic scandals, and they often refrained from opening other ambassadors' dispatches.[130] The Council of

Ten was also extremely diligent when it came to delivering the official letters sent by the sultan to other European rulers. For instance, when they realized that such an imperial letter addressed to the king of France had accidentally been placed in the bailo's mailbag, they quickly forwarded it to France and informed the French ambassador in Istanbul as well as Sokollu Mehmed Pasha that the letter had been transmitted to Paris by express courier.[131] Moreover, the council was aware of the risks involved in carrying enemy correspondence during wartime; in 1566 they ordered both the bailo in Istanbul and the orator in Vienna not to accept letters from the Austrian ambassador, who wanted to use Venetian diplomatic couriers in the Vienna-Venice and Venice-Istanbul route. The Ten simply feared repercussions if the Ottomans intercepted these letters.[132]

The Ottomans themselves used the Venetian postal service even when writing to their own officers.[133] During the siege of Malta (1565), when they momentarily lost communication with their fleet, they asked Venice to transmit their messages.[134] In 1588 Gevherhan Sultan, the daughter of Selim II, sent a letter to her son Mustafa, the governor of Clissa, with the Venetian mail.[135] It should be added, however, that occasions when the Ottomans used Venetian couriers for correspondence within the empire were exceptions because the empire already had a perfectly functioning courier system stretching throughout the "well-protected domains."[136]

Correspondence between Ottoman spies and their employers in Istanbul was occasionally realized through the Venetian postal system as well. The baili carefully went through the letters in the mailbag that arrived from Venice in order to detect intelligence reports that were disguised as merchant letters and sent to the Ottoman grandees under pseudonyms or via intermediaries. In September 1585, for instance, the Venetian *Inquisitori di Stato* warned bailo Lorenzo Bernardo that Marrano power broker David Passi had agents in Venice and throughout Europe, and added that these were regularly writing letters to him.[137] Bernardo should check the letters submitted to the Jews of Istanbul and those written by Passi's agents in order to learn their content and the identity of their recipients in Venice.[138] In 1601 bailo Agostino Nani discovered the letters of a certain Lodovico Veggia, who was sending intelligence reports from Rome to Grand Admiral Cigalazade Yusuf Sinan Pasha. Thanks to the bailo's discovery, the Ottoman agent was detained in Rome.[139]

The "Honorable Spy": Necessary Qualities in a Diplomat-cum-Spymaster

As numerous examples drawn from archival sources suggest, the Venetian baili were expert spymasters who gathered information from a variety of sources. Espionage was part of their diplomatic function—they were regarded as "honorable spies."[140] They organized and led a well-functioning intelligence network with competent spies and well-connected informants in key positions. Their diplomatic status enabled them to freely contact the Ottoman authorities as well as other European ambassadors with whom they exchanged information, even though most of the time in their dispatches to their superiors in Venice they talked more about receiving than giving information. But they did give away information; in fact, the Ottomans considered them their main source of information regarding things European.[141]

Obviously, this information "exchange" was politically motivated and beyond words of courtesy and diplomatic finesse; both sides weighed each other and tried to gain the upper hand. Still, this disingenuous exchange was a necessary evil, a practice in which both the Ottoman grandees and the Venetian baili were allied. It was not a zero-sum game where one's loss was another's gain but rather a mutually beneficial relationship in which two powers, mostly on good terms with each other, shared information. It would be a truism to state that most of the time both sides manipulated the information and shared what suited their interests. But this observation should not lead us to conclude that it was all a charade. Nor were these negotiations merely a series of perfectly executed maneuvers; there was always room for error. Both the Ottoman grandees and the Venetian baili were quick to read between the lines and make the most of unintentionally revealed information. Finally, sometimes even the highest-ranking Ottoman officers willingly leaked information in order to steer the imperial policy toward the "right" path; in an empire rampant with factional rivalries, the baili easily penetrated state secrets through the fissures made by internal divisions within the Ottoman ruling elite.[142]

Being an effective spymaster required a number of traits. First, the baili had to manage a large intelligence network composed of spies operating in the field and informants in every level of the Ottoman administrative and military apparatus. Moreover, they had to supervise and inspire their embassy personnel—most important, the dragomans and the secretaries who had more practical experience in Ottoman politics thanks to their long years of service in Istanbul and who could thus be of much help to Venetian diplomatic and information-gathering efforts. Furthermore, the baili also acted as postmasters. It fell on their shoulders to organize the safe transmission of the gathered information to the relevant authorities by recruiting couriers and keeping tabs on the actions of these not-so-trustworthy figures. They were also asked to check the letters of others, carried by these couriers, for sensitive information. Finally, the baili organized Venice's counterintelligence in the Ottoman capital. They spied on the troublesome figures who could act against the Serenissima's interests, such as the Venetian exiles, the *banditi*. Moreover, they uncovered the identities and the missions of Ottoman spies who were set for Europe and alerted the authorities.[143]

The baili's sphere of activity was not limited to the Ottoman capital; they also coordinated intelligence activities in the *Stato da Mar*. Without delay, they informed the Venetian authorities in Crete, Cyprus, and the Ionian Islands each time an Ottoman fleet left the Dardanelles or when they were informed of other important political and military developments in the Ottoman capital.[144] Those authorities and the Venetian consuls in major Ottoman ports in turn sent information to the baili, sharing the results of their own information-gathering efforts. Needless to say, the baili quickly passed them on to their colleagues in the west.[145]

In addition to the leadership and managerial skills, diplomatic adroitness was also another essential quality. Whether between the Venetian baili and the Ottoman grandees or among the European diplomats themselves, diplomatic negotiations in Istanbul concentrated as much on information exchange as conflict resolution. Regularity and consistency were also vital. Information quickly lost its relevance as the balance of power between rivaling factions swiftly changed and imperial policy swung from one side to the other. In 1565 anxious senators reminded bailo Soranzo with an almost unanimous vote (174-2-1) that he should not leave them without a letter for more than fifteen days.[146]

We do not know how much the baili followed the developments in the techniques of cryptography and steganography; it was their secretaries and scribes who performed these tasks. We do have evidence, however, that some could not help micromanaging their chancery and thus gained some practical experience of breaking ciphers. In 1617, for instance, Almoro Nani managed to conclude from the characters used in the cipher in two intercepted spy letters that these were addressed to the Austrian ambassador. His prediction proved useful, especially in light of the fact the Venetians could not decipher those letters.[147]

Gathering information was only one of the baili's tasks as spymasters; it was in fact the easiest one. Information was free for all in Istanbul; the question was to separate fact from rumor and reliable intelligence from dis- or misinformation. Sixteenth-century Istanbul's intelligence community was filled with swindlers and crooks who constantly tried to capitalize on central governments' eagerness for political secrets. A seasoned spymaster had to filter out the bad intelligence, information with "such little foundation."[148] Various channels of information allowed the baili to verify the gathered information. Their other Ottoman informants, always in rivalry with each other, quickly revealed false information. The baili could, moreover, rely on their numerous spies in the city, other European diplomats and moles in the Ottoman government who leaked official documentation.

Having filtered out the false information, the baili should also prioritize the most relevant intelligence in order not to send too much information for the Venetian decision makers to sort and absorb. In his seminal work on Philip II's grand strategy, Geoffrey Parker delineated how such an "information overload" paralyzed the Spanish government;[149] this would have been even more damaging for a republic such as Venice, where decisions were made with the participation of a larger number of people. Moreover, information had to be transformed into intelligence; as experienced diplomats and acute observers of Ottoman politics, it was the baili's métier to contextualize raw information within the larger framework of Ottoman strategy and factional politics.[150]

The efficiency of the baili in gathering information was of utmost importance for Venetian decision makers, who were always eager to keep abreast of political and military developments in the capital of a threatening empire, a formidable foe as well as a useful ally. The Venetian authorities had confidence in their baili's skills as spymasters. These experienced diplomats, who were entrusted with one of the most prestigious posts in the Venetian diplomatic corps, were given full autonomy in running their information-gathering network.[151] They freely spent the resources allocated to them on informants, recruited spies at will, and coordinated the intelligence missions. Most important, it fell on their shoulders to deal with the embassy's staff and troublesome information brokers of dubious background and loyalties.

In dealing with such sleazy characters, who were always suspected of duplicity and intrigue, the baili had to demonstrate immense leadership qualities in all their functions, as consuls, diplomats, and spymasters. Their role as intelligence leaders was especially significant because there were no inherited organizational structures and attitudes that established espionage's modus operandi. Without formal training or a clear distinction between these functions, the efficiency of the diplomatic mission in gathering intelligence depended more on personal traits of a bailo than would be the case in the twentieth century. In spite of early signs of specialization that characterized the office of the permanent ambassador, the baili had wide discretionary powers; they had to improvise, take the initiative, and produce ad hoc solutions to problems simply because there were few guidelines helping them while recruiting spies, organizing intelligence missions, and engaging in disinformation and counterintelligence.

In a sense, then, the baili's leadership was premised on their personal and professional traits and connections. Any attempt to find continuities and discontinuities with contemporary typologies of Western leadership risks distorting the time-specific meaning and functions of intelligence leadership in a society and for a state that are different from those in which modern intelligence operates. Unfortunately, documents at our disposal do not allow us to go into more details. Even though the Venetian archives house a relatively rich corpus of diplomatic documents, the succinct and to-the-point nature of early modern correspondence prevents an in-depth analysis of the leadership qualities that the baili demonstrated during specific espionage missions.

We can state in the end, though, that their efforts produced handsome results; it was thanks to them that early modern Venice became an "information clearinghouse" concerning things Ottoman.[152] The baili's regular dispatches were read out in the Senate. Their secret letters for the exclusive eyes of the Council of Ten informed the Serenissima's diplomatic strategy. Lastly, their final reports at the end of their tenure, the famous *relazioni*, hardly remained limited to the Venetian senators; they were (illegally) copied and sold throughout Europe. The centrality of Venice and of the figure of the ambassador for the circulation of information in Europe is evident from the popularity of these reports, which became a major source of information on the Ottoman Empire up until the nineteenth century. Their influence on modern historiography is palpable in the works of prominent historians such as Leopold von Ranke and Joseph von Hammer-Purgstall.[153]

The baili's efficiency in penetrating Ottoman state secrets is so impressive that even today, almost two centuries after the penning of Hammer-Purgstall's magnum opus, Ottomanists, including the author of this chapter, continue to rely on their observations.[154] Their access to privileged circuits of information is all the more surprising in a secretive political culture in which decision making was confined to the smallest possible group.[155] Apparently, even though the principle of the inaccessibility of *esrâr-ı saltanat* (literally "secrets of sovereignty"; i.e., Tacitus's *arcana imperii*) prevailed in written works,[156] in the realm of oral communication, even top-secret information was available to well-connected political actors, including foreign ambassadors, first and foremost the Venetian baili.

Notes

I would like to thank Maria Pia Pedani, Levent Kaya Ocakaçan, and Ioanna Iordanou for their comments.

1. Pierre Sardella, *Nouvelles et spéculations à Venise: au debut du XVIe siècle* [News and speculations in Venice at the beginning of the sixteenth century] (Paris: Librarie Armand Colin, 1948); Hans J. Kissling, "Venezia come centro di informazioni sui Turchi" [Venice as a center of information on the Turks], in *Venezia, centro di mediazione tra Oriente e Occidente, secoli XV–XVI: Aspetti e problemi* [Venice, center of mediation between the Orient and the Occident in the fifteenth and sixteenth centuries: Aspects

and problems], ed. Hans Georg Beck et al., (Florence: L. S. Olschki, 1977), 1:97–109; Paolo Preto, *I servizi segreti di Venezia* [The secret services of Venice] (Milano: Il Saggiatore, 2010; 1st ed., 1994), 87–95; Robert Mantran, "Venise: centre d'informations sur les turcs" [Venice: Center of information on the Turks], in *Venezia, centro di mediazione*, 1:111–16; and Peter Burke, "Early Modern Venice as a Center of Information and Communication," in *Venice Reconsidered*, ed. John Martin and Dennis Romano (Baltimore, MD: Johns Hopkins University Press, 2000), 389–419.

2. Marino Sanudo, *I diarii di Marino Sanuto (MCCCCXCVI-MDXXXIII) dall' autografo Marciano ital. cl. VII codd. CDXIX-CDLXXVII* [The diaries of Marino Sanuto] (Venice: F. Visentini, 1879), 58 vols.

3. According to Garrett Mattingly, the early modern state looked to its diplomats for two things: allies and information. Garrett Mattingly, *Renaissance Diplomacy* (1958; repr., New York: Dover Publications, 1988), 95. While Bacigalupe states that diplomacy and espionage are "twin brothers" [Miguel Angel Echevarría Bacigalupe, *La diplomacia secreta en Flandes, 1598–1643* [Secret diplomacy in Flanders, 1598–1643] (Leioa-Vizcaya: Argitarapen Zerbitzua Euskal Herriko Unibertsitatea, 1984), 33], Carnicer and Marcos have gone as far as claiming that espionage was the real reason for the existence of resident embassies and that the ambassadors' diplomatic functions merely provided a legal cover for their information-gathering activities [Carlos Carnicer and Javier Marcos, *Espías de Felipe II: los servicios secretos del imperio español* [Spies of Philip II: The secret services of the Spanish Empire] (Madrid: La esfera de los libros, 2005), 146]. All the monographs specializing on early modern espionage accentuate the diplomats' role in gathering, verifying, and analyzing information. See Charles Howard Carter, *The Secret Diplomacy of the Habsburgs, 1598–1625* (New York: Columbia University Press, 1964), chap. 10; Bacigalupe, *La diplomacia secreta*, 33–35; Lucien Bély, *Espions et ambassadeurs au temps de Louis XIV* [Spies and ambassadors in the time of Louis XIV] (Paris: Libraire Arthème Fayard, 1990), 116–17; Alan Marshall, *Intelligence and Espionage in the Reign of Charles II, 1660–1685* (Cambridge: Cambridge University Press, 1994), chap. 7; Preto, *I Servizi Segreti*, 123–28, 197–209; Alain Hugon, *Au service de Roi Catholique: "Honorable Ambassadeurs" et "Divins Espions"—répresentation diplomatique et service secret dans les relations Hispano-Françaises de 1598 à 1635* [In the service of the Catholic king: "Honorable Ambassadors" and "Divine Spies"— Diplomatic representation and secret service in Hispano-French relations from 1598 to 1635] (Madrid: Casa de Velázquez, 2004), 125–30; Jean-Michel Ribera, *Diplomatie et espionnage: les ambassadeurs du roi de France auprès de Philippe II du traité du Cateau-Cambresis (1559) à la mort de Henri III (1589)* [Diplomacy and Espionage: The ambassadors of the king of France at the court of Philip II from the Treaty of Cateau-Cambresis (1559) to the death of Henri III (1589)] (Paris: Honoré Champion Editeur, 2007), part 2; and Carnicer and Marcos, *Espías de Felipe II*, 49–58. Also see articles in Béatrice Perez, ed., *Ambassadeurs, apprentis espions et maîtres comploteurs: les systèmes de renseignement en Espagne à l'époque moderne* [Ambassadors, apprentice spies and master-plotters: The system of information gathering in Spain in the early modern period] (Paris: Presses de l'université Paris-Sorbonne, 2010).

4. Carlo Coco and Flora Manzonetto, *Baili veneziani alla Sublime Porta* [The

Venetian baili at the sublime porte] (Venezia: Stamperia di Venezia, 1985); Eric R. Dursteler, "The Bailo in Constantinople: Crisis and Career in Venice's Early Modern Diplomatic Corps," *Mediterranean Historical Review* 16 (2001): 1–30; and Eric R. Dursteler, *Venetians in Constantinople: Nation, Identity, and Coexistence in the Early Modern Mediterranean* (Baltimore, MD: Johns Hopkins University Press, 2006).

5. Şefik Peksevgen, "Secrecy, Information Control and Power Building in the Ottoman Empire, 1566–1603" (PhD diss., McGill University, 2004), chap. 2.

6. John-Paul Ghobrial, *The Whispers of Cities: Information Flows in Istanbul, London and Paris in the Age of William Trumbull* (Oxford: Oxford University Press, 2013), 72.

7. Archivio di Stato di Venezia [Archive of the State of Venice, hereafter ASV], *Senato, Archivio Proprio Costantinopoli* [Senate, Archive relating to Constantinople, hereafter *APC*], fil. 5, c. 340v (March 9, 1552).

8. A renegade is a convert to another religion.

9. Dursteler, *Venetians in Constantinople*, 168.

10. ASV, *Senato, Dispacci Costantinopoli* [Senate, Dispatches from Constantinople, hereafter *SDC*], fil. 4, c. 136v (July 9, 1569).

11. *SDC*, fil. 32, c. 129r (September 29, 1590).

12. *SDC*, fil. 31, cc. 453r–454v (August 18, 1590).

13. Joshua M. White, "Fetva Diplomacy: The Ottoman Şeyhülislam as Trans-Imperial Intermediary," *Journal of Early Modern History* 19 (2015): 199–221.

14. *SDC*, fil. 21, cc. 464v–465r (July 12, 1585). On Saadeddin's role in Ottoman decision making, see Baki Tezcan, "The Ottoman Mevali as 'Lords of the Law,'" *Journal of Islamic Studies* 20 (2009): 383–407, here 398–99n34, 402.

15. *SDC*, fil. 32, cc. 177v–179v (October 18, 1590).

16. *SDC*, fil. 4, c. 119r (June 25, 1569).

17. Mehmed shared information regarding the military situation in the East and diplomatic negotiations with the Austrians. *SDC*, fil. 32, cc. 138v–139r (October 8, 1590). This was not the first time he provided the bailo with crucial intelligence; ten months before, he had informed him of the lack of materials in the Arsenal. *SDC*, fil. 30, c. 263r (December 23, 1589).

18. *SDC*, fil. 31, c. 453v (August 18, 1590); fil. 32, c. 138v (October 8, 1590).

19. Emrah Safa Gürkan, "Touting for Patrons, Brokering Power and Trading Information: Trans-Imperial Jews in Sixteenth-Century Constantinople," in *Detrás de las apariencias. Información y espionaje (siglos XVI–XVII)* [Behind appearances: Information and espionage (XVI–XVII centuries)], ed. Emilio Sola Castaño and Gennaro Varriale (Alcalá de Henares: Universidad de Alcalá, 2015), 127–51.

20. Maria Pia Pedani, ed., *Relazioni di ambasciatori veneti al Senato tratte dalle migliori edizioni disponibili e ordinate cronologicamente, vol. XIV: Costantinopoli, relazioni inedite (1512–1789)* [Reports of the Venetian ambassadors for the senate, taken from the best available editions and ordered chronologically, vol. 14: Constantinople, unedited reports (1512–1789)] (Turin: Bottega d'Erasmo, 1996), 341; *SDC*, fil. 23, c. 1v (March 3, 1586), fil. 22, cc. 122r–123r (October 2, 1588), fil. 28, cc. 168r–168v (November 17, 1588), 326r–326v (December 30, 1588); and ASV, *Senato,*

Secreta, Deliberazioni Costantinopoli [Senate, secret, deliberations about Constantinople; hereafter *Deliberazioni Costantinopoli*], reg. 8, c. 94v (November 14, 1592).

21. *SDC*, fil. 2, c. 135r (July 10, 1567). The Venetians considered Joseph Nasi responsible for the outbreak of the war of 1570–73 and the fire in the Venetian Arsenal in 1569.

22. *SDC*, fil. 2, c. 398r (January 19, 1567, *more Veneto* [hereafter m.v.: The Venetian year started on March 1, so January 1567 in the Venetian calendar actually refers to January 1568. The same rule applies to February as well]).

23. Benjamin Arbel, *Trading Nations: Jews and Venetians in the Early Modern Eastern Mediterranean* (Leiden: E. J. Brill, 1995), 79–80.

24. *SDC*, fil. 67, c. 255r (July 25, 1609).

25. Francesca Lucchetta, "Il medico del bailaggio di Costantinopoli: fra terapie e politica (sec. XVI–XVI)" [The physician of the Bailate in Constantinople: Between therapy and politics], *Quaderni di Studi Arabi* [Books of Arab studies] 15 (1997) suppl., 5–50. In 1585 Lorenzo Bernardo received information from Valentino regarding Ahmed Pasha's health and the issue of a ship he seized from the captain general of the Venetian fleet (*Provveditore dell'Armata*). *SDC*, fil. 22, c. 331r (December 24, 1585).

26. The imperial naval facility in Istanbul. Even though there were other arsenals in the empire, most of the Ottoman fleet was built and equipped there.

27. A corsair is a privateer.

28. Emrah Safa Gürkan, "Fooling the Sultan: Information, Decision-Making and the 'Mediterranean Faction' (1585–1587)," *Journal of Ottoman Studies* 45 (2015): 57–96.

29. On this neglected corsair–turned–grand admiral, see Antonio Fabris, "Hasan 'il Veneziano' tra Algeria e Costantinopoli" [Hasan "the Venetian" between Algiers and Constantinople], *Quaderni di Studi Arabi* 5 (1997): 51–66.

30. *SDC*, fil. 28, cc. 265r (December 17, 1588), 434r (January 27, 1588, m.v.); and fil. 30, c. 236v (December 23, 1589).

31. *SDC*, fil. 29, c. 402v (July 21, 1589).

32. *SDC*, fil. 28, cc. 58r–60v (September 24, 1588), 434r (January 27, 1588, m.v.), 497r–498r (February 25, 1588, m.v.); fil. 29, cc. 87r–87v (April 4, 1589); 133v–135v (April 27, 1589), 207r–207v (May 13, 1589); and fil. 30, cc. 249v (December 9, 1589), 317v (June 22, 1589), 335v (January 20, 1589, m.v.).

33. *SDC*, fil. 21, cc. 197r–201r (April 29, 1585).

34. *SDC*, fil. 22, c. 225v (November 13, 1585).

35. *APC*, fil. 5, c. 207v (September 19, 1551).

36. *SDC*, fil. 4, c. 246v (October 10, 1569).

37. *SDC*, fil. 31, cc. 453r–454v (August 18, 1590); and Horatio Brown, ed., *Calendar of State Papers Relating to English Affairs in the Archives of Venice* [hereafter *COSP*], vol. 8 (London: Her Majesty's Stationery Office, 1894), no. 1015 (February 16, 1590, m.v.).

38. *APC*, fil. 5, c. 46r (February 1550, m.v.).

39. *SDC*, fil. 23, c. 547v (July 8, 1586).

40. For an example of how well informed the baili were regarding the Ottoman fleet's destinations in the Mediterranean, see *SDC*, fil. 1, cc. 207r–207v (July 4, 1566).

41. Dursteler, *Venetians in Constantinople*, chap. 3.

42. "Orator" was one of the terms used for diplomats throughout the Renaissance. Mattingly, *Renaissance Diplomacy*, 26.

43. Sanudo, *I diarii*, vol. II, col. 612. He was most probably trying to obtain the revocation of his banishment.

44. *APC*, fil. 5, c. 46r (February 1550, m.v.).

45. *APC*, fil. 5, c. 26v (November 25, 1550).

46. *SDC*, fil. 2, cc. 398r, 398v (January 19, 1567, m.v.).

47. *SDC*, fil. 28, c. 287r (December 19, 1588).

48. ASV, *Consiglio dei dieci, Parti Secrete* [Council of Ten, secret proceedings; hereafter *Parti Secrete*], reg. 11, cc. 179r–179v (January 15, 1578, m.v.).

49. *SDC*, fil. 29, c. 402v (July 21, 1589).

50. *SDC*, fil. 31, c. 453r (August 18, 1590).

51. Emrah Safa Gürkan, "The Efficacy of Ottoman-Counter-Intelligence in the Sixteenth Century," *Acta Orientalia Academiae Scientiarum Hungaricae* [Oriental reports of the Hungarian Academy of Sciences] 65 (2012): 1–38, here 19–23.

52. *SDC*, fil. 5, cc. 93v–94r (May 1, 1570).

53. *SDC*, fil. 4, c. 264r (January 4, 1569, m.v.).

54. *SDC*, fil. 22, c. 323r (December 11, 1585).

55. *COSP*, vol. 8, nos. 1015 (February 16, 1590, m.v.), 1030 (March 16, 1591).

56. *SDC*, fil. 30, c. 380v (January 20, 1589, m.v.).

57. *Parti Secrete*, reg. 8, cc. 114v–115v (May 23, 1568).

58. *SDC*, fil. 4, c. 268v (January 21, 1569, m.v).

59. Cristian Luca, "Documentary Notes Relative to the Kinships of Levantines and Venetians with the Princely Families from Wallachia and Moldavia (16th–17th Centuries)," in *Românii în Europa medievală: (între Orientul bizantin şi Occidentul latin): studii în onoarea profesorului Victor Spinei* [Romans in Medieval Europe (between the Byzantine East and the Latin West): Studies in honor of Professor Victor Spinei], ed. Dumitru Teicu and Victor Spinei (Brăila: Ed. Istros, 2008), 653–75, here 654–56.

60. *APC*, fil. 5, c. 72v (April 29, 1551).

61. *APC*, fil. 5, c. 332r (March 4, 1552).

62. ASV, *Capi del Consiglio dei dieci, Lettere di Ambasciatori* [Heads of the Council of Ten, letters of the ambassadors; hereafter *Lettere Ambasciatori*], b. 3, fols. 162–64 (November 13, 1568).

63. *SDC*, fil. 30, c. 240v (December 9, 1589).

64. Eric Dursteler, *Renegade Women: Gender, Identity, and Boundaries in the Early Modern Mediterranean* (Baltimore, MD: Johns Hopkins University Press, 2011), 23.

65. It was Maria Pia Pedani who first discovered Beatrice's Muslim name. ASV, *Provveditori sopra Ospedali e luoghi pii diversi* [Superintendents of hospitals and various pious places], f. 46, "Commissaria Fatma hatun"; and Maria Pia Pedani, "Safiye's Household and Venetian Diplomacy," *Turcica* 32 (2000): 9–31; here 26.

66. Maria Pia Pedani-Fabris, "Veneziani a Costantinopoli alla fine del XVI secolo," *Quaderni di Studi Arabi* 15 (1997): 67–84; and Pedani, "Safiye's Household," 25–27.

For Beatrice's letter indicating that she was at Venice's service, see *Lettere di Ambasciatori*, b. 6, c. 140 (February 26, 1592, m.v.).

67. Dursteler, *Renegade Women*, 21–23.

68. *SDC*, b. 44, copia, reg. 11, cc. 183–84 (November 7, 1596). I would like to thank Prof. Pedani for pointing out this document.

69. Emrah Safa Gürkan, "Mediating Boundaries: Mediterranean Go-Betweens and Cross-Confessional Diplomacy in Constantinople, 1560–1600," *Journal of Early Modern History* 19 (2015): 107–28, here 111–16.

70. *SDC*, fil. 23, c. 180r (April 16, 1586).

71. *SDC*, fil. 2, cc. 437r–438r (February 2, 1567, m.v.); and *APC*, fil. 5, cc. 169r–169v (July 19, 1551).

72. *SDC*, fil. 5, c. 316r (December 30, 1570).

73. *APC*, fil. 5, c. 380r (May 10, 1552); *SDC*, fil. 25, cc. 170r, 171r–v (April 16, 1587); and fil. 32, cc. 52v–53r (September 4, 1590).

74. Vestiges of the Catholic merchants trading in the city since Byzantine times, these Franks were allowed to live in Istanbul after its fall to the Ottomans in 1453, and thus they became Ottoman subjects. Eric Dursteler, "Latin-Rite Christians in Early Modern Istanbul," in *Osmanlı İstanbulu I: I. Uluslararası Osmanlı İstanbulu Sempozyumu Bildirileri, 29 Mayıs–1 Haziran 2013, İstanbul 29 Mayıs Üniversitesi* [Ottoman Istanbul I: Proceedings of the 1st International Ottoman Istanbul Symposium, 29 May–1 June 2013, Istanbul 29 May University], ed. Feridun Emecen and Emrah Safa Gürkan (Istanbul: İstanbul 29 Mayıs Üniversitesi Yayınları, 2014), 137–46.

75. For instance, in 1588 Giovanni Moro sent his dragoman to contact his informants on Siyavuş Pasha. *SDC*, fil. 28, cc. 326r–326v (December 30, 1588).

76. *APC*, fil. 5, c. 207v (September 19, 1551).

77. *APC*, fil. 5, c. 116r (June 6, 1551).

78. *SDC*, fil. 2, cc. 399r–399v (January 19, 1567, m.v.).

79. *Lettere di Ambasciatori*, b. 6, fol. 1 (March 5, 1581).

80. On the Brutti family, their Mediterranean-wide connections, and their kinship with Sinan Pasha, see Noel Malcolm, *Agents of Empire: Knights, Corsairs, Jesuits and Spies in the Sixteenth-Century Mediterranean World* (London: Allen Lane, 2015). For Cristoforo, see chap. 19.

81. *Lettere di Ambasciatori*, b. 6, fol. 51 (December 21, 1582).

82. *Lettere di Ambasciatori*, b. 5, fol. 163; and Malcolm, *Agents of Empire*, 269.

83. *SDC*, fil. 1, cc. 76r–79v; and fil. 26, cc. 428r–429v, 430r–431r.

84. *SDC*, fil. 2, cc. 421r, 428r–433r; fil. 3, cc. 193r–193v, 197r–199r; fil. 22, cc. 175r–176v, 470r; fil. 30, cc. 341r, 343r–345v; fil. 31, cc. 219r–220v; and *APC*, fil. 5, c. 238v.

85. *SDC*, fil. 3, cc. 1r–4v, 197r–199r.

86. *SDC*, fil. 1, c. 215v; fil. 22, cc. 361r, 362r–365r; fil. 23, c. 499r; and fil. 32, cc. 45r–45v.

87. *SDC*, fil. 1, c. 218r.

88. Filippo de Vivo, *Information and Communication in Venice: Rethinking Early Modern Politics* (Oxford: Oxford University Press, 2007), 33–36.

89. *Parti Secrete*, reg. 8, cc. 137v–139r (January 5, 1568, January 18, 1568, m.v.).

90. *SDC*, fil. 26, cc. 424r (February 23, 1587, m.v.), 428r–429v (February 23, 1587, m.v.).

91. *SDC*, fil. 1, cc. 86r–86v (April 13, 1566).

92. *SDC*, fil. 1, cc. 82r–82v (April 13, 1566).

93. *Parti Secrete*, reg. 8, cc. 118r–118v (June 4, 1568).

94. *SDC*, fil. 3, c. 344v (November 22, 1568).

95. *SDC*, fil. 2, c. 399r (January 19, 1567, m.v.).

96. *SDC*, fil. 2, cc. 400r–400v (January 19, 1567, m.v.).

97. *Parti Secrete*, fil. 20, unpaginated document dated August 13, 1578. Zecchini or sequin is the name of the Venetian gold coin or ducat. In use since 1284, it was made of 3.5 grams of almost pure gold (.997 fine).

98. *SDC*, fil. 21, c. 113v (March 29, 1585).

99. *SDC*, fil. 21, cc. 384r, 387r–388r (June 22, 1585).

100. *SDC*, fil. 1, c. 218r (July 20, 1566).

101. *SDC*, fil. 1, c. 215v (July 20, 1566).

102. On the career of Hacı Murad, a Mediterranean go-between who wore several professional hats (an imperial *çavuş*, an Ottoman diplomat, Uluc Ali's kahya, the governor of Madiyyah [Ott. Midye]), see Jean Canavaggio, "Le 'Vrai' visage d'Agi Morato" [The "real" face of Agi Morato], *Les Langues Néo-Latines* [The neo-Latin tongues] 239 (1981): 22–38; Emilio Sola and José F. de la Peña, *Cervantes y la Berbería: Cervantes, mundo turco-berberisco y servicios secretos en la epoca de Felipe II* [Cervantes and Barbary: Cervantes, the Turco-Berber world and secret services in the age of Philip II] (Madrid: Fondo de Cultura Economica, 1995), chap. 8; and Güneş Işıksel, "Hacı Murad (Agi Morato): An Elusive Dignitary Active in the Second Half of the Sixteenth Century," *Journal of Ottoman Studies* 47 (2016): 247–63.

103. *SDC*, fil. 1, cc. 461r–462r (February 2, 1566, m.v.).

104. *SDC*, fil. 2, cc. 338r, 398r; and *APC*, fil. 5, c. 34r (January 1, 1550, m.v.).

105. *SDC*, fil. 4, c. 165r (July 23, 1569).

106. *SDC*, fil. 3, c. 124v (June 14, 1568).

107. *SDC*, fil. 4, c. 112r (May 11, 1569).

108. *SDC*, fil. 81, c. 116r (April 30, 1616) refers to a Suliman Granatino, quoted by Tijana Krstić, "Contesting Subjecthood and Sovereignty in Ottoman Galata in the Age of Confessionalization: The *Carazo* Affair, 1613–1617," *Oriento Moderno* [Modern Orient] 93 (2013): 422–53, here 431.

109. *Parti Secrete*, reg. 9, cc. 54v–55r (February 20, 1569, m.v.).

110. For an example, see *Parti Secrete*, reg. 10, cc. 26v–26r (May 30, 1572).

111. Eventually, Germini would fall short of Venetian expectations. *Parti Secrete*, reg. 12, cc. 45v–46r (September 23, 1580).

112. *Lettere di Ambasciatori*, b. 3, fol. 85–88 (January 13, 1566, m.v.).

113. *Parti Secrete*, reg. 4, cc. 82v–83r (November 7, 1537).

114. *SDC*, fil. 4, c. 82r (May 14, 1569); and fil. 5, c. 93r (May 1, 1570).

115. See Emrah Safa Gürkan, "Espionage in the 16th Century Mediterranean:

Secret Diplomacy, Mediterranean Go-Betweens and the Ottoman-Habsburg Rivalry" (PhD diss., Georgetown University, 2012), chaps. 2 and 5.

116. For instance, see ASV, *Inquisitori di Stato* [State inquisitors; hereafter *IS*], b. 416, unpaginated document dated November 30, 1591. Venetian ambassadors and spies in other capitals informed their government of spies that other powers dispatched to Istanbul so that the Signoria could quickly warn its baili. *Deliberazioni Costantinopoli*, reg. 7, cc. 140r (January 14, 1588, m.v.), 145v (January 26, 1588, m.v.).

117. For more on this network, see Emrah Safa Gürkan, "Espionage in the 16th Century Mediterranean," chap. 5.

118. Even though there were couriers going back and forth between Istanbul and the Habsburg Naples, this did not provide a regular channel of transmission, and Spanish spies used the Venetian public mail as well. One of them, Juan Segui de Menorca, complained to bailo Lorenzo Bernardo that his letters were being detained in Venice and that this was a great discomfort to Habsburg intelligence efforts. He then wanted to use Bernardo's diplomatic mail, but the bailo flatly refused him any assistance. He instead opened his parcel (*plichato*) and sent his enciphered letters to Venice (*IS*, b. 416, unpaginated document dated November 30, 1591). Bernardo moreover stopped paying Menorca's salary because the Spanish ambassador who appointed him, Giovanni Margliani, had passed away. Owing to the lack of a permanent Spanish diplomatic mission in Istanbul, Menorca had nobody to vouch for him. Archivo General de Simancas [General archive of Simancas; hereafter AGS], Papeles de Estado [State papers; hereafter *E*] 1090, fol. 8 (September 10, 1588); *E* K 1675, fol. 21 (January 19, 1591).

119. Emilio Sola Castaño, *Uchalí: El Calabrés tiñoso, o el mito del corsario muladí en la frontera* [Uluc Ali: The miserable Calabrian, or the myth of a renegade corsair in the borderlands] (Barcelona: Edicions Bellaterra, 2011), 376.

120. *APC*, fil. 5, cc. 36v–37v (January 18, 1550, m.v.).

121. *SDC*, fil. 31, cc. 456v–457r (August 18, 1590). The Marranos were Spanish Jews who had been forced to convert to Christianity but still practiced their old faith in secret.

122. P. Augusto Tormene, "Il bailaggio a Costantinopoli di Girolamo Lippomano e la sua tragica fine" [The bailate of Girolamo Lippomano in Constantinople and his tragic end], *Nuovo archivio veneto* [New Veneto Archive], n.s. 3, t. 6 (1903), 375–431; n.s. 4, t. 7 (1904), 66–125, 288–333; and t. 8 (1904), 127–61.

123. For a spy sent to the Arsenal, see *APC*, fil. 5, c. 46r (February 1550). For another sent to Phillipolis (Plovdiv) to spy on the marching Ottoman army, see *SDC*, fil. 1, cc. 207r (July 4, 1566), 215r (July 20, 1566).

124. *SDC*, fil. 2, c. 398r (January 19, 1567, m.v.).

125. On Venetian mail service to Istanbul, see Luciano de Zanche, "I vettori dei dispacci diplomatici veneziani da e per Costantinopoli" [The carriers of Venetian diplomatic dispatches to and from Constantinople], *Archivio per la storia postale, comunicazioni e società* [Archive for the history of the mail, communications and society] 1 (1999): 19–43; and Luciano de Zanche, *Tra Costantinopoli e Venezia: dispacci di stato*

e lettere di mercanti dal basso medievo alla caduta della Serenissima [Between Constantinople and Venice: State dispatches and merchant letters from the late medieval ages to the fall of the Serenissima] (Prato: Istituto di Studi Storici Postali, 2000). Eric Dursteler puts forward an interesting argument: the Venetians took pains to ensure their monopoly on information flow between Istanbul and Europe so that they could maintain their republic's political relevance and defend its economic status. Eric R. Dursteler, "Power and Information: The Venetian Postal System in the Early Modern Mediterranean," in *From Florence to the Mediterranean: Studies in Honor of Anthony Molho*, ed. Diogo Curto et al. (Florence: Olschki, 2009), 601–23, here 602.

126. *SDC*, fil. 23, cc. 370v–372r (May 15, 1586), 391r (May 28, 1586).

127. *Parti Secrete*, reg. 8, cc. 82v–83r (April 9, 1567), 83r–83v (April 17, 1567).

128. Karl Nehring et al., eds., *Austro-Turcica, 1541–1552. Diplomatische Akten des habsburgischen Gesandtschaftverkehrs mit der Hohen Pforte im Zeitalter Süleymans des Prächtigen* [Austro-Turcica, 1541–1552: Records of Habsburg diplomatic relations with the sublime porte in the age of Süleyman the Magnificent] (Munich: Oldenburg, 1995), 539, 571, 591–92; and María José Rodríguez-Salgado, "Eating Bread Together: Hapsburg Diplomacy and Intelligence-Gathering in Mid Sixteenth-Century Istanbul," in *Detrás de las apariencias*, 73–100; here 94.

129. In 1587 the annual cost of the Venetian mail service was 5,705 ducats. Dursteler, "Power and Information," 615.

130. When the Austrian ambassador was detained by the Ottomans in 1551, for instance, bailo Navagero could not give him a letter that was sent either by Ferdinand I or the Austrian ambassador in Venice. Navagero instead sent back the letter, unopened and in good condition (*ben conditionata*), to Venice. *APC*, fil. 5, c. 193v (August 29, 1551).

131. *Parti Secrete*, reg. 9, c. 11v, 14r–14v (July 19, 1569).

132. *Parti Secrete*, reg. 6, cc. 160r–160v (May 29, 1566), 160v–161r (April 30, 1566), 161v (May 30, 1566).

133. For other examples of Ottoman correspondence carried by Venetian couriers, see Dursteler, "Power and Information," 604.

134. *Parti Secrete*, reg. 8, c. 79v (February 18, 1566, m.v.). Still, during the siege of Malta there were couriers going back and forth between the Ottoman navy and Istanbul. Selânikî Mustafa Efendi, *Tarih-i Selânikî* [The history of Selânikî], ed. Mehmet İpşirli (Ankara: Türk Tarih Kurumu, 1999), 1:9.

135. *SDC*, fil. 28 cc. 125v (October 22, 1588), 133r–133v.

136. The Sultana sent this letter through Venetian hands because she wrote it at the bailo's behest. The letter urged Mustafa to punish his men who were molesting the Venetians across the frontier.

137. Chosen from the members of the Council of Ten, three state inquisitors dealt with many tasks, including protecting state secrets. Therefore, they supervised spies and informants.

138. The bailo responded that he could not know for certain which ones were written by Passi because the "Consul of the Jews" in Istanbul brought the letters all

together in one pile. From his other sources the bailo acquired the information, however, that Passi had agents in Ancona and that his brother was in Venice. The only letters he could intercept were the ones that Passi directly gave the bailo's secretary to be mailed to the lagoon. Even then, fearful of Passi's power in the Ottoman capital, he did not dare open these letters; instead, he sent them to the State Inquisitors. See *IS*, b. 148, fol. 1 (September 25, 1585); and b. 416, unpaginated documents dated January 8, 1585, m.v., March 25, 1586, and August 2, 1590.

139. *Parti Secrete*, reg. 14, cc. 128v (September 22, 1601), 129r–129v (December 14, 1601).

140. This term was originally coined by the French writer and diplomat François de Callières. *De la Manière de négocier avec les souverains* [On the manner of negotiating with princes] (Amsterdam: La compagnie, 1716), 30: "We call an ambassador an honorable spy [*honorable espion*] because one of his primary responsibilities is to discover the secrets of the Courts where he is and he fails in his duties if he does not undertake the necessary spending to win over those who could inform him [translation is mine, there is already an English translation of the book (A. F. Whyte, *The Practice of Diplomacy* [London: Constable, 1919]), but it provides only a rough translation].

141. Gürkan, "Espionage in the 16th Century Mediterranean," 403–5.

142. On these factional rivalries that became more evident especially after 1579, see Günhan Börekçi, "Factions and Favorites at the Courts of Sultan Ahmed I (r. 1603-1617) and His Immediate Predecessors" (PhD diss., Ohio State University, 2010).

143. *Parti Secrete*, reg. 5, cc. 100v–101r (May 16, 1543); *SDC*, fil. 21, c. 523v (August 5, 1585); and *IS*, b. 416, unpaginated documents dated September 28, 1621, and January 6, 1621, m.v.

144. *SDC*, fil. 23, c. 585r (August 6, 1586); and fil. 25, c. 141v (April 4, 1587).

145. *SDC*, fil. 3, c. 234r (September 19, 1568); and fil. 4, c. 213r (September 30, 1569).

146. *Deliberazioni Costantinopoli*, reg. 3, cc. 24r–24v (November 17, 1565).

147. *IS*, b. 416, unpaginated document dated October 28, 1617.

148. *APC*, fil. 5, cc. 36v–37v (January 18, 1550, m.v.).

149. Geoffrey Parker, *The Grand Strategy of Philip II* (New Haven, CT: Yale University Press, 1998), 21–31, 65–71, and conclusion.

150. For an example, see *SDC*, fil. 28, cc. 286v–287r (December 19, 1588).

151. Salvatore Carbone, *Note introduttive ai dispacci al Senato dei rappresentanti diplomatici veneti: Serie: Costantinopoli, Firenze, Inghilterra, Pietroburgo* [Introductory notes to the despatches to the Senate of the Venetian diplomatic representatives: Series: Constantinople, Florence, England, Petersburg] (Roma: Quaderni della rassegna degli archivi di stato, 1974), 25; and Dursteler, "Bailo in Constantinople," 2.

152. Dursteler, "Power and Information," 601.

153. Donald E. Queller, "The Development of Ambassadorial Relazioni," in *Renaissance Venice*, ed. J. R. Hale (Totowa: Rowman and Littlefield, 1973), 174–96, here 176; Vivo, *Information and Communication*, 57–70; Gino Benzoni, "Ranke's Favourite Source: The *Relazioni* of Venetian Ambassadors," *Syracuse University Library*

Associates Courier 22 (1987): 11–26; and Maria Pia Pedani, "Note di storiografia sull'impero ottomano," *Mediterranea. Ricerche storiche* [The Mediterranean: Historical Researches] 34 (2015): 445–58, here 450–54.

154. Emrah Safa Gürkan, "Fonds for the Sultan: How to Use Venetian Sources for Studying Ottoman History," *News on Rialto* 32 (2013): 22–28.

155. Peksevgen, "Power, Information Control," 114–19, 132–33.

156. This discreet attitude is most obvious in official chronicles. Even though some of these were written by major political figures, they are extremely reluctant to delve into internal divisions, factional struggles, and decision-making processes, instead portraying the government as in harmony save only in times of crisis.

4 A Perfect Spy Chief?

Feliks Dzerzhinsky and the Cheka

Iain Lauchlan

Feliks Edmundovich Dzerzhinsky (1877–1926) was the undisputed master-mind behind the formation of the Soviet security services, leading the organs of state security (the Cheka and OGPU) from their inception on December 7, 1917, till his death on July 20, 1926.[1] He has continued to be revered, in both ruling circles and among wide swathes of the general public in Russia, ever since. Even Nikolai Bukharin, the most prominent victim of Stalin's purges—crimes carried out by Dzerzhinsky's heirs in the Lubianka—retained his admiration for "Iron Feliks" till the end and blamed the degeneration of the Soviet secret police on the fact that "Dzerzhinsky is no more; the wonderful traditions of the Cheka have gradually receded into the past, those traditions by which the revolutionary idea governed all its actions, justified cruelty toward enemies, safeguarded the state against any counter-revolution. For this reason, the organs of the Cheka won a special trust, a special honor, authority and respect."[2] Not even Stalin could topple the cult of Dzerzhinsky, though he did on occasion try to rein it in.[3]

Feliks Dzerzhinsky is alone among the USSR's founding fathers still to enjoy the approval of Russia's ruling elites in the twenty-first century. The Russian Federation's domestic (FSB) and foreign (SVR) espionage and counterintelligence agencies are proud to acknowledge themselves as direct descendants of Dzerzhinsky's espionage and counterintelligence organization—in history books, cinema, and the press.[4] Russian state security staff to this day still celebrate the foundation of the Cheka every twentieth of December. They are decorated with awards created for the Cheka during the civil war. They train at Moscow's Dzerzhinsky Academy (founded in 1921), aspire to join the elite special forces' Dzerzhinsky Division (founded in 1924), and continue to refer to themselves as *chekisty*.[5] When the oligarch Boris Berezovsky was interrogated by Vladimir Putin in the Lubianka in 1999, he noticed that the FSB chief had a bust of Dzerzhinsky on his desk.[6] In 2007 the Russian magazine *Ogonëk* reported that Dzerzhinsky's was the most popular portrait on Internet poster sites, outselling even that of Putin.[7] In the same month the Moscow offshoot of the *Wall Street Journal* asserted that a *"chekist* education" in the KGB was far more useful than a Harvard MBA as a track to success in contemporary Russia.[8] Over half of those polled in Moscow in November 2013 supported the return of the infamous Vuchetich statue of Dzerzhinsky back to its old spot in Lubianka Square (where it stood from 1958 to the fall of the Soviet Union in 1991), and consequently the Moscow city council has agreed to do just this if an official referendum on the issue shows support.[9]

1877-1917: The Apprenticeship of an Ideal *Chekist*

The admiration and respect awarded to Feliks Dzerzhinsky appear to be based on his distinctive impact on the practice of espionage and counterintelligence in the Soviet Union.[10] The exemplary career of "Iron Feliks" was a key element in training for Soviet spies during the Cold War, as one KGB defector recalled: "The activities of the Vecheka during the first years of Soviet power in Dzerzhinsky's days were studied in detail. Dzerzhinsky himself was held up as an ideal *chekist*."[11] Yet Dzerzhinsky was a spy chief for just eight years. His influence on Soviet espionage and counterintelligence was profound not just because of his practical contributions to the construction of the security *apparat* but also as a result of the moral example of his turbulent life. As the Soviet poet laureate Vladimir Mayakovsky declared: "To the youth pondering how to live, on whom to model his life, I would say this, without hesitation, model it on Comrade Dzerzhinsky."[12] Feliks Dzerzhinsky knew this all too well: "Do you know what makes me powerful?" he asked the Central Committee in 1926 just hours before his death. "The fact that I do not spare myself . . . that is why everybody here loves me, that is why you believe in me." There was a rumble of approval throughout the audience, and a voice from the center of the auditorium called out, "Correct!"[13]

The personal struggles "Iron Feliks" endured in the forty years of his life before he became head of the Cheka formed the basis of this self-sacrificing image. His experiences in these years bear a resemblance to the background of John Le Carré's imaginary "perfect spy":

> You have loyalty and you have affection. But to what? To whom? I don't know all the reasons for this. Your great father. Your aristocratic mother. . . . And maybe you have put your love in some bad places now and then. . . . Yet you also have morality. You search. What I am saying is . . . for once nature has produced a perfect match. You are a perfect spy. All you need is a cause. . . . All

the junk that made you what you are: the privileges, the snobbery, the hypocrisy, the churches, the schools, the fathers, the class systems, the historical lies, the little lords of the countryside, the little lords of big business, and all the greedy wars that result from them, we are sweeping them away forever, for your sake. Because we are making a society that will never produce such sad fellows as Sir Magnus [the eponymous "perfect spy"].[14]

Feliks also had an imposing and later absent father (with a noble pedigree stretching back over two hundred years) and a doting aristocratic mother (claiming kinship with the Polish national hero Tadeusz Kościuszko). Young Feliks, a sincere and profoundly moral child (whose best subject at school was Canon Law as he planned to train as a Catholic priest),[15] had philanthropic loyalty and affection in abundance. But, like Le Carré's perfect spy, these loyalties and affections outwardly shifted over the course of his life: from Polish nationalism[16] to internationalist revolution (as cofounder of the Polish and Lithuanian branch of the Marxist Social Democratic Party in 1898).[17] This shift was driven by collisions with little lords of the countryside in the rural estate near Minsk where he grew up; with bullying schoolmasters of Vilna where he studied, where schoolboy informers were rewarded, where pupils were banned from chatting in their native tongue, and where Catholic children were forced to attend Orthodox church services; collisions with priests who "spread darkness and preach submission";[18] collisions with the little lords of big business in his time working in the factory sweatshops of the Baltic region; and finally his prison cell view of the "insanity and horrors" of the greedy "war to end all wars" from 1914 to 1917.[19] In lashing out at these authority figures, the historical lies, the class system, the hypocrisy, Dzerzhinsky avoided the easy option of emigration and the compromises of émigré factionalism. Instead he chose to endure for over twenty years a secret life of fight and flight in the revolutionary underground, mostly inside the Russian Empire: a Manichaean world of comradeship and betrayal, the absolute freedom of rebellion and the miserable horror of eleven years in tsarist prison camps.[20]

Thus, before the revolution Dzerzhinsky confronted rather than evaded the contradictions in his background, the dualities in his life, to forge his own personal code of honor: "militant humanism."[21] This ethos apparently provided a moral compass for the new generation of revolutionary policemen caught in a terrible paradox: they were expected to annihilate the old world of which they were a part and create a better world through the base methods of violence, surveillance, and betrayal.[22] In other words—to paraphrase Raymond Chandler's formula for the ideal detective—the *chekisty* were expected to navigate the mean streets of revolution without themselves being mean; neither tarnished nor afraid, they were expected to be men of honor

Photo 4.1 Feliks Dzerzhinsky. (*Rossiiskii gosudarstvennyi arkhiv sotsial'no-politicheskoi istorii* [*RGASPI, The Russian State Archive of Social and Political History*], Moscow)

employed in a dishonorable profession.[23] How could they achieve this? Dzer-zhinsky's solution was through fatalism—if they embraced their doomed fate, they would be impervious to fear or self-interest: "the fruits of the revolution should not go to us, but to the next generation."[24] Regarding this the Soviet dissident Andrei Sinyavsky recognized the irony that the cult of Dzerzhinsky aimed to supplant and subvert Judeo-Christian values by borrowing much of its rhetoric and rationale from the same source:

> The chief murderer, manager of the prisons and the torture, had to be a man with a crystal-clear soul. In staining it with blood, he became in the eyes of his worshippers a truly great martyr who had sacrificed himself on the altar of revolutionary cosmogony, for the creation of a new world and a new man. Hence the surprising similarity between Dzerzhinsky and Christ: both gave themselves to redeem man's sins. Except that Christ redeemed man's sins with his death and resurrection, whereas the new saint, Dzerzhinsky, takes sins

upon himself—mass murder and torture—which he commits in the name of the creation of a Heavenly Kingdom on earth. So that in Soviet iconography the Crucified Lord is replaced by a Holy Executioner.[25]

The October Revolution of 1917 was the moment when the revolutionary saint found a practical way to advance his chosen cause: the construction of a society that would never again produce such sad fellows as Mr. Dzerzhinsky. But what sort of "perfect spy" had this apprenticeship created? A spy, it seems, who picked up three invaluable skills: contempt for death (in his early twenties Feliks had been diagnosed with tuberculosis and given only a few years to live),[26] a belief in the utility of violence (he later reproached the squeamishness of émigré intellectuals, Lenin included, who had not "experienced the revolution in a practical way"),[27] and the necessity of conspiracy (his frequent stays in prison taught him that "all the prisoners in my vicinity are the victims of informers").[28] Audacity, ruthlessness, and cunning might well be seen as perfect qualities for a spy chief, but in the case of Feliks Dzerzhinsky very little separated these virtues from recklessness, cruelty, and paranoia.

December 1917: Praetorian Guard

We can see a similar paradox, whereby Dzerzhinsky's greatest attributes were also his greatest flaws, when we look at the circumstances surrounding the creation of the Cheka. The original Soviet security police grew out of a group of ad hoc security guards headed by Dzerzhinsky from the summer of 1917, acting as odd-job men for the Bolshevik leader: organizing Lenin's escapes to Finland and his security in the Smolny Institute and liquidating armed resistance to the October coup in Petrograd. Their first major tasks after the official creation of the Cheka in December 1917 were the investigations into attempts on Lenin's life a month later and posting security guards around the Kremlin when the Bolshevik government moved there in the spring of 1918. This work demanded a kind of unthinking devotion that "Iron Feliks" considered his chief virtue: Lenin, it was often said, "was the only authority for Dzerzhinsky."[29] The Cheka boss likened himself to "a faithful hound ever ready to tear apart the villain."[30] While this clearly had its advantages for the Bolshevik leader, the idea that this is a desirable quality of a "perfect spy" is dubious. Historians widely agree that the chief flaw of the worst Soviet spy chief of all, Nikolai Yezhov, was that he was "the diligent executor of Stalin's wishes . . . [who never] exceeded Stalin's control in any way."[31] The fact that Yezhov employed the security police as "cogs in a terrible machine"[32] that "delivered what Stalin and his Politburo wanted"[33] merely shows that he faithfully followed a tradition begun by the perfect Bolshevik spy chief, Feliks Dzerzhinsky.

There was a second problem: Lenin kept the Cheka close to exercise strict control, but the information it supplied regarding security threats had a clear impact on his worldview. The master began to take on some of the traits of his loyal bloodhound. "Lenin has become quite insane," Leonid Krasin complained in 1918, "and if anyone has influence over him it is only 'Comrade Feliks' Dzerzhinsky, an even greater fanatic, and, in essence, a cunning piece of work, who scares Lenin with counter-revolution and the idea that this will sweep us all away."[34] Dzerzhinsky established a symbiotic bond between intelligence chief and head of state whereby a paranoid leader promoted a paranoid organization, and the paranoid organization made the leader more paranoid. As the finance commissar, Grigory Sokol'nikov, later complained to Dzerzhinsky: "The more resources your agents receive, the more they exaggerate [the significance of] their work. This is the peculiar characteristic of your extremely important, but also dangerous, institution."[35] If we look at the praise lavished on the Cheka by other Soviet politicians when they occupied senior posts (e.g., Trotsky in 1917–19,[36] Zinoviev and Kamenev in 1922–23,[37] Bukharin in 1926–27[38]), it seems that whoever gained power was likely to become a fan of *chekist* measures. The declassified Kremlin visitors' books showed that Stalin spent more time with his spy chiefs Nikolai Yezhov and Lavrenti Beria than any other official, with the exception of Viacheslav Molotov.[39] Molotov claimed that "in the end, the decision [to launch the Terror of 1937–38] was based on trust in the GPU's [*sic*] word."[40] There is some archival evidence to support this: documents discovered in 1992 showed that Stalin acted in tandem with the security services in launching the "mass operations" of 1937.[41]

Spring 1918: Esprit de Corps

Dzerzhinsky's emphasis on the virtues of loyalty can be seen most clearly in the rationale behind his selection of the first cohort of agents for his new organization in the spring of 1918. The Cheka was the only branch of the Soviet state that issued a blanket ban on former tsarist officials entering its service. Dzerzhinsky ordered his officers on February 21, 1918, "to recruit only Party comrades in all but exceptional cases" and to monitor staff lists to make sure no "former-*okhranniki* and gendarmes" managed to sneak back into the secret police.[42] This was a deliberate policy: to counter voices "raised objecting that the [Extraordinary] Commissions were operating in accordance with recycled gendarmerie instructions from Tsarist times."[43] The total overhaul may seem self-evident considering the regime change, but it is unusual. Hitler's Gestapo, for example, inherited almost all of its personnel from the Weimar Republic's security police; the staff profile of the police in revolutionary France showed remarkable continuities through the various upheavals from the 1780s to the 1820s (Joseph Fouché is a classic case in point); and the transition from the KGB to the FSB has shown similar stability (e.g., Vladimir Putin).

A survey of the sixty-nine highest-ranking *chekists* in 1920 found that all were Communist Party members and that fifty had joined before the October Revolution.[44] The preference for prerevolutionary party veterans persisted throughout the 1920s.[45] Consequently, most of the top-level security staff up to 1937 had been recruited from a very specific pool of individuals (mostly prerevolutionary comrades of Dzerzhinsky from the northwestern provinces of the tsarist empire) in a specific period (1917–19) and in a very specific context (civil war). This meant they were all of roughly the same age in 1918 (their mid-thirties) and from a similar geographical, social, and ethnic background. The highest-ranking staff consisted of six Poles (two of them Jewish), three Latvians, eight Russians (one of them Jewish, one brought up abroad), one Ukrainian, one Armenian, and one Georgian.[46] Stephen Wheatcroft has shown that it was "the same group of individuals" recruited from this milieu who were at the heart of the violence not just in the civil war but also during Collectivization and the Great Terror.[47] The operational chiefs of the mass operations in 1937 were not outsiders brought in by Nikolai Yezhov, but Genrikh Yagoda's former assistants G. E. Prokof'ev and Ia. S. Agranov and a coterie of *chekisty* surrounding the man behind the Shakhty trial and dekulakization—Yefim Yevdokimov.[48] The clique that came out on top in the aftermath of the Great Terror in 1938 (under Beria) began their careers, like the Yevdokimov circle, together in the Cheka on the periphery *and* also mostly came from national minorities in the regions of their birth.[49]

The specific geographical roots and context of recruitment of the early *chekisty* had, as in the case of Dzerzhinsky, a specific impact on their temperaments. Those he chose were usually veterans of the revolutionary struggle on the fringes of the tsarist and Soviet empires, where state power was weakest and methods were bloodiest. The party members here were more doers than thinkers: rabble-rousers, smugglers, bank robbers, murderers, jailbirds, gangsters, and above all else, conspirators.[50] "In our Chekas," Dzerzhinsky boasted, "the majority of workers are old revolutionaries who passed through the tsarist autocracy's school of hard knocks [*surovaia shkola*]."[51] Even left-wing supporters of the regime could see the flaw in this: "The only temperaments that devoted themselves willingly and tenaciously to this task of 'internal defense' were those characterized by suspicion, embitterment, harshness, and sadism. Long-standing social inferiority complexes and memories of humiliations and suffering in the Tsar's jails rendered them intractable, and since professional degeneration has rapid effects, the Chekas inevitably consisted of perverted men tending to see conspiracy everywhere and to live in the midst of perpetual conspiracy themselves."[52]

These experiences also left a profound sense of alienation: the *chekisty* claimed to think and act as if they came not just from a different place but also from a different species and a different time. Nadezhda Mandelstam, for example, after being interrogated by Dzerzhinsky's closest collaborator, Yakov Peters, in the late 1920s, noted that he "behaved like a person of a superior race who despised physical weakness and the pathetic scruples of intellectuals. . . . The chekists were the avant-garde of the 'new people', and they had indeed basically revised, in the manner of the Superman, all ordinary human values."[53] The Cheka's status as something outside the norm—literally extra-ordinary—was emphasized by anachronistic rhetoric: "We, like the Israelites," wrote the Cheka's chief ideologue, Martin Latsis, "have to build the Kingdom of the Future under constant fear of enemy attack."[54] They were frequently referred to as *oprichniki* (literally "those whose are separate") after Ivan the Terrible's original terrorist-enforcers, and in a manner that suggested they were supernatural beings from ancient times: "in the perception of enemies, trembling at his very name, Dzerzhinsky figures as some sort of demon, some sort of wizard of Bolshevism."[55] As with pagan spirits, even mentioning *oprichniki* was treated by Soviet citizens with a kind of superstitious dread; all kinds of elision and allusion were used: "uninvited guests," "night-time visitors," "silent intruders." Isaac Babel referred to them as "sacred people."[56] Their name, wrote Solzhenitsyn, "like that of a jealously guarded deity, cannot ever be mentioned. You are there; everyone feels your presence; but it is as though you didn't exist."[57] In 1918 above all else *chekist* rhetoric harked back to the French Revolution: their license to kill was justified with a decree on "The Socialist Fatherland in Danger!" on February 21, 1918. Lenin frequently referred to Dzerzhinsky as a "proletarian Jacobin." And nearly a decade later Bukharin was to repeat this in his eulogy to the "First *Chekist*,"[58] while Stalin compared the OGPU to Robespierre's Committee of Public Safety.[59] This sense of alienation (of geography, culture, occupation, time, and temperament) was a dangerous kind of dissociative state; it psychologically enabled the new spies to act outside socially determined moral norms.

September 1918: True Believers

Allusions to the French Revolution came to the fore in Dzerzhinsky's Proclamation of the Red Terror of September 1918. In this his organization embodied the vital difference in the mind-set of police repression by the Whites and the Reds: for the latter the outbreak of random violence was historically sanctioned and seamlessly incorporated into the Leninist understanding of revolution as civil war,[60] whereas it sat awkwardly with White claims to represent "Russia, one and indivisible." This excused the Cheka in advance for the inevitable collateral damage. As Solzhenitsyn observed, "The imagination and spiritual strength of Shakespeare's evildoers stopped short at a dozen corpses. Because they had no ideology."[61] Dzerzhinsky suffered no such qualms. "Terror is an absolute necessity in times of revolution," he told the press in June 1918. "The defense of the revolution cannot take into account that it may harm particular individuals."[62]

This ideological approach to security policing shows a distinct difference between Dzerzhinsky's new police ethos and the post-Enlightenment norm. The Cheka was "a direct organ of the Party, subject to Party directives and Party control."[63] Consequently, Dzerzhinsky's prime directive was not the protection of a legal system, a state order, or even simply a leader but rather the defense of a version of the world described in a set of party-approved sacred texts. In both dictatorships and democracies the model for most investigative police forces over the past two centuries (at least in theory, however shoddily adhered to) has been to proceed via inductive reasoning: the investigation comes before the verdict. In contrast to this, back in the USSR the Marxist-Leninist canon already provided the conclusions, as immutable as the fixed Earth in medieval Christian cosmology. Consequently, investigations were not pursued to discover the truth but rather to validate it. Bukharin was wrong when he said the Soviet security police employed "medieval methods."[64] Their methods were technically modern, using all the latest tools: telephones, telegraphs, typewriters, universal citizen registration, cross-referenced card catalogues, photographs, fingerprints, phone taps, social science, and psychology, and so on. He was closer to the truth in his subversive aside at the 1938 show trial: "The confession of the accused is a medieval principle of jurisprudence."[65] Solzhenitsyn agreed: "Like medieval torturers, our interrogators, prosecutors, and judges agreed to accept the confession of the accused as the chief proof of guilt."[66]

It has often been pointed out that the method of extracting confessions to validate theory only became the norm during the Great Terror, that it was the rational product of practical time constraints (and is indeed a common failing in security forces under pressure).[67] Nevertheless, the ethos that confession was a valid police method was rooted from the start in the fact that the highest authority for the Cheka was Marxist-Leninism, not empiricism. This inquisitor's job was to make the "facts" fit the ideologically correct verdict rather than vice versa. Dzerzhinsky's assistant, Martin Latsis, later admitted that the enemy "plots" they used to justify the Proclamation of the Red Terror were "fictitious" but that these fantasies revealed a higher truth.[68] In his Cheka manifesto he advised: "When interrogating, do not seek material evidence or proof of the accused's words or deeds against Soviet power. The first question you must ask is: what class does he belong to, what education, what upbringing, origin or profession does he have? These questions must determine the accused's fate. This is the sense and the essence of the Red Terror."[69] Marxist dogma provided scientific rules predicting objective political allegiance; the class struggle drove all observable phenomena, like Aristotle's prime mover directing the planets in perfectly predictable circles. As enforcers of this reality the security police suggested the first show trials in 1921. Their purpose was to provide explanations of why events failed to unfold as scientifically predicted. Their complexity merely confirmed the thoroughness of the security service's investigations, like the erudition of a Scholastic monk constructing a syllogism.[70] This early Cheka ethos endured even after the mortal threat of the civil war receded; for example, in the mass sweep of intellectuals in 1922 the *intelligenty* found themselves sentenced to exile first and interrogated only afterward.[71] The targets for the expulsion were decided in accordance with Dzerzhinsky's typology of intellectuals.[72]

And typologies were very important. Ideology imposed itself on the mindset of the security police through strict rules on the terminology to be used in their reports, which "contain no literary invention or embellishment, nor any rhetorical devices, but they do have their own characteristics: way of expression, mode of thought, language, syntax, lexicon and intonation."[73] Unlike tsarist-era informers, even unofficial—that is, secret—employees of the Cheka were expected to follow an officially approved template when submitting their reports; "conferences" were organized to coach them on how to write in the acceptable language of Bolshevism.[74] Prescribed terminology determined that people were sentenced according to their category rather than their crime: whites, kulaks, bandits, wreckers, hooligans, and so on. This might sound like the predetermined "aliens/other" categories ruthlessly persecuted by all modern dictatorships. However, in the Soviet case these were subjective categories, more like that of "witch" or "heretic" centuries earlier, which could be applied to anyone. Terminology also redefined the actions of the security police: they did not "punish," they "repressed" and "destroyed." The infamous NKVD *operativnyi prikaz* (operational order) no. 00447 of July 1937 is often mistranslated into English as a "punitive" (*karatel'naia*) measure, when in fact the original term was "repressive" (viz. *operatsiia po repressirovaniiu*). The distinction is important. The Red Terror, Latsis wrote, "does not judge the enemy, it strikes him."[75] Early GPU directives preserved the Cheka's revolutionary conception of repression: exile was defined "not as a judicial punishment, but as a measure of social defense."[76]

As belief was internalized over time, the cognitive tension between *chekist* language and the data they collected grew. This process has been highlighted by Vladlen Izmozik's study of the security police reports over the course of the 1920s whereby "the OGPU's information acquired an ever-greater significance for the leadership of the country, and came to be considered the most complete and reliable of any government institution," because it "became gradually less objective."[77] The job of the rank-and-file security police was to fit observations into preexisting party-approved categories; this demanded manufacturing confessions for increasingly elaborate conspiracies, like Ptolemaic astronomers demonstrating the eccentric movements of planets with a bewildering array of epicycles. In 1937 the complexity reached critical mass, where "language slipped from everyone's control, and anyone could be labelled a 'Trotskyist' or 'Bukharinist' and thus be isolated and destroyed."[78] The breakdown in reason was mirrored by the breakdown in language, as exemplified when Vyshinsky's courtroom hyperbole regarding mad dogs, demons, pygmies, vampires, and so forth exhausted itself: "There exist no words with which one could depict the monstrousness of the crimes committed."[79] This links order no. 00447 (a final reckoning with the enemy "once and for all time") to the "revolutionary millenarian" movements studied by Norman Cohn, which arose in the twilight of the medieval world, when social crises viewed through a biblical prism looked like heralds of the apocalypse: "Above all, calamities caused by unseen or unknown agencies — plague or famine, gross inflation or mass unemployment . . . may then produce an emotional disturbance so widespread and acute, such an overwhelming sense of being exposed, cast out and helpless, that the only way in which it can find effective relief is through . . . a sudden, collective and fanatical pursuit of the millennium."[80]

1919-1920: Soldier Spies

The language of *chekism* also shows that Dzerzhinsky did not think like an ordinary policeman, because he did not consider himself to be an ordinary policeman. "Iron Feliks" represented the new professional ideal — sleeping on a camp bed, with a pistol under his pillow; living on standard issue rations in military billets; decked out in a practical leather overcoat (part of a consignment originally intended for the British air force, requisitioned to protect *chekisty* from the cold, dirt, blood, and typhus flea) and in an army tunic, riding boots, and cavalry cap. Dzerzhinsky considered himself to be a "soldier of the revolution . . . appointed to a post in the front line."[81] Latsis stated that the Cheka was not a police force but "the battle organ of the party of the future," what Yezhov would later refer to as "the armed vanguard of the party."[82] As such Dzerzhinsky repeatedly insisted that their operations, like those of the Red Army against enemy forces, "cannot be controlled by justice officials."[83] Stalin concurred: "Self-criticism would threaten the existence of the OGPU and be the ruin of *chekist* discipline," he told Dzerzhinsky's successor, Viacheslav Menzhinsky, on the eve of Collectivization, "do not forget that the OGPU is a military organization."[84]

This was not empty rhetoric. By 1919, when the civil war began to rage in earnest, the Cheka borrowed heavily from military techniques. As Peter Holquist has shown, "What distinguished the Soviet regime was not its use of this or that practice. What distinguished the Bolsheviks is the extent to which they turned tools originally intended for total war to the new ends of revolutionary politics."[85] Holquist argues that Cheka surveillance and police practices were taken not from the tsarist police but from the Imperial Russian army.[86] The Cheka's first mass operation—"Decossackization," the deportation in April 1919 of an estimated 300,000 people—was more akin to the actions of an invading army than a police measure; it was carried out to secure the southern front against the White armies.[87]

The military mind-set meant that the Cheka seemed to lose its raison d'être when the civil war ended. In January 1920 Dzerzhinsky announced that they would abandon the use of the death penalty, and talks were afoot to abolish the institution entirely. But in the spring guerrilla actions against the Bolsheviks broke out in rural areas of Samara, Tambov, Voronezh, and Tula, and the security police began killing without trial once more.[88] After this Dzerzhinsky, while fighting a guerrilla war in Ukraine, defended the Cheka's right to carry out extrajudicial executions in cases of "terrorist acts and open rebellion . . . [and] for bandits and spies."[89] Martin Latsis's experiences fighting "on the internal front" against guerrillas in Ukraine formed the basis of his tracts on *chekism*.[90] Yakov Peters was a veteran of military operations versus "bandits" in the North Caucasus and *basmachi* in central Asia from 1920 to 1922. It is no accident that the operational chief of the Great Terror, Yefim Yevdokimov, cut his teeth in the guerrilla skirmishes against Nestor Makhno in 1920; after that he continued to use counterinsurgency techniques against bandits in Ukraine and North Caucasus throughout the 1920s. When on active operational duty he was responsible for more than half of the OGPU's extrajudicial executions under the New Economic Policy (NEP) and spearheaded not just the first Stalinist show trial but the first Stalinist mass operation—"Dekulakization"—in 1930.[91] Just to the south the Cheka boss, Lavrenti

Beria, also developed Stalinist policing as a form of bandit-war gangsterism. In an area where Bolshevik rule was weak and the opposition well armed and genuinely dangerous, he fought fire with fire: assassinating political opponents inside the party, taking the family members of rebels hostage, forcing prisoners to denounce themselves in show trials, organizing secret executions and mass burials in unmarked graves, infiltrating the opposition with phony partisans at home and *agents provocateurs* abroad, and so on.[92]

1921: The Paranoid Style

Guerrilla war justified the continued existence of this supposedly *extraordinary* wartime commission because it blurred the distinction between war and peace. As guerrilla war dissolved into what Dzerzhinsky called *banditizm* ("banditism"),[93] it had a further blurring effect: political opposition spilled over into the economic sphere. Dzerzhinsky was able to capitalize on this from 1921 onward because, in addition to his posts as head of the Cheka and the NKVD, he held a number of senior positions in economic affairs.[94] The rationale behind the Cheka's expansion into what should have been non-political matters went as follows: "In connection with the liquidation of the fronts [i.e., the end of the conventional war] and the shift of all our energies to the task of internal construction, the tactics of the White Guards and anti-Soviet parties of all varieties has changed, in recent times all their efforts and attention have turned towards the work of disrupting our economic policies, mainly through bandit gangs and organising minor uprisings on behalf of the counter-revolutionary cause."[95] "Banditism" was a catchall term, implying that economic crimes were a hidden form of political dissent: in acts of banditry counterrevolutionaries often worked in cahoots with capitalist racketeers; racketeers worked with criminal gangs to obtain their goods and protect their operations; and criminal gangs were involved in violent robberies and the pilfering of government supplies. As a result, even the pettiest crook risked being accused of the political crime of "banditism," liable to summary execution.

This mind-set, where petty crime was linked through a conspiratorial chain to political opposition, was expressed in a joint circular by Dzerzhinsky and Viacheslav Molotov in February 1921: "Having lost the battle on the external front, the counterrevolution is focusing its efforts on overthrowing Soviet power from within. It will use any means to attain this goal, drawing on all of its experience, all of its techniques of betrayal."[96] In other words, they asserted that the enemy became more secretive, devious, and vicious the closer it came to defeat. This is a clear precursor to Stalin's theory of the intensification of the class struggle.[97] Indeed, it provoked a fundamental disagreement between Nikolai Bukharin and Feliks Dzerzhinsky in the autumn of 1924, four years before the former fell out with Stalin over much the same issue: the advance of socialism, Bukharin argued, should be matched by the advance "toward a more liberal form of rule: fewer acts of repression, more rule by law, more discussion, self-government."[98] Dzerzhinsky called this "a concession to Nepmanism, Philistinism, and a virtual rejection of Bolshevism."[99]

Dzerzhinsky's pursuit of borderland bandits in 1921 had one further blurring effect: it muddied the waters separating foreign and domestic enemies. As bandit gangs weakened, the more determined among them fled from the Baltic region, Ukraine, the Caucasus, and Turkestan across the Soviet borders into Finland, Poland, Turkey, Persia, and Afghanistan and made contact with British and French intelligence.[100] As a result, foreign espionage was not just metaphorically connected to domestic opposition, it was geographically contiguous, tangibly linked. The typical "foreign" spy by 1921 was not a British agent shuttled into Moscow like a visitor from another planet but a Soviet citizen plodding into Bukhara on a camel.[101] The first extensive networks of Soviet espionage abroad were established in 1921—in Afghanistan, Persia, and Turkey—to chase émigré bandits seeking support from foreign governments.[102] The Soviet view of the world in 1921 was a fearful one: it was clear that the fires of revolution would not overwhelm Russia's neighbors in the near future, and consequently the fragile republic was surrounded by hostile states, secretly plotting, they believed, the destruction of the great Soviet experiment.[103] The rebellion at Kronstadt in March of that year seemed to vindicate Dzerzhinsky's warning that the gravest threats came from collaboration between the enemy outside and disillusioned citizens within.[104]

1922: The Dzerzhinsky Ballet

In the wake of Kronstadt, with the dual threat of enemies within and without in mind, Dzerzhinsky conceived a new peacetime role for the Cheka: uncovering conspiracies and ensnaring foreign spies. This resulted in celebrated stings such as the "Trust" and "Sindikat" operations, which seemed to show that domestic woes were the result of foreign subterfuge.[105] However, the foreign agents captured (most famously Boris Savinkov and Sidney Reilly) were of negligible importance. The real targets for this spectacle were Communist supporters who had begun to doubt the necessity of preserving the vast espionage apparatus in peacetime. The Kronstadt revolt had shown that the real danger to Communism was not the rebels' foreign connections but the fact that Communist Party members shared the rebels' concern that "the gruff commands of the Cheka *oprichniki* are all the working man of Soviet Russia has won after so much struggle and suffering."[106] Émigré publications attacking the Soviet state in 1922 focused on the fact that the regime "has in reality rebuilt the recently destroyed tsarist *okhranka*."[107] Similar criticisms had surfaced inside the party intermittently throughout the civil war and were cryptically alluded to by the Workers' Opposition in 1920, the Platform of the 22 in 1922, and the Platform of the 46 in 1923.[108] Dzerzhinsky was forced to take measures to avoid the total dissolution of the Cheka between 1922 and 1924: "To counteract these attitudes we need to review our practices, our methods, and eliminate everything that can feed such attitudes." He recommended to his deputy Menzhinsky:

> We should use searches and arrests more carefully, with better incriminating evidence or by mobilizing popular Party support for us. . . . We must pay attention to the struggle for popularity among peasants, organizing help for them in the struggle against hooliganism and other crimes. And in general, we need to plan measures to gain support among workers and peasants and mass Party organizations. In addition, once again, we need to pay attention to our information summaries so that they provide the members of the Central Committee with an accurate picture of our work.[109]

One might conclude from this that Dzerzhinsky was repenting of his old ways and recommending a change in the security methods to bring them in line with conventional peacetime Western police norms. In fact, it was the opposite; he was playing his last trump card. The Cheka's critics, he argued, suffered from the misapprehension that the Lubianka operated on the same principles as security police forces in bourgeois countries, merely protecting the state. The Cheka, he claimed, was in fact a new kind of organization, an intermediary connecting the party and the people; hence the need for more scrupulous methodology, hence the celebrated "sting" operations exposing vast conspiracies, not for their own sake, but to "counteract" the negative attitudes toward the Cheka among Communists and to "mobilize popular support."[110] The Lubianka-orchestrated celebration of the Cheka's fifth anniversary in December 1922 staged in Moscow's Bolshoi Theatre was the launchpad of this campaign for popular support. The Tenth Congress of Soviets, also meeting in the Bolshoi, voted that same month to erect a monument to Feliks Dzerzhinsky in Moscow.[111] The émigré press recognized in these celebrations that Dzerzhinsky's truly unique contribution to espionage (what John Le Carré would later call the "secret theater" of our age) was his talent for *grand guignol*:

Among all their worthy predecessors, neither Benckendorff, nor Plehve, nor Stolypin, nor even Durnovo, hit upon the wonderful idea of staging public celebrations for *okhranniki*, spies and executioners in the Imperial Theaters. The Moscow symphony orchestra has produced a ballet of intoxicating gestures, colors and sounds in praise of the rather different gestures, colors and sounds in the basements of the Cheka. It is a truly unique pageant in cynicism. But the outer zest of the *Chekistskii ballet* should not distract us from the real significance of these "Jubilee Celebrations": the very existence of the Jubilee itself proves that, even after six years, the Bolshevik dictatorship is incapable of weakening the gendarme apparatus for one second.[112]

Even Soviet supporters grasped the macabre theatrical essence of "*chekism*." We can see this from the original design for the statue of "Iron Feliks" (based on a sketch of him from life by Vera Mukhina in 1925), which was scheduled to be erected in Lubianka/Dzerzhinsky Square at the end of the 1930s but was never completed. It is very different from the Vuchetich version, that solid and watchful policeman in the long raincoat, erected in 1958. Mukhina's model depicted Dzerzhinsky as a lean, cruel, and mournful figure in peasant blouse, clutching a sword of impossible length; instead of facing away from the Lubianka, his intense stare was supposed to be directed at the police headquarters. In this version he looked more like a menacing character from an old Muscovite fairy tale. The effect was intentional. Mukhina's biographer, Olga Voronova, has shown that the statue stood in a typical ballet pose and that its appearance was based on Mukhina's sketches of the fantastical villains in contemporary productions of *La Sylphide* and *La Bayadère*.[113]

Mukhina played with these mythic motifs because she aimed to present not just a historical figure but also an archetype. Feliks Dzerzhinsky is quite clearly the most inspirational and influential intelligence leader Russia has ever possessed. In less than a decade he defined the ideals of the Soviet intelligence *apparat*, aspects of which have survived the fall of Communism inside the Russian security services to this day. In stark contrast to the Western model of intelligence leadership offered in the introduction to this book, the reasons he was so influential correspond on many levels with Carlyle's "great man" theses and Weber's observations on the importance of "charisma." The theatrical presentation of Dzerzhinsky in Soviet propaganda dramatized his qualities as the Soviet spy chief par excellence, a timeless Carlylean hero. Aspects of Carlyle's typology of heroes (divinity, prophet, poet, priest, scholar, and king) can be seen in the celebration of Dzerzhinsky's audacity, ruthlessness, and cunning; his special relationship with the leader; the otherness of his agents; their ideological purity, military toughness, and mysterious ability to penetrate a hidden world of conspiracy.[114] Dzerzhinsky and company claimed that their connection to the people was the unique ingredient and the purported secret of their success: "The fact that we discovered the secret conspiratorial threads and the counter-revolutionary bandit and speculation organizations was not thanks to some Sherlock Holmes sitting in the Cheka, but was due to the fact that the Cheka was a revolutionary organ of struggle for the defense of the revolution and was closely coupled to the party and the working class."[115] Feliks Dzerzhinsky was venerated as the personification of the mystical bond between police and people: "Enemies do not understand, cannot understand, the truth that Dzerzhinsky's 'satanic all-roundedness,' his 'good luck,' flow from the fact that all the greatness and all the might of our class, its passionate will to struggle and to victory, its deepest creative forces, were embodied in Dzerzhinsky."[116]

Dzerzhinsky was a great success in creating a potent justification for the central role of intelligence in Soviet statecraft and a role model for those who have served the Lubianka ever since. Yet his creation was ultimately a catastrophic ethos for a modern espionage and counterintelligence organization. It formed the neotraditionalist core of Stalinism whereby the appeal to popular opinion tapped into premodern resources (denunciation, patron-client networks, totems, and taboos) in the pursuit of modern ends (nation-building, social classification and transformation, technological progress, etc.).[117] The result was not a modern intelligence machine but rather a deadly mutation of one: a fusion of science and superstition. When let off the leash, *chekist* operations easily developed into a centrally directed form of mob rule, far more potent and unpredictable than the apparatus of a reactionary police state. Far from offering us the exemplary life of a perfect spy, Feliks Dzerzhinsky's career and contributions to the world of espionage are a cautionary tale.

Notes

1. As George Leggett, in what remains the most authoritative history of the Cheka, phrased it: "all evidence points to Dzerzhinsky being the author of the Vecheka concept. . . . On the consistent showing of Lenin's pre-October doctrine, nothing could have been further from his intention, at that time, than the introduction of a political police system." George Leggett, *The Cheka: Lenin's Political Police* (Oxford: Oxford University Press, 1981), 19.

2. From Bukharin's "Letter to a New Generation of Party Leaders," memorized by his wife in February 1937 and reproduced in her memoirs, A. Larina, *This I Cannot Forget* (London: Pandora, 1994), 343.

3. Rossiiskii Gosudarstvennyi Arkhiv Sotsial'no-Politicheskoi Istorii, Moscow [Russian State Archive of Social and Political History; hereafter RGASPI], f.558, op.11, d.1120, ll.29–32: Stalin's speech to the Military Council on June 2, 1937, in which he said Dzerzhinsky had in 1922 been "an active Trotskyist who tried to use the GPU in defence of Trotsky." Stalin rejected Menzhinsky's proposal on November 14, 1932, to

create an award for service to the OGPU titled "The Order of Feliks Dzerzhinsky." See RGASPI, f.558, op.1, d.5284, l.1.

4. The first example of this was the Cheka's weekly newspaper (*Yezhenedel'nik VChK* [The weekly newspaper of the VChK]), which ran for just two months during the period of the Red Terror. They gathered a collection of documents glorifying their activities in *Krasnaia kniga VChK* [The red book of the VChK] (Moscow: Politizdat, 1920). One of the signals for the revival of the cult was the republication of the Cheka weekly in V. K. Vinogradov, ed., *VChK upolnomochena soobshchit'* [The VChK is authorized to report] (Moscow: Kuchkovo pole, 2004). The FSB and its foreign intelligence equivalent, the SVR, have published self-serving historical accounts. See Y. M. Primakov et al., eds., *Ocherki istorii rossiiskoi vneshnei razvedki* [Essays on the history of Russian external intelligence], 6 vols. (Moscow: Mezhdunarodnye otnosheniia, 1996–2007). The FSB museum in the Lubianka, now open to tourist groups, provides a rather selective presentation of the history of the Russian secret police. And the more popular publications on the Cheka promoted by the FSB and KGB in Moscow and Minsk range from the glossy—such as *Feliks Dzerzhinskii: K 130-letiiu so dnia rozhdeniia* [Feliks Dzerzhinsky: On the 130th anniversary of his birth] (Moscow: Kuchkovo pole, 2007) and V. A. Sobolev et al., eds., *Lubianka 2: Iz istorii otechestvennoi kontrrazvedki* [Lubianka 2: A history of Russian counterintelligence] (Moscow: Mosgorarkhiv, 1999)—to the sentimental, such as A. A. Plekhanova and A. M. Plekhanov, eds., *"Ia vas liubliu . . ." Pis'ma Feliksa Dzerzhinskogo Margarite Nikolaevoi* ["I love you . . ." Feliks Dzershinsky's letters to Margarita Nikolaeva] (Moscow: Kuchkovo pole, 2007). KGB literary and cinema prizes were introduced in March 1979; they were discontinued in 1988 but revived by the FSB in 2000 and expanded in 2001 and 2006.

5. See Mikhail Sokolov, "Kul't spetssluzhb v sovremennoi Rossii" [The cult of the special forces in contemporary Russia], *Neprikosnovennyi zapas* [Emergency ration] 42 (2005).

6. Stephen Lee Myers, "Father of KGB Might Return to Headquarters," *New York Times*, September 17, 2002.

7. "Vysoko poveshennye litsa" [The most popular posters], *Ogonëk* [The light], November 5–11, 2007, 45.

8. Oleg Chernitskii and Vladimir Fedorin, "KGB luchshe MBA: chto daet biznesu chekistskoe obrazovanie" [KGB is better than MBA: The advantages of a chekist education], *Smart Money: Analiticheskii delo ezhenedel'nik* [Smart money: Weekly business analysis], November 5, 2007, 64–84.

9. Tom Balmforth, "'Iron Feliks' Inching Back to Old KGB Headquarters," *Radio Free Europe / Radio Liberty*, June 13, 2015, accessed January 9, 2016, http://www.rferl.org/content/feliks-dzerzhinsky-statue-kgb-moscow-cheka/27070211.html.

10. Most Russian-language biographies focus on his career as head of the Cheka/OGPU; for example, A. M. Plekhanov, *Dzerzhinskii: Pervyi Chekist Rossii* [Dzerzhinsky: Russia's first *chekist*] (Moscow: Olma Media grupp, 2007). See also A. S. Ivanov, *Neizvestnyi Dzerzhinskii* [The unknown Dzerzhinsky] (Minsk: Valev, 1994); and S. A. Kredov, *Dzerzhinskii* (Moscow: Molodaia gvardiia, 2013). There are numerous

Polish-language biographies of Dzerzhinsky, again concentrating on his role as spy chief. Poland mostly produced hagiographies in the Soviet era; for example, T. Daniszewski, *Feliks Dzierżyński nieugiety bojownik o zwyciestwo socjalizmu* [Feliks Dzerzhinsky: A steadfast fighter for socialism] (Warsaw: Ksiazka i Wiedza, 1951); Jan Sobczak, *Feliks Dzierżyński romantyk rewolucji* [Feliks Dzerzhinsky: The romantic revolutionary] (Warsaw: Ksiazka i Wiedza, 1974); Jerzy Ochmanski, *Feliks Dzierzynski, 1877–1926* (Poznan: Wydawn. Poznańskie, 1977); and Janusz Teleszynski, *Gorejacy plomien Feliks Dzierżyński, 1877–1926* [Feliks Dzerzhinsky: The burning flame, 1877–1926] (Warsaw: Wydawnictwo Ministerstwa Obrony Narodowej, 1977). Polish demonographies appeared both before the Soviet regime in Poland and after its fall. See Bogdan Jaxa-Ronikier, *Dzierżyński: Czerwony kat* [Dzerzhinsky: The red cat] (Warsaw: Polska Zjednoczona, 1933); and Jerzy S. Łątka, *Krwawy apostoł. Feliks Dzierżyński* [Feliks Dzerzhinsky: The bloody apostle] (Kraków: Społeczny Instytut Historii, 1998).

11. Aleksei Myagkov, *Inside the KGB: An Exposé by an Officer of the Third Directorate* (Richmond, Surrey, UK: Foreign Affairs Publishing, 1974), 47.

12. This is quoted in most Russian biographies of Dzerzhinsky. It is given particular prominence in the 130-year anniversary hagiography *Feliks Dzerzhinskii: K 130-letiiu*, 146.

13. Feliks Dzerzhinskii, *Izbrannye stat'i i rechi, 1908–1926* [Selected articles and speeches, 1908–1926] (Moscow: Gospolitizdat, 1947), 375.

14. John Le Carré, *A Perfect Spy* (London: Hodder and Stoughton, 1986), 551–52.

15. "Feliks loved Jesus very much," his sister Jadwiga later claimed. "His commandments were deeply embedded in his heart . . . and [even after becoming an atheist] he continued to respect Christ." Quoted in *Argumenty i fakty* [Arguments and facts], July 19, 2006.

16. See RGASPI, f.76, op.4, d.17, l.2, in which Dzerzhinsky admitted in 1922 that "as a young boy, I dreamt of a cap of invisibility and of killing all Muscovites."

17. See Robert Blobaum, *Feliks Dzierżyński and the SDKPiL: A Study of the Origins of Polish Communism* (New York: Columbia University Press, 1984).

18. Feliks Dzerzhinsky, Letter to his sister Aldona, October 6, 1902, in *Prison Diary and Letters* (Honolulu, HI: University Press of the Pacific, 2002), 176.

19. Dzerzhinsky, Letter to his wife Zosia, November 20, 1916, in *Prison Diary and Letters*, 284.

20. On the impact of his childhood on his later career see Iain Lauchlan, "Felix before the Fall: A Biographical Approach to Understanding Stalinism," in *International Newsletter of Communist Studies Online* 19, no. 26 (2013): 48–61.

21. Elaboration on the meaning of this term, often used in Soviet propaganda, can be found in a late Stalinist school textbook: L. I. Timofeev, *Russkaia sovetskaia literatura. Uchebnoe posobie dlia 10-go klass srednei shkoly* [Soviet-Russian literature: A handbook for the tenth class of middle school], 8th ed. (Moscow: Gos UPI Ministerstva Prosveshcheniia, 1953), 130. For a wider discussion of the term, see Julie Fedor, *Russia and the Cult of State Security: The Chekist Tradition, from Lenin to Putin* (New York: Routledge, 2011), 18.

22. As one of Dzerzhinsky's contemporaries put it: "The men of my generation . . . cannot help the sensation of having lived on the frontier where one world ends and another begins." Victor Serge, *Memoirs of a Revolutionary* (New York: NYRB, 2012), 444.

23. Raymond Chandler, "The Simple Art of Murder," *Atlantic Monthly*, December 1944, accessed May 1, 2016, http://www.en.utexas.edu/amlit/amlitprivate/scans/chandlerart.html.

24. Dzerzhinsky's letter to Lunacharsky, January 21, 1921, on the creation of orphanages, quoted in A. I. Valakhanovich, *Feliks Edmundovich Dzerzhinskii* (Minsk: Nauka i tekhnika, 1997), 128.

25. Andrei Sinyavsky, *Soviet Civilization: A Cultural History* (New York: Arcade Publishing, 1991), 128. The cult of Dzerzhinsky showed similarities to Anatoly Lunacharsky's contention that Jesus was the first Communist and that "if Christ were alive now he would be a Bolshevik." See Dimitry V. Pospielovsky, *A History of Soviet Atheism in Theory, and Practice, and the Believer* (Basingstoke, UK: Macmillan, 1987), 94–95.

26. He took the news stoically: "He who lives as I do," he told his sister, "cannot live very long." Feliks Dzerzhinsky, Letter to his sister, Aldona, October 21, 1901, in *Prison Diary and Letters*, 143.

27. Dzerzhinsky's response to Lenin's April Theses quoted in Leon Trotsky, *History of the Russian Revolution*, trans. Max Eastman (Chicago: Haymarket Books, 2008), 236–37.

28. Feliks Dzerzhinsky, Diary entry, May 9, 1908, in *Prison Diary and Letters*, 27.

29. I. N. Steinberg, *In the Workshop of the Revolution* (London: Victor Gollancz Ltd, 1955), 71–72.

30. Dzerzhinsky, *Prison Diary and Letters*, 290. On the recurrent image of the "guard dog on a chain," see Donald Rayfield, *Stalin and His Hangmen* (London: Penguin, 2005), 200; and Fedor, *Russia and the Cult of State Security*, 8.

31. O. V. Khlevniuk, *Politbiuro: Mekhanizmy politicheskoi vlasti v 1930-e gody* [The Politburo: The mechanics of political power in the 1930s] (Moscow: ROSSPEN, 1996), 210.

32. Nikolai Bukharin, quoted in Boris I. Nicolaevsky, *Power and the Soviet Elite* (London: Pall Mall Press, 1965), 18–19.

33. Paul Gregory, *Terror by Quota: State Security from Lenin to Stalin* (New Haven, CT: Yale University Press, 2009), 254.

34. Leonid Krasin, quoted in Rayfield, *Stalin and His Hangmen*, 64.

35. Quoted in V. S. Izmozik, *Glaza i ushi rezhima: Gosudarstvennyi politicheskii kontrol' za naseleniem Sovetskoi Rossii v 1918–1928 godakh* [The eyes and ears of the regime: State political control over the inhabitants of Soviet Russia, 1921–1928] (St. Petersburg: Izd. St Peterburgskogo Universiteta, 1995), 111.

36. In 1918 Trotsky advocated organizing a show trial for the tsar and famously warned "the guillotine will await our enemies." Leggett, *The Cheka*, 54.

37. See, for example, their hearty participation in the Cheka's fifth anniversary celebrations: "Na prazdnike GPU" [On the GPU holiday], *Pravda* [Truth], December 18, 1922.

38. See Bukharin's obituary to Dzerzhinsky in *Pravda*, July 21, 1926, and his articles celebrating the tenth anniversary of the Cheka in *Pravda*, December 18, 1927, and *Izvestia* [The news], December 20, 1927.

39. A. V. Korotkov and A. A. Chernobaev, eds., "Posetiteli kremlevskogo kabineta I. V. Stalina: Zhurnaly (tetradi) zapisi lits, prinyatykh pervym gensekom 1924–1953 gg" [Visitors to Stalin's Kremlin office: The general secretary's visitors' book, 1924–1953], *Istoricheskii arkhiv* [Historical archive], 1994, no. 6; 1995, nos. 1–6; 1996, nos. 1–6; 1997, no. 1.

40. V. M. Molotov, *Molotov Remembers: Conversations with Felix Chuev* (Chicago: I. R. Dee, 1993), 263.

41. First published in *Trud* [Labour], no. 88, June 4, 1992. Reproduced in V. N. Khaustov et al., *Lubianka. Stalin i GUGB NKVD, 1937–1938* [The Lubianka: Stalin and the GUGB NKVD, 1937–1938] (Moscow: Demokratiia, 2004), 273–81. On the other "mass operations," see N. Vert and B. Mironenko, *Massovye repressii v SSSR, Istoriia Stalinskogo Gulaga* [Mass repressions in the USSR: A history of the gulag under Stalin] (Moscow: ROSSPEN, 2004): 1:267–68, 305–8.

42. M. Latsis, *Chrezvychainye komissii* [The extraordinary commissions] (Moscow: Gosizdat, 1921), 11.

43. Vasily Mitrokhin, *"Chekisms": A KGB Anthology* (London: Yurasov Press, 2008), xvii.

44. Tsentral'nyi Arkhiv Federal'noi Sluzhbi Bezopasnosti, Moscow [The central archive of the Federal Security Service, hereafter TsAFSB], f.1, op.4, d.6, l.160: "Iz otcheta mandatnoi komissii 4-i konferentsiia ChK, 6 Fev. 1920."

45. TsAFSB, f.2, op.10, d.190, l.351: Lubianka to regional GPUs in October 1927 on the importance of the "most responsible work" going to party members who had joined before the Revolution. On continuity of personnel from 1920s to 1930s, see K. V. Skorkin and N. V. Petrov, *Kto rukovodil NKVD, 1934–1941* [Who directed the NKVD, 1934–1941] (Moscow: Zvenia, 1999), 498.

46. Leggett, *The Cheka*, 258–59. According to one account in September 1918, Russians accounted for only 30 percent of staff in the Lubianka headquarters. See Gregory, *Terror by Quota*, 63. On the lower-level Cheka rank and file being mostly Russian, see Alter Litvin, "The Cheka," in Edward Acton et al., eds., *Critical Companion to the Russian Revolution, 1914–21* (London: Hodder Arnold, 1997), 318–19.

47. Stephen G. Wheatcroft, "Agency and Terror: Evdokimov and Mass Killing in Stalin's Great Terror," *Australian Journal of Politics and History* 53, no. 1 (2007): 20.

48. M. P. Frinovskii, N. Nikolaev-Zhudrin, I. I. Dagin, V. M. Kursky, and Minaev-Tsikanovskii. The team would be executed at the same time: February 1940. See ibid., 40.

49. L. P. Beria (Mingrelian), M. D. Bagirov (Azerbaijani), Vladimir Dekanozov (a Georgian who grew up in Baku), M. M. Gvishiani (Armenian), Bogadan Z. Kobulov (Armenian), Vsevolod Nikolaevich Merkulov (a Russian-Armenian born in Azerbaijan), Solomon Mil'shtein (Polish Jew), Avksentii Rapava (Mingrelian), Nikolai M. Rukhadze (Georgian), Shota Sadzhaia (Mingrelian), Lavrenti Tsanava (Mingrelian), and S. A. Goglidze (Georgian).

50. Litvin, "The Cheka," 318. In 1920 over half of the Cheka's officials had no more than a primary education, and just 1 percent were university educated.

51. Dzerzhinsky's speech at the Fourth Cheka Conference, February 6, 1920, TsAFSB, f.1, op.4, d.6, ll.142–44.

52. Serge, *Memoirs*, 84.

53. Nadezhda Mandelstam, *Hope against Hope: A Memoir* (London: Harvill Press, 1999), 79–80.

54. Quoted in Merle Fainsod, *How Russia Is Ruled* (London: Harvard University Press, 1970), 426.

55. Obituary to Feliks Dzerzhinsky in *Pravda*, July 23, 1926. For an excellent summary of these themes see Fedor, *Russia and the Cult of State Security*, chap. 1.

56. Quoted in ibid., 6. See also Mandelstam, *Hope against Hope*, 4–6; and Kevin Moss, "Bulgakov's Master and Margarita: Masking the Supernatural and the Secret Police," *Russian Language Journal* 38, nos. 129–30 (1984): 115–31.

57. Alexander Solzhenitsyn, *The Gulag Archipelago* (London: Harvill Press, 1974), 148–49.

58. "Rech' tov. N. I. Bukharina," *Pravda*, July 24, 1926.

59. Stalin speech to visiting foreign workers on November 5, 1927, quoted in Fainsod, *How Russia Is Ruled*, 423.

60. For Lenin's November 7, 1918, summary of the role of the Cheka, see "Rech' V. I. Lenina, proiznesennaia v klube VChK" [V. I. Lenin's speech in the VChK club], in V. Vinogradov et al., eds., *Arkhiv VChK: Sbornik dokumentov* [The VChK archive: A collection of documents] (Moscow: Kuchkovo pole, 2007), 92–93. See also Israel Getzler, "Lenin's Conception of Revolution as Civil War," *Slavonic and East European Review* 74, no. 3 (1996).

61. Solzhenitsyn, *Gulag Archipelago*, 174.

62. Quoted in E. J. Scott, "The Cheka," *St Antony's Papers*, no. 1 (1956): 8.

63. *Iz istorii VChK. Sbornik dokumentov* [A history of the VChK: A collection of documents] (Moscow: Politizdat, 1958), 250.

64. Quoted in Larina, *This I Cannot Forget*, 343.

65. Bukharin's last appeal, March 12, 1938, in *Report of Court Proceedings in the Case of the Anti-Soviet "Block of Rights and Trotskyites"* (Moscow: Izdanie NKIu, 1938), 667–68.

66. Solzhenitsyn, *Gulag Archipelago*, 101.

67. See Gregory, *Terror by Quota*, 202–18, on confession as the product of the need for "simplified methods" to speed up productivity.

68. W. H. Chamberlin, *The Russian Revolution, 1917–1921* (London: Macmillan, 1935), 68.

69. Latsis, quoted in Fainsod, *How Russia Is Ruled*, 426.

70. Dzerzhinsky proposed a "model trial" of the Socialist Revolutionaries in a letter to Lenin on December 28, 1921. See Marc Jansen, *A Show Trial under Lenin: The Trial of the Socialist Revolutionaries, Moscow 1922* (London: Springer, 1982), 27–28.

71. M. A. Osorgin, *Vremena* [The times] (Paris, 1955), 180–82.

72. RGASPI, f.76, op.3, d.303, ll.1–3, September 5, 1922.

73. Mitrokhin, *Chekisms*, xix.

74. RGASPI, f.17, op.12, d.259, ll.17–22.

75. Quoted in Fainsod, *How Russia Is Ruled*, 426.

76. Gosudarstvennyi Arkhiv Rossiiskoi Federatsii, Moscow [State archive of the Russian Federation, hereafter GARF] f.393, op.43, d.80, l.420, October 1, 1923.

77. Izmozik, *Glaza i ushi rezhima*, 130, 134.

78. J. Arch Getty and Oleg Naumov, *The Road to Terror: Stalin and the Self-Destruction of the Bolsheviks* (New Haven, CT: Yale University Press), 378. See, for example, Yagoda's 1935 speech in David R. Shearer, *Policing Stalin's Socialism: Repression and Social Order in the Soviet Union* (New Haven, CT: Yale University Press, 2009), 23: "a hooligan, a robber, a bandit—is he not the real counter-revolutionary?" Shearer (ibid., 26) contrasts this to the 1930 report of the Russian Republic's NKVD (i.e., a non-*chekist* police official), A. A. Tolmachev, whose report on crime "contained no politicized language, no references to anti-Soviet elements, and the categories of crimes were laid out in a straight-forward literally descriptive manner [describing even banditry as a criminal problem]."

79. *Report of Court Proceedings in the Case of the Anti-Soviet "Block of Rights and Trotskyites"* (Moscow: Izdanie NKIu, 1938), 696.

80. Norman Cohn, *The Pursuit of the Millennium: Revolutionary Millenarians and Mystical Anarchists in the Middle Ages* (Oxford: Oxford University Press, 1970), 314.

81. Dzerzhinsky, letters May 27 and August 29, 1918, and April 15, 1919, in *Prison Diary and Letters*, 291–94.

82. Latsis, *Chrezvychainye komissii*; and A. I. Kokurin and N. V. Petrov, *Lubianka: Organy VChK-OGPU-NKVD-NKGB-MGB-MVD-KGB, 1917–1991* [Lubianka: The organs of the VChK] (Moscow: Demokratiia, 2003), 413.

83. Dzerzhinsky, 1921, quoted in ibid., 413–14.

84. Stalin to Menzhinsky, September 16, 1929, in Gregory, *Terror by Quota*, 211.

85. Peter Holquist, "Violent Russia, Deadly Marxism? Russia in the Epoch of Violence," *Kritika* 4, no. 3 (Summer 2003): 651.

86. Peter Holquist, "'Information Is the Alpha and Omega of Our Work.' Bolshevik Surveillance in Its Pan-European Context," in *The Structure of Soviet History: Essays and Documents*, ed. Ronald Suny (New York: Oxford University Press, 2003), 55.

87. Gregory, *Terror by Quota*, 29. See also Peter Holquist, "To Count, to Extract, and to Exterminate: Population Statistics and Population Politics in Late Imperial and Soviet Russia," in *A State of Nations: Empire and Nation-Making in the Age of Lenin and Stalin*, ed. Terry Martin and Ronald Suny (New York: Oxford University Press, 2001), 114–23.

88. V. N. Khaustov, *Lubianka: Stalin i VChK-GPU-OGPU-NKVD, 1922–1936* [Lubianka: Stalin and the VChK-GPU-OGPU-NKVD, 1922–1936] (Moscow: Demokratiia, 2003), 349.

89. Dzerzhinsky to the Politburo, January 13, 1921, TsAFSB, f.2, op.1, d.244, l.95.

90. See M. Latsis, *Dva goda bor'by na vnutrennom fronte* [Two years of struggle on the internal front] (Moscow: Gosizdat, 1920). On mass executions in Ukraine after the end of the civil war in 1920–21, see A. M. Plekhanov, *VChK-OGPU v gody*

NEP, 1921–1928 [The VChK-OGPU in the NEP era, 1921–1928] (Moscow: Kuchkovo pole, 2006), 127.

91. Khaustov, *Lubianka*, 38–40; and Wheatcroft, "Agency and Terror," 28. Statistics from O. B. Mozokhin, "Statistika repressivnikh organov VChK-OGPU (1921-1934)" [Statistics on the repressive organs of the VChK-OGPU (1921–1934)], *Voennyi Istoricheskii Arkhiv* [Military history archive], nos. 6–12 (June–December 2004); A. Papchinskii and M. Tumshis, *Shchit, raskolotii mechom: NKVD protiv VChK* [The shield and sword divided: NKVD versus VChK] (Moscow: Sovremennik, 2001), 193–96; and Lynne Viola, "The Role of the OGPU in Dekulakization, Mass Deportations, and Special Resettlement in the 1930s," *The Carl Beck Papers in Russian and East European Studies*, no. 1406 (Pittsburgh, January 2000). For Molotov on the leading role of the provincial OGPU, see RGASPI, f.17, op.2, d.441, ll.50 and 56. For Yevdokimov's operational command, see TsAFSB, f.2, op.9, d.21, ll.393–94.

92. Amy Knight, *Beria: Stalin's First Lieutenant* (Princeton, NJ: Princeton University Press, 1993), 33–41. See also Boris Baikov, "Vospominaniia o revoliutsii v Zavkavkaz'i (1917–1920 g.g.)" [Recollections of the revolution in the Caucasus], *Arkhiv Russkoi Revoliutsii* [Archive of the Russian Revolution], vol. 9 (Berlin); and Evgenii Dumbadze, *Na sluzhbe cheka i kominterna* [In the service of the Cheka and the Comintern] (Paris, 1930), 58. It is estimated that 80 percent of executions were not even reported.

93. The Cheka deliberately employed the term *banditizm* ("banditism") rather than *banditstvo* (banditry), implying that it was an ideological rather than merely criminal phenomenon.

94. He was People's Commissar for Transport, head of the Commission for Improving the Lives of Children, chairman of the Workers' Defence Council and the main economic body, Vesenkha. For an excellent collection of documents detailing Dzerzhinsky's instructions in this sphere from 1921–22, see Plekhanov, *VChK-OGPU v gody NEP*, 532–50, 556, 577–78, 582–83, 585–86, 591–92.

95. G. A. Trushin, Special Vecheka Plenipotentiary (PPVChK), telegram to all branches of the security police on intensifying the struggle against "banditism," June 8, 1921, in Plekhanov, *VChK-OGPU v gody NEP*, 561.

96. RGASPI, f.17, op.84, d.228, l.52.

97. On this theory see J. V. Stalin, *Works* (Moscow: Gosizdat, 1954), 12:37–42.

98. RGASPI, f.76, op.3, d.345, ll.2–2ob.

99. Ibid., l.1.

100. G. S. Agabekov, *GPU: Zapiski chekista* [GPU: Notes of a *chekist*] (Berlin: Strela, 1930), 67–87, 116, 119.

101. The British Empire was indeed aiming to infiltrate spies into the Soviet Union in this way. See, for example, the list of India Office Records cited in Giles Milton, *Russian Roulette: How British Spies Thwarted Lenin's Global Plot* (London: Hodder and Stoughton, 2013), 355–57.

102. Primakov, *Ocherki istorii*, 2:242–43.

103. For the classic study of the connection between the belief in an omnipresent conspiracy and the terror, see G. T. Rittersporn, "The Omnipresent Conspiracy: On Soviet Imagery of Politics and Social Relations in the 1930s," in N. Lampert and

G. T. Rittersporn, *Stalinism: Its Nature and Aftermath: Essays in Honour of Moshe Lewin* (London: Macmillan, 1992).

104. See *Kronshtadtskaia tragediia 1921 goda, dokumenty v dvukh knigakh* [The Kronstadt tragedy: A collection of documents in two volumes] (Moscow: ROSSPEN, 1999). One exception was Iakov Agranov's report of April 5, 1921, which failed to toe the party line about a foreign conspiracy. See Israel Getzler, "The Communist Leaders' Role in the Kronstadt Tragedy of 1921 in the Light of Recently Published Archival Documents," *Revolutionary Russia* 15, no. 1 (June 2002): 22–44.

105. See, for example, Dzerzhinsky's assertion that supply problems in Siberia were the result of saboteurs supported by the Japanese government, and his request that further powers be granted to the Cheka to deal with the problem. See RGASPI, f.76, op.3, d.237, l.3, Dzerzhinsky to Yenukidze, January 2, 1922.

106. *Izvestiia vremennogo komiteta* [The provisional government news], March 8, 1921: "Za chto my boremsia" [What we are fighting for]. See *Pravda o kronshtadte* [The truth about Kronstadt] (Prague: Volia Rossii, 1921), accessed May 1, 2016, http://soviethistory.msu.edu/1921-2/kronstadt-uprising/kronstadt-uprising-texts/rebels-what-are-we-fighting-for/.

107. TsAFSB, f.2, op.1, d.795, l.26, cutting from *Dni* [Days], December 29, 1922. See also *Che-Ka: Materialy po deiatel'nosti chrezvychainykh komissii* [The Cheka: Materials on the activities of the extraordinary commissions] (Berlin: Izd. tsental'nogo biuro, 1922).

108. See R. V. Daniels, *The Conscience of the Revolution: Communist Opposition in Soviet Russia* (Cambridge, MA: Harvard University Press, 1960); and George Leggett, "The Cheka and a Crisis of Communist Conscience," *Survey* 25 (1980). On the closure of the weekly Cheka newspaper due to party criticism, see RGASPI, f.17, op.2, d.5, ll.1–1ob. Kamenev, Krylenko, Riazanov, Bukharin, Beloborodov, Piatakov, Petrovsky, Smirnov, Sokol'nikov, and Olminsky, among others, all attacked it between 1918 and 1924. Trotsky wanted the Red Army to handle state security. See V. Nekrasov, *Trinadtsat "zheleznykh" narkomov: Istoriia NKVD-MVD, 1917–1982* [Thirteen "iron" commissars: A history of the NKVD-MVD, 1917–1982] (Moscow: Versty, 1995), 84.

109. December 24, 1924, RGASPI, f.76, op.3, d.345, ll.1–1ob. For similar instructions, see Dzerzhinsky to Unshlikht, September 5, 1922, RGASPI, f.76, op.3, d.303, ll.1–3.

110. In fact, in this regard the Cheka ethos was not new. See the Third Section's fiftieth anniversary jubilee report published in V. Bogucharskii, "Tret'e otdelenie o samom sebe" [The Third Section on itself], *Vestnik Yevropy* [The European herald] (March 1917).

111. On the planning and stenographic records of the celebratory meeting of December 17, 1922, see TsAFSB, f.1, op.6, d.160, ll.1–50. Extracts have been published in Vinogradov, *Arkhiv VChK* [Archive of the VChK], 613–26.

112. TsAFSB, f.2, op.1, d.795, *Vyrezki iz inostrannoi pressy* [Folder: Cuttings from the foreign press], ll.25–26, press cutting from *Dni*, December 28, 1922. The GPU provided a list of the editorial staff of *Dni*, among others—P. B. Aksel'rod, G. Aronson, A. Belyi, A. M. Gor'kii, Iu. O. Martov, V. M. Chernov, and N. N. Sukhanov.

113. Inna Skliarevskaia, "Balet Vera Mukhinoi" [Vera Mukhina's ballet], *Peterburgskii teatral'nyi zhurnal* [The St. Petersburg theatrical journal], no. 4 [62], 2010, accessed April 12, 2017, http://ptj.spb.ru/archive/62/music-theatre-62/balet-very-muxinoj/.

114. Thomas Carlyle, *On Heroes, Hero-Worship and the Heroic in History* (1840), accessed April 12, 2017, http://www.kouroo.info/kouroo/Carlyle/HEROES/12may40.pdf.

115. *Izvestia*, December 18, 1927.

116. "Nad grobom Dzerzhinskogo" [Over Dzerzhinsky's coffin], *Pravda*, July 23, 1926. For examples of the Dzerzhinsky cult, see *Feliks Dzerzhinskii, 1926–31: Sbornik statei* [Feliks Dzerzhinsky, 1926–1931: A collection of essays] (Moscow: Politizdat, 1931).

117. On neotraditionalism see, in particular, Ken Jowitt, *New World Disorder: The Leninist Extinction* (Berkeley: University of California Press, 1992), 121–58.

5 The Consummate Careerist

Erich Mielke, the German Democratic Republic's
Minister for State Security

Paul Maddrell

Erich Mielke served as the minister for state security of the German Democratic Republic (GDR) from 1957 to 1989, making him one of the longest-serving intelligence chiefs in history. He was one of the most important people in the State Security Ministry (or Stasi) for even longer than that since it was he who, in 1949, chose the ministry's senior officers as the Stasi was being formed. In reality, he was as much a servant as a leader: he was able to preside over the Stasi for forty years because he was the loyal functionary of two superiors, the East German Communist Party, known as the Socialist Unity Party (Sozialistische Einheitspartei Deutschlands, SED), and the Soviet security service, the KGB (Komitet Gosudarstvennoi Bezopasnosti: Committee for State Security). He imposed on his ministry obedience to the party and loyalty to the Soviet Union. Since the Stasi was very much the KGB's creation, the mentality and methods of the two agencies were the same. Mielke's role as minister was to impose on the Stasi the political culture of the SED and the organizational culture of the KGB. Although he was a mediocre leader, his role in the Stasi's history was nonetheless important.

When the Stasi was created by a law of the GDR's parliament, the Volkskammer, in February 1950, Mielke was a strong candidate for the position of minister. He was not chosen because he did not enjoy the confidence of the Soviets, who then dominated the fledgling East German security agencies. Wilhelm Zaisser became the first GDR minister for state security because the Soviets trusted him. When Zaisser was dismissed in July 1953, he was succeeded by another German Communist, Ernst Wollweber, who also enjoyed the Russians' confidence more than Mielke did. Only when the Russians allowed the East German Communist leader, Walter Ulbricht, to choose his own security minister did Mielke achieve that position, which he did in November 1957. Significantly, he achieved it as Ulbricht's placeman.

This chapter will consider, first, why Mielke held the position of minister for state security for so long and, second, how well he led the Stasi.

The Servant of Two Masters: Mielke's Longevity as Minister

The position of GDR state security minister was, politically, a very sensitive one. The appointee had to safeguard both East German and Soviet interests. The first two ministers failed to satisfy both of these masters. Mielke succeeded in doing so (though in easier circumstances), which is why he lasted so long in the position.

Zaisser, the first state security minister, was appointed to the position owing to his loyal service to the USSR: he was a long-serving agent of the Soviet military intelligence service, the GRU (Glavnoye Razvedivatelnoye Upravleniye: Main Intelligence Directorate), who had commanded one of the International Brigades during the Spanish Civil War and had been employed in political reeducation work among German prisoners of war during the Second World War. He was dismissed because the popular uprising of June 17, 1953, which the Stasi failed either to predict or to prevent, humiliated the East German Communist regime and discredited him. Wollweber, his successor, had also demonstrated his loyalty to the Soviet Union as head of a maritime sabotage organization during the years of the Nazi regime. During the war he took refuge in Sweden, but the Nazis forced the Swedish government to imprison him, which wrecked Wollweber's health. He was an intelligent, assertive, and decisive man who reorganized the Stasi and improved its effectiveness. Though a successful minister, he was fired in 1957 because the East German leader, Walter Ulbricht, wanted his own man at the Stasi's helm. Wollweber's health was so bad that he could not put up much of a fight. The Soviet Communist regime was willing to allow Wollweber to fall because its policy, after the fright of the Hungarian Uprising in 1956, was to improve the legitimacy of the satellite regimes by giving them more freedom of action. It therefore allowed Ulbricht to have his way.[1]

Mielke succeeded Wollweber. The KGB had misgivings about Mielke, considering him deceitful; the KGB *rezident* (station chief) in the GDR from 1953 to 1957, Yevgeni Pitovranov, considered him "crafty and insincere."[2] Mielke had tried to conceal aspects of his past, such as his brother's suicide in 1955. He had also spent the war in France, where the Soviets had had no contact with him. Residence in the West was always a black mark in their book because it exposed people to Western influence. To make matters worse, Mielke had been interned by the Germans when they occupied Vichy France, and the Soviets did not know for how long he had been in their hands. The two most

Photo 5.1 Erich Mielke (third from left, in grey uniform). The photograph was taken in January 1970. Mielke was here attending a reception hosted by the GDR's leader, Walter Ulbricht (extreme left), to celebrate the Stasi's twentieth anniversary.
Source: *Der Bundesbeauftragte für die Unterlagen des Staatssicherheitsdienstes der ehemaligen Deutschen Demokratischen Republik (BStU, The Federal Commissioner for the Records of the State Security Service of the Former German Democratic Republic)*

important Soviets in East Germany—Colonel General Vasili Chuikov, the head of the Soviet Control Commission, and his political adviser Vladimir Semyonov—were both sufficiently concerned about Mielke's time in France to report it to Stalin in January 1950, when the matter of who the East German minister of state security should be came before the Soviet Politburo.[3] The Soviets finally acquiesced in 1957 to Mielke's appointment because Ulbricht insisted.

Mielke overcame this mistrust, which was one of the great successes of his career. Since we have no access to the KGB's records, we do not know precisely when or how he won their confidence. Nevertheless, it is clear that he stayed in office for so long because his subservience satisfied the leaders of the SED and the success of his ministry satisfied the Russians. By the early 1970s, at the latest, he enjoyed the Soviets' favor. They gave him their highest honor, the Order of Lenin, four times: first in 1973, then in 1982, then in 1985, and for the last time in 1987. It is noteworthy that the Order was first awarded to him late in his career in GDR state security—after sixteen years as minister (half of his time in that position). He was also awarded the USSR's Order of the Red Banner four times.[4] In 1987, the USSR's president, Andrei Gromyko, also awarded him the honorary title of "Hero of the Soviet Union."[5] General Secretary Erich Honecker was firmly of the view that, during his leadership of the SED, Mielke was held in high regard in Moscow.[6]

The main reason his stock rose with the Soviets was evidently that he sought consistently to meet their security needs. Ernst Wollweber had disagreed with the KGB about how much surveillance was needed in the GDR, arguing that the regime was secure and that the Stasi's full-time staff and informer network could both be reduced in size.[7] Mielke, by contrast, shared the Soviets' concern about Western ideological influence and pressed for very extensive social surveillance carried out by a very large informer network—indeed, he may have gone even further than the Soviets wanted in expanding his ministry and its stock of informers. The Stasi's main task became to ward off Western ideological influence, which Mielke damned as *politisch-ideologische Diversion* (political-ideological diversion, or PID for short). The KGB agreed with him on the importance of the task and even adopted the term itself.[8] The Soviet regime, from Khrushchev down, was alarmed at the upsurge in opposition and the collapse in the authority of the satellite regimes that de-Stalinization had produced. The Soviet leaders realized that the satellite regimes' standing as Soviet puppets made them deeply unpopular with their peoples. In an attempt to reduce this unpopularity, they gave the satellites more freedom of action. However, they also insisted that strong efforts be made to secure the satellite peoples from harmful Western influences; the same policy was pursued in the Soviet Union itself. Simple institutional interest also pressed for such a policy. The KGB had no interest in maintaining that the Soviet regime was secure and, in the absence of real opposition, tended to invent it.[9] It could do so because that message was very welcome at the top of the party.

The same combination of insecurity and political dogmatism on the part of the Communist leadership and the institutional interest of the security service was at work in the GDR. Mielke personified both tendencies. Under his leadership of the Stasi, any criticism of the regime or "actually existing Socialism" was unacceptable and was ascribed to a counterrevolutionary movement directed by the Western intelligence services.

Under Mielke, the Stasi followed the KGB's lead in security policy and worked closely with its Soviet partner, supplying it with much valuable information. Throughout the 1960s the KGB was as concerned as Mielke about the extent of Western influence on the Soviet Bloc, including the GDR. It was concerned about all the ways in which Western ideas seeped into the bloc: tourism (particularly trips by Eastern Europeans to the West), letter-writing, scientific and cultural exchanges, political propaganda, and most of all, radio and television broadcasts. In the KGB's eyes, there were no greater enemies than Radio Liberty and the World Service of the BBC. Evidently relying on figures provided by the Hungarian security service, the Államvédelmi Hatóság (ÁVH), the KGB's view in the 1960s was that more than 20 percent of young Hungarians listened to Western radio broadcasts. For the KGB, as for Mielke, any nonconformity with the party line was unacceptable; it classified such nonconformity as either "harmful attitudes" or "hostile acts." The two categories together encompassed all criticism of Communist society, and statistics were kept on both. The KGB reported that in 1965 and 1966 young people in Hungary had been guilty of approximately 87,000 "harmful attitudes" and "hostile acts."[10]

Mielke's conservative Communism chimed exactly with the outlook of Yuri Andropov, who served as chairman of the KGB from 1967 to 1982. Andropov had been Soviet ambassador to Hungary when the revolution broke out there in 1956, and from then on he had been convinced that dissidence, which he saw as ideological subversion encouraged and organized by the West, represented a grave threat to the Soviet Bloc. The outbreak of the Prague Spring in Czechoslovakia in 1968 confirmed him in this belief. Mielke worked closely with Andropov, who for his part cultivated Mielke, recognizing the Stasi's importance and prizing both Mielke's reliability and the stability his ministry had created in the GDR. The KGB and Stasi signed important agreements on cooperation during Andropov's time as KGB chairman, reflecting his respect for the Stasi and its achievements.[11]

From 1967 until Andropov's death in 1984 the Stasi marched in step with the KGB in its efforts to defeat dissidence. The Stasi's readiness to get rid of dissidents by depriving them of their GDR citizenship, rather than by imprisoning them, followed the KGB's example. The trend began in the USSR with the dispatch of Viktor Krasin into exile in 1973 and that of Alexander Solzhenitsyn in February 1974 (Andropov had wanted to expel Solzhenitsyn from the USSR since he had won the Nobel Prize for Literature in 1970).[12] The GDR followed suit in November 1976, when the singer Wolf Biermann was deprived of his citizenship while on tour in West Germany.[13]

Indeed, from the 1960s until the collapse of the SED regime, the Stasi's policy toward dissidence was that of the KGB. Both regimes sought to preserve the fiction that they enjoyed public support. They tried to refrain from brutal repression and mass arrests, and adhered to legality, at least for as long as it suited them. They sought to prevent dissidence or unwelcome developments (such as applications to emigrate) from manifesting themselves rather than suppress them once they appeared. Surveillance rose in importance as a way of obtaining early warning of them. The security services made much greater efforts to intimidate dissidents to rethink their plans and would-be emigrants to withdraw their applications. By contrast, less use was made of arrests and prosecutions; the prosecutions that did take place were very carefully prepared. Well-known dissidents were often publicly discredited rather than prosecuted. From the mid-1960s on, the KGB publicly used the English word "dissidents" to describe such people, in an attempt to present them as agents of Western intelligence services and as people under foreign influence rather than as true representatives of Soviet public opinion.[14] The danger of Western espionage was energetically publicized to provide an excuse for the prohibition on most Soviet and East German citizens traveling abroad. The ideas conveyed by the Western mass media were damned as "ideological sabotage" designed to undermine the Communist regimes, and the media themselves were presented as under the control of the Western secret services.[15]

Mielke's efforts in the 1960s to improve the education and professional training of Stasi officers also followed the KGB's lead. A telling example is the trend on the part of Stasi interrogators from the 1960s on to make greater use of psychological influence to win the cooperation of their victims (Mielke had himself been a brutal interrogator in the 1950s). Again, from Khrushchev's time onward, the KGB's insistence on observing "Socialist legality"—or seeming to, at least—was the reason for this move away from brutality to a more correct approach.[16]

The emphasis on surveillance rather than trials did not suit Mielke's aggressive, brutal personality. He was characteristically heavy-handed in building up his service and its informer network. By the 1980s, the Stasi, with its staff of 80,000, had one security official for every 180 GDR citizens; the KGB, by contrast, had one security official for every 600 Soviet citizens.[17] Mielke deliberately created a service that closely resembled its Soviet parent.

Mielke's stock undoubtedly also rose with the Soviets because of his service's impressive record in maintaining the GDR's security. The threat the KGB most feared was political subversion, and here the GDR's record was good. Unlike Poland or Hungary or Czechoslovakia, from 1953 to 1989 the GDR did not experience any popular uprising or repudiation of Communism on the part of the regime. The Soviets were also morbidly afraid of the prospect of an American nuclear attack; gathering military intelligence became the top priority of the Stasi's foreign intelligence collection in the mid-1970s, and the East Germans achieved striking successes. The Soviets were very impressed by the military intelligence they collected, particularly on the North Atlantic Treaty Organization (NATO), the NATO forces in Western Europe, and their weaponry. The intelligence obtained by the Stasi's best sources was even better than that obtained by the KGB's spies in NATO. The Warsaw Pact's forces were, accordingly, very well informed about the NATO forces in Western Europe; if it had come to war, they would have greatly profited from this intelligence. Knowing its value, Mielke presented the best intelligence to

Andropov personally.[18] He was here taking credit for successes for which he was certainly not responsible. He was fortunate that it was he who was minister when, in the late 1950s, the Stasi's Hauptverwaltung Aufklärung (HVA) first started to achieve real success in collecting high-grade intelligence in West Germany.

The KGB was also impressed by the Stasi's successes in counterintelligence: it penetrated the intelligence services of West Germany and managed to arrest a very large number of Western spies, thereby enhancing the security of not only the GDR but the rest of the Soviet Bloc as well.[19] The Stasi's counterintelligence units worked closely with Soviet counterintelligence agencies (both of the KGB and GRU) in the USSR and East Germany. By the late 1950s the Stasi's counterintelligence departments were so skillful that even the United States' Central Intelligence Agency (CIA) has paid tribute to them.[20] Mielke, who was heavily involved in counterintelligence, can take some of the credit for his ministry's skill in this field.

In sum, it was under Mielke's leadership that the Stasi established itself as the second most important security service in the Soviet Bloc; unlike other satellite security services, it was a genuine partner of the KGB, not a mere subordinate. Mielke expected—and got—deference from KGB officers. The success of his ministry secured his position as minister.[21]

How Well Did Mielke Lead the Stasi?

For a remarkably long period Mielke led an organization that contributed substantially to the political stability of the GDR and the military capability of the Warsaw Pact. Does it follow from this that he was an able leader?

Multiple Actors in the Security Field

Assessing the skill with which Mielke ran his ministry is complicated by two factors. The first is that the Stasi quickly became a large organization and ended up a very large one; in 1989 it had a staff of 102,000. Its qualities derived from the skills of its staff at all levels. Even the minister was only one player on a big team. That said, he was never a nonentity; he could not be so since the ministry was run on the military model of a single commander: the minister dominated the ministry. He could give orders to any Stasi officer, regardless of rank, bypassing the ministry's official hierarchy. Mielke exploited his position to the full, maintaining his connection with his senior officers via a battery of telephones in his office and demanding news from them every morning. Under his predecessor, Wollweber, the Kollegium, the Stasi's highest body, had been an important forum for discussion and collective decision making;

though it still met under Mielke, he did not use it to take advice or make decisions together with his officers.[22] He was a bully who raged at his subordinates and badgered them with phone calls and demands. Egotism and insecurity drove him to try and dominate others, and the Stasi's authoritarian structure and culture enabled him to do so. The minister was also the political leadership's chief intelligence adviser; the information it received on the GDR and the outside world from the Stasi reached it by way of Mielke's desk and represented one of its principal sources of information.

The second factor is that security was such a crucial issue for the GDR that several actors were involved in the making of security policy. The most important were the Soviets. They dominated the ministry for most of the 1950s, and it operated under their direction to the very end. It was they who built it up from scratch, teaching the staff how to do their jobs. Their influence was everywhere. Mielke was one of their pupils; there is no evidence that he had any involvement in intelligence work before 1945, and all he knew he learned from Soviet instructors. It was they who gave the Stasi its character; its operations were straightforward copies of their own. Even before Mielke became its chief, it was a big organization with a large network of informers that aimed at conducting comprehensive surveillance of society. Soviet oversight of the Stasi placed limits on Mielke's authority to the very end. Since the Stasi's foreign intelligence service, the HVA, worked principally for the USSR rather than the GDR and was ably led by a chief, Markus Wolf, who had strong Soviet support, it enjoyed a measure of independence from Mielke. It was Wolf, rather than Mielke, who was responsible for the service's success. In its early years it was run directly by the Soviets, who chose its staff.[23]

The subordination of the Stasi to the Socialist Unity Party also placed limits on Mielke's authority: decisions on important matters of intelligence or security had to be referred to the party's first secretary (always jealous of his authority, Mielke largely excluded his nominal superior, the Central Committee secretary in charge of security questions, from actual decision making). The Politburo's Security Commission (from 1960 called the National Defense Council) also considered security matters.[24] Within those limits, Mielke was a very authoritative minister who had the last word on much that the Stasi did.

Personality

What were Mielke's qualities? He had an enormous capacity for hard work.[25] He enjoyed robust good health, which he maintained carefully and which enabled him to remain long in office. His self-discipline was considerable; his work routine was punishing, and he was rarely seen drunk. He had intelligence, but it was very ordinary. He left school at sixteen because he found the work too difficult.[26] Nevertheless, he had enough intelligence to do the job of minister for state security. He had cunning and some talent for organization. His intellectual shortcomings did not stand in the way of the Stasi's success: security work does not require high intelligence but rather diligence, thoroughness, and painstaking attention to detail. Mielke had all these qualities. He was greatly assisted by the GDR's strict security regime and by the Stasi's strong esprit de corps and sense of being an elite guard serving the party. He was a disciplinarian, obsessed with hierarchy, rank, and medals. The discipline he imposed on his staff was so strict that it was a form of bullying; his men were afraid of Mielke. They were disciplined for trivial matters, such as drinking too much and having affairs and car crashes. Any infringement of the ministry's strict code of silence about its work led to disciplinary proceedings.[27] Over time, the Stasi's staff became very disciplined. Mielke played a role in this, but his enthusiasm for disciplinary action shows what a petty man he was. Moreover, much of the improvement in discipline that the Stasi actually needed had already been done before Mielke's time as minister by his predecessor Ernst Wollweber.

Markus Wolf claims that Mielke had no capacity for long-term planning, for which he relied on others.[28] The intellectual ordinariness of the Stasi's staff was such that an able, refined man like Wolf appeared to those who dealt with him to be an outstanding figure. For the same reasons, the poetry-writing Yuri Andropov stood out among his colleagues in the KGB (Wolf also had literary leanings). For all his success as an intelligence chief, Wolf's abilities were not outstanding ones.[29] One reason Mielke enjoyed authority as minister was that he resembled his subordinates more than Wolf did. For all his ordinariness, Mielke left his mark on the Stasi and the history of the GDR—he was an ordinary man who mattered.

One of his key attributes was his unscrupulousness. Mielke was a criminal, as every Communist police chief had to be. For him, as for all Communist political police chiefs, guilt was political: an enemy was whoever stood in the party's way. The party's will was law. Nevertheless, he was a *dedicated* criminal. A passionately political man, he was a convinced Marxist-Leninist, and like all Marxist-Leninists, he believed that society was his enemy and had to be reformed by force. Any measure was justified, however criminal, if it served the cause of building a Communist society. His first notable political act was his participation in the murder of two Berlin policemen in August 1931. He was a political criminal for the rest of his long life (he died in May 2000 at the age of ninety-two).

Although Mielke certainly had qualities, they were not great enough to give him a large share of responsibility for the Stasi's success. Little of that can be put down to him; he was an archetypal Soviet political policeman of the post-Stalin era. The most that can be said for him as minister is that from the early

1950s he played a significant role in turning a youthful and inexperienced staff into what was, ten years later, a successful security service. His other great achievement was to develop his career.

For all Mielke's authoritarian style of leadership, the Stasi's success resulted from the skill, commitment, and loyalty of its staff. It maintained its security very well: there were few Western agents in its ranks. This success secured its informer network in the West: the Stasi was able to build up and run an excellent human informer network in the Federal Republic, and West Germany's intelligence agencies had no idea how deeply they had been penetrated. Mielke played little role in this. Between their creation in the early 1950s and dissolution in 1989–90, the Stasi and the VA/NVA (the intelligence service of the East German army[30]) ran informer networks among West Germans totaling some twelve thousand people. Approximately half of these people reported to the HVA. A further six thousand reported to other departments of the Stasi and to the VA/NVA.[31] The HVA in fact owed its success in collecting valuable intelligence not to the number of its spies but to its skillful, well-planned recruitment of agents and their adroit infiltration into suitable targets.[32] If anything, as Mielke grew older, he hampered the success of the HVA since he became more cautious and fearful of diplomatic incidents. From 1974, when the West German chancellor, Willy Brandt, was brought down by the exposure of an HVA spy, Günter Guillaume, in the federal chancellery, Mielke and Honecker put pressure on the HVA to avoid any diplomatic incident, even if it had to dispense with a good source to do so. The HVA called this "Guillaume syndrome."[33]

Mielke played a bigger role in the expansion of the Stasi's domestic network of informers, though the roles of the party's two leaders—Walter Ulbricht (party first secretary from 1950 until 1971[34]) and Erich Honecker (first secretary from 1971 until 1989)—were as important as his own. In the mid-1950s, before Mielke became minister, the Stasi's domestic informer network already numbered between 20,000 and 30,000 people. It was substantially expanded in the 1960s, and in 1968 stood at 100,000 people. At its peak in the mid-1970s, it was made up of about 180,000 people, the great majority of them men. By 1989, when the regime fell, its size had fallen somewhat to 173,000 people, but it still represented a little more than 1 percent of the East German population. Depending on the district, the Stasi had an informer for between every 80 and 160 people.[35]

The main reason for such an absurdly huge network was the acute insecurity of the GDR, which always lacked legitimacy and popular support and throughout its existence faced the subversive challenge of West Germany's society, economy, and state. Three conservative Communists at the top of the GDR regime—Ulbricht, Honecker, and Mielke—furthermore decided a huge network was necessary to improve the GDR's security. Mielke's narrow-minded, dogmatic Communism, combative character, and mistrustful personality inclined him toward intensifying surveillance and intimidation rather than countenancing reform. Since Communism could not be wrong, the Socialist Unity Party's ruling group tended to blame all criticism and weakness on the hostile machinations of the class enemy rather than on the failings of Communism itself, thus making the class enemy a security problem. Mielke was one of the most aggressive exponents of this line of thinking; his profound mistrust of the East German population and aggressive determination to achieve as much control as possible over it supplied some further impetus for the recruitment of an immense informer network. He constantly hammered home to his officers the need for comprehensive social surveillance (in Stasi language, this was called the "Who is who?"—*Wer ist wer?*—question). This reflected the mixture of aggression and insecurity characteristic of the dogmatic Communist.

Their reasoning went as follows: since Communism was correct, it was bound to triumph (they therefore overestimated its subversive appeal); since it was so subversive, the class enemy would have to make every possible effort to defeat it, which it had to be doing (even if evidence for this was lacking).[36] Communists were, by their very nature, deluded. Whether the GDR ever was genuinely totalitarian—that is to say, sought and achieved total control of society—is a much-disputed question. However, one thing is certain: total control is what Mielke wanted. As Jens Gieseke has rightly observed, if the concept of totalitarianism did not already exist, anyone researching Mielke's psychology would have had to invent it.[37]

As soon as he became minister, Mielke sought consistently to increase his ministry's size and responsibilities. He intensified domestic repression, pressing for the expansion of the Stasi's informer network. These efforts reflected not only his dogmatic Marxism-Leninism and aggressive desire for as much control over East German society as possible, but also his determination to increase his power by making himself indispensable to his superiors. He was a power-seeking intriguer. From the late 1950s, on Ulbricht's instructions, he expanded the Stasi and its informer network not only to clamp down hard on dissatisfaction and unrest but also to ensure that surveillance acted prophylactically, preventing Western "political-ideological diversion" from having any effect on East German society. His policy of "preventive" security, which utterly failed, represented an extreme view of what GDR security required. Until the mid-1960s the regime was too concerned with Ulbricht's economic reform policy for Mielke to obtain the resources he needed. However, the ministry's staff and informer network grew from then on. The Prague Spring, in 1968, gave the SED leaders a severe shock. From then on the conservatives in the Politburo were in the driving seat, and Mielke was given the resources he needed to place society under ever wider surveillance and interfere even more in it. From the early 1970s, as détente proceeded, the prospect of closer relations with West Germany caused him and the new first secretary, Honecker, further alarm. Neither was willing to countenance any liberalization—least of all one forced by the West—of the Communist system.[38]

Mielke did not merely order measures against the regime's opponents; he was personally involved in their persecution. In the 1950s, before he became minister, the divisions of the Stasi for which he was responsible were the main security departments and the trials department, Line IX, which prepared prosecutions of dissidents and spies for trial, chiefly by interrogation.[39] Line IX was the core of the Stasi's apparatus of political repression. Mielke often took part in interrogations and proved a pitiless and threatening interrogator. He spent many nights in the 1950s in the Stasi's investigative prison in Berlin-Hohenschönhausen, interrogating prisoners. Throughout his time as minister he had a close relationship with Line IX. He displayed the same enthusiasm for disciplining his staff. Of course, once again he was merely taking to an extreme a responsibility imposed on him by the party. The Stasi's immense emphasis on political education and disciplinary action was required by the party, which needed the Stasi to be an utterly reliable instrument of political repression. The party organization in the Stasi concerned itself not only with the political reliability of the ministry's staff but also with their private lives; its supervision of them was another reason why the staff was so disciplined and little penetrated by the Western intelligence services.[40]

Mielke's Marxism-Leninism affected the Stasi for the worse in its capacity of intelligence provider to the SED leadership. Of course, there were no independent press or media in the GDR, as a Communist state; the leadership's only sources of information were official ones, which provided information colored by Marxism-Leninism and the party's policies. The Stasi did little to correct this tendency. While the information it provided to the party leaders was among the best available to them, the ministry still did not make clear the extent of popular criticism. Mielke was responsible for this, though here again he acted as the leadership's agent. Reporting on East German public opinion was the most sensitive type of reporting for the Stasi. Since the party claimed to represent the working class, which formed the overwhelming majority of East Germans, the Stasi could not present the population as dissatisfied with the regime. Presenting public opinion as it really was would have undermined the party's claim that Marxism-Leninism rested on a scientific understanding of society, and thus weakened the legitimacy of its rule. The ministry would have risked being seen as an opposition within the party. It would thus have been in danger of infringing the ban, in force since Lenin's time, on the formation of intra-party factions. In fact, the party leadership insisted on not being told what the real situation in the GDR was; it wanted to be told that the construction of a Communist society was proving a success and that all problems came from the outside world. Mielke acquiesced in this because he was an orthodox Marxist-Leninist who believed this paranoid, self-satisfied conspiracy theory and because it was the only way to keep his job, which was his main aim.

He himself acted as the filter through which these reports passed—or did not pass—to the leadership. He frequently forbade that particular reports were sent to the party. From the time he became minister, the Stasi's intelligence assessment staff (from 1965 called the Zentrale Auswertungs- und Informationsgruppe, ZAIG) reported on only those matters the party wanted it to report on. It reported to the party leadership on East German public opinion only a few times each year; its reports consistently played down the extent and severity of popular dissatisfaction over the GDR's many failings. Criticism was always presented as coming from a minority, particularly of the working class. The ZAIG's reporting assumed that the major threat to the GDR came from Western subversion. Most of the reports that went to the leadership (72%) between 1959 and 1989 were foreign intelligence reports, prepared by the HVA, on developments in the Western and developing worlds. Reports on events within the GDR tended to be about security matters—either attacks on the GDR's security by enemy forces (usually in the West or under Western influence) or industrial accidents or economic mismanagement.[41]

Reporting on the state of the economy was another very sensitive matter. Once again, his handling of it demonstrates that Mielke cared more about his position than the GDR's well-being. The SED Politburo always tended to make light of the GDR's economic difficulties and take too optimistic a view of its economic performance. Save in the regime's last days, Mielke did not challenge this in the Politburo, even though he knew full well by the early 1980s that the GDR had grave economic problems.[42] In 1980 officers of the Stasi's Line XVIII, responsible for the security of the East German economy, were told to prepare a report on the state of the economy. They were given access to the most sensitive economic records and reported that the economy was on the point of collapse. Mielke's response was to threaten them with expulsion from the party if they did not moderate their conclusions. They duly did so.[43]

Some of the Stasi's brutality is to be attributed to Mielke personally. In 1984, in front of his officers, he openly expressed frustration that he could not have some of East Germany's dissidents shot.[44] He was fully involved in Stasi efforts in the 1950s to kidnap defectors from its own ranks and those of the police and bring them back to the GDR for trial and punishment. The punishment was usually a long term of imprisonment; sometimes it was death. Among the Stasi's victims was at least one of Mielke's own enemies, Robert Bialek, the former chief political officer of the embryonic East German army, the Barracked People's Police (Kasernierte Volkspolizei), who fled to the West in 1953.[45] He was not the only one behind this policy; Ernst Wollweber was equally merciless.[46] Indeed, the Stasi's entire culture, inherited from its Soviet parent, was one of violence in the service of the party. This is why Mielke felt so at home there. It has also been alleged that in 1950 he personally murdered another German Communist, Willi Kreikemeyer, who might have provided damning information about Mielke's time in France, but there is no convincing evidence to support this claim.[47] Into the 1980s traitors within the Stasi—people who spied for Western intelligence services or planned to flee to the West—were executed, even though the GDR had abolished capital punishment a decade before. The last such execution was that of Werner Teske, an HVA officer, in 1981.[48] Mielke's aim was to deter any defection from their ranks and thus to maintain the security of the ministry.

Mielke had no qualms about ordering his ministry to give training and other assistance to vicious Marxist-Leninist national liberation movements in the third world and to terrorist organizations such as the Palestine Liberation Organization (PLO), the African National Congress, and the Baader-Meinhof Gang. For a quarter of a century, starting in the early 1960s, the Stasi helped to build up the security services and police of brutally repressive regimes in the developing world. Its first foray into the third world was to Ghana, where Stasi officers helped to establish that state's post-independence security agencies in the 1960s. In the 1970s the ministry gave security assistance both to Marxist regimes in Africa and the Middle East—those of Angola, Ethiopia, Mozambique, and South Yemen—and to third world dictators who were seen as worthwhile friends (Idi Amin in Uganda and Francisco Macías Nguema in Equatorial Guinea). The Mozambican and South Yemeni regimes both put their enemies in concentration camps. There were large teams of Stasi advisers in Ethiopia and South Yemen. In the 1980s the Stasi gave security assistance to the Soviet-backed Communist regime in Afghanistan and the Sandinista regime in Nicaragua.

These partnerships with regimes in the developing world naturally led to support for terrorist organizations closely connected with them. Baader-Meinhof Gang terrorists found refuge in the GDR, with the regime's knowledge and assistance, from 1977 on. The Stasi helped them to obtain training in terrorist techniques at PLO camps in Jordan, Lebanon, and South Yemen. It was complicit in crimes the Gang carried out. It also helped Libyan and Palestinian terrorists to murder American servicemen in the attack on the La Belle discotheque in West Berlin in 1986; the ministry knew in advance of the plan for the attack and helped the terrorists transport their explosives to West Berlin. While Mielke would certainly have secured Honecker's approval for this, the decision was also his and reflected his vicious combativeness. He regarded the Baader-Meinhof Gang as an instrument with which to destabilize his main enemy, West Germany. West German Communists were, from the mid-1970s, trained in insurgency techniques in the GDR, just in case the Federal Republic descended into civil strife. Another notorious terrorist, the Venezuelan Ilyich Ramírez Sánchez (known as "Carlos the Jackal"), also found sanctuary in the GDR.[49]

This viciousness harmed the GDR's international standing throughout its short life and helped to bring about its end. George H. W. Bush, the former director of Central Intelligence who became president of the United States in 1989 and strongly supported West Germany's drive for the unification of the two German states from the end of that year, has written in his memoir of that time of his hostility to the GDR and the reasons for it. Writing of a visit he made to West Germany in 1983 as vice president, he recalls:

> I already felt an abhorrence for the German Democratic Republic before this trip. In my CIA days I had seen that East Germany was among the very worst offenders when it came to training terrorists or destabilizing countries. They were perhaps the most aggressive of all in the spying business and would stop at nothing to further their ends. It was the East Germans to whom the Soviets turned to carry out a lot of the ugliest missions. They were the chief bully of the East bloc.[50]

The judgment "the chief bully of the East bloc" applies well to Mielke personally. As his record shows, he was cruel and unscrupulous. There is no evidence of sadism, however; nor is there evidence from any time of his life that points to psychological imbalance. His mental faculties were in steep decline in his last years as minister, but he does not seem to have been fully senile. Despite his failing mental powers, he was still sufficiently compos mentis to realize, in 1989, that Gorbachev's reform policy was encouraging popular opposition in the GDR that was capable of overthrowing the regime. When Leonid Shebarshin, the head of the KGB's First Chief Directorate (PGU), its foreign intelligence service, visited the GDR in 1989, Mielke told him that Gorbachev's reform policy threatened the very existence of the Communist regimes.[51] He gave the same warning that summer to Sergei Kondrashev, one of Shebarshin's senior officers who was vacationing in the GDR, and asked him to pass it on to KGB chairman Vladimir Kryuchkov for transmission to Gorbachev himself.[52] Meeting his officers that summer, Mielke asked them whether there would be a popular uprising.

A careerist, Mielke lusted for office and power. He was still trying to stay in power in 1989, when he was eighty-one. Like the Soviet security chief

Lavrenti Beria before him, he showed cunning by ingratiating himself with his political superiors in the GDR's ruling Socialist Unity Party and the Russians. His success in cultivating them—particularly the leading KGB officials—was the greatest success of his career. He consistently sought to make himself and his ministry appear indispensable in their eyes. He cultivated the SED first secretaries he served obsequiously. His state security ministry obtained Western luxury goods for the Socialist Unity Party leaders just as the KGB did for the Soviet Communist Party's elite (its *nomenklatura*). It even stole such goods from packages sent by West Germans to their East German relatives and friends.[53]

A cunning man, Mielke understood that every senior Communist official had to be a courtier. He displayed political gifts. He always took care to present himself as loyal to the Socialist Unity Party's first secretary. He was always asking senior officials who dealt frequently with the first secretary for the latest news about him. In fact, he betrayed both of the first secretaries he served. He supported Erich Honecker's attempt to overthrow Walter Ulbricht and later supported Egon Krenz's move to overthrow Honecker.[54] He also abandoned his chief, Wilhelm Zaisser, in 1953, when circumstances and Walter Ulbricht turned against the then minister for state security.[55] Seeing that his moment had come, he actively cooperated with Ulbricht when the latter tried in 1957 to drive Wollweber out of the position of minister. So self-important was Mielke that it took him a long time to accept Honecker as his leader—when he had to toast the first secretary, he did so leaving Honecker's name out or mispronouncing it. Instead, he regarded the KGB chairman, Yuri Andropov, as his chief.[56]

His position as minister for state security gave him very good knowledge of the party *nomenklatura*, which he exploited skillfully.[57] He carefully collected damaging information on his party rivals so as to get the better of them in the struggle for power, but he never challenged the political elite. Mielke was careful in how he presented himself to others. Wolf relates that in their discussions Mielke always portrayed himself as a true friend of the Soviet Union.[58] When Gorbachev introduced his reform policy in the Soviet Union, Mielke trod a careful path, publicly proclaiming his loyalty to the Soviet leader and his policies while not distancing himself from his own party leadership's very obvious dislike of them. Although Mielke displayed skill, it was no more than an application of the time-honored maxim "Sniff out, suck up, survive." The Russians rightly read him as an insincere careerist.

The Functionary

Mielke was, above all, a functionary: a man who implemented the will of others. He was the instrument by which Walter Ulbricht and the KGB imposed their will on the Stasi. It is telling that when he finally achieved the position he craved, that of full member of the Politburo, he said little in Politburo meetings. He claimed that this was for security reasons; in reality, he could contribute little to the Politburo's decision making. He became the third most important man in the GDR not because he was able but because his job was so important.

His superiors used Mielke above all to ensure that they were served by a loyal and capable political police. From the earliest days of his time in the police he had responsibility for selecting suitable police officials, weeding out unsuitable ones, and training the police in the Marxist-Leninist worldview.[59]

Obsequious toward his superiors, Mielke bullied his subordinates mercilessly. He was an authoritarian minister whose outbursts of temper grew worse as he got older. His self-importance was vast.[60] His treatment of his subordinates was also condescending: he called them by their surnames and used the familiar form ("*Du*") to address them, whereas most of them had to call him "comrade minister" and use the polite form ("*Sie*") when speaking to him.[61] His birthday parties were spectacular demonstrations of self-importance. They took place at a country estate outside Berlin that served as Mielke's hunting lodge. The guests were serenaded at dinner by a choir of the Stasi's armed force, the "*Wachregiment* Feliks Dzerzhinsky."[62]

Mielke owed his authority to his position, not his abilities. He does not impress as a leader of men (he led very few women since there were few in his ministry). That said, his unquestioned authority as minister from 1957 to 1989 had a beneficial impact on the Stasi, which was not as racked by internal politics and infighting as the KGB. Mielke's ministry had an authoritative head—albeit a mediocre, old, and increasingly senile one. He was loyal to the first secretary (at least most of the time), and the first secretary in turn supported him, as did the KGB.

The GDR relied heavily on Mielke. Such a fragile state could only survive thanks to a powerful, ruthless political police; the Stasi was therefore created in 1949–50, as the GDR itself was being founded. Since the Stalinists who led the SED were convinced of the correctness of Marxism-Leninism, any criticism of the regime or Communist society among East Germans was regarded as the subversive work of the class enemy rather than a natural development. Suppressing it therefore became a task for the Stasi, whose minister steadily rose in importance and influence until by the mid-1980s he was the third most powerful man in the state after the party leader Erich Honecker and the overseer of the economy Günter Mittag. Together with the KGB, the SED, and his own officers, Mielke did play a role in making the Stasi the effective security service it was. It always bore his brutal stamp. However, rather than he being the making of it, it was the making of him.

Conclusion

Throughout all his years in the Stasi, Mielke followed a few simple rules: satisfy both the Russians and the party; ingratiate yourself with the party leader for as long as he is in firm control of the party; keep a close eye out for dissent by assembling the best force of informers you can; and maintain the ministry's security—by political education, disciplinary measures, and if necessary, kidnapping and murder. He had the ambition, diligence, combativeness, cunning, and good health to follow these rules successfully, which kept him in office for thirty-two years.

His greatest success was to win the KGB's backing. The Russians became strong supporters of his because he was an exponent of the conservative Communism in which they believed. He was just as committed as they were to fighting the "class enemy," both in the GDR and beyond its borders, and created a security regime to do this that resembled theirs. By the 1960s they were impressed with the degree of security that the Stasi had achieved in the GDR. He imposed an extremely strict security regime with the brutal aggression that so characterized him. Ehrhart Neubert's judgment on him is a good one: "Mielke personified the criminal energy of the Stalinist communists from the 1930s until the end of the GDR."[63]

Notes

1. See Jan von Flocken and Michael F. Scholz, *Ernst Wollweber: Saboteur-Minister-Unperson* (Berlin: Aufbau-Verlag, 1994).

2. David Murphy, Sergei Kondrashev, and George Bailey, *Battleground Berlin: CIA vs. KGB in the Cold War* (New Haven, CT: Yale University Press, 1997), 293.

3. Ibid., 130–32, 292–93.

4. Heribert Schwan, *Erich Mielke: der Mann, der die Stasi war* [Erich Mielke: The man who was the Stasi] (Munich: Droemer Knaur, 1997), 375–86.

5. Wilfriede Otto, *Erich Mielke–Biographie: Aufstieg und Fall eines Tschekisten* [Erich Mielke—biography: Rise and fall of a *chekist*] (Berlin: Dietz Verlag, 2000), 445.

6. Reinhold Andert and Wolfgang Herzberg, *Der Sturz: Erich Honecker im Kreuzverhör* [The fall: Erich Honecker cross-examined] (Berlin: Aufbau-Verlag, 1990), 376.

7. von Flocken and Scholz, *Ernst Wollweber*, 151, 175, 185.

8. Jens Giesecke, "Erich Mielke (1907–2000). Revolverheld und Oberster DDR-Tschekist," in *Konspiration als Beruf: Deutsche Geheimdienstchefs im Kalten Krieg* [Secrecy as an occupation: German secret service chiefs in the Cold War], ed. Dieter Krüger and Armin Wagner (Berlin: Christoph Links Verlag, 2003), 253.

9. Amy Knight, *The KGB: Police and Politics in the Soviet Union* (Boston: Unwin Hyman, 1988), 53–54.

10. Christopher Andrew and Vasili Mitrokhin, *The Mitrokhin Archive: The KGB in Europe and the West* (London: Allen Lane / Penguin Press, 1999), 324–25.

11. See, for example, Otto, *Erich Mielke–Biographie*, 370–74, 375–76.

12. Andrew and Mitrokhin, *Mitrokhin Archive*, 405–14.

13. Ehrhart Neubert, *Geschichte der Opposition in der DDR 1949–1989* [History of the opposition in the GDR 1949–1989] (Bonn: Bundeszentrale für Politische Bildung, 1997), 224–27. The regime had already in 1973 invited Biermann to leave the GDR and settle in the Federal Republic.

14. Andrew and Mitrokhin, *Mitrokhin Archive*, 400.

15. Knight, *The KGB*, 200–14.

16. Ibid., 193–97.

17. Gieseke, "Erich Mielke (1907–2000). Revolverheld und Oberster DDR-Tschekist," 259.

18. Jens Gieseke, *Der Mielke-Konzern: Die Geschichte der Stasi, 1945–1990* [The Mielke business: The history of the Stasi, 1945–1990] (Munich: Deutsche Verlags-Anstalt, 2006), 217–21; and Schwan, *Erich Mielke*, 137.

19. Paul Maddrell, "Im Fadenkreuz der Stasi: Westliche Spionage in der DDR. Die Akten der Hauptabteilung IX," *Vierteljahrshefte für Zeitgeschichte* 61, no. 2 (2013): 141–71.

20. Murphy, Kondrashev, and Bailey, *Battleground Berlin*, 351–52.

21. Oleg Kalugin, *Spymaster: My 32 Years in Intelligence and Espionage against the West* (London: Smith Gryphon, 1994), 173–74.

22. Werner Großmann, *Bonn im Blick: die DDR-Aufklärung aus der Sicht ihres letzten Chefs* [Bonn in view: The GDR foreign intelligence service from the perspective of its last head] (Berlin: Das Neue Berlin, 2001), 113, 177.

23. Jens Gieseke, *Die hauptamtlichen Mitarbeiter der Staatssicherheit: Personalstruktur und Lebenswelt, 1950–1989/90* [The staff of the State Security Service: Their personnel structure and the world they lived in, 1950–1989/90] (Berlin: Ch. Links Verlag, 2000), 165.

24. See Armin Wagner, *Walter Ulbricht und die geheime Sicherheitspolitik der SED: der Nationale Verteidigungsrat der DDR und seine Vorgeschichte (1953 bis 1971)* [Walter Ulbricht and the secret security policy of the SED: The National Defense Council of the GDR and its early history (1953 to 1971)] (Berlin: Ch. Links Verlag, 2002); and Wagner, "Der Nationale Verteidigungsrat als sicherheitspolitisches Exekutivorgan der SED," in *Staatspartei und Staatssicherheit. Zum Verhältnis von SED und MfS* [State Party and State Security: On the relationsip between SED and MfS], ed. Siegfried Suckut and Walter Süß (Berlin: Ch. Links Verlag, 1997), 169–98.

25. Markus Wolf, *In Eigenem Auftrag: Bekenntnisse und Einsichten* [On my own behalf: Avowals and insights] (Berlin: Schwarzkopf and Schwarzkopf, 1999), 214–15.

26. Schwan, *Erich Mielke*, 51.

27. Gieseke, *Die hauptamtlichen Mitarbeiter der Staatssicherheit*, 354–59, 545–46; and John O. Koehler, *Stasi: The Untold Story of the East German Secret Police* (Boulder, CO: Westview Press, 1999), 330.

28. Wolf, *In Eigenem Auftrag*, 215.

29. Alexander Schalck-Golodkowski, *Deutsch-deutsche Erinnerungen* [German-German recollections] (Reinbek bei Hamburg: Rowohlt Verlag, 2000), 235–36.

30. Nationale Volksarmee: National People's Army. "VA/NVA" stands for Verwaltung Aufklärung / Nationale Volksarmee: Intelligence Directorate, National People's Army.

31. Georg Herbstritt, *Bundesbürger im Dienst der DDR-Spionage: Eine analytische Studie* [Citizens of the Federal Republic in the service of GDR espionage: An analytical study] (Göttingen: Vandenhoeck and Ruprecht, 2007), 84.

32. Peter Siebenmorgen, *"Staatssicherheit" der DDR: Der Westen im Fadenkreuz der Stasi* ["State Security" of the GDR: The West in the Stasi's sights] (Bonn: Bouvier Verlag, 1993), 130–31.

33. Großmann, *Bonn im Blick*, 120.

34. The Socialist Unity Party's leader was known as the general secretary from 1950 to 1953 and from 1976 to 1989. From 1953 to 1976 he was known as the first secretary.

35. Gieseke, *Der Mielke-Konzern*, 114–16.

36. Großmann, *Bonn im Blick*, 159, 178.

37. Gieseke, *Die hauptamtlichen Mitarbeiter der Staatssicherheit*, 15.

38. Ibid., 227–30, 293–96, 368–69, 536–37.

39. Karl Wilhelm Fricke and Roger Engelmann, *"Konzentrierte Schläge": Staatssicherheitsaktionen und politische Prozesse in der DDR, 1953–1956* ["Concentrated blows": State Security operations and political trials in the GDR, 1953–1956] (Berlin: Ch. Links Verlag, 1998), 107.

40. Gieseke, *Die hauptamtlichen Mitarbeiter der Staatssicherheit*, 155; and Silke Schumann, *Parteierziehung in der Geheimpolizei. Zur Rolle der SED im MfS der fünfziger Jahre* [Party training in the secret police: On the role of the SED in the Stasi of the 1950s] (Berlin: Ch. Links Verlag, 1997), 83–84.

41. Jens Gieseke, "Annäherungen und Fragen an die 'Meldungen aus der Republik,'" in *Staatssicherheit und Gesellschaft* [State Security and society], ed. Jens Gieseke (Göttingen: Vandenhoeck and Ruprecht, 2007), 81–87, 92–93, 97; and David Childs and Richard Popplewell, *The Stasi: The East German Intelligence and Security Service* (London: Macmillan Press, 1996), 179.

42. Schalck-Golodkowski, *Deutsch-deutsche Erinnerungen*, 149, 153, 230; and Wolf, *In Eigenem Auftrag*, 169.

43. Maria Haendcke-Hoppe-Arndt, "Wer wußte was? Der ökonomische Niedergang der DDR," in *Rückblicke auf die DDR* [The GDR in retrospect], ed. Gisela Helwig (Cologne: Edition Deutschland Archiv/Verlag Wissenschaft und Politik, 1995), 125–26.

44. Gieseke, *Die hauptamtlichen Mitarbeiter der Staatssicherheit*, 451.

45. See Michael Herms and Gert Noack, *Aufstieg und Fall des Robert Bialek* [Rise and fall of Robert Bialek] (Berlin: edition ost, 1998). Bialek was kidnapped by the Stasi in West Berlin in February 1956 and taken to East Berlin, where he is believed to have died in captivity.

46. Gieseke, *Die hauptamtlichen Mitarbeiter der Staatssicherheit*, 206–8.

47. See Wolfgang Kießling, *"Leistner ist Mielke." Schatten einer gefälschten*

Biographie ["Leistner ist Mielke." Shadows of a falsified biography] (Berlin: Aufbau Taschenbuch Verlag), 1998.

48. Childs and Popplewell, *The Stasi*, 81, 161.

49. Ibid., *The Stasi*, 136–41; and Michael Müller and Andreas Kanonenberg, *Die RAF-Stasi-Connection* [The RAF-Stasi connection] (Berlin: Rowohlt, 1992), 73–75.

50. George Bush and Brent Scowcroft, *A World Transformed* (New York: Alfred A. Knopf, 1998), 183.

51. Großmann, *Bonn im Blick*, 159.

52. Murphy, Kondrashev, and Bailey, *Battleground Berlin*, 397.

53. Schalck-Golodkowski, *Deutsch-deutsche Erinnerungen*, 215–27.

54. Wolf, *In Eigenem Auftrag*, 27.

55. Childs and Popplewell, *The Stasi*, 56.

56. Wolf, *In Eigenem Auftrag*, 179–82.

57. Ibid., 77.

58. Ibid., 35.

59. Gieseke, *Die hauptamtlichen Mitarbeiter der Staatssicherheit*, 69–70.

60. Kalugin, *Spymaster*, 174.

61. Großmann, *Bonn im Blick*, 177.

62. Schalck-Golodkowski, *Deutsch-deutsche Erinnerungen*, 237–38.

63. Neubert, *Geschichte der Opposition in der DDR*, 95.

6 Markus Wolf

From the Shadows to the Limelight

Kristie Macrakis

During the Cold War, Markus Wolf (1923–2006), chief of East German foreign intelligence (the HVA, Hauptverwaltung Aufklärung), was known as "the man without a face," a man of mystery who avoided the media. He was so elusive that for most of the Cold War West German intelligence did not even have a recent picture of him. It was not until 1979, when defector Werner Stiller identified him in an observation photograph, that Western German intelligence knew what he looked like. The photograph was then provided to *Der Spiegel*, West Germany's equivalent to *Time* or *Newsweek*, and the magazine displayed Wolf's image as its cover photograph. Although he then finally had a face, Wolf never appeared in public as the head of East German intelligence. He did not go public until the fall of the Berlin Wall in November 1989 when he courted the media with a new mission and new career.

In this chapter, I will argue that Markus Wolf was an effective Eastern Bloc spy chief who exemplified Soviet Communism's principle of strict secrecy when it came to intelligence leadership. Unlike American espionage during much of the Cold War, complete secrecy, and the associated avoidance of the media, was the fundamental principle of the intelligence profession. East Germany and the rest of the Soviet Bloc was a closed society, not an open one like the United States with freedom of the press and other hallmarks of democracy. After the fall of the Berlin Wall, however, Wolf took on a new leadership role—that of spokesman and advocate for his former staff members as well as a public book author. While he was now in the limelight, he used the opportunity to manipulate the media for his former staff members as well as out of egotism.

The example of Markus Wolf offers a window on the difference between intelligence leaders in the Eastern Bloc and the West during the Cold War. What role did national (I will argue he represented an Eastern Bloc, not a German, style), institutional (the HVA as part of the Ministry for State Security),

Photo 6.1 Markus Wolf (second from right, striking the glass of the GDR's leader Walter Ulbricht with his own). The photograph was taken in January 1970. Wolf was here attending a reception hosted by Ulbricht to celebrate the Stasi's twentieth anniversary. Source: *Der Bundesbeauftragte für die Unterlagen des Staatssicher heitsdienstes der ehemaligen Deutschen Demokratischen Republik (BStU, The Federal Commissioner for the Records of the State Security Service of the former German Democratic Republic)*

and historical (divided Germany in the Cold War) factors play in defining Wolf as a leader? Although Wolf was a public enigma during the Cold War, he was an admired leader within his espionage fiefdom as well as in the West. What qualities did he possess that earned him the respect of his subordinates? Finally, I will show that Wolf's leadership mattered until the Ministry for State Security / HVA became an ossified bureaucracy in its later years. When intelligence services become huge and unwieldy bureaucracies, an intelligence leader loses significance and power and becomes a ceremonial figurehead.

Although Wolf's career offers a window into larger issues surrounding Cold War spy chiefs, he was also unique in the annals of intelligence history for two reasons: Not only was he the longest-serving spy chief in history, he was also the youngest. He became head of foreign intelligence at the age of twenty-nine and served for thirty-four years, providing plenty of time to become a legend and earn the respect of friends and foes alike.

Unlike the Western model, Wolf as intelligence chief was not answerable to the Politburo or oversight committees when it came to potential abuses of intelligence. Behind the Iron Curtain there were no senate select committees, no media watchdogs, and no public accountability. The society was secretive, the government was secret, and more appropriately, intelligence and state security were top secret.

It should not come as a surprise that intelligence leaders and their institutions value secrecy. Even in the United States, the land of intelligence leaks, secrecy was still highly valued up to the Church Committee hearings in the 1970s. Furthermore, the United States had a unique media ethos; leaks became increasingly commonplace. In contrast to the West, the Eastern Bloc kept to a strict secrecy ethos, in part because it was more totalitarian, in part because the party controlled the media and the party was always right, and in part because secret intelligence is meant to stay secret.

The Making of an Obedient Communist Spy Chief

Markus Wolf never planned on becoming a spy, let alone a spy chief for thirty-four years. When I interviewed him, he told me, "Actually I wanted to become an aerospace engineer and was interested in a scientific-technical profession."[1] But the party was always right and continued to put him where it needed him during turning points in politics, thus shaping his career. Even though he had had other career plans, once he became a spy chief he did the job with "great passion and aplomb."[2]

Unlike many other Eastern Bloc intelligence leaders or functionaries, Wolf came from a bourgeois intellectual family—not a farmer's or worker's family as did all of the other East German Ministry for State Security leaders. Because he was born into an intellectual Jewish family in Hechingen, a town in the western part of Germany, Markus Wolf's biography diverges considerably from most of the other intelligence leaders in the Eastern Bloc. This did not matter to his colleagues, who recognized that he had earned his passage to East Germany because he had had to flee the Nazis.

His family background helped facilitate his rise as a trusted Communist functionary and protected him later as a spy chief. His father, Friedrich Wolf, a noted Communist playwright and physician, moved the family to the Soviet Union after Adolf Hitler's rise to power in 1933. During the period of exile in Moscow, Wolf initially attended the German Karl Liebknecht School, but later, wanting to become an aerospace engineer, he entered the Moscow Institute of Airplane Engineering. After five semesters of studying aerospace engineering he was told to join the Comintern—the Communist International—where he was trained for the "secret war against the Hitler regime in Germany."[3] He learned how to conduct undercover work behind enemy lines and was filled with Communist ideology, studied the history of the workers' movement, and learned about Marxism-Leninism in depth. He was also trained to "follow orders without question."[4] This might be difficult for Westerners to understand, but dedicated Communists thought that "the party was always right."

Wolf's recruitment was part of the Soviet effort to find Germans with ties and loyalty to the Soviet Union to send back to Germany after the war. It was a small pool. From the time the war ended in 1945 until he retired, Wolf held posts ordinarily occupied by more senior people. He had been groomed for them from an early age.

Just as the party had sent him to the Comintern school, it also sent him to the German Communist radio school in Moscow. He was ordered to become a journalist after the Comintern school closed in 1943. When Wolf arrived in Moscow, two of his friends from the school joined him. Like Wolf, Wolfgang Leonhard and Helmut Gennys were part of the Communist elite. From Moscow's perspective, they seemed suitable and destined for greatness. Now they were near the leadership center of the exiled German Communist Party.[5]

In his 1951 curriculum vitae Wolf writes that "the party leadership (Gen. Pieck u. Ulbricht)" sent him to "Institute 205," a secretive-sounding former Comintern school that now housed various Communist Party radio stations. Many years after the fall of the Berlin Wall, Wolf explained in his memoir that he was asked to join the "German People's Broadcasting Station" (*Deutscher Volkssender*), the German Communist Party station, as an announcer and commentator because his father was a famous author.[6] He learned his new journalism trade from the more experienced German journalists at the station and was also a radio announcer. But more important for his later career, he also hobnobbed with future East German leaders like Wilhelm Pieck, Walter Ulbricht, and Anton Ackermann.[7]

Wolf's first postwar assignment as a Berlin radio announcer was to cover the trials of Nazi war criminals in Nuremberg, Germany, in the fall of 1945. He reported on the events for the Soviet-controlled Berlin radio as "Michael Sturm" (in English, "Michael Storm"). In fact, Wolf's Nuremberg ID picture was the first picture to land in the CIA's file on him. It was also to be the last for a very long time.

At some point during his time in Berlin, Wolf brought up his unfinished aeronautic engineering studies in Moscow, but Ulbricht told him, "We are not building airplanes in the Soviet Union now, we are working in areas that are necessary here in Berlin."[8] Wolf never did graduate or obtain a degree from a university. For Ulbricht, everyone had a function or task, and Wolf followed orders well. He was called back to Moscow in 1949, and at the age of twenty-six he became first counselor to the ambassador at the GDR embassy in Moscow. Despite his youth and previous training as a journalist, one of his greatest assets was that he was seen as a Russian. Indeed, one of the reasons he succeeded and survived in his career was that the Russians trusted him completely. He was Moscow's man in East Berlin. Not only did they trust him, but according to a former deputy, his Russian was so good he was often asked to speak at Soviet meetings in East Berlin.[9]

Given his closeness to the German Communist Party leadership in exile, it is not surprising that Anton Ackermann called him back to East Berlin to work at the new Foreign Political Intelligence Service (Aussenpolitischer Nachrichtendienst, APN). What is surprising is that Wolf had no intelligence training or experience outside the Comintern school. But, again, he followed his orders. The APN operated under the cover of an institute for economics (Institut für Wirtschaftswissenschaftliche Forschung, IWF). According to Wolf, when he arrived there were eight staff members and four Soviet liaison officers. The new foreign intelligence service was modeled on Soviet intelligence and emphasized political and scientific-technical intelligence collection. Ackermann "was and remained his mentor,"[10] taking Wolf under his wing and training him in the art of intelligence.

Either Ackermann must have been supremely impressed with Wolf or there were no other viable candidates, because when Ackermann fell ill in 1952 and wanted to devote more time to his Politburo duties, he recommended the twenty-nine-year-old Wolf as his replacement. This was after only one year on the job.

Gerhard Heidenreich, one of the former old Communist "illegals" who ran the Institute for Economic Research, also played a role in Wolf's quick rise to leadership. According to Heidenreich, Wolf never opposed Ulbricht openly, while he privately supported Ackermann, who was expelled from the Politburo and fired as acting minister of foreign affairs in October 1953 because he opposed Ulbricht. It was this ability to speak out of two sides of his mouth while not openly criticizing his superiors—like many diplomats—that helped Wolf to survive for so long as spy chief. Heidenreich admired Wolf and said in an interview that "he was a friend of the Soviet Union and absolutely trustworthy."[11]

Wolf Survives the Vulkan Affair

Right before the Easter holiday, on April 9, 1953, Gotthold Kraus, an IWF deputy head of department and mole for the CIA, defected to West Germany. He brought a list of thirty-eight agent names to the West along with knowledge of the IWF and Markus Wolf. Although Kraus was the CIA's Berlin Base mole, the agency shared the information with West German counterintelligence. The West Germans dubbed this operation "Vulkan," or "Volcano" in English. It was indeed IWF's "baptism by fire" as well as Wolf's baptism ceremony. It was his first crisis, but he survived it unscathed. The minister for state security, Wilhelm Zaisser, simply told him: "Mischa, you have to learn more and more about many things."[12]

One of the reasons he survived was his youth; another was that he was Moscow's man in East Berlin. Aside from following orders well, Wolf's youth allowed the Soviet advisers to boss him around without resistance. Some of the valuable papers Kraus brought with him to the West included the minutes to a meeting the day after Stalin's death. The papers revealed that Wolf, who admitted he was a Stalinist at the time, sat in a two-hour meeting with the Soviets before reporting back to his IWF staff. According to the vague reports, when Wolf did report back, he simply conveyed what the Soviets wished and recommended that it be carried out.[13]

As a result of Kraus's defection, the CIA was also able to learn more about Markus Wolf and find out what he looked like. Curiously, the mole never took Wolf's picture or passed one on. Instead, the CIA, having learned that Wolf reported from the Nuremberg trials, asked an analyst in the graphics registry to screen over one thousand pictures from the Nuremberg trials available at the National Archives. She then selected sixteen pictures that might be Wolf. Kraus was able to identify "without a doubt" Mischa Wolf at the age of twenty-two to twenty-three.[14]

Even though the CIA eventually found a picture of Wolf, West German intelligence and the media did not have one. When *Der Spiegel* broke the story about the IWF, they named Wolf publicly for the first time as the "Head of the Soviet Zone's Institute for Economic Research located in East Berlin at Luisenstrasse 4."[15]

Apparently West German intelligence thought they had a picture of Wolf dating back to 1959. It was not published in the media until the magazine *Der Spiegel* printed it in 1979 as part of the Werner Stiller story. It is a curious picture as it does not resemble other pictures of Wolf. It appears not to be Wolf at all—his nose is smaller; he is wearing nickel, intellectual-looking glasses and has an arrogant look on his face. Even so, this was to be the only picture West German intelligence thought they had of Markus Wolf until 1979, which was why he began to be known as the "man without a face" by Western intelligence and the media.

The CIA and West German counterintelligence also learned from the mole that "Ackermann thought a great deal of WOLF, and so did the Russians. . . . ULBRICHT was not in favor of his appointment as head of the IWF. ACKERMANN and the Russians, however, were able to overrule ULBRICHT. He was known in the IWF as 'Genosse [Comrade] Mischa.'"[16]

Given the Soviets' history of gerontocracy, it is surprising that Ackermann's deputies—Richard Stahlmann or Gustav Szinda (both veteran

Communists)—were not chosen. Stahlmann, who was already sixty-one years old, "gracefully accepted the role as Wolf's deputy." (Szinda was fifty-five, a good age for a leader.) Wolf later said that Stahlmann was "the true organizer of our foreign intelligence" who stood "side by side with Soviet intelligence." In fact, Wolf always had two Soviet advisers by his side, who were as "drunk by . . . zealousness and philosophizing" as he was (in other words, intoxicated by Communist ideology and its implementation).[17] This would suggest that Wolf was a bit of a puppet at first, operated by his senior colleagues and Soviet intelligence.

Interestingly, at the time Wolf became head of East German foreign intelligence, West German intelligence existed only as the Gehlen Organization and was run and financed by the United States of America. Not until 1956 did the Gehlen Organization become an official West German intelligence agency (the Federal Intelligence Service, or Bundesnachrichtendienst [BND] in German). Reinhard Gehlen, a German Wehrmacht officer, remained the head until he reached retirement age in 1968.

Another key to Wolf's success as a leader was probably his unflappable personality. When I interviewed him about the HVA's Sector for Science and Technology, he was totally calm when I mentioned the defector Werner Stiller, unlike his colleagues in the sector who turned red in the face with anger when I mentioned the name. Wolf told me coolly: "He's not my friend."[18]

There are also earlier pieces of evidence showing that he was always sedate—even a West German dossier described his manner this way. Indeed, Kraus indicated in the 1950s that "he speaks calmly and intelligently. . . . [Kraus] has never seen him really excited." Second, his old friend from Comintern days, Wolfgang Leonhard, pegged him as "the type of clever, calm functionary who stands in the background, who sees everything as a big chess game when other comrades take it seriously, fight for it and are enthusiastic about it."[19]

Given Wolf's successful use of the "Romeo" method and charm with women, I am often asked what he was like in person. I found him easy to talk to, very smart, and remarkably down-to-earth for a mythical spy chief. He was more intellectual and well-spoken than the other officers I had talked to. He was very helpful and often anticipated my questions before I asked them. Since he knew I was interested in scientific-technological intelligence (S&TI), he asked if he could put me in touch with the head of the sector. Although I had already talked to the head of the S&TI sector, I did not find him as forthcoming with information as Wolf. Many years later I learned that he had indeed called Horst Vogel and told him about me and that I was "very good."

Given these character traits, it was surprising that he seemed very Eastern European in his mind-set and manners since his focus was on the West.

When I arrived at the café meeting, he was sitting in a chair with his suit jacket over his shoulders. He also projected some former Eastern European ways of doing things. For example, at the time I interviewed him, Germans did not need a visa to visit the United States for a short stay, yet he was looking for an invitation from me to come to America. (Of course, Wolf would have been apprehended if he had tried to travel.)

As Wolf grew into the role of spy chief, other personality traits emerged that seemed to contribute to the respect he earned from his staff members. They included "a confident manner, his intellectual aura, and . . . his aloofness."[20] Gabriele Gast, one of Wolf's prized agents in the BND, also thought that Wolf had a "certain aura" or charisma and that he was aware of "his effect" on people. Gast did not find him as aloof as her own spy chief, BND president Gerhard Wessel, who had more of a military bearing appropriate to his background, but of course, she met Wolf at many informal, vacation-style meeting places like the Yugoslavian coast.[21]

One of his former deputies thought Wolf was a great leader because he was "highly intelligent," he knew how to "interact with people," he did not boss people around, he "listened," and was "not arrogant." His successor, Werner Großmann, described him as a "strategic thinker." Two former deputies— one his successor, Großmann—also described him as a "buddy." Interestingly, both deputies lived in the same bungalow-style apartment building as Wolf in the Oberseestrasse in the Obersee lake district of East Berlin. Therefore, Wolf was not just a boss but also a friend they knew intimately—their experience of him was "up close and personal."[22]

But Wolf had a darker personality trait that became clear to me when I interviewed him for my book *Seduced by Secrets*. He told me that the key to successful agent recruitment was "using human weaknesses." When I mentioned a journalist friend, he said "journalists are there to be used."[23] Probably his most sordid manipulation of human weaknesses was the famed "Romeo" method. Wolf and his staff sent male case officers to Bonn and used them to seduce lonely women secretaries with access to top-secret files. Wolf's flippant remark to critics of the method: "the affairs produced many happy marriages."[24] And even a couple of emotionally scarred women and a suicide, we might add.

For Wolf, the Romeos represented just one of a handful of motivations for spying, including ideology, money, frustrated ambitions, and personal attraction. The idea was to use any one of the motivations to exploit that human weakness. The Romeo method does not appear to be a brilliant innovation masterminded by Wolf (unlike the KGB's use of women "swallows"). If anything, it shows that the HVA was male-dominated. It just so happened that the HVA sent a lot of males to work in West Germany, as Wolf admits in the German-language version of his memoir: "most of the scouts that we sent to the West were single men."[25]

Interestingly, in my analysis of the CIA-acquired Rosenholz materials containing the code names and real names of agents, the motivations mentioned previously are listed, and the term used for what came to be known as the Romeo method is "personal attraction." This motivation went both ways—men could recruit women and women could recruit men. In addition, it helped to recruit an agent if he or she took a liking to the case officer and a friendship developed without a sexual relationship. Moreover, none of the secretaries who worked for the science and technology sector did it for love; rather, ideology and money were the most common motivations.[26]

Not everyone liked Markus Wolf. Some former staff members said he possessed the same "weaknesses of all power politicians." They found him "unapproachable, often subtly arrogant, cold and calculating, and [he] never let success leave his gaze. He cultivated a cult around himself . . . that flattered his sense of self."[27] Peter Richter and Klaus Rößler continue that he often placed by his side and advanced weak people so that he looked good. In the end, this contributed to the decline of the service, they claim. There is also no doubt that Wolf did not fit the typical GDR personality because of his intellectual and bourgeois background.

After the Vulkan affair, Wolf reorganized the APN/IWF, making it more decentralized with offices scattered around East Berlin. In the spring of 1953 the APN/IWF became part of the Ministry for State Security under Wilhelm Zaisser. It became Department XV in the ministry and was renamed HVA in 1956. After Zaisser was dismissed in July 1953, Ernst Wollweber became the Stasi's chief, only to be succeeded in 1957 by Erich Mielke, who stayed on as the "man who was the Stasi" until 1989.[28]

After the crises of the 1950s subsided, the HVA started to thrive under Wolf. His foreign intelligence service certainly profited from the division of Germany. East and West Germany shared the same language and culture. Operatives did not have to learn a new language or even travel very far to reach the institutions they penetrated. In that respect, West Germany was an easy target. The late 1950s were considered the Golden Age of the HVA as Wolf sent migrant-agents in the stream of citizens fleeing to the West. The migrant-agents were sometimes students groomed to work in the political and scientific nerve centers of West Germany, both in Bonn and at nuclear power centers. By the 1960s, the students had penetrated West Germany's most important institutions, and the service was thriving.

During the 1960s a couple of HVA spies were caught in West Germany, and Wolf's name came up again in the media, especially the BND's favorite magazine for leaking information—*Der Spiegel*. Two notable cases from the

1960s included Harold Gottfried, an atomic spy, and Hannsheinz Porst of the famed West German photography shops.

Porst found the dapper and well-dressed Wolf, who wore "well-cut suits," to be warm in a distant way with a good sense of humor, describing him as cultured and refined. He enjoyed his company because he could talk about ideas that did not "belong to the official repertoire." Even though Porst was a millionaire, Wolf charmed him into spying for East Germany in order to direct him into spying against a political party. Porst secretly joined the East German Socialist Unity Party (SED) in 1958 and became a mole in West Germany's liberal Free Democratic Party (FDP). Porst did not recognize the division of Germany and provided financing to both parties; his motto was "I'm a millionaire and a Marxist."[29]

This big case brought Wolf into the limelight again and provided fodder for his legend to grow. According to *Der Spiegel*, West German counterintelligence dossiers described Wolf in this way: "Wolf possesses an excellent memory, is unusually intelligent, combines his sharp intellect with kindness and camaraderie, and never uses an ordering tone of voice. He never raises his voice, and he has a calm worldliness. He is confident and ironic but not hurtful."[30]

The Günter Guillaume Affair

Even though Markus Wolf was an enigma in the West during the Cold War, there were several other intelligence fiascos that brought his service and his name into the media. In fact, whenever an agent was caught or someone defected, Wolf's name was mentioned in the media. Most notable, because of its impact on international affairs, was the unmasking of Günter Guillaume as a spy working as an assistant to West German federal chancellor Willy Brandt. The affair had unintended consequences.

The HVA sent Günter Guillaume and his wife Christel to West Germany in 1956 with the flow of migrants. They were supposed to establish themselves and worm their way into political circles. They joined West Germany's Social Democratic Party (SPD), and by 1972 Günter had become Chancellor Willy Brandt's personal aide, with access to the federal chancellor's secrets. Willy Brandt, Germany's first left-of-center chancellor for forty years, resigned his post when Guillaume was exposed as a spy for the HVA. Though Wolf is often praised for planting an agent in the chancellor's office, he admits that Brandt's resignation was entirely unintended, and the affair represented one of the HVA's biggest failures. Of course, the scandal made headline news, and Wolf was in the press again.[31]

In a 1974 article in *Der Spiegel* about the Guillaume affair, the author noted that the "HVA-Chief Wolf is both admired and feared professionally by his intelligence adversaries in the West." Not only that, but a former BND head of department considered the "Wolf apparatus the best currently functioning secret service."[32] Indeed, planting an agent in the federal chancellery was seen as a great success, and Wolf's HVA had already secured its reputation as one of the world's best spy agencies by the 1970s.

The Defection of Werner Stiller

On January 18, 1979, Werner Stiller, an officer in the HVA's Sector for Science and Technology, defected in West Berlin to West Germany. Wolf's deputy called him the next day, his birthday, to tell him the news. Like most people in his position confronted with such news, he cursed. But his letting off steam did not match Erich Mielke's reaction when he called Wolf to inform him that his speeches were now in the enemy's hands. Mielke screamed into Wolf's ear on the emergency phone: "What a f- - - - - -g shambles! We might as well just invite the enemy to attend our meetings and be done with it! You all make me sick."[33]

After his arrival in West Berlin, West German intelligence moved Stiller to a high-security apartment building in Munich near the Pullach headquarters of the BND. Stiller's debriefing lasted a little more than a year. As part of the debriefing process, the BND laid some pictures before him, and Stiller confirmed Wolf's identity in Swedish observation photographs of Wolf with his second wife, Christa, in Stockholm. Swedish authorities had become suspicious of the distinguished-looking East German named Dr. Kurt Werner and dispatched an agent to take his picture along with his wife (it turned out that he was meeting a NATO agent as well as Dr. Friedrich Cremer, who was the SPD Mayor of Lengfurt). Now, for the first time, West German intelligence had an up-to-date picture of Markus Wolf. Rather than keep the picture for its files, the BND leaked it to *Der Spiegel*. The "man without a face" had become visible to all. Wolf's image was plastered all over the West German news media, including a cover story on Stiller's defection published in *Der Spiegel* in March 1979.[34]

West German intelligence was elated; the Stiller defection was a real coup, and they celebrated it for many years after that. This glee was reflected in the comments made in the numerous interviews I conducted with West German security officials about Werner Stiller for my book on East German scientific and technological espionage. Their enthusiasm and triumphalism is also reflected in the subtitle to the major *Der Spiegel* article used by the BND for propaganda purposes: "The most important defector from spy central in the GDR lugged suitcases full of secret files and microfilms to the West—a painful defeat for Gen. Markus Wolf's East Berlin foreign espionage unit."[35] Yet again, Wolf was mentioned as the responsible leader.

Although Wolf was called the "man without a face" in the West, Wolf says "he never felt like a man without a face." Later, many years after his retirement, he claimed that anyone could have seen him at East German parades in Berlin. "That no photos of me existed has more to do with the incompetence of Western journalists. I sat in the first row of every May parade. If a Western journalist had asked a GDR colleague who Mischa Wolf is, then there would have been photos earlier."[36] It is doubtful that an East German journalist would have tipped off a Western journalist, and besides, there were no photographs of Markus Wolf in East German newspapers and magazines either. I scoured the whole news archive of *Neues Deutschland* (the organ of the Socialist Unity Party and the most visible and widely circulated newspaper in the GDR), and it mentions him only a few times when he was promoted to general and the Socialist Unity Party congratulated him on his sixtieth birthday. He was also pictured in *Neues Deutschland* at the funeral in 1982 of his brother Konrad Wolf, the noted film director. *Der Spiegel* noted the publication of this picture as an "embarrassing slip-up" for the Socialist Unity Party's "PR-Work."[37] By the 1980s Wolf was increasingly in the limelight.

Although the press makes a big deal about the lack of a picture, the issue really boils down to the fact that East Germany was a closed society draped with a thick cloak of secrecy. As part of the state's control of Communist society, the East German media were state-run and thus under the party's control. East German newspapers did not leak secrets; therefore, their intelligence agencies did not have to stand up for themselves in the state-run media.

Even with the two major setbacks of the Guillaume affair and the Stiller defection in the 1970s, Wolf's reputation only grew. But unfortunately, so did the service's bureaucracy. From these two cases it was clear that the HVA had well-placed agents in industry and government offices. As Oleg Kalugin, a former KGB general, noted: "The East German foreign intelligence agency, headed by the brilliant Markus Wolf, had so deeply penetrated the West German government, military and secret services that all we had to do was lie back and stay out of Wolf's way."[38]

Other glowing assessments praised Wolf's spy agency for acquiring the lion's share of material for their hungry big brother, the Soviet Union. According to BND sources, 80 percent of the assessments of NATO that the Soviet Union received from its Eastern European satellites came from East Germany.[39]

Wolf was highly respected in his service and in the West. In another secret dossier kept by the BND he is described as an "excellent intelligence man, possesses outstanding leadership qualities, very good rhetoric and is very convincing." Further, the East German Ministry for State Security respected him because of his "competency, [and] he never talks to subordinates in a tone that would suggest orders from above, he criticizes the situation not the person, is understanding and can listen, and is eloquent."[40]

Did Other Spy Chiefs Have a Face?

Markus Wolf was famously called the "man without a face," but most postwar intelligence chiefs in Europe tried to avoid the limelight. By contrast, American spy chiefs had no problem displaying their face in the media. In fact, Allen Dulles made the cover of *Time* magazine in 1953 on the occasion of his appointment as CIA chief, with his trademark pipe and a cloaked man with a dagger in the background.[41] Feature stories followed in other newspapers and magazines.

It is difficult to make comparisons between Wolf and his counterparts in West Germany, because during Wolf's tenure there were *six* BND chiefs with ever-decreasing terms and ever-increasing visibility: Reinhard Gehlen (1956–68), Gerhard Wessel (1968–78), Klaus Kinkel (1979–82), Eberhard Blum (1982–85), Heribert Hellenbroich (August 1–August 27, 1985), and Hans-Georg Wieck (1985–90). Unlike in Markus Wolf's case, any scandal led to the dismissal of a West German intelligence chief.

One of the biggest scandals that led to dismissal is the case of Heribert Hellenbroich. He lasted only twenty-seven days as BND president because Hans Joachim Tiedge defected to the East on his watch (August 19, 1985). Hellenbroich had been head of the Bundesamt für Verfassungsschutz (BfV), West Germany's counterintelligence service, from 1983 to 1985; Tiedge was employed there as a counterintelligence official. Despite Tiedge's alcoholism and psychological degeneration after the death of his wife, Hellenbroich kept him on in counterintelligence. When the scandal broke in 1985, Hellenbroich's picture was on the cover of *Der Spiegel*.

The fact that Wolf's time as chief was the equivalent of the tenure of six West German intelligence chiefs also says something about the difference in leadership. While many of the BND presidents after Wessel's term were ceremonial and long-serving bureaucrats that led the agencies, Wolf's hand as leader was felt for many years, allowing him more time to develop a legendary reputation.

West Germany was not the only country in which spy chiefs had shorter terms. Other democracies like the United Kingdom and the United States displayed the same pattern. One thing is clear: the earlier postwar leaders like Gehlen, Wessel, Dick White (chief of SIS, 1956–68), and Allen Dulles (DCI, 1953–61), all served longer terms—about ten years each—than intelligence chiefs in Western democracies in the later Cold War. This reflected the growing bureaucratization of spy agencies and the decreasing importance of a spy chief, who increasingly became ceremonial figureheads.

Wolf's Longevity

Markus Wolf was the longest-lasting spy chief in history, partly because he had an early start as the youngest spy chief in history. Unlike his West German counterparts, for example, he was not of retirement age after ten years of service. In fact, he was probably just reaching his stride at the ten-year mark in 1963.

I have already mentioned some of Wolf's personality traits and the importance of Soviet support in Wolf's success and longevity. Another important factor was his family background, which gave him a further layer of "untouchability." Not only was he the son of Friedrich Wolf, the acclaimed old Communist and playwright, but his brother Konrad Wolf was an important artist and filmmaker in the GDR.

Wolf's long years of leadership were pockmarked with successes and failures. The failures—usually defections or the arrest of agents—generally made headline news. While Wolf may have not been pictured in the stories about arrested agents or defectors, his name was always in the press.

Unlike many Western spy chiefs, Wolf also ran some of his own agents. In his memoir, he said he did this, in part, to break up the boredom of the bureaucratic life of an intelligence chief.[42] Many of the agents he ran were high-profile ones. Aside from Porst, the most notable Western agents he ran were Klaus Kuron (who was a counterintelligence official in the BfV engaged in operations against the GDR from 1962 to 1990, when he was caught) and Gabriele Gast (who by 1989 had advanced to head of the BND's analytical department producing analyses on the Soviet Union). Kuron and Gast had been recruited by other officers, while Wolf met and debriefed them. But when Wolf was younger, he actually recruited and ran his own agents. He often met with agents in a fancy villa in Dresden, where he wined and dined them, or abroad in neutral countries. And, of course, he met several high-profile agents during his fateful visit to Sweden in 1978.

Into the Limelight

By the early 1980s Wolf was ready to step down as chief of the HVA. His goal was to retire on his sixtieth birthday in 1983, but the elderly Mielke was against it because he thought he might be pushed out owing to his own age. The real catalyst for Wolf's exit, however, was the death in 1982 of his younger brother Konrad, whom he adored.[43]

Werner Großmann, Wolf's successor, first heard about his wish to retire in the sauna with trusted colleagues. In the sauna one talks privately about "God and the World" (*Gott und die Welt*—everything under the sun).[44] Although Wolf had become a legend in his own time, he still felt like he worked in the shadows while his father and his younger brother basked in the public glory of authorship and filmmaking. Furthermore, he had never wanted to become a spy chief. He wanted out. With the death of his brother in 1982, he had a new mission: to complete Konrad Wolf's project. He felt compelled to write up his younger brother's idea to produce a film or write a book about boyhood friends called *The Troika*: three friends who grew up on different sides of the Cold War—one in the Soviet Union, Konrad Wolf in the GDR, and the other, George Fischer, in the United States—but met up in the United States forty years later.[45]

In his memoir, Großmann relates that Wolf slowly started to pass on many of his administrative and operational duties to him as Wolf retreated more and more from the ministry. Großmann became his first deputy and Wolf groomed him as his successor. However, Mielke would not budge. Eventually, Wolf only attended ceremonial events and Großmann ran the daily affairs of the HVA. He even started writing his books at the office.[46] It was not until the BND tried to recruit Wolf's second wife, Christa, who was vacationing in Bulgaria, that Mielke started to soften his stance. He realized that Wolf's womanizing in prudish East Germany threatened national security. Wolf's official retirement date was November 15, 1986, but Großmann says he never saw him in the office after March 1986.[47]

Großmann's description of Wolf's motivation to retire is corroborated by evidence at the time. On October 8, 1986, Wolf wrote a letter to Minister Mielke in which he confirms that he groomed Großmann as his successor to ensure "continuity in leadership." Officially, in his personnel file, Wolf also claims that he wanted to write a history of the HVA, but in reality, he worked on his book *The Troika* at first.[48] It was published three years after his retirement in March 1989. The major sensation in the book was that he broke with Stalinism. Even though the Berlin Wall had not been breached, both East and West German newspapers covered the book's release. This was Wolf's first step into the limelight.

The official reason provided to the SED Politburo and the National Defense Council of the GDR was that Wolf retired for "health reasons."[49] After the fall of the Wall—in numerous interviews and in his own autobiography—Wolf sets forth other reasons for his wish to leave the ministry, including self-serving, high-sounding motivations in which he foresaw the bankruptcy of the system. There is no contemporaneous evidence to corroborate this.

The next step into the limelight occurred after the fall of the Berlin Wall. At a huge rally calling for change at the Alexanderplatz in East Berlin on November 4, 1989, Wolf stepped up to the podium and emerged as an unlikely reformer. He called for reforms in "his party"—the SED. He still believed in Communism but now embraced Gorbachev's reforms like *perestroika* and *glasnost*. Karl Wilhelm Fricke, otherwise critical of Wolf and the Ministry for State Security, writes that Wolf showed "civic courage" because he acknowledged that he had served the Ministry of State Security as a general for thirty-four years and wanted to protect his former staff members from blanket censure. These claims were met with both cheers and hisses.[50]

Soon after this rally, Wolf emerged as a spokesman for his former staff at the HVA. He went to great lengths to distance the HVA from the repressive excesses of the Ministry for State Security. He stated repeatedly in numerous interviews that the HVA operated like any other foreign intelligence service. More important, he refused to become a traitor by divulging information to the West. He refused to talk about any agents that had not yet been exposed and caught by Western intelligence. Wolf related in his memoir that he even refused a pitch by the CIA to resettle in California if he provided them with the names of big cases.[51]

The CIA's overture came in May 1990. Central Intelligence Agency officers reminded Wolf that his time was running out because Germany would be unified in October that year and he would become a wanted man. Shortly before October 3, 1990, the day of unification, Wolf fled to Moscow via Austria hoping to find asylum there. He was very disappointed in the unresponsiveness of the Soviet Union, which he had served so faithfully for thirty-four years. Former colleagues and current politicians were not willing to help him or his staff avoid prosecution. He returned to Germany and presented himself to German prosecutors. On September 24, 1991, he was apprehended at the border and spent eleven days in jail.

Wolf's legal situation was controversial. While West Germans thought he should be prosecuted for treason, he claimed he could not betray his own country since he operated out of East Germany. In the end, he won that battle and was convicted only of two kidnappings dating back to the 1950s and early

1960s. The judgment was a suspended sentence of two years in jail and a fine in 1997. He never spent any more time in prison.[52] The West German justice system withdrew the judgment against him and other leaders, and he continued writing books and providing interviews to the media.

Wolf did not publish his long-awaited memoir until 1997, instead teasing the public and espionage aficionados with books like the *Secrets of Russian Cooking*, published in 1995. His new profession was author and media personality: from 1989 to the time of his death in 2006 he wrote six books. He gave hundreds of interviews and relished the limelight. No longer invisible, Wolf became the public face of East German foreign intelligence — an urbane, smooth spokesman for his "scouts for peace" as well as for the cruder apparatchiks who ran East Germany and the HVA bureaucracy.

Conclusion

Given the foregoing narrative, it would seem Markus Wolf was a successful and admired spy chief for thirty-four years. He was an unmistakable product of a nearly extinct era when ideology shaped leaders. Born into a worldly and intellectual German-Jewish family, his career was shaped by the crucible of the Stalinist Soviet Union, his adopted homeland until he returned to East Germany after the Second World War. With his unflappable, calm personality, his Communist zeal and loyalty to the Soviet Union, his youth, his family background, and a diplomatic talent for talking out of both sides of his mouth, he survived scandals that would have quickly put him out of office in the West. These characteristics also made him an effective intelligence leader.

Just as Wolf was the product of German roots and a Soviet upbringing, so too was his service, the HVA, a hybrid of German efficiency and Soviet Communist bureaucracy. Over decades, it also acquired a wealth of intelligence experience. With the advantage of operating in a divided Germany against an open society with a common culture, language, and heritage, Wolf's service penetrated West Germany with moles and agents in practically all walks of life, from the military to rival intelligence agencies.

Despite inborn advantages, there is no doubt that Wolf's leadership and his personality traits helped shape the success of the service and its image abroad during and after the fall of the Berlin Wall. For Wolf, Cold War espionage was a big chess game, where pawns were manipulated by preying on their human weaknesses. Although cynical and manipulative, Wolf earned the respect of his adversaries through his successes and charming but down-to-earth personality. He also absorbed the Russian hospitality of his youth; he even cooked Russian food for his guests and agents, personalizing his interactions.

Unlike his counterparts in the West, Wolf was a "man without a face" primarily because of the influence of the Soviet Bloc way of conducting intelligence. His style of leadership was formed by the national context of a Communist East Germany shaped by the Soviet Union, the institutional context of a hybrid intelligence agency, and the historical context of the division of Germany and the Cold War. Although Wolf as leader was shaped by his times, his personality contributed to his image and success. It must be remembered that Wolf was also unique in the annals of intelligence history because of his youth and resulting longevity.

Part of the reason he survived so long was his youth in his early career. Later, the HVA became synonymous with Wolf, and Eastern Bloc leaders tended to serve long terms. Unlike in the West, scandal did not lead to ouster. When I asked his former deputy and successor, Werner Großmann, why Wolf survived so long, he replied that "he was exceptionally suited and was highly respected by the party leadership." He also had good contacts because he came from the Wolf family.[53]

As long as the HVA was a smaller and less bureaucratic agency, a leader played a significant role in shaping the agency and inspiring its staff. When, by the 1980s, it became a big, lumbering bureaucracy, leadership at the top was less important. This is illustrated by the assumption of Werner Großmann of the position of HVA chief when Wolf retired. His job entailed much more bureaucracy, and he was pegged a bureaucrat (perhaps unfairly so, as he was also quite personable in conversation); he saw himself as a pragmatist in contrast to the idealist Wolf.[54]

The expansion of intelligence bureaucracies was not unique to the HVA. The last decade of the Cold War and the post-9/11 world has seen the proliferation of intelligence agencies and the expansion of staffing. As intelligence agencies get bigger, they become more bureaucratic and institutionalized. Department heads, sub-department heads, and deputies proliferate. Spy chiefs become less important. In our own era in the United States, there are so many intelligence agencies and ever-changing leaders it is hard to keep track of them. Moreover, leaders never seem to last very long, and it is hard to remember their names. This is detrimental to the conduct of intelligence, and Wolf's story is a lesson for future intelligence agencies to learn.

Notes

1. Kristie Macrakis interview with Markus Wolf, March 1995. For biographical background about Markus Wolf, see Alexander Reichenbach, *Chef der Spione: die Markus-Wolf Story* [Spy chief: The Markus Wolf story] (Stuttgart: Deutsche Verlags-Anstalt, 1992); and Leslie Colitt, *Spymaster: The Real-Life Karla, His Moles, and the East German Secret Police* (New York: Addison-Wesley, 1995), as well as more recent

short book chapters. See, for example, Karl Wilhelm Fricke, "Markus Wolf (1923): Drei Jahrzehnte Spionagechef des SED-Staates" [Markus Wolf (1923): Spy boss for three decades of the SED-State], in *Konspiration als Beruf: Deutsche Geheimdienstchefs im Kalten Krieg* [Secrecy as an occupation: German secret service chiefs during the Cold War], ed. Dieter Krüger and Armin Wagner (Berlin: Ch. Links Verlag, 2003), 284–309; Nicole Glocke and Peter Jochen Winters, *Im geheimen Krieg der Spionage: Hans-Georg Wieck (BND) und Markus Wolf (MfS)—Zwei biografische Porträts* [In the secret espionage war: Hans-Georg Wieck (BND) and Markus Wolf (MfS)—two biographical portraits] (Halle [Saale]: Mitteldeutscher Verlag, 2014), 231–493.

2. Macrakis interview with former deputy who wished to remain anonymous, April 28, 2015, Berlin.

3. Markus Wolf, *Freunde Sterben Nicht* [Friends don't die] (Berlin: Das Neue Berlin, 2002), 72.

4. Markus Wolf with Anne McElvoy, *Man without a Face: The Autobiography of Communism's Greatest Spymaster* (New York: Random House, 1997), 33. Although I used the German and English editions of Wolf's autobiography in the research for this article, I cite the English edition, if the passage is the same, to accommodate the English-speaking audience. The German edition is not coauthored with Anne McElvoy and has additional material on German topics. For example, there is a whole chapter on Herbert Wehner in the German edition. For the German edition, see Markus Wolf, *Spionagechef im geheimen Krieg: Erinnerungen* [Spy chief in the secret war: Memoirs] (Munich: List Verlag, 1997).

5. Ibid., 90.

6. Ibid., 44.

7. BStU (Stasi archive), Cadre File, KS, 60003/90, 76; ibid., 90–91.

8. Hans-Dieter Schütt, *Markus Wolf: Letzte Gespräche* [Markus Wolf: Last conversations] (Berlin: Das Neue Berlin, 2007), 139.

9. Macrakis interview with former deputy, April 28, 2015, Berlin.

10. Staff numbers from Wolf, *Man without a Face*, 45; and Wolf, *Freunde Sterben Nicht*, 96.

11. Leslie Colitt, *Spymaster*, 56.

12. Wolf, *Man without a Face*, 59. "IWF's Baptism by Fire" is a section heading in David E. Murphy, Sergei A. Kondrashev, and George Bailey, *Battleground Berlin: CIA vs. KGB in the Cold War* (New Haven, CT: Yale University Press, 1997), 139. See also Benjamin B. Fischer, "Markus Wolf and the CIA Mole," *Center for the Study of Intelligence Bulletin* 10 (Winter 2000): 8–9.

13. Documents reproduced in Donald P. Steury, ed., *On the Front Lines of the Cold War: Documents on the Intelligence War in Berlin, 1946–1961* (Washington, DC: CIA History Staff, Center for the Study of Intelligence, 1999), 287–302.

14. Ibid. Document IV-8: "Pictures of Mischa Wolf," April 9, 1957 (MORI: 145204), 304–5.

15. "Die Vulkanisierten" [The vulcanized], *Der Spiegel*, April 22, 1953, 5.

16. Steury, *On the Front Lines of the Cold War*, 305.

17. Benjamin B. Fischer, "*Bruderorgane* [Brother organs]: The Soviet Origins of East German Intelligence," in *The Stasi at Home and Abroad: Domestic Order and Foreign Intelligence*, ed. Uwe Spiekermann (Washington, DC: German Historical Institute, suppl. 9, 2014), 151–69, here 159. See also Richard Meier, *Geheimdienst ohne Maske* [Secret service without a mask] (Berlin, 1992), 147. Quotation from Reichenbach, *Chef der Spione*, 63.

18. Macrakis interview with Markus Wolf.

19. Steury, *On the Front Lines of the Cold War*, 304. See also Wolfgang Leonhard, *Die Revolution entlässt ihre Kinder* [The revolution lets its children go] (Cologne: Kiepenheuer and Witsch, 1981), 576; and Reichenbach, *Chef der Spione*, 10.

20. Werner Großmann, *Bonn im Blick: die DDR-Aufklärung aus Sicht ihres letzten Chefs* [Bonn in view: The GDR Foreign Intelligence Service from the perspective of its last head] (Berlin: Das Neue Berlin, 2001), 119.

21. Gabriele Gast, *Kundschafterin des Friedens: 17 Jahre Topspionin der DDR beim BND* [A scout for peace: 17 years as a top GDR spy in the BND] (Frankfurt/Main: Eichborn, 1999), 189.

22. Macrakis interview with former deputy, April 28, 2015, Berlin; and interview with Werner Großmann, April 29, 2015.

23. Macrakis interview with Markus Wolf, 1994, Berlin.

24. Remark made in many TV interviews. See also obituary by Mark Landler, "Markus Wolf, German Spy, Dies at 83," *New York Times*, November 10, 2006, http://www.nytimes.com/2006/11/10/world/europe/10wolf.html?. For a book on the Romeo method, see Marianne Quoirin, *Agentinnen aus Liebe* [Agents for love] (Frankfurt/Main: Eichborn, 1999).

25. Wolf, *Spionagechef im geheimen Krieg* (Munich: List Verlag, 1997), 150.

26. Kristie Macrakis, *Seduced by Secrets: Inside the Stasi's Spy-Tech World* (New York: Cambridge, 2008), 84–86.

27. Peter Richter and Klaus Rößler, *Wolfs West-Spione: Ein Insider-Report* [Wolf's spies in the West: An insider report] (Berlin: Elefanten Press, 1992), 131–32.

28. Heribert Schwan, *Erich Mielke: der Mann, der die Stasi War* [Erich Mielke: The man who was the Stasi] (Munich: Droemer Knaur Verlag, 1997).

29. "Porst-Prozess" [Porst trial], *Der Spiegel*, no. 18 (1969): 100–106.

30. Ibid., 106.

31. Wolf, *Man without a Face*, 189. See also "DDR-Spion im Kanzleramt" [GDR spies in the chancellor's office], *Der Spiegel*, no. 18 (1974): 20–31, here 28.

32. Ibid.

33. Kristie Macrakis, *Seduced by Secrets*, 64–65; and Wolf, *Man without a Face*, 176–78.

34. Wolf, *Man Without a Face*.

35. "DDR-Geheimdienst enttarnt: die Spione des Markus Wolf" [The GDR secret service revealed: Markus Wolf's spies], *Der Spiegel* 33, no. 10 (March 1979): 70–83, here 70. Several former intelligence and counterintelligence officials with whom I spoke expressed elation about the Stiller defection.

36. Markus Wolf, *Die Kunst der Verstellung: Dokumente, Gespräche, Interviews* [The

Art of disguise: Documents, conversations, interviews], ed. Günther Drommer (Berlin: Schwarzkopf and Schwarzkopf, 1998), 110, 316.

37. Keyword search in *Neues Deutschland* archive. *Neues Deutschland*, November 12, 1982; and "General ohne Gesicht" [General without a face], *Der Spiegel*, January 24, 1983.

38. Oleg Kalugin, *Spymaster: My Thirty-Two Years in Intelligence and Espionage against the West* (New York: St. Martin's Press, 1994), 195.

39. Benjamin B. Fischer, *"Bruderorgane,"* 164.

40. Reichenbach, *Chef der Spione*, 10.

41. "The Man with the Innocent Air," *Time* 62, no. 5 (August 3, 1953): 14.

42. Wolf, *Man without a Face*, 110.

43. This point is stated in Wolf's memoir and the short biographies and is confirmed in Wolf's personnel file: BStU, KS, 600003/90, 59. Two former deputies underscored how much he adored his brother.

44. Macrakis interview with Werner Großmann, April 29, 2015. This is also mentioned in Großmann's autobiography, *Bonn im Blick*, 98.

45. Großmann, *Bonn im Blick*, 109–10. I also noticed how much Wolf's brother and family meant to him during my first interview.

46. Macrakis interview with Werner Großmann, April 29, 2015.

47. Ibid., 117.

48. BStU, KS 60003/90, 59.

49. Peter Jochen Winters, in Glocke and Winters, *Im geheimen Krieg der Spionage*, 422.

50. Serge Schmemann, "Old Master Spy in East Berlin Tells Why He Backs Changes," *New York Times*, November 22, 1989, A14; and Karl Wilhelm Fricke, "Markus Wolf (1923)," 306.

51. Wolf, *Man without a Face*, 9.

52. Rudolf Hirsch, *Der Markus Wolf Prozeß: Eine Reportage* [The Markus Wolf trial: A report] (Berlin: Brandenburgisches Verlagshaus, 1994).

53. Macrakis interview with Werner Großmann, April 29, 2015.

54. He describes himself as a pragmatist in his memoir and in an interview with the author, April 29, 2015.

7 "The Dossiers"

Reinhard Gehlen's Secret Special Card File

Bodo V. Hechelhammer

Reinhard Gehlen (1902–79) was the head of the German Federal Intelligence Service, the Bundesnachrichtendienst (BND).[1] Gehlen was the first president of the BND from 1956 until 1968, and before that head of its predecessor, the so-called Gehlen Organization. Gehlen achieved a promotion from head of an organization under US tutelage to president of the BND, a legal part of the West German state. During these years of organizational consolidation he outmaneuvered his potential intelligence opponents and rivals and gained the ear of Chancellor Konrad Adenauer (1876–1967) and his trusted state secretary Hans Globke (1898–1973).[2] Gehlen, as head of the foreign intelligence service, developed an especially close relationship with Globke as part and parcel of providing the conservative government of the Federal Republic of Germany with information on domestic as well as foreign affairs. In fact, Reinhard Gehlen placed West Germany's political elite under surveillance throughout the 1950s and 1960s.

The focus in this chapter is on the "dossiers," or to be more precise, the secret special card file of the first president of the BND. Behind the term "dossiers" lies the accusation of Gehlen improperly collecting information about politicians and dignitaries of the Federal Republic of Germany throughout his presidency. To understand Gehlen's secret special card file, it is necessary to understand its creator; similarly, understanding the "dossiers" helps us to understand how Gehlen led the BND.

The public learned about the existence of the special card file as a result of West Germany's Guillaume committee of inquiry of 1974. The case of the famous spy Günter Guillaume (1927–95), an intelligence agent in West Germany for East Germany's foreign intelligence service, was not the only subject of parliamentary investigation in the early 1970s.[3] The committee of inquiry also had to deal with the accusation that the BND under Reinhard Gehlen had conducted domestic intelligence activities contrary to its competence

Photo 7.1 Reinhard Gehlen, undated photograph, but from the 1970s after his retirement as BND president. (*Bundesnachrichtendienst [Federal Intelligence Service, Germany]*)

as a foreign intelligence service, which had been documented in dossiers on certain people. The media wrote that there had been BND dossiers on the eating, drinking, and sexual habits of a least fifty-four leading figures in politics, academia, and the military.[4] Others suggested that there were as many as six hundred such dossiers containing potentially incriminating material about politicians the BND had monitored both within and outside West Germany.[5] Horst Ehmke (born 1927), state secretary of the federal chancellery from 1969 until 1972, summed it up in a public statement dating from autumn 1974: It was "a jolly good collection," but it had been beyond the competence of a foreign intelligence service to collect it.[6] Even though these dossiers were supposedly destroyed at his directive in 1970, some copies of them resurfaced several years later.

Reinhard Gehlen made a public attempt to qualify what had been said before, claiming that these files had just been stored in a special place, and therefore were "special files," but that they were not "dossiers" on public figures and that he had kept them for personal use only. Concerning the origin of the information contained in the files, he pointed out that they had been collected lawfully within West Germany and were not the product of illegal domestic intelligence-collection activities: "They mainly contained secondary information, the by-products of foreign intelligence collection. Sometimes they contained gossip and tittle-tattle . . . secondary information that is," said Gehlen.[7]

The Guillaume committee of inquiry stated in its final report in early 1975 that "as far as the special card file . . . is concerned, it cannot be established that this file was the result of domestic intelligence collection activities conflicting with [the service's] mission. However, the taking of evidence did not result in a final assessment as only some of the files were still available."[8] It was impossible to evaluate the special card file because information about the matter was missing. What was this special card file? What was the content of the "dossiers," and about whom were they compiled? For example, did they, as has been assumed recently, concern the public prosecutor in the federal state of Hesse, Fritz Bauer (1903–68), who played a key role in initiating the Frankfurt Auschwitz trials (1963–65)?[9] Did they also contain intimate details, and were they possibly used to influence politics? These questions have been asked repeatedly and discussed at length yet have not been answered since 1974.[10]

In this chapter, I would like to provide a few preliminary answers to them. The secret special card file was terminated and does not exist any more inside the BND or in its archives. Some dossiers were transferred to other departments of the service, and others were shredded. In the archives, "destruction reports" and "handover protocols" were found; some documents that had belonged to the special card file were found in files all over the BND archive. With this information, it is now possible to reconstruct the structure of the card file and the content of some of the dossiers.

The Origins of the Secret Special Card File

In the beginning of the Gehlen Organization, the special card file was just one among many other filing systems. Reinhard Gehlen had set up the filing system of his organization on the basis of the principle of isolation, and in a deliberately decentralized way.[11] During his tenure, there were allegedly about one hundred different card files containing information on various people or topics in use simultaneously.[12]

But what were the origins of the special card file? Two different origins have been identified. First of all, when the Gehlen Organization started its work for the United States after the end of World War II, counterespionage was among its official tasks. As part of its intelligence work, the organization had to establish contacts with numerous authorities and institutions—municipal administrations, the police, and so on. For security reasons and also to uncover and fend off Communist infiltration, information on any contact person was collected and held in card files. Contacts with staff of other government bodies, especially with officials of all political parties in West Germany, were always noted, among other reasons because of their GDR contacts—for instance, via the "Eastern Bureaus" of the West German parties the Christian Democratic Union (CDU), the Social Democratic Party (SPD), and the Free Democratic Party (FDP)—but also to obtain information on their political attitude and reliability.[13] The main points of interest were the person's anti-Communist convictions and their attitude toward the Gehlen Organization, and also whether and how they could be of use to the agency. At the end of the day, the task of "counterintelligence" proved useful as an ostensible authorization and justification of the service's activities.

Second, the special card file is rooted in Reinhard Gehlen's anti-Communist ideology. He was firmly convinced that the remnants of the resistance group the "Red Orchestra"—that is to say, groups of people who had maintained contacts with the Soviet Union before 1945—were still active in the Federal Republic of Germany.[14] The "Red Orchestra" was a name given by the Gestapo to an anti-Nazi resistance movement in Berlin as well as to Soviet espionage rings operating in German-occupied Europe and Switzerland during World War II. Whole departments of Gehlen's organization were tasked with collecting and evaluating intelligence on the "new Red Orchestra," known internally by the German code word *Fadenkreuz* (crosshairs). At the beginning of the 1950s, for instance, Reinhard Gehlen was absolutely convinced that the CDU politicians Ernst Lemmer (1898–1970) and Jakob Kaiser (1888–1961) were Soviet agents and that the SPD politicians Adolf Grimme (1889–1963) and Herbert Wehner (1906–90) were in touch with the remaining members of the "Red Orchestra."[15] The circle of suspects grew larger and larger. Eventually, people associated with the anti-Nazi resistance movement like Otto John (1909–97), Friedrich Wilhelm Heinz (1899–1968), and Hans Joachim Oster Jr. (1914–83), son of the leading resistance figure Hans Oster (1887–1945), were also suspected.[16] Curiously enough, all of them at some point were competing with Gehlen's organization in their respective functions as heads of other West German intelligence agencies. Otto John was the first head of West Germany's domestic intelligence service, the Federal Office for the Protection of the Constitution (Bundesamt für Verfassungsschutz, BfV), from 1950 to 1954. And Friedrich Wilhelm Heinz built up his own intelligence service for the West German federal chancellery. These people were the subjects of some of the earliest traceable dossiers of the special card file.

Even when the BfV, which was responsible for domestic intelligence collection and counterintelligence, was founded in 1950, practically nothing changed. The case of Otto John, among others, who mysteriously surfaced in the GDR in July 1954, affirmed Gehlen's conviction that the BND had to take an interest in domestic matters, as all other agencies were apparently infiltrated by the Soviet Union. This conviction that conspiracy and infiltration were rife and were undermining the state was held by many for some years to come. In the years immediately following the war, such thoughts fell on fertile ground with the Americans as well as the West German government. Without any doubt there had been Soviet attempts to infiltrate West German government agencies. However, Gehlen came up with ever-new suspicions and flights of fancy. In retrospect, one of his leading analysts, who was regarded as brilliant by his colleagues and who was tasked with analyzing the intelligence on the "Red Orchestra" for Gehlen, called the latter's beliefs "irrational fancies" and "pitiable." According to him, they were "part of a world that could have been invented by Kafka, where treason and clandestine contact with traitors seemed just natural conduct."

The *Sonderkartei* (Special Card File)

After the BND was founded, Dr. Hans Globke, state secretary in the federal chancellery, saw his own file while on one of his visits to the BND headquarters in Pullach.[17] The only thing he found fault with was the fact that too many people had access to such sensitive information on individuals of special interest. He was by no means against the existence of such a card file; he was only against the way the files were stored and how much access was given to them.

There is a letter dating from 1953 by "40/A," the counterintelligence department, to "30," Reinhard Gehlen, that shows just how necessary such a special card file seemed to people with the suspicious mind-set described previously. On the basis of intelligence provided by the General Representation "L" in Karlsruhe, the letter said that Globke's claim to have been forced to write the legal commentary on the Nuremberg Laws was wrong. He was described as an "ice-cold person, who does not care . . . which power he serves, as long as he can enjoy the power a leading bureaucrat has." Gehlen made a note by hand: "40/A is ordered to immediately destroy the original report by 'L' and drafts of this memo, as well as to make sure that the information is not entered into the card file."

Thus, Gehlen ordered the removal of files of important people from the central card file department of the BND and their transfer to a special filing cabinet in the BND president's house. This cabinet was kept by a special assignments department in the president's staff until the end of Gehlen's tenure; this team was first known as "363/II" and then as "106/II," important organizational units of the presidential staff. Only the president was allowed to use the special card file, which was located one floor above his office. Only a few members of his staff had access to it. The special card file was even physically separated from the remaining staff by a separate access door. The person responsible for the special card file was Annelore Krüger (1922–2012), a long-standing confidant whom Gehlen felt he could trust absolutely.[18] Even though reports on public figures could still be stored in other card files, especially significant reports were transferred to the special card file and held there only. Therefore, it turned from a BND card file into an exclusive personal card file of Reinhard Gehlen, which allowed him to be quickly and accurately informed whenever necessary—for example, before he set off to meetings at the federal chancellery in Bonn.

The End of the Card File

With the end of the Gehlen era came the end of the special card file. His successor Gerhard Wessel (1913–2002) immediately removed the 106/II department from the president's staff and transferred its head, Ms. Krüger, to a branch office. After this reorganization, he also had the president's house, House 37, renovated. Consequently, the files had to be removed from House 37 and were transferred to a strong room in the neighboring building (37c).[19] It was during this reorganization that Wessel learned of the existence of the special card file, which had not been handed over to him by Gehlen. Wessel felt it necessary to act immediately, particularly because at the end of May 1968 the federal chancellery had tasked a commission chaired by civil servant Reinhold Mercker to conduct an internal investigation of the state of affairs at the BND. As early as June 7, 1968, Wessel ordered all departments of the BND holding documents on public figures to inspect these and establish whether they were complete and in keeping with the BND's charter. He also ordered that all documents not related to the BND's mission be passed to himself so that they could be destroyed later. All other documents were to be passed on to appropriate organizational units of the BND. The liquidation of the special card file took around twenty months, with the inspection of the first files of the special card file being completed as early as August 8, 1968, and the last recorded inspection taking place on March 25, 1970.

Collecting and analyzing domestic intelligence was not the actual mission of the foreign intelligence service, but a law specifying the mission of the BND was only passed in 1990. The origins of the special card file lay in the time when the Gehlen Organization was working under the patronage of the American intelligence services—up to 1949 under the aegis of the US Army and to 1956 under that of the Central Intelligence Agency (CIA). Consequently, from the 1950s the West German federal chancellery determined the BND's mission.

Gerhard Wessel did not immediately inform the federal chancellery about the special card file. He only informed the new head of the federal chancellery, Horst Ehmke, one week after Willy Brandt (1913–92) was elected the fourth chancellor of the Federal Republic on October 27, 1969. At first, Ehmke requested an overview of the special card files, asking Wessel to provide him with examples. The BND president did so on December 9, 1969, supplying a list of fifty-four names and four "random samples."[20] The list was compiled alphabetically, from Wolfgang Abendroth (1906–85) to Siegfried Zoglmann (1913–2007), as it was supposed to provide only an overview of the card file's contents. The samples presented four politicians as a cross section of the parliamentary groups represented in West Germany's parliament, the Bundestag: Rainer Barzel (1924–2006, CDU), Carlo Schmid (1896–1979, SPD), Friedrich Zimmermann (1925–2012, Christian Social Union/CSU), and Siegfried Zoglmann (1913–2007, FDP). After having inspected the files, Ehmke agreed with Wessel's proposal that they be destroyed.

Now the documents were combined into dossiers with very similar content: On April 17, 1970, 616 documents were gathered into 52 dossiers, and three days later another 388 documents into 70 dossiers.[21] The card file was not fully destroyed, as the BND president did not order a search for all file cards. In particular, he did not order a search for duplicates of the dossier documents. Thus, some dossier documents were found a few years later, around 1973 or 1974, preserved on microfilm. Even today, it is possible that some dossier documents, unrecognized as such, have remained in the files in the BND archives.

Reconstruction of Contents

What were the contents of the special card file? According to what we know now, it related to at least 210 people. The corresponding dossiers contained up to 220 documents consisting of as many as 500 pages.[22] The contents of the files were not identical; they contained single items of information on a certain person—for example, newspaper articles, notes of conversations, statements they had made about the BND, information on defamation campaigns, and personal correspondence. Intimate personal details have so far not been found in the special card file, even though this kind of information did exist in other filing systems. In the course of the special card file's destruction, about 1,100 documents were destroyed (in 1970 and 1973), and about the same number of documents were handed over to other organizational units of the BND.[23]

The first documents inspected in 1968, which were also the most numerous, were ones on Franz Josef Strauß (1915–88), the famous Bavarian politician, and the last ones inspected in 1970 concerned Hans Hubert von Löfen (born 1914), a member of the SPD's Eastern Bureau.

Files were compiled according to specific instructions from the federal chancellery, but Gehlen also collected information on people independently. He first and foremost collected information on West German public figures like politicians, important civil servants, journalists, and military officers. Such people were of particular interest to him because he had personal meetings with them or had to provide information on them to the federal chancellery. He did not target in particular any political party represented in the West German parliament; according to my calculations, about 39 percent of the politicians on whom he collected information were members of the SPD, 36 percent were members of the CDU, 9 percent were members of the CSU, and 14 percent were members of the FDP. Moreover, information was collected about foreign nationals with an intelligence background—for example, the Soviet spy Rudolf Ivanovich Abel (1903–71). In addition to that, Gehlen was interested in a few of the members of his own staff, intelligence assets, and other high-profile contacts or informants of his service: the card file contains documents on at least ten members of staff, such as Carl-Theodor Schütz (1907–85), and it contains more than fourteen operational files—for example, on Hans-Joachim Rechenberg (1910–77) and on Richard Christmann (1905–89).[24] Other dossiers concerned media organizations: the West German troops' newspaper *Deutsche Soldatenzeitung*, the publishing house Axel-Springer-Verlag, and the news magazine *Der Spiegel* and its publisher Rudolf Augstein (1923–2002).[25] We will now examine seven short examples that display the diverse content of the special card file.

Franz Josef Strauß

Franz Josef Strauß was the chairman of the CSU, a member of the federal cabinet in various ministerial positions, and for a long time the minister-president of the state of Bavaria. There were at least 220 documents, with a length of about 500 pages dating from 1957 to 1967, on Franz Josef Strauß, with the majority of them consisting of information on "defamation campaigns" against him. Some of the documents dealt with his relationship with the BND and his requests to the BND for information. As an example, a note of a conversation in 1962 on the "Fibag scandal" describes how Strauß, "who [made] quite a depressed impression, . . . seemed worried about the outcome of the

Fibag process."[26] The "Fibag scandal" of 1961–62 was a West German political scandal in which then minister of defense Strauß was accused of corruption because he had reportedly advised an American colleague to award the Fibag (*Finanzbau Aktiengesellschaft*) company a contract to construct thousands of apartments for the American military in West Germany. In 1962 a parliamentary commission was formed to investigate the allegations. Not only did the BND use its intelligence information to brief Strauß on the Fibag affair, but it was also used to give him political protection. The BND informed him as early as possible about foreign and domestic affairs that closely concerned him.

Hans Globke

There were at least forty-six documents consisting of roughly fifty pages dating from 1954 to 1962 concerning Hans Globke. It is easy to summarize them, as they all dealt with defamation campaigns against him and insults to him. The BND's main focus was the trial of Adolf Eichmann in Jerusalem in 1961. Reinhard Gehlen always reported himself and quickly to the state secretary of the federal chancellery on anything like this that took place.[27] Especially in the unstable early phase of the Federal Republic it was extremely important for Hans Globke to know whether something was happening that conflicted with the government's interests. Gehlen and Globke had almost daily contact with each other for years. That was a political symbiosis. Gehlen warned Globke whenever campaigns against him were coming up.

Herbert Wehner

Herbert Wehner was a former member of the Communist Party who joined the SPD after World War II. He served as federal minister of intra-German relations from 1966 to 1969 and thereafter as chairman of the SPD parliamentary group in the Bundestag until 1983. There were at least thirty-seven documents on him dating from 1953 to 1964, concerning, for example, his visit to the Yugoslav head of state Josip Tito (1892–1980) in 1957 and incriminating material on him from Denmark, regarding events that had occurred when Wehner had been in exile in Moscow from 1937 to 1941 and then moved to Scandinavia, where he was arrested and interned for espionage. There is a note dated November 1958 criticizing the hostile reaction of the GDR to the (in its view, unjustifiable) sitting of the Bundestag in West Berlin (Allied territory) and Wehner's suitability as an "all-German spokesperson." What is interesting is the BND's position: it voiced its opposition to Wehner's speaking out on the reunification question before the Bundestag; here again, it was getting involved in domestic affairs without authority. There are other notes of conversations from 1958 that concern only domestic affairs, especially in connection with the deteriorating relationship between Fritz Erler and Wehner on the issue of West German remilitarization, and criticism from within the SPD parliamentary group of Wehner who, his critics claimed, would systematically try to influence the party's grassroots on this issue. What is particularly interesting is that the information was just for Gehlen himself and came from the ongoing reporting on Wehner. Because of his Communist past, the BND collected information about him until late into the 1960s.

Willy Brandt

Eight documents were found relating to Willy Brandt, the leader of the SPD from 1964 to 1987 and chancellor of the Federal Republic of Germany from 1969 to 1974. All came from the time when he was the governing mayor of (West) Berlin. The subjects of some of these documents were an alleged secret meeting between Wehner and Brandt; the statements of a journalist in April 1961 on the meeting the previous month between Brandt and US president John F. Kennedy; and a conversation in about November 1966 between Brandt and Soviet ambassador to the GDR Pyotr A. Abrassimov. There were also file cards on all of Brandt's aliases. One document from 1950 with a reference to his card in a different file provided the Gehlen Organization with intelligence information characterizing Brandt as having a "leading position within the SPD's Eastern Bureau. Great worker, but real swot."[28] A briefing for the BND president from 1958 deals with a dispute between Brandt and the mayor of the West Berlin district of Kreuzberg, Willy Kressmann (1907–86). Criticizing his fellow SPD member Brandt, Kressmann said that "Brandt and many others will in time leave Berlin together with the Allies if the Berlin crisis reaches a peak. Apart from that, Berlin is only a stepping stone for him to other political functions. It has been the Allies and the Berlin SPD that have talked Berliners into having him as Mayor."[29] But the BND also collected information about Willy Brandt at the express request of Konrad Adenauer. The minutes of a meeting between the BND president and the federal chancellor in June 1960 state: "Question about the career and evolution of Mayor Brandt. Does he have [an] intelligence background?"[30] On the other hand, the BND also reported to Brandt (for example, in 1961) on investigations undertaken by the Poles about his past in Norway (Brandt had fled to Norway in 1933, when the Nazis came to power, to escape arrest by the Gestapo). At the end of the notes, the BND considered how Brandt himself could be informed more quickly about such events, as Gehlen had promised this. The example of Willy Brandt illustrates the political sensitivity of the special card file and also how Reinhard Gehlen reacted to the growing importance of Brandt beyond Berlin.

Wolfgang Döring

There were at least thirty-one documents, around sixty-six pages dating from 1954 to 1963, on Wolfgang Döring (1919–63), an FDP politician in North Rhine-Westphalia. Almost all of them, however, were reports of meetings with the BND because Döring had been handled as a special asset under the cover name "Dora." He had been in contact with the BND since 1955 in the context of counterintelligence investigations, especially because of the FDP's talks with officials of East Germany's Liberal Democratic Party of Germany and his meetings with nationals of satellite states of the Soviet Union and the Soviet ambassador to the Federal Republic of Germany.

Rudolf Augstein

There were at least eleven documents consisting of nearly nineteen pages dating from 1953 to 1964 on Rudolf Augstein, one of the most influential West German journalists and founder and part-owner of the magazine *Der Spiegel*.[31] The subjects of some of these documents were the "planned exclusion of A.[ugstein] from the FDP," "A.'s appearance before an editorial conference of the *Süddeutsche Zeitung*," and the "financial losses for Augstein and Kindler."[32] These subjects suggest concern with exclusively domestic matters. To make it clear, the collection and exploitation of intelligence information about the financial situation of a news magazine and the editorial board's decision making was not the result of any order from the West German government. Gehlen gathered information on *Der Spiegel* and sought sources in its editorial staff to obtain forewarning of any stories about the federal government or his own service (from the early 1950s *Der Spiegel* published articles critical of the Gehlen Organization and its relations with the federal chancellor's office).[33]

Elisabeth Noelle-Neumann

As far as is known, there is only one document in the card file about Elisabeth Noelle-Neumann (1916–2010), a celebrated West German political scientist and founder of the public opinion research organization Institut für Demoskopie Allensbach. This document dating from July 1960 is, however, quite revealing because it can be reconstructed completely: on Tuesday, June 28, 1960, BND president Gehlen had his weekly meeting with Chancellor Adenauer in the chancellery, the minutes of which were prepared by the BND. Item 6 reads: "Federal Chancellor pointed to the opinion research center Institut für Meinungsforschung in Allensbach. He said the owner Ms. Neumann was a communist. He would like to know what else is known about the institute and its background."[34] On July 20, the BND informed the head of the federal chancellery, Hans Globke, presenting its findings on Ms. Noelle-Neumann and the Allensbach Institute in a letter that was then stored in the special card file.[35] In this letter, the BND stated that "the head of the Allens-bach Institute, Dr. Noelle-Neumann, had no connection whatsoever to Ms. Buber-Neumann, the former communist party (KP) functionary that the federal chancellor probably had in mind."[36] The letter continues, "There are no disadvantageous findings on the institute, its head and its staff. We are not in a position to give a well-founded assessment of the institute's work. How-ever, we do have the impression that the institute is striving for an objective approach in dealing with its tasks."[37]

Despite claims to the contrary, so far no documents have been found on the Hessian public prosecutor Fritz Bauer (mentioned previously). This might be a case of confusion because there definitely was a dossier on the CDU politi-cian Fritz Baier (1923–2012), and the BND had information on Willy Brandt's confidant Leo Bauer (1912–72), but this was covered by the press as early as the 1970s.

Conclusion

Although the special card file has its origins in intelligence collection on personal contacts of members of the West German public service and on the "Red Orchestra," the collection of personal information grew larger and larger and expanded to include more and more people. To control access to it, the card file was transferred to the president's house, where it turned from a general BND card file into the private card file of Reinhard Gehlen. He felt he needed such information, not to have political influence over people, but to strengthen his position within the politics of the Federal Republic of Germany as he served West German chancellor Konrad Ade-nauer assiduously. His aim was, by means of domestic reporting, to make his organization the only West German intelligence service of importance. The reports always reflected the policy objectives of the BND, with the surveil-lance being only a means to an end. Gehlen succeeded in his aim because he alone had sensitive, politically valuable intelligence that he could provide the federal government quickly, enabling internal problems to be detected early and appropriate solutions found. This information concerned not only foreign and security policy issues but also information on domestic actors (indeed, it chiefly concerned these). This is the only possible explanation for the fact that Federal Minister Strauß and, above all, the state secretary of the federal chancellery Hans Globke were regularly provided with informa-tion that they could use in their efforts to make themselves indispensable. For this purpose, contrary to Gehlen's claim, the BND did not rely only on secondary information that made its way into the agency's hands. Quite the opposite: intelligence was collected deliberately too. While his collection of information on West German political figures was not illegal, it served Gehlen's purposes and those of his political masters rather than the cause of West Germany's defense. Chancellor Adenauer and Globke, the head of his chancellery, benefited from this additional intelligence because the BND's information was obtained early and was relevant to policy. Reinhard Gehlen tried to wield political influence not just on his own behalf but also to benefit the conservative government, which obtained an advantage in being better informed about the views of its partners and opponents on domestic and foreign affairs.

In a conversation with officers of the GDR's Ministry of State Security, the penetration agent Heinz Felfe (1918–2008)—who from 1951 to 1961 worked as a mole in the BND for the Soviet Union's principal foreign intelligence service, the KGB's First Chief Directorate—referred accurately to the use Globke and Gehlen made of one another. His comment, which can be found in a record of the Stasi's counterintelligence department (Hauptabteilung II), was that the BND "was used by Globke as a sort of private detective institute for the federal chancellery and for Chancellor Adenauer." The special card file indeed resembled a compass needle of Reinhard Gehlen's priorities, which he adjusted to the magnetic field of government politics in order to position his organization, and especially himself, as indispensable fixed points on the domestic policy map of West Germany.

Notes

1. Reinhard Gehlen, *Der Dienst: Erinnerungen, 1942–1971* [The service: Memoirs, 1942–1971] (Mainz-Wiesbaden: von Hase and Koehler, 1971); Dieter Krüger, "Reinhard Gehlen (1902–1979). Der BND-Chef als Schattenmann der Ära Adenauer," in *Konspiration als Beruf: Deutsche Geheimdienstchefs im Kalten Krieg* [Secrecy as an occupation: German secret service chiefs in the Cold War], ed. Dieter Krüger and Armin Wagner (Berlin: Ch. Links Verlag, 2003), 207–36; and Bodo Hechelhammer, "'Die Dossiers.' Reinhard Gehlens geheime Sonderkartei," in *Die Geschichte der Organisation Gehlen und des BND, 1945–1968: Umrisse und Einblicke. Dokumentation der Tagung am 2. Dezember 2013* [The history of the Gehlen Organization and the BND, 1945–1968: Outlines and insights. Documents of the conference on 2 December 2013], ed. Jost Dülffer, Klaus-Dietmar Henke, Wolfgang Krieger, and Rolf-Dieter Müller (Marburg: UHK, 2014), 81–90.

2. Norman J. W. Goda, "The Gehlen Organization and the Heinz Felfe Case. The SD, the KGB, and West German Counterintelligence," in *A Nazi Past: Recasting German Identity in Postwar Europe*, ed. David A. Messenger and Katrin Paehler (Lexington: University Press of Kentucky, 2015), 271–94.

3. Günter Guillaume was an assistant to federal chancellor Willy Brandt (1913–92). He was arrested as a spy for the GDR on April 24, 1974. After that, Brandt resigned.

The West German Federal Parliament appointed a commission of inquiry on June 6, 1974. See 7. Wahlperiode, Drucksache 7/3246, *Bericht und Antrag des 2. Untersuchungsausschuss zu dem Antrag der CDU/CSU betr. Einsetzung eines Untersuchungsausschusses*–Drucksache 7/2193 [Report and application of the 2nd investigative committee concerning the application of the CDU/CSU concerning the appointment of an investigative committee—Printed Record 7/2193], 5; and Eckhard Michels, *Guillaume, der Spion: Eine deutsch-deutsche Karriere* [Guillaume, the spy: A German-German career] (Berlin: Ch. Links Verlag, 2013), 252.

    4. Rudolf Augstein, "Bei späterem Bedarf," *Der Spiegel* [The mirror] 42, October 14, 1974, 27; and Stefanie Waske, *Nach Lektüre vernichten. Der geheime Nachrichtendienst von CDU und CSU im Kalten Krieg* [Destroy after reading: The secret intelligence service of the CDU/CSU in the Cold War] (München: Carl Hanser Verlag, 2013), 181.

    5. "Geheimpapier: Ein korruptes Unternehmen," *Stern* [Star] 27, no. 41 (1974): 160; Diethelm Damm, "Lehren aus den Affären mit dem Bundesnachrichtendienst (BND)," in *Vorgänge* [Events] 55, no. 1 (1982): 27; Heinz Felfe, *Im Dienst des Gegners. Autobiographie* [In the service of the enemy: Autobiography] (Berlin [Ost]: Verlag der Nationen, 1988), 290–309; and Stefanie Waske, *Mehr Liaison als Kontrolle. Die Kontrolle des BND durch Parlament und Regierung, 1955–1978* [Liaison rather than supervision: The supervision of the BND by parliament and government, 1955–1978] (Wiesbaden: VS Verlag für Sozialwissenschaften, 2009), 228–29.

    6. Eduard Neumaier, "Es war eine dolle Sammlung," *Die Zeit* [Time] 43, October 18, 1974, 11–13.

    7. Ludger Stein-Rueggenberg, "Reinhard Gehlen: Der BND wird ruiniert," in *Christ und Welt* [Christ and the world], October 18, 1974; and Reinhard Gehlen, *Verschlusssache* [Classified information] (Mainz: von Hase and Köhler, 1980), 42–47.

    8. 7. Wahlperiode, Drucksache 7/3246, *Bericht und Antrag des 2. Untersuchungsausschuss zu dem Antrag der CDU/CSU betr. Einsetzung eines Untersuchungsausschusses*–Drucksache 7/2193, 89.

    9. Hans Leyendeck, "Reise in eine andere Galaxis," in *Süddeutsche Zeitung* [South German newspaper], January 14, 2011, 7.

    10. Ibid.

    11. Magnus Pahl, *Fremde Heere Ost. Hitlers militärische Feindaufklärung* [Foreign armies East: Hitler's military reconnaissance of the enemy] (Berlin: Ch. Links Verlag, 2012), 112–14.

    12. *Vermerk "Vorbeugender Geheimschutz"* [Note "preventive secrecy"], August 26, 1974, BND-Archives, 100.496, 2.

    13. Nachlass Dr. Klausner, BND-Archives, N17/1, 156–58.

    14. Gerhard Sälter, *Phantome des Kalten Krieges. Die Organisation Gehlen und die Wiederbelebung des Gestapo-Feindbildes "Rote Kapelle"* [Phantoms of the Cold War: The Gehlen Organization and the revival of the Gestapo enemy image of the "Red Orchestra"] (Berlin: Ch. Links Verlag, 2016), 468–75.

    15. Schreiben, December 1974, National Archives and Records Administration (NARA), *Gehlen, Reinhard*, Record, Box 41, 230/86/22/06; and Henry Leide,

NS-Verbrecher und Staatssicherheit. Die geheime Vergangenheitspolitik der DDR [Nazi criminals and the GDR State Security: The GDR's secret policy on the past] (Göttingen: Vandenhoeck und Ruprecht, 2006), 301–18.

16. BND-Archives, 104.110.

17. Jürgen Bevers, *Der Mann hinter Adenauer. Hans Globkes Aufstieg vom NS-Juristen zur grauen Eminenz der Bonner Republik* [The man behind Adenauer: Hans Globke's rise from Nazi lawyer to grey eminence of the Bonn Republic] (Berlin: Ch. Links Verlag, 2009).

18. Bodo Hechelhammer and Susanne Meinl, *Geheimobjekt Pullach: Von der NS-Mustersiedlung zur Zentrale des BND* [Secret target Pullach: From Nazi model settlement to BND headquarters] (Berlin: Ch. Links Verlag, 2014), 210–12.

19. Statement Eberhard Blum, October 25, 1974, BND-Archives, 4.701 [not paginated]; *Protokoll der 18. Sitzung des 2. Untersuchungsausschusses der 7. Wahlperiode. Aussage des Zeugen Wessels* [Minutes of the 18th session of the 2nd Investigative Committee of the 7th Parliament: Testimony of the witness Wessel], PA-DBT, October 9, 1974, 177; and Waske, *Mehr Liaison als Kontrolle*, 229–30.

20. Horst Ehmke, "Mein Eindruck war, dass es eine Sache war, die Präsident Wessel bedrückte, dass er die Dinge aus dem Verkehr gezogen hatte, bei sich gesammelt hatte und dass er jetzt, bevor es zur Vernichtung kam, politische Rückendeckung haben wollte," *Protokoll der 18. Sitzung des 2. Untersuchungsausschusses der 7. Wahlperiode. Aussage des Zeugen Horst Ehmke* [Minutes of the 18th session of the 2nd Investigative Committee of the 7th Parliament: Testimony of the witness Horst Ehmke], PA-DBT, October 9, 1974, 82; and Waske, *Mehr Liaison als Kontrolle*, 182.

21. Letter Pr, November 11, 1975, BND-Archives, 40.212 [not paginated].

22. BND-Archives, 1.188; and Waske, *Mehr Liaison als Kontrolle*, 231.

23. Letter IV to Ref/Pr, April 16, 1970, BND-Archives, 4.701, 232f.; and Waske, *Mehr Liaison als Kontrolle,* 232–34.

24. Erich Schmidt-Eenboom and Matthias Ritzi, *Im Schatten des dritten Reiches. Der BND und sein Agent Richard Christmann* [In the shadow of the Third Reich: The BND and its agent Richard Christmann] (Berlin: Ch. Links Verlag, 2011).

25. Erich Schmidt-Eenboom, *Undercover. Wie der BND die deutschen Medien steuert* [Undercover: How the BND controls the German media] (München: Droemer-Knauer Verlag, 1999).

26. Letter 27 VK to 106, May 8, 1962, BND-Archives, digital copy, 120.006, 371.

27. Letter 40/A to 30, September 17, 1953, BND-Archives, digital copy, 120.623, 1.826.

28. Card file, 1950, BND-Archives, 1.216 [not paginated].

29. Notice, 1958, BND-Archives, digital copy, 120.603, 2037.

30. Minutes of meeting with federal chancellor, July 1, 1960, BND-Archives, digital copy, 120.616, 56-58.

31. File on Rudolf Augstein, BND-Archives, 1.188 [not paginated].

32. Card file on Augstein, Rudolf, BND-Archives, 102.288 [not paginated].

33. See, for example, "Des Kanzlers lieber General," *Der Spiegel* 39 (1954), 12–25.

34. Notice of the BND, June 28, 1960, BND-archives, 120.616, digital copy, 24f.

35. Letter of the BND, July 20, 1960, BND-Archives, 120.616, digital copy, 55–61.

36. Letter of the BND president to Dr. Globke, July 20, 1960, BND-Archives, 120.616, digital copy, 56–58.

37. Anlage zu Nr. 903/60, July 10, 1960, BND-Archives, digital copy, 58–60.

8 India's Cold War Spy Chiefs

Decolonizing Intelligence in South Asia

Paul M. McGarr

In August 1947, Britain's colonial administration lowered the Union Jack and departed from South Asia having failed to bequeath newly independent India an intelligence apparatus that was fit for the purpose. In contrast to the progressive transfer of political power from the colonizer to the soon-to-be-decolonized that had occurred in the subcontinent after 1945, the handover of intelligence and security responsibilities was precipitate and problematic. Indian leaders had been afforded ever-greater authority and influence over internal policy once the Attlee government had reluctantly come to accept that, in South Asia at least, Britain lacked both the means and the will to suppress the forces of postwar nationalism. In the intelligence sphere, the transfer of command from British to Indian hands occurred on a far shorter timescale and on a much more limited basis. To a degree, this was unsurprising, given that a large proportion of the colonial intelligence effort in South Asia had long been directed at undermining and discrediting the same nationalist figures who assumed prominent positions in India's pre-independence transitional governments.[1]

Nonetheless, in the immediate aftermath of India's independence, the nation's fledgling intelligence service, the Intelligence Bureau (IB), lacked adequate manpower, training, agent networks, and an institutional knowledge of modern intelligence practice. Matters were not helped by the distribution of meager intelligence assets between the two new sovereign states of India and Pakistan. In the wake of the subcontinent's partition, many Muslim intelligence officers elected to leave secular India and pledge their allegiance to Mohammad Ali Jinnah's Muslim League government in Pakistan. Moreover, inside India, different agencies with a stake in the country's civil and military intelligence operations competed fiercely with each other for resources and patronage, fostering discord and inefficiency within the national intelligence community. Notably, the work of IB's central and provincial networks overlapped with India's state police forces, each of which fielded its own small intelligence force. In addition, the nation's three armed services each deployed their own intelligence wings and jealously defended the autonomy and operational independence of military intelligence units.[2]

In March 1949, Vallabhbhai Patel, India's home minister, provided some insight into the scale of the intelligence vacuum that the British had left in the subcontinent. Speaking with journalists, Patel confirmed that on assuming control of India's Home Ministry in 1946, he had discovered that intelligence files "were absolutely closed to Indians. When I [Patel] became Home Minister, my dossier and those of all the Congress members had already been destroyed, for when I attempted to discover what they thought about me, I found absolutely nothing. They [the British] did not give us any information, either with regard to their past actions, or their manner of procedure, or their secret organizations; in short, they did not let us see or know anything."[3]

In short, as Patel confirmed, his department had been compelled "to create the 'Intelligence Department' afresh in every detail."[4] The significant intelligence void facing India's government was made all the more troubling by a series of urgent national security issues pressing in on the Home Ministry. Specifically, New Delhi was anxious to curtail outbreaks of communal violence and reassure the country's substantial Muslim minority by keeping a firm lid on simmering Hindu nationalism.[5] Equally, Indian officials were concerned to negate the subversive threat posed by a large and well-supported Communist Party of India.[6] Externally, Indian territorial disputes with Pakistan, principally over the former princely state of Kashmir, demanded the constant attention of hard-pressed intelligence officers.

To meet an increasing demand from anxious political masters for intelligence on a diverse range of threats, IB turned to the Indian Police Service in an effort to build much-needed capacity. With backgrounds in conventional policing, many of IB's new officers found the transition to intelligence work especially challenging. One former Indian intelligence officer has noted that the first cohort of IB recruits proved "totally at sea. Trained in and accustomed for long years to the use of police executive powers, they were at a complete loss in a set-up which first stripped them of their uniform and their powers and then asked them to show results."[7]

The lot of India's intelligence officers was complicated further by the ambivalent attitude, at best, that many of the nation's political elite evinced toward their work. One senior IB officer subsequently attested that India's first premier, Jawaharlal Nehru, entered office with "a strong prejudice against Intelligence." Nehru's suspicion of intelligence agencies was commonly attributed to the harassment and oppressive surveillance that Britain's colonial security apparatus had inflicted on his family during the nation's long struggle for independence. Once installed as independent India's prime minister, Nehru continued to express reservations that "Indian Intelligence was still dependent on the British and was following old British methods taught to the Indian Officers in pre-independence days, and was also dishing out intelligence which the British continued to supply to it."[8] Indeed, well into the 1950s, Nehru was to be found complaining to his friend, and India's last viceroy, Lord Louis Mountbatten, about the usefulness of the product that he received from IB. "I always read our Intelligence reports very critically and I am not prepared to accept them as they are," Nehru confided. "I have had a good deal of experience of the police and of Intelligence from the other side to be easily taken in by the reports we get."[9]

That is not to say that Nehru failed to recognize India's pressing need to develop a new and effective intelligence service. In November 1947, reflecting on the communal disturbances that were then engulfing the country, the Indian leader underlined to his chief ministers "the necessity for developing intelligence services. This is very important, both from the provincial and the central points of view. It is not easy to develop a good intelligence service suddenly as the men employed must be carefully chosen. Our old intelligence system has more or less broken down as it was bound to, because it was meant for other purposes, chiefly in tracking Congressmen and the like. The new intelligence service will have to be built differently."[10]

In fact, the man Nehru, or more accurately, Vallabhbhai Patel, selected to manage the IB's transition from a colonial to postcolonial intelligence service had been earmarked for the post back in March 1947. On taking control of the Home Ministry in the dying days of the British Raj, Patel wasted little time in identifying candidates to become the first Indian director of IB. In Patel's mind, the appointment of an Indian director of the Intelligence Bureau (DIB) would not only serve as a symbol of British retreat but also, and more important, ensure that the extensive colonial security apparatus would pass into nationalist hands before a formal transfer of constitutional power. Once stripped of its eyes and ears in India, any last-minute change of heart on the part of the British would be rendered utterly futile. The colonial intelligence service in India had been instrumental in sustaining British rule.

Having considered a number of candidates, Patel selected Tirupattur Gangadharam Sanjeevi Pillai, commonly known as Sanjeevi, to be India's first spy chief. Sanjeevi had joined the Indian Police Service in Madras, in southern India, in September 1922. During a tumultuous prewar period that saw the Indian Congress Party under the leadership of Mohandas Gandhi and Nehru campaign for *swaraj*, or independence, Sanjeevi rose steadily through the ranks of the Madras police. In 1946, following distinguished service in the Madras Special Branch and Criminal Investigation Department (CID), Sanjeevi was promoted to the post of deputy inspector general of Madras Police. Within a year, Sanjeevi was posted to New Delhi and in April 1947 was formally appointed DIB. Writing to Omandur Ramaswamy Reddy, premier of the Madras presidency, the largest and most important administrative region in southern India, Patel apologized for ordering Sanjeevi north at that time, stating that he knew "that you can ill-afford to spare him, but it is of paramount necessity that we should have a first-class officer as Director. After a great deal of search we have been able to find in him a suitable person."[11]

In fact, some of Sanjeevi's colleagues in IB found their new boss to be a distant and difficult character. K. Sankaran Nair, a fellow native of Madras who would go on to forge a long and highly distinguished career in Indian intelligence, respected Sanjeevi for his intellect and the high professional standards that he demanded from IB officers. Nair was less impressed by Sanjeevi's prickly temperament and air of assertive self-confidence that bordered on conceit.[12] A propensity to lapse into fits of willful arrogance would, ultimately, lead Sanjeevi to fall foul of his political masters and bring his tenure as DIB to an abrupt and inglorious end.

The formidable concatenation of acute challenges and inadequate resources that Sanjeevi inherited as DIB would, however, have strained the nerves of even the most assured individual. In large part, the British had rolled up their colonial intelligence structure before they departed from South Asia. It fell to Sanjeevi to fill the resulting intelligence chasm, both inside and outside India, by training new cadres of IB officers and recruiting intelligence sources from scratch. The IB's responsibilities post-1947, in operational terms, at least, remained much as they had been before the transfer of power. The remit of Sanjeevi's organization was to identify, analyze, and report on threats to Indian national security. Indian intelligence had traditionally retained little capacity for direct intervention or covert action, at home or abroad.[13] Unsurprisingly, the splintered and inchoate intelligence organization inherited by Sanjeevi struggled to cope in the midst of the widespread communal violence and political turmoil that followed the Indian subcontinent's partition. Observing events from afar, Guy Liddell, deputy director of the British Security Service, criticized IB's "complete lack of intelligence about what is going on in various parts of India." "D.I.B is not," Liddell observed acidly in October 1947, "even a shadow of its former self."[14]

Sanjeevi set about addressing inadequacies in IB's ranks by recruiting a new cadre of intelligence officers directly from India's most prestigious universities. The scheme aimed to draw the best and brightest students into IB

and, in the longer-term, groom them for senior positions within the organization. Sanjeevi's innovation floundered, however, in the face of stiff resistance
from established officers who, like the DIB, had followed a traditional route
into IB through the Indian Police Service.[15] At the same time, Sanjeevi antagonized influential political figures within the ruling Congress government, and
the country's military hierarchy, by seeking new and broad executive powers
for his organization. Having direct personal experience of an oppressive British intelligence system, many in the Congress Party, Patel included, feared
that Sanjeevi's grab for power threatened to place IB beyond the legislative
scrutiny appropriate in a democracy. Moreover, a concurrent bid by the DIB
to secure control over all intelligence matters, civil and military, met with a
firm rebuff from India's armed forces. Air Marshal Sir Thomas Elmhirst, who
continued to run the Indian Air Force after 1947, observed that Sanjeevi had
provoked "a certain amount of trouble" by seeking to assert his authority over
the country's Joint Intelligence Committee (JIC). Having suggested to his
military colleagues that the DIB should not only chair the JIC but "control all
Intelligence—internal, external, military, naval and air," Sanjeevi was curtly
instructed that such a proposal was unthinkable and that he should "concern
himself with internal security and with the running of a certain number of
agents into adjacent territory."[16]

Having suffered a series of domestic setbacks, Sanjeevi looked abroad in
an effort to bolster IB's fortunes. In December 1948, he traveled to London to
hold discussions with the British Security Service, otherwise known as MI5.
Guy Liddell, MI5's deputy director, noted that his Indian colleague was "obviously appalled by the size of his task. He [Sanjeevi] told me pathetically that
the Indian Government expected him to know everything well in advance."
Having listened to Sanjeevi's complaints that political jealousies inside the
ruling Congress Party threatened to cripple the authority and effectiveness
of IB as a national intelligence agency, Liddell reflected with surprise that
his counterpart appeared to be seeking "almost dictatorial powers." Political
pressure to deliver results quite beyond the capabilities of IB, Liddell mused,
appeared to have induced Sanjeevi to contemplate the creation of "an enormous Gestapo, which will cost the country a great deal of money and may well
be corrupt and inefficient."[17] Back in India, Bill U'ren, MI5's resident security liaison officer, who under an agreement reached between Liddell and
Patel back in 1947 facilitated intelligence exchange between London and New
Delhi, agreed that Sanjeevi had set himself "an almost impossible task." In an
effort to appease his political superiors, U'ren confirmed that the DIB had
not only placed IB officers in all of India's provinces but was simultaneously
running agents directly from New Delhi without the knowledge of local staff.

Such a step-up, MI5 reasoned, would foster confusion and encourage discord between the center and India's regions, stoking "local jealousies" and compromising intelligence capabilities.[18]

Sanjeevi went on to establish a close collaborative relationship with MI5. In June 1950, U'ren's successor in India, Eric Kitchen, emphasized to London that the DIB wasted "no opportunity of stressing the value which he places on maintaining our relationship on a professional and personal basis."[19] Relations between the Security Service and IB on Sanjeevi's watch became so close that London thought nothing of approaching the DIB to request help in collecting intelligence behind the Iron Curtain. In July 1949, the British Secret Intelligence Service, or MI6, was under criticism for its dearth of sources inside the Soviet Union. In an effort to improve British intelligence coverage of the USSR, MI5 approached Sanjeevi to inquire whether IB would be willing to employ Indian citizens traveling to the Soviet Union in an attempt to cultivate sources of information.[20] Indeed, Liddell was to crow that in intelligence terms, "India is relying more and more on us [MI5] and they could not do without our S.L.O. there at all. This is satisfactory."[21]

Less acceptable to the British was an apparent reluctance on the part of Sanjeevi to fully appreciate the magnitude of the Communist threat in India. In the view of British diplomats in India, the DIB failed to comprehend the transnational direction and wider regional threat posed by Communist activity in Asia. Rather, to British alarm, Sanjeevi seemed to take a more circumscribed approach to Communism inside India, considering it to be little more "than a radical and possibly violent Indian political movement, aimed against the present Congress Government."[22] In contrast, the British were alarmed that Communist influence in India appeared to be on the rise and "exert[ing] a considerable indirect political influence by swaying Indian outlook towards the left." Commenting on this difference in outlook, Alexander Symon, Britain's deputy high commissioner in India, concluded that

> his [Sanjeevi's] opinions serve the . . . purpose of showing us how very far the Director of the Intelligence Bureau has yet to go in his Communist education. He seems to regard the movement as a purely internal nuisance to be classed with any other political body in India and he shows no signs of regarding Communism as an international conspiracy aimed at the Sovietization of Asia and the World. His views seem to me to be somewhat superficial.[23]

The intelligence services of the United States, and above all, the Central Intelligence Agency (CIA), proved eager to provide Sanjeevi with a corrective lesson in the insidious menace of international Communism. In early 1949, the DIB was invited to Washington for talks with the Federal Bureau of Investigation (FBI) and CIA. Before Sanjeevi's arrival in North America, Howard Donovan, counselor at the US embassy in New Delhi, forwarded the State Department a biographical sketch of the head of Indian intelligence. Sanjeevi, Donovan noted, "is a man of dignified appearance and bearing. He speaks excellent English and is obviously a man of good family and background. He is a Hindu, but is not a vegetarian. . . . He never uses alcohol in any form . . . and he does not smoke. . . . The subject's chief hobbies are gardening and astrology."[24]

It is difficult to conceive of an individual more removed from the hackneyed and stereotypical image of a rugged and swashbuckling Cold War intelligence officer. But while Sanjeevi was certainly no James Bond, he did, in American eyes at least, have one important asset. The DIB was, the US embassy in Delhi reported, thought to be, "very close to Prime Minister Jawaharlal Nehru."[25] In fact, Sanjeevi was not nearly as intimate with the Indian premier as US officials believed. Revealingly, the DIB's visit to the United States did not get off to a propitious start. India's ambassador in Washington, and Nehru's sister, Vijaya Lakshmi Pandit, took exception to the intelligence chief's failure to advise her of his presence in America. On taking the matter up with her brother, the irritated Pandit was assured by Nehru that she had been "perfectly justified" in protesting at Sanjeevi's behavior. "I was greatly annoyed myself," Nehru added. "As a matter of fact I saw Sanjeevi before he went away and laid great stress on his contacting you and keeping in touch with you throughout his visit."[26]

The principal purpose of Sanjeevi's visit to the United States was to study the operations and methods of the Federal Bureau of Investigation and the state police.[27] Building external intelligence capability represented a secondary concern. Early that year, Sanjeevi had formed an overseas intelligence branch within IB. Initially, two officers were recruited from outside IB to work for the organization under diplomatic cover as first secretaries in India's embassies in Paris and Bonn. The DIB hoped to glean information from the CIA on foreign intelligence operations.[28] Ahead of Sanjeevi's arrival in Washington, Loy Henderson, the United States' ambassador in New Delhi, cautioned US intelligence officials that Sanjeevi's visit was likely to have "wide ramifications in our over-all relations with India."[29] At the time, India's security and intelligence forces were battling to suppress a violent Communist-led insurrection in Telegana, in the south of the country. American diplomats were hopeful that the ongoing threat posed by militant Communism inside India would encourage Sanjeevi to solicit advice and support from his counterparts in the United States.

Sanjeevi wished, above all, to replicate the intimate relationship that the IB had established with MI5, and draw on the internal security expertise and counterespionage experience of the FBI and its enigmatic director, J. Edgar Hoover. The Indian intelligence supremo confided to Loy Henderson that he had "been looking forward with particular enthusiasm to meeting and having a heart-to-heart with . . . J. Edgar Hoover." To Henderson's mortification, however, Sanjeevi subsequently confirmed that he had been left "boiling with resentment" by the off-hand manner in which the imperious Hoover had received him. The "deep-seated pique" that Hoover stirred in Sanjeevi was evident when the latter made it plain to a shocked Henderson that "if a liaison was contemplated [between US and Indian intelligence services] even remotely involving the F.B.I. . . . he [Sanjeevi] would not only advise against us making such a proposal but would personally oppose it if it were made."[30]

In contrast, the CIA went out of its way to please and impress Sanjeevi. Having been warmly welcomed and lavishly entertained by senior agency figures—including Col. Richard Stilwell, chief of the agency's Far East division; Kermit "Kim" Roosevelt, shortly to achieve notoriety for his exploits in Iran; and director of Central Intelligence, Roscoe Hillenkoetter—Sanjeevi came away from Washington with a notably positive impression of the CIA.[31] Significantly, and to the CIA's satisfaction, the head of IB embraced the agency's offer to explore "the possibility of establishing an official liaison on Communist matters."[32] Sanjeevi's experience in the United States was to cast a long shadow over Indo-US intelligence liaison and, more broadly, Washington's Cold War relationship with New Delhi. The DIB's visit to North America ensured that it would be the CIA, and not, as Sanjeevi had intended, the FBI, that became India's strategic intelligence partner.[33] Co-opting Sanjeevi as a tacit American Cold War ally was deemed all the more important by US officials given what they considered to be "the supercilious and smug approach of the members of the Nehru dynasty toward the US and Americans in general." State Department officers responsible for South Asia identified a whiff of condescension in their interactions not only with Jawaharlal Nehru but also Vijayalakshmi Pandit, and Nehru's cousin, Braj Kumar Nehru, then executive director at the World Bank.[34]

Within a matter of months, however, American plans for Sanjeevi were rendered superfluous. In July 1950, Sanjeevi was sacked as DIB and sent back to the police service in Madras. Over the previous two years, Nehru had harbored a growing unease at the quality of the product that he was receiving from the Intelligence Bureau, a state of affairs that the Indian premier never failed to communicate to Sanjeevi.[35] The DIB had also made a powerful enemy in Krishna Menon, India's high commissioner in the United Kingdom and one of Nehru's staunchest political allies and closest confidants. Much as he had done with Pandit in the United States, Sanjeevi alienated Menon by arranging to meet with MI5 in London without the high commissioner's prior knowledge. Furthermore, by informing Patel of criticisms that Menon had leveled at the home minister in the course of private discussions with Sanjeevi, the DIB sparked a political furor in New Delhi.[36] More important, India's intelligence chief's abrasive manner, appetite for power, and aptitude for political controversy exhausted the goodwill of Patel and fatally depleted his currency inside the Home Ministry.[37]

In Sanjeevi's place, Patel appointed Bhola Nath Mullik as India's second DIB. Mullik had been working in New Delhi as deputy director of IB since September 1948. Inside India's intelligence community, Mullik had earned the reputation as an exceptionally industrious individual, with firm opinions yet a genuine concern for the welfare of subordinates.[38] Articulate and politically astute, Mullik had been elevated to the post of DIB over the heads of several more senior candidates within the Indian government bureaucracy.[39] Mullik's rapid rise to the top of Indian intelligence did not pass without comment or criticism. Y. D. Gundevia, India's foreign secretary, took a dim view of the new DIB, characterizing him as a sycophant incapable or unwilling to speak truth to power.[40] Further afield, Guy Liddell found Mullik to be a much less agreeable personality than his opposite number in Pakistan, Kazim Raza. To Liddell's mind, Mullik was "rather shifty" and less "balanced and intelligent" than his deputy in IB, Madan Hooja.[41] While he considered Mullik's personality as "not a very pleasant one," Liddell attributed the DIB's asperity, in part, to "the fact that as a rather young man he has been put into a very big job and is a little conscious of his position."[42]

Under Mullik's direction, the IB enhanced its influence in the upper echelons of the Indian government. One prominent contemporary observer of the Nehru governments has attributed the increased political power accumulated by IB to Mullik's personal relationship with Nehru. "Access to, and the confidence of the Prime Minister, were the prerequisite of influence in the Government in those days," it has been noted, "and Mullik enjoyed them to the full."[43] Moreover, Mullik's control of security dossiers on many of Nehru's closest colleagues and political adversaries, coupled with the increasingly important role played by intelligence in domestic Indian politics, ensured that India's premier had good reason to keep his spy chief close at hand. Much as Sanjeevi had before him, however, Mullik's accumulation of bureaucratic authority was greeted with concern among the senior ranks of India's armed forces. In particular, a suspicion festered in military circles that the DIB was feeding false information to Nehru regarding purported military plots against the civil government, in a bid to reinforce IB's standing at the expense of the army.[44]

Abandoning Sanjeevi's measured attitude to the subversive threat posed to India by Communism, Mullik ensured that IB adopted a much more aggressive approach on this issue.[45] In May 1958, when Roger Hollis, director-general of MI5, visited India, he recorded with satisfaction that the DIB's appraisal of the danger posed by Communist subversion in the subcontinent was much closer to the British Security Service's position than that of the Indian government.[46] Dismissive of Sanjeevi's plans to extend IB's operations in Europe, Mullik instead focused on improving his organization's external intelligence-gathering resources in countries abutting India, which he believed served India's national security interests best.[47] Accordingly, Mullik concentrated IB's limited capacity for covert action on Pakistan and threats to Indian national security posed by armed irredentist movements in Nagaland and Mizoram, which lay on India's northeastern borders with Burma and China.[48]

One significant point of continuity between India's first and second DIBs lay in the field of foreign intelligence liaison. Mullik continued Sanjeevi's practice of maintaining close collaborative relations between IB and MI5. In 1951 Mullik traveled to London to attend the second Commonwealth security conference alongside colleagues from Canada, Australia, New Zealand, South Africa, Pakistan, and Ceylon. Over the subsequent decade, MI5 officers conducted regular visits to IB headquarters and outstations across India while Indian intelligence officers traveled to London to attend British security courses. Indeed, the intimacy of ties between the British and Indian intelligence communities was such that in 1957 Mullik confided to Roger Hollis, "In my talks and discussions, I never felt that I was dealing with any organization which was not my own."[49] Mullik played up the criticisms that he would encounter in New Delhi if the scale and scope of IB's interaction with Western intelligence agencies were to become known to his political masters. In reality, it is more plausible to conclude that Jawaharlal Nehru was fully aware of the nature of IB's relationship with MI5 and the CIA, and elected to turn a blind eye to it on the ground of expediency.

Revealingly, by the end of the 1950s, as India's relationship with the People's Republic of China deteriorated sharply, the IB chose to "look the other way" as CIA aircraft transited through Indian airspace in support of agency-sponsored resistance operations in Chinese-controlled Tibet, and CIA operatives spirited the Dalai Lama out of Lhasa and into northern India following an abortive Tibetan uprising in 1959.[50] By the early 1960s, the CIA had a sizable, growing, and active in-country presence in India. Having initially operated from a single "station," or base of operations, in New Delhi, the agency progressively extended the geographical scope of its activities, establishing a network of smaller outstations in Bombay, Calcutta, and Madras. One contemporary American observer in India recorded that local agency personnel appeared active "more than anything else in getting inside the [ruling] Congress Party for purposes of information or influence."[51] In 1959 the CIA worked with the Congress Party to remove a democratically elected Communist Party of India administration in the southern Indian state of Kerala. By secretly channeling funds to Congress Party functionaries and local anti-Communist labor leaders, the CIA helped to destabilize, and eventually dislodge, Kerala's Communist government.[52] In July 1961, the extent to which American intelligence cooperation with India had evolved under Mullik was brought home to John Kenneth Galbraith, the US ambassador in New Delhi. Galbraith was surprised, and faintly amused, when, in the course of being introduced to local dignitaries in southern India, a man stepped forward and exclaimed exuberantly, "Mr. Ambassador, I am the superintendent of police here in Madras. I would like to tell you that I have the most satisfactory relationship with your spies."[53]

The defining moment of Mullik's intelligence career occurred in the late autumn of 1962. Under Mullik, IB had continued to develop as an essentially domestic security service with a notably limited capacity to run external intelligence-gathering operations. Such capabilities as IB did have outside India were deployed preponderantly to counter perceived threats from Pakistan. From the late 1950s, despite a sharp decline in New Delhi's relations with Beijing, which brought a long, simmering border dispute between Asia's two most populous nations to the fore, little of IB's attention was directed toward China. In part, Mullik's decision not to focus more on Chinese intentions with respect to India was reflective of a wider political blind spot in Nehru's government. The Indian premier himself, and his influential defense minister, Krishna Menon, were preoccupied by territorial disagreements with Pakistan, and more especially the Kashmir dispute. A marked reluctance existed among senior Indian policy makers to contemplate a looming Chinese threat.[54] As a result, when the Chinese People's Liberation Army swept into northern India in October 1962, routing the Indian Army in the process, the Indian government, its people, and not least, Mullik's IB, responded with a mixture of bewilderment and dismay.[55]

India's military humiliation claimed a swathe of prominent victims. Shattered by the very public repudiation of his China policy, Nehru's political power ebbed away, his health suffered, and he died in office, in May 1964, an embittered and much diminished figure. Krishna Menon's mismanagement of India's defense portfolio saw him hounded out of office. Mullik, too, never recovered from the stigma associated with IB's failure to anticipate the timing and scale of China's military assault on India, an episode widely characterized as the most momentous and overt intelligence failure in the country's history.[56] He lingered on as DIB until 1964, during which time he belatedly sought to rebalance Indian intelligence capabilities away from an overweening preoccupation on Pakistan. Drawing on support from Western intelligence partners, most notably the CIA, the IB equipped and trained a clandestine warfare unit to monitor Chinese military supply routes into Tibet. Under an agreement reached between Mullik and James Critchfield, chief of the CIA's Near East operations, Langley furnished support to the Indo-Tibetan Special Frontier Force (SFF), a unit modeled on the US Army Green Berets, or special forces. From the winter of 1964, SFF operations along the Sino-Indian border were coordinated by a joint Indo-US command center in New Delhi. The IB went on to mount a joint operation with the CIA to insert nuclear-powered surveillance equipment on two of India's Himalayan peaks in a bid to collect data on Chinese atomic tests.[57]

The damage inflicted by the 1962 Sino-Indian border war on Mullik's reputation as a spy chief, however, proved terminal. Mullik's efforts to shape the historical narrative of the conflict through the publication of books with such evocative titles as *Chinese Betrayal* proved largely facile and counterproductive.[58] These self-serving accounts, intended to pin the blame for the 1962 debacle on others, served Mullik's interests badly. How naive, some critics charged, for a senior intelligence officer to accuse the Chinese so publicly of betrayal. Surely, had China not behaved as any nation-state would in the circumstances and looked to advance its national interest? It was Mullik, the DIB's detractors have continued to assert, who "betrayed" his own foolishness and ineptitude by daring to suggest otherwise.[59]

A notably positive legacy of Mullik's controversial tenure as DIB lay in his ability to identify and develop intelligence officers of exceptional ability. In this regard, the emergence of Rameshwar Nath Kao—first as an IB officer of uncommon skill and resourcefulness and later as the inaugural chief of India's external intelligence service, the Research and Analysis Wing (R&AW)— stands as the preeminent case in point. In the context of Indian intelligence, Kao was somewhat of a hybrid. Born into a family of upper-caste Kashmiri pandits, after graduating from Lucknow and Allahabad universities with degrees in English literature, Kao went on to join the Indian Police Service in 1940. After serving for seven years as a police officer, following India's independence Kao transferred to the IB.[60] Widely respected by colleagues at home and abroad as an unassuming and modest individual blessed with a tough and subtle intellect, Kao was revered above all for his uncompromising professionalism and acute analytical brain.[61] In the course of a distinguished intelligence career that spanned four decades, R. N. Kao emerged as modern India's supreme spy chief. Under Kao's leadership, Indian intelligence played a crucial role in the 1971 Indo-Pakistani War and the emergence of Bangladesh as a sovereign state. In addition, Kao adroitly utilized India's intelligence agencies to further New Delhi's interests in Afghanistan, assist postcolonial African countries in the creation of intelligence and security organizations, offer covert support to the African National Congress' anti-apartheid struggle in South Africa, and nullify threats posed to the Indian state from insurgents closer to home, in Mizoram and Nagaland.[62]

From the very beginning of Kao's intelligence service, he benefited from the existence of a close personal connection with the Nehru political dynasty. Kao's family hailed from Allahabad in northern India, the home of the Nehru clan. During her childhood, Kao's mother had been an intimate of Kamala Nehru, Jawaharlal Nehru's wife. Kao's father-in-law, A. N. Mulla, an eminent lawyer, became a colleague and friend of Motilal Nehru, the future Indian premier's father. As a Kashmiri Brahmin, Kao was born and raised in the same social and cultural milieu as the Nehru family.[63] While Kao's contemporaries never questioned his effectiveness as an intelligence officer of the highest caliber, his social connections with the all-powerful Nehru family certainly helped to ease his path to the very top of India's intelligence hierarchy. When Kao joined the IB in 1948 as an assistant director for security, it is notable that he was posted to act as personal security officer to Jawaharlal Nehru.[64]

In April 1955 Kao's undoubted abilities as an intelligence officer and the confidence that he inspired in India's prime minister were demonstrated by the *Kashmir Princess* incident. An extremely sensitive and potentially incendiary episode in China's Cold War relations with the United States, the *Kashmir Princess* crisis had developed after the Communist Chinese government chartered an Air India "Super Constellation" aircraft to ferry officials from Hong Kong to a conference of nonaligned nations held in the Indonesian city of Bandung. The Chinese premier, Zhou Enlai, was scheduled to travel to Bandung on the Indian aircraft. On April 11, 1955, the *Kashmir Princess* crashed into the Indian Ocean en route to Indonesia, with the loss of all its passengers and all but three of its Indian aircrew.[65] Zhou's life was saved by a last-minute change of travel plans. Following the disaster, the Chinese government charged that the *Kashmir Princess* had been sabotaged by nationalist Chinese agents who, with the CIA's support, planned to assassinate Zhou.[66] Coming at a point when the United States' relations with China were under great strain owing to mounting tension in the Taiwan Straits, Nehru gave Kao the delicate task of investigating the aircraft's loss.

Unraveling the facts behind its midair disintegration was to prove problematic and politically difficult. Kao had to work with, and secure the trust of, a Chinese government that was convinced of America's complicity in bringing down the *Kashmir Princess*.[67] Moreover, he had to liaise with security forces in Hong Kong and British intelligence services as a consequence of the plane's departure from UK sovereign territory. Not least, open speculation that the CIA had, in some way, been involved in the loss of the Indian airliner necessitated engaging in discussions with the agency's headquarters in Langley. Kao skillfully negotiated the turbulent political waters of his assignment and emerged from the investigation with his reputation and prestige considerably enhanced. The Chinese government was impressed by the proficiency and apparent objectivity with which Kao went about his work.[68] Moreover, the British officials in Hong Kong praised the Indian intelligence officer for the "moderating influence" that he had brought to bear on the enraged Chinese authorities.[69] All in all, Kao's professionalism and pragmatic good sense helped to extract much of the diplomatic sting from a potentially explosive Cold War intelligence imbroglio.

Toward the end of the 1950s Kao's standing as an intelligence troubleshooter received a further boost after he completed a special overseas assignment in Africa. In 1958 Kwame Nkrumah, prime minister of the newly independent West African state of Ghana, approached Nehru at a Commonwealth prime ministers' conference to request Indian support in establishing an intelligence organization. In common with most postcolonial states, a lack of qualified or experienced personnel had compelled Ghana to retain British administrators in senior government positions, including ones in security and intelligence. British officials had persuaded Nkrumah to permit an MI5 security liaison officer to continue working in the country in a countersubversion and internal security capacity. Nkrumah was keen, however, to reduce his government's dependence on MI5, and Kao was given the task of creating a Ghanaian intelligence service from scratch. Working under the cover provided by the Indian High Commission in the country's capital, Accra, Kao distinguished himself by helping to establish the Foreign Research Service Bureau (FRSB), Ghana's first independent intelligence service.[70]

The biggest triumph of Kao's career, however, occurred after he was promoted to lead one of India's intelligence agencies. In 1965, following a brief war between India and Pakistan over the disputed state of Kashmir, further discord surfaced between the IB and the Indian armed services over the quality of the Intelligence Bureau's product and the scope of its responsibilities. A move by the Indian army, supported by the Indian defense minister, Y. B. Chavan, to encroach on IB's intelligence remit was successfully rebuffed. However, an ensuing political debate developed in India over the appropriate role and structure of a modern intelligence service. Indira Gandhi, Nehru's daughter, who had assumed the position of Indian prime minister in January 1966, saw domestic political advantages in transferring IB's foreign intelligence responsibilities to a new external intelligence organization. Reflecting on the rationale for restructuring Indian intelligence, P. N. Haksar, principal secretary to the prime minister and one of Gandhi's political confidants, noted at the time, "The case for separating the 'internal' Intelligence Organisation from 'external' Intelligence is obvious enough. . . . Intelligence requires astute and sophisticated correlation of political, economic, historical and psychological factors which cannot be done by those trained under Police discipline."[71]

Having commissioned Kao to examine how precisely a new external intelligence arm might function, Gandhi subsequently accepted the former's recommendation to establish an "Indian CIA," with the innocuous nomenclature "the Research and Analysis Wing." The new organization was to report to the cabinet secretariat and fall under the prime minister's direct control. Moreover, on making the decision to inaugurate the R&AW, Gandhi promptly decreed that Kao would serve as its first head, or secretary.[72]

In the face of fierce opposition from IB, Kao calmly and efficiently integrated India's external intelligence infrastructure into his new organization. On September 21, 1968, the R&AW officially came into being with a skeleton staff composed of a couple of hundred officers drawn from the ranks of IB. Within little more than a year, Kao managed the remarkable feat of transforming the R&AW from a paper project into a fully operational intelligence service.[73] A natural innovator and assiduous student of tradecraft, Kao looked for inspiration and guidance from the CIA; the Israeli intelligence service, Mossad; and French, British, and Japanese colleagues in the external intelligence world. Incorporating best practice from around the globe, the R&AW developed an economic intelligence unit; a science and technology section; codebreaking and satellite monitoring capabilities; a psychological warfare component, the information division; and even a public relations arm.[74]

In 1971, under Kao's direction, the R&AW played a pivotal role in India's third military conflict with Pakistan since independence and contributed to the transformation of East Pakistan into the sovereign state of Bangladesh. Specifically, the R&AW furnished India's policy makers and armed services with intelligence on Pakistan's politico-military intentions and capabilities; trained Bengali "freedom fighters" for operations inside East Pakistan; established contact with Bengali officials working for the Pakistani government and persuaded many to switch allegiance and support an independent Bangladesh; and mounted a psychological warfare operation to discredit Pakistan's military regime in the eyes of world opinion.[75] Reflecting on the effectiveness of the R&AW's performance, one Indian government official observed prosaically that "1971 was the year of the first test for the R&AW, which was very closely involved with the Bangladesh and Pakistan operations. The results achieved during this period justified the decision of the Government to set up a new foreign intelligence organization on modern lines."[76] In fact, the events of 1971 had proved a triumph for Kao and the R&AW, both of whom, as one Indian intelligence officer later reflected, became "the toast of the [Indian] policymakers."[77]

In the years that followed, successive Indian governments tasked the R&AW with an ever-increasing number of additional responsibilities. These encompassed areas as diverse as the collection and dissemination of economic intelligence as well as those relating to developments in advanced conventional armaments, nuclear weaponry, and the connected fields of science and technology. Equally, as Indian government officials acknowledged, the R&AW rendered "valuable service by maintaining secret liaison with other friendly foreign intelligence services in matters of common interest. This has often helped in reaching political understanding with different countries, in dealing with problems of international terrorism, and also providing an absolutely secure channel of direct communication, without diplomatic protocol, between the heads of governments."[78] Indeed, it was perhaps in the field of international intelligence liaison that the combination of Kao's assured and urbane personality and shrewd professionalism served India's interests best.

Under Kao, the R&AW developed strong and productive relationships with counterparts in the United States, Canada, the United Kingdom, France, West Germany, Israel, and Japan, and also with Soviet and Eastern European intelligence agencies. In the Indian Ocean region and Persian Gulf, Kao cooperated closely with France's Service for External Documentation and Counter-Espionage (SDECE) and Iran's SAVAK to explore ways of collecting intelligence on the United States.[79] Elsewhere, and notably in northern Burma, when it suited India's purposes, Kao and the R&AW worked alongside the CIA to limit Chinese influence in Southeast Asia.[80] When serving as director of Central Intelligence between 1976 and 1977, the future American president, George H. W. Bush, became a firm friend of Kao. Writing to Kao in June 1984, when serving as vice president in the Reagan administration, Bush noted that he had "consistently found our conversations to be informative and valuable." Revealingly, Bush went on to stress the extent to which "we have used our personal communications in the past to pass informal information between our two governments." Political problems then bedeviling Indo-US relations, the vice president intimated, might best be resolved by utilizing well-established intelligence channels rather than normal diplomatic means.[81]

In point of fact, the political connections that had served Kao so well earlier in his career had, by the mid-1970s, begun to redound to his disadvantage. Above all, Indira Gandhi's declaration of a state of national emergency in India in 1975 (it lasted until 1977) saw the prime minister's political opponents accuse her intelligence chief of exceeding his powers, undermining democracy, and facilitating a police state. Although Kao's critics could furnish no evidence to support charges of impropriety on the part of the R&AW, a perception became established in the Indian press, and among sections of the government bureaucracy, that the intelligence organization had allowed itself to become politicized and had collaborated with Gandhi in suppressing opposition to her government. In April 1977, with Gandhi now out of office, one Indian government official recorded that

> there has been a series of articles in newspapers and journals, making various speculations about the Research & Analysis Wing and Sri R. N. Kao. . . . All of them are ill-informed. . . . In these publications, gross and serious charges have also been made against Sri Kao, as well as the R&AW, accusing them of going beyond the charter of their duty and interfering in internal politics. These include allegations of tapping telephones of . . . Gandhi's political opponents, exercizing surveillance over opposition leaders, maintaining confidential dossiers about them, and a host of bizarre stories.[82]

By the middle of that year, the momentum that had gathered in India behind rumors of the R&AW's impropriety had reached a point where many public commentators openly questioned the agency's continued viability.[83] Kao was personally enmeshed in a web of scurrilous accusations and was the subject of hostile press comment. Saying that he knew "for a fact" that charges leveled against Kao were baseless, P. N. Haksar nonetheless lamented that the R&AW's chief had "paid dearly by being unwittingly drawn into the cross-fire of political controversy."[84]

Kao stepped down as the head of R&AW before 1977 came to an end. Returning briefly to serve an undistinguished term as senior adviser to Indira Gandhi at the beginning of the 1980s, with a remit covering security and intelligence matters, Kao slipped quietly into permanent retirement following Gandhi's assassination in 1984. Of late, a trend among erstwhile Indian intelligence officers to revisit their careers in print has led to Kao's memory being revived in the contemporary Indian imagination. In the late 1960s, India's first generation of external intelligence officers were dubbed the "Kao boys," in honor of their chief. These former colleagues of Kao, in particular, have sought to cast him in the role of "unsung hero," whose "monumental" contributions to the security of the Indian state and the broader intelligence community have been shamefully undervalued.[85] Certainly, Kao's record of achievement, first as a field officer of uncommon proficiency and flair, and latterly as an intelligence leader of rare insight and innovation, marks him out as India's foremost spy chief.

Notes

1. R. K. Yadav, *Mission R&AW* (New Delhi: Manas Publications, 2014), 24.

2. Bhashyam Kasturi, *Intelligence Services: Analysis, Organisation and Functions* (New Delhi: Lancer Publishers, 1995), 25.

3. Patel interview from March 1949 in *Le Courrier des Indes* [The mail of the Indies], May 29, 1949, attachment to R. H. Ingersoll to Joseph S. Sparks, "Indian Intelligence Service," July 11, 1949, Record Group (RG) 59, Office of South Asian Affairs India Affairs, 1944–57, Lot file 57D373, Box 2, Folder Memo Book 1949, US National Archives, College Park, Maryland (USNA).

4. Patel interview from March 1949 in *Le Courrier des Indes*, May 29, 1949, attachment to R. H. Ingersoll to Joseph S. Sparks, "Indian Intelligence Service," July 11, 1949, RG59, Office of South Asian Affairs India Affairs, 1944–57, Lot file 57D373, Box 2, Folder Memo Book 1949, USNA.

5. Y. D. Gundevia, *Outside the Archives* (New Delhi: Sangam Books, 1984), 208–9.

6. "'Reds Hinder Nation's Advance,' Says Nehru," *Hindustan Times*, January 13, 1960.

7. Yadav, *Mission R&AW*, 24.

8. B. N. Mullik, *My Years with Nehru, 1948–1964* (New Delhi: Allied Publishers, 1972), 57.

9. Nehru to Mountbatten, September 18, 1954, New Delhi, *Selected Writings of Jawaharlal Nehru* (*SWJN*), ed. Ravinder Kumar and H. Y. Sharada Prasad (New Delhi: Oxford University Press, 2000), 26:221–23.

10. Jawaharlal Nehru, November 2, 1947, New Delhi, in *Letter to Chief Ministers, 1947–1964*, vol. 1, *1947–1949*, ed. G. Parthasarathi (New Delhi: Oxford University Press, 1985), 10–11.

11. Kasturi, *Intelligence Services*, 26.

12. K. Sankaran Nair, *Inside IB and RAW: The Rolling Stone that Gathered Moss* (New Delhi: Manas Publications, 2013), 90.

13. Kasturi, *Intelligence Services*, 27.

14. October 15, 1947, Liddell Diaries (LD), 85–88, KV/4/469, United Kingdom National Archives, Kew, London (UKNA).

15. Yadav, *Mission R&AW*, 26.

16. May 5, 1948, LD, 90–92, KV/4/470, UKNA.

17. December 7, 1948, LD, 204, KV/4/470, UKNA.

18. December 9, 1948, LD, 205, KV/4/470, UKNA.

19. Christopher Andrew, *The Defence of the Realm: The Authorized History of MI5* (London: Allen Lane, 2009), 443.

20. July 6, 1949, LD, 141, KV/4/471, UKNA.

21. May 23, 1950, LD, 91, KV/4/472, UKNA.

22. C. H. Masterman to A. C. B. Symon, March 2, 1948, FCO 37/521, UKNA.

23. A. C. B. Symon to Paul Patrick, February 14, 1948, DO 133/128, UKNA.

24. Howard Donovan, "Biographical Document on Sanjeevi," May 16, 1949, appendix to J. C. Satterthwaite to James E. Webb, June 15, 1949, RG59, Office of South Asian Affairs: India Affairs 1944–57, Lot file 57D373, Box 2, Folder Memorandum to the Secretary 1949, USNA.

25. J. C. Satterthwaite to James E. Webb, June 15, 1949, RG59, Office of South Asian Affairs: India Affairs 1944–57, Lot file 57D373, Box 2, Folder Memorandum to the Secretary 1949, USNA.

26. Jawaharlal Nehru to Pandit, May 20, 1949, Vijaya Lakshmi Pandit Papers (VLPP), Subject File 60, Nehru Museum and Memorial Library New Delhi (NMML); Jawaharlal Nehru to Vijaya Lakshmi Pandit, June 22, 1949, VLPP Subject File 60, NMML.

27. J. C. Satterthwaite to James E. Webb, June 15, 1949, RG59, Office of South Asian Affairs: India Affairs, 1944–57, Lot file 57D373, Box 2, Folder Memorandum to the Secretary 1949, USNA.

28. Kasturi, *Intelligence Services*, 27.

29. Satterthwaite to Webb, June 15, 1949, Lot file 57D373, Box 2, Folder Memorandum to the Secretary 1949, RG 59, USNA.

30. Loy W. Henderson to Joseph S. Sparks, April 17, 1950, and Richard W. Klise to Loy Henderson, April 18, 1950, RG59, Office of South Asian Affairs: India Affairs 1944–57, Lot file 57D373, Box 2, Folder Official Informal Jan-May 1950, USNA.

31. Joseph S. Sparks to Loy W. Henderson, July 8, 1949, RG59, Office of South Asian Affairs: India Affairs 1944–57, Lot file 57D373, Box 2, Folder Official Informal July 1949, USNA.

32. Loy W. Henderson to Joseph S. Sparks, April 17, 1950, and Richard W. Klise to Loy Henderson, April 18, 1950, RG59, Office of South Asian Affairs: India Affairs 1944–57, Lot file 57D373, Box 2, Folder Official Informal Jan-May 1950, USNA.

33. J. C. Satterthwaite to James E. Webb, June 15, 1949, RG59, Office of South Asian Affairs: India Affairs 1944–57, Lot file 57D373, Box 2, Folder Memorandum to the Secretary 1949, USNA.

34. Joseph S. Sparks to Loy W Henderson, July 8, 1949, RG59 Office of South Asian Affairs: India Affairs 1944–57, Lot file 57D373 Box 2 Folder Official Informal July 1949, USNA.

35. Kasturi, *Intelligence Services*, 27.

36. See Nehru to Krishna Menon, January 5, 1949, 385; and Nehru to Vallabhbhai Patel, January 6, 1949, 386, *SWJN*, 2nd series, vol. 9, ed. S. Gopal (New Delhi: Oxford University Press, 1990).

37. Nair, *Inside IB and RAW*, 90.

38. Ibid., 95.

39. Neville Maxwell, *India's China War* (London: Pelican, 1972), 335; and Kasturi, *Intelligence Services*, 27.

40. Gundevia, *Outside the Archives*, 211–12.

41. May 11, 1951, LD, 70, KV/4/473, UKNA; August 3, 1951, LD, 135, KV/4/473, UKNA.

42. May 17, 1951, LD, 73, KV/4/473, UKNA.

43. Maxwell, *India's China War*, 335.

44. Nair, *Inside IB and RAW*, 98.

45. Ibid., 98.

46. Andrew, *Defence of the Realm*, 445–46.

47. Nair, *Inside IB and RAW*, 94.

48. B. Raman, *The Kaoboys of R&AW: Down Memory Lane* (New Delhi: Lancer, 2007), 7–8.

49. Andrew, *Defence of the Realm*, 444–45.

50. See Kenneth Conboy and James Morrison, *The CIA's Secret War in Tibet* (Lawrence: University Press of Kansas, 2002); and John Kenneth Knaus, *Orphans of the Cold War: America and the Tibetan Struggle for Survival* (New York: PublicAffairs, 1999).

51. Rosenthal to Salisbury, undated, Box 159, CIA Series 1965–66, Harrison Salisbury Papers, Butler Library, Columbia University (BLCU).

52. Ellsworth Bunker, Oral History, June 18, and July 17, 1979, BLCU, 67–68.

53. John Kenneth Galbraith, "The Year of the Spy (in a Manner of Speaking)," *New York Times*, January 5, 1986.

54. Gundevia, *Outside the Archives*, 211–12; and Nair, *Inside IB and RAW*, 98–99.

55. Yaacov Vertzberger, "Bureaucratic-Organizational Politics and Information Processing in a Developing State," *International Studies Quarterly* 28, no. 1 (1984): 69–95.

56. See Manoj Shrivastava, *Re-Energising Indian Intelligence* (New Delhi: Vij Books, 2013), 53; and Stephen P. Cohen and Sunil Dasgupta, *Arming without Aiming: India's Military Modernization* (Washington, DC: Brookings Institution, 2013), 47.

57. See Robert Komer to McGeorge Bundy, October 14, 1965, Box 13, Folder 6 Bundy, McG—Decisions 1965–66, National Security Files (NSF), Robert W. Komer Papers; and Walt Rostow to President Johnson, April 30, 1966, Folder "India's Unconventional Warfare Force," NSF, Lyndon B. Johnson Library (LBJL), Austin, TX. See also M. S. Kohli and Kenneth Conboy, *Spies in the Himalayas: Secret Missions and Perilous Climbs* (Lawrence: University Press of Kansas, 2003); and Knaus, *Orphans of the Cold War*, 265–76.

58. B. N. Mullik, *My Years with Nehru: The Chinese Betrayal* (New Delhi: Allied Publishers, 1971).

59. K. Shankar Bajpai, "The Unlearned Lesson of 1962," *The Hindu*, November 2, 2012, accessed November 2, 2012, http://www.thehindu.com/opinion/lead/the-unlearned-lesson-of-1962/article4055276.ece.

60. Rameshwar Nath Kao, Secretary, Cabinet Secretariat and Director of General Security, FCO 37/1923, "Leading Personalities in India 1977," UKNA; and Yadav, *Mission R&AW*, 17.

61. Rameshwar Nath Kao, Secretary, Cabinet Secretariat and Director of General Security, FCO 37/1923, "Leading Personalities in India 1977," UKNA; and P. H. Gore Both to Lord Home, April 5, 1961, DO 201/12, UKNA.

62. Raman, *Kaoboys of R&AW*, 26

63. Yadav, *Mission R&AW*, 27.

64. Ibid., 18.

65. Nehru to N. Raghavan, April 12, 1955, New Delhi, *SWJN*, ed. Ravinder Kumar and H. Y. Sharada Prasad (New Delhi: Oxford University Press, 2001), 28:33.

66. Nehru to N. R. Pillai, April 22, 1955, Bandung, *SWJN*, 28:334.

67. Nehru discussion with Chou En-lai, April 26, 1955, Bandung, *SWJN*, 28:335–37.

68. Yadav, *Mission R&AW*, 19.

69. A. Grantham to Foreign Secretary, No. 784, August 17, 1955, FO 371/115143, UKNA.

70. Nair, *Inside IB and RAW*, 123–25.

71. P. N. Haksar, "Prime Minister's Secretariat," September 14, 1967, Subject File 119, III Instalment, P. N. Haksar Papers, NMML.

72. Nair, *Inside IB and RAW*, 152–55.

73. Ibid., 152–55.

74. Yadav, *Mission R&AW*, 19.

75. Raman, *Kaoboys of R&AW*, 10.

76. Minute to P. N. Haksar, April 30, 1977, Subject File 57, I and II Instalment, P. N. Haksar papers, NMML.

77. Raman, *Kaoboys of R&AW*, 22.

78. Minute to P. N. Haksar, April 30, 1977, Subject File 57, I and II Instalment, P. N. Haksar papers, NMML.

79. Raman, *Kaoboys of R&AW*, 43–44.

80. Ibid., 20.

81. George Bush to R. N. Kao, June 19, 1984, Country File India 1984 [1] [OA-ID 19779], George Bush Library, College Station, TX.

82. Minute to P. N. Haksar, April 30, 1977, Subject File 57, I and II Instalment, P. N. Haksar papers, NMML.

83. Vappala Balachandran, *National Security and Intelligence Management: A New Paradigm* (Mumbai: Indus Source Books, 2014), 67.

84. P. N. Haksar, April 30, 1977, Subject File 57, I and II Instalment, P. N. Haksar papers, NMML.

85. Yadav, *Mission R&AW*, 21; and Raman, *Kaoboys of R&AW*, 26.

9 Emir Farid Chehab

"Father of the Lebanese Sûreté Générale"

Chikara Hashimoto

Emir Farid Chehab was the longest-serving chief in the history of the Sûreté Générale, the Lebanese security service, and is remembered as *Bay al Amn al Aam* (Father of the Sûreté Générale).[1] Emir Chehab headed the agency during Lebanon's turbulent nascent period between 1948 and 1958, and during his tenure as chief it emerged as one of the leading intelligence and security services in the Middle East. The organization played a crucial role in safeguarding the internal security of postwar Lebanon. Emir Farid Chehab was an active intelligence chief: in addition to developing and directing the Sûreté, he ran his own private network of agents, liaised with foreign intelligence and security counterparts, and was also involved in day-to-day operations, including activities outside Lebanon. He was a Middle Eastern cold warrior, fighting against Communist movements in the region owing to his belief that Communism was detrimental to Middle Eastern values and culture. He also fought for Lebanon's independence against the radical Arab nationalist movement associated with Egyptian leader Gamal Abdel Nasser.

Personality

Emir Farid Chehab was born sometime between 1905 and 1911 to the Chehab family, a Maronite Christian family of noble ancestry, who have held the title of emir (prince) since at least the eleventh century. He was the son of Emira Maryam Chehab (granddaughter of the last ruler of Lebanon) and Emir Hares Sayyed Ahmad Chehab (honorary member of the Turkish parliament) in Hadeth, Mount Lebanon.[2] The Chehabs are a prominent noble Lebanese family from the Bani Quraish tribe, descended from the tribe of the Prophet Mohammed. In the seventeenth century, part of the family converted to Christianity, so the family consisted of both Muslims and Christians.[3] General

Photo 9.1 Emir Farid Chehab, the "Father of the Lebanese Sûreté Générale." (*Hares Shehab and Youmna Asseily, son and daughter of Farid Chehab*)

Fuad Chehab, the third president of Lebanon (1958–64) after independence, was also from the Chehab family and a cousin of Emir Chehab.[4] Emir Chehab as a Maronite Christian leaned toward Christian beliefs but rarely went to church. He also kept his distance from the clergy, who had a political role in Lebanon.[5]

With a law degree from Saint Joseph University in Beirut, Emir Chehab started his career in 1930 as a detective in the colonial police in Lebanon. Thanks to a series of successful investigations that resulted in the uncovering and arrest of members of underground criminal organizations, he quickly earned a reputation for breaking up illegal gambling rings in Lebanon.[6] By using unconventional methods of disguise—such as a rich Arab tribesman, a merchant, and a Bedouin, changing clothes and wearing a false mustache—and sometimes using provocative methods to uncover the truth or prove his suspicions, he was described as an adventurous master of disguise.[7] Transferring from the colonial police in 1939, he entered the Sûreté Générale and soon rose to be assistant to the director-general, heading the counterintelligence and anti-Communist sections at the same time. In February 1941, he was imprisoned on allegations that he had contacted officials of Nazi Germany. After his release from a six-month solitary confinement without trial, he was rearrested as a political prisoner and imprisoned for a further period of eighteen months.[8] Emir Chehab later recounted the reasons for the arrests as intragovernmental fighting under the French mandate as well as some strong but unreasonable antagonism toward him from his seniors.[9]

Following Lebanon's independence and a direct request from President Bechara El-Khoury, he was released in October 1943 and reinstated to his previous position at the Sûreté. In the following year, he acted as a liaison officer between the Palestine police and the Lebanese security forces. In September 1945, he was appointed director-general of the Judicial Police. In addition to the position he already held, he was appointed by President El-Khoury in October 1947 as governor of the Beqaa Valley in Lebanon to end a postwar state of chaos there and bring order. Within three months of his appointment, he had successfully restored law and order without a single shot being fired.[10] In January 1948, as the security situation in Beirut deteriorated, he was recalled to the capital and became director-general of the Sûreté Générale. He remained in the position until September 1958.[11] Although his religious background as a Maronite Christian was certainly important to his appointment, his prestigious family connections had a less significant role in preventing other candidates from becoming the director-general. Emir Chehab was primarily chosen not for his title and family connections but rather owing to his long-established experience and expertise in the field of internal security. Above all, he was trusted by President El-Khoury, who highly prized his extraordinary professional abilities and diligence in discharging his duties since his return to the Sûreté in 1943.[12]

Emir Chehab was a gifted spy chief. Sir Patrick Coghill, former director of the Jordanian Criminal Investigation Department (CID) who remained a close friend of Chehab's, described him as "an able police officer and a most charming and delightful person."[13] According to Nicolas Nassif, the author of the official history of the Sûreté Générale, he was a prince in both his style and behavior.[14] He was certainly talented in various ways, with a lively interest in many subjects: he took part in judo and fencing, played musical instruments, and mastered seven languages in his free time.[15] Learning foreign languages was his way of understanding the cultures of his friends and foes—he could even sing the national anthem of the Soviet Union by heart.[16] He had a good sense of hospitality that made him many personal friends inside and outside Lebanon and brought him renown across the country.[17] His thirst for knowledge and his childhood interest in reading detective novels was the cornerstone of his entry into the world of detectives and spies.[18]

Emir Chehab did not belong to a particular political party, but he was a firm anti-Communist and opposed to pan-Arab nationalism;[19] despite his Levantine heritage, he was pro-Western and looked to the West for intellectual advancement and sympathy. His political vision was therefore more Occidental than Oriental.[20] Nevertheless, his anti-Communism and hostility to pan-Arab nationalism came from his pragmatism as well as his patriotic commitment to a free and independent Lebanon. Owing to his acute and realistic understanding that Lebanon was not a powerful state in the region, he considered its destiny to be almost entirely dependent on others. He believed strongly that Lebanon should resist any intervention in its internal affairs on the part of foreign powers and that Lebanon should retain its pluralistic identity, with all its people working together for "the greater good of Lebanon." Following both his political instinct and Lebanon's long-standing political tradition, he believed that Lebanon's multiconfessional society should be watched over by Christian elites. He believed that as long as the Christians retained certain political and military privileges, the West would not abandon Lebanon.[21] While he considered Communism to be in principle constructive, he regarded it as completely incompatible with the culture of the Middle East. Chehab was of a very independent nature and believed in the freedom of the individual.[22] Likewise, he considered pan-Arab nationalism and other radical nationalist movements instigated by Gamal Abdel Nasser to be detrimental to the already fragile multiconfessional society of Lebanon. Emir Chehab thus decided to fight them.[23] While his attitudes and stance were shared by his Western counterparts, mostly the British, he nevertheless looked down on the Americans, deeming them "temperamentally incapable of understanding the complexities of the Levant."[24] He also kept some distance from the French, perhaps because of his experiences under the French mandate.

Developing the Concept of Security

Lebanon was the regional center of political intrigue, espionage, and underground activities in the postwar period.[25] Keith Wheeler, *Time* magazine's Middle East correspondent at the time, called postwar Lebanon the "busiest rendezvous for political and mercantile intrigue."[26] According to Yaacov Caroz, former deputy chief of Israel's Mossad (Institute for Intelligence and Special Operations), Lebanon was "not only the scene of inter-Arab struggles" but also "an international centre for espionage and secret 'duels.'"[27] Owing to its political neutrality and tolerance, the Soviet and Eastern European legations maintained in Lebanon their largest diplomatic and trade delegations in the Middle East. Lebanon was also home to the highest reported number of Communist members and sympathizers in the Middle East.[28] Intelligence officers, exiled politicians, journalists, and oil businessmen were all stationed in Beirut, from which they operated throughout the entire region.[29]

During the period of Emir Chehab's tenure as a spy chief, political violence and upheavals were commonplace in Lebanon. Lebanon's politics and security were powerfully affected by external factors in the region and were also manipulated by foreign powers, which intervened actively in the country. From the Arab defeat in the Arab-Israeli War of 1948, Lebanon's domestic politics were not only aligned according to religious sectarianism but were also complicated by the chronically unstable conditions of Lebanon's neighbor, Syria, where a series of coups d'états occurred during the period. The first coup d'état in Syria, led by Col. Husni al-Za'im in 1949, prompted a revolt in Lebanon by Antoun Saadeh, founder of the Syrian Social Nationalist Party (SSNP), who subsequently escaped to Syria after his failure to overthrow the Lebanese government. Antoun Saadeh was later extradited and executed in Lebanon in the same year. In 1951 Prime Minister Riad El-Solh was assassinated by an SSNP member in revenge for Antoun Saadeh's execution.[30] From the mid-1950s onward, political violence in Lebanon intensified with the rise of radical Arab nationalist movements. To make matters worse, the internal affairs of Lebanon were targeted by two powerful camps in the region throughout the period and became entangled in their political designs: the Hashemite dynasties of Jordan and Iraq, owing to their respective desires for a united Greater Syria and Iraq's "Fertile Crescent plan" to unite Iraq, Syria, Lebanon, and Jordan; and anti-Hashemite forces led by Egypt and Saudi Arabia, which tried to pull Lebanon in the opposite direction.[31] Political violence reached a crisis point in 1958, when Egyptian leader Gamal Abdel Nasser established the United Arab Republic of Egypt and Syria. Thereafter, money and arms poured in from Damascus for the rebels who had risen up against the pro-Western president Camille Chamoun. In 1958 political turmoil began that fragmented Lebanon and would lead to the civil war in the 1970s.

Facing these political and security challenges to Lebanon's fragile society, Emir Chehab directed the Sûreté Générale against certain political groups as subversive elements in postwar Lebanon. These groups included the Lebanese and Syrian Communist parties, the SSNP (also known as the Parti Populaire Syrien, or Syrian Popular Party), the Islamic Hizb ut-Tahrir (Party of Liberation), the Muslim Brotherhood, and the Kurdish and Armenian minority groups.[32] These political parties were a security concern for Emir Chehab as they were not only subversive in nature but also maintained a close connection with foreign countries. His greatest concern was underground Communist activities in Lebanon and their connection with the Soviet Union. Emir Chehab's understanding of Communism as the cause of instability in Lebanon was founded on his thorough study of Communist ideology and its key figures, such as Karl Marx, Friedrich Engels, Vladimir Lenin, Leon Trotsky, and Joseph Stalin.[33] From his official and private sources, Emir Chehab had a very clear understanding of underground Communist activities in Lebanon and the methods of Soviet espionage and subversion in the region.[34] He was particularly concerned that the Soviets would use minority groups, such as the Kurds and Armenians, as a means to contact local Communist Party leaders and instigate subversive activities in the region.[35] This concern was supported by information obtained from the capture and the interrogation of Communists, and also justified by evidence provided by the Sûreté's Iraqi counterpart, the Criminal Investigation Department (CID).[36]

According to one account, Emir Chehab's private sources included very senior figures within the Lebanese Communist Party who provided him with both strategic and tactical intelligence on Communist activities in Lebanon. In addition to being informed about the party's organizational structure and membership and local Communist branches, Emir Chehab was aware of the most confidential discussions and disagreements among key policy makers within the party and the party's affiliation and connections with the Soviet Union.[37] The official history of the Sûreté notes that at his instruction the agency arrested Antoine Tabet, a Maronite candidate and prominent Lebanese Communist, at the beginning of the June 1957 general election and released him on the day after the election.[38] From the start of his leadership, Emir Chehab also made sure that the Lebanese armed forces were free of Communist infiltration. He achieved this through collaboration with his cousin, Gen. Fuad Chehab, commander of the Lebanese army, later president of Lebanon (1958–64).[39]

The Baghdad Pact was signed in 1955, committing Iran, Iraq, Pakistan, Turkey, and the United Kingdom to cooperation to prevent Soviet expansion into the Middle East. This prompted Emir Chehab's sights to turn to another subversive front in Lebanon—radical Arab nationalist movements associated with and instigated by the Egyptian leader Gamal Abdel Nasser. Emir Chehab considered Nasser's Egypt an ally of the Soviet Union but saw the alliance as unequal and exploitative. Despite being feted as a champion of the Arab world by Radio Cairo, to Emir Chehab Nasser was only detrimental to the independence of postwar Lebanon and a proxy of the Soviet Union. As Nasser grew closer to the Eastern Bloc, he first suspended and subsequently terminated anti-Communist measures taken in the region by the Arab League.[40] Emir Chehab saw that Nasser was merely serving the interest of the Soviet Union.[41] As Nasser's popularity grew and the Syrians allied with Nasser, Emir Chehab felt that Lebanese independence was increasingly threatened by internal subversion. Through his own sources of intelligence, Emir Chehab was also aware in the mid-1950s of Egyptian efforts at subversion in Lebanon. His most secret source, the wiretapping of the Egyptian embassy and local politicians, revealed that the Egyptian ambassador and military attachés in Lebanon were instigating subversive activities and even supplying arms and explosives to the local politicians and politically motivated activists opposed to the Lebanese president Camille Nimir Chamoun.[42] While the Egyptian military attachés were expelled on the ground of their subversive activities, the turmoil led to intervention on the part of the United States, which landed its armed forces in Lebanon in 1958.[43]

As Intelligence Chief

As the chief of the Sûreté Générale, responsible for monitoring all subversive activities in the country, Emir Chehab was very well informed about such activities across the region. He was considered a key Middle Eastern source of intelligence by journalists, diplomats, and intelligence officers. Keith Wheeler called him "probably the smoothest, shrewdest and best informed hawkshaw in the eastern end of the Mediterranean basin."[44] Indeed, under his tenure the Sûreté Générale had a web of espionage networks across the region and operated not only inside but also outside Lebanon.[45] It also enjoyed access to sensitive information—including telexes, letters, and phone calls of foreign embassies—from wiretapping, which Emir Chehab had maintained a particular interest in since his service in the Judicial Police.[46]

In addition to official sources of the Sûreté, Emir Chehab had an extensive network of private agents. He recruited informers, including receptionists and bartenders at the St. George Hotel, a hub of intelligence rendezvous and political conspiracies, and security guards at the airport who could unofficially monitor the movements of foreigners.[47] He also maintained a female agent disguised as a Communist sympathizer. She wore a leather belt decorated with the Communist flag and headed a parade in support of the Soviet Union. She later reported to Emir Chehab about her contact with the Lebanese Communist Party and its activities.[48] Emir Chehab met his private informers away from his office—mostly in public places or at his quiet villa in Al Hadath, Mount Lebanon.[49] His private agent networks reached not only across Lebanon but also throughout the Middle East, stretching from Lebanon's immediate neighborhood, such as Syria, Jordan, and Palestine, to far-off Morocco, Turkey, Kuwait, Iraq, Saudi Arabia, and Egypt.[50] In addition, Chehab's personal fount of intelligence was topped off by liaising with foreign intelligence services. He personally liaised with his Iraqi, Jordanian, Turkish, and Iranian counterparts while promoting internal security in the region.[51] He was also the first point of contact for Western intelligence services wishing to conduct operations from Lebanon.[52]

Emir Chehab made a number of significant contributions to the development of the Sûreté Générale and the internal security of postwar Lebanon.
Under the French mandate, the Lebanese and Syrian police and intelligence
services were organized in accordance with the French system of intelligence
organization.[53] Internal security was maintained by the combined security
apparatus of the Gendarmerie, police, and Sûreté Générale. The Gendarmerie
was a military police that served as an auxiliary to the armed forces and was
charged with dealing with small-scale disorder; the police was intended for
urban and traffic duties and was responsible for investigating ordinary crimes;
and the Sûreté Générale dealt with subversive activities, principally handling
border control and the monitoring of foreigners in the country.[54] From the
concession of the French mandate in 1923 until 1948, internal security in Lebanon had been maintained by the police, and the Sûreté Générale had mainly
been subordinate to it.[55] While the Sûreté Générale was reorganized under
Edward Abu Jaoude, its first director (1945–48), there was no significant
change in the organization inherited from the French mandate. Moreover, an
ethic of professionalism did not exist. Abu Jaoude, who was considered inefficient and dishonest, was dismissed from the position by President El-Khoury
because he had received, through one of his relatives, large bribes from Jewish diamond merchants in Palestine.[56] At Chehab's insistence and thanks to
the trust in him of Lebanon's president, the Sûreté Générale was granted the
authority to deal with subversive activities in the country and emerged as the
leading security force in independent Lebanon.

During Chehab's tenure as chief, the Sûreté was reorganized and transformed into a modern security service. Under his direction, it identified and
defined subversive threats to newly independent Lebanon and worked to con-
strain and suppress Communist and radical pan-Arab nationalist movements
in the country. New counterespionage and countersubversion sections were
created to tackle these subversive threats.[57] Its information security and physical security were enhanced by the compartmentalization of the Sûreté. Within
a year of his appointment, new Sûreté buildings were placed at his disposal,
and Emir Chehab separated them into different sections, restricting public
access to secret sections. The secret sections were further compartmentalized
for information security.[58] The organization also introduced a modern card-
index record-keeping system at its registry with the help of Britain's Security
Service (often known as MI5).[59]

The reorganization and maintenance of Lebanon's internal security was not
easy. MI5 deputy director-general Guy Liddell once described Emir Chehab
as "an intelligent man trying to achieve an almost impossible task."[60] Lebanon's population is divided between Maronite Christians, Sunni Muslims, and

Shiite Muslims, and this multicultural setting complicated his work. Long-established traditions, the Constitution of 1926, and the National Pact of 1943 provided the Lebanese political system with the principle of a fair division of posts in the state apparatus: the country's president was a Maronite; its premier a Sunni Muslim; the Speaker of the House a Shiite Muslim; and parliamentary seats were divided between Christians and Muslims in a six-to-five ratio.[61] Like the rest of the state apparatus, the Sûreté was headed by a Maronite Christian and comprised officers from different sectarian communities.[62] There were "wheels within wheels" at the Sûreté in the late 1940s, wherein officers were loyal not only to the postwar nation-state but also to their respective sects.[63] Owing to these complexities within the agency, Emir Chehab could trust only a limited number of officers, especially on sensitive matters—no more than five of the one hundred Sûreté officers.[64] His trusted officers were not necessarily confined to Maronite Christians but came from different ethnic and religious backgrounds and had been working with Emir Chehab since the 1930s.[65] By appointing them to key positions, such as the counterespionage, countersubversion, and wiretapping sections, Emir Chehab established his own circle of trusted lieutenants within the Sûreté and received intelligence reports directly from these officers. The most delicate material, like that gained through wiretapping, which Emir Chehab considered the most valuable source of intelligence, was not shared outside this trusted circle. Emir Chehab was ultimately the only analyst in the Sûreté.[66] Throughout the period, to overcome this sectarian issue in the Sûreté, Emir Chehab directly involved himself in the recruitment process. He investigated candidates' potential and loyalty at their interview, asking the question, "What is your feeling towards Lebanon, and what can you do for it?"[67]

Emir Farid Chehab also maintained his own eyes and ears within the Sûreté Générale. His informants watched and reported on the activities of officers and their loyalty to the agency, and Emir Chehab punished unprofessionalism harshly.[68] He nevertheless worked to ensure that the government gave the staff of the Sûreté the recognition, dignity, working conditions, and environment that they deserved.[69] He was dictatorial and feared to some extent but always widely respected inside his organization.[70] He was also very hands-on, directly training officers in surveillance operations, investigation, tradecraft, and recruitment.[71] He gave his officers undertaking risky operations false identities and confiscated guns intended for self-defense.[72] The official history of the Sûreté notes that his ideas, rules, and professionalism became its foundation and underpinned the professionalism of its officers and that without him the Sûreté would have been a much weaker organization.[73]

Foreign Liaison in Anti-Communist Measures

One of the remarkable roles Emir Chehab played as a spy chief was his cooperation with foreign intelligence and security services concerning the regional security of the Middle East. His willingness to liaise with his foreign counterparts came directly from his commitment to the independence of postwar Lebanon. Emir Chehab held a firm conviction that the subversive activities of international Communism had to be dealt with by international efforts. Owing to the nature of international Communism—that is to say, its transnational character, direction by the Soviet Union, and objective of world revolution—Lebanon was incapable of countering this subversive threat alone. Despite the fact that Communist activities were prohibited throughout the Middle East, except in Israel, the postwar Lebanese government had little political commitment to counter the threat owing to its political neutrality and its status as the freest country in the region.[74] However, the Sûreté Générale did engage in anti-Communist measures, arresting Communists and confiscating subversive publications and the printing machines of alleged subversive activists and groups. (Subversive publications were the main tool of Communist activists agitating among local populations against their own governments.) For instance, an illegal publication, *Akhbar*, was believed to have a circulation of "about 10,000 copies a day" in Lebanon.[75] However, Emir Chehab found it difficult to intercept and confiscate subversive (i.e., illegal) publications in the country. Some materials were smuggled into Lebanon from outside the jurisdiction of the Sûreté Générale, which made it impossible to eradicate the roots of the subversive activities it targeted.[76] The printing presses of these illegal publications were reported to be located either in the Soviet Union or in the local Soviet legation itself, against which the Sûreté Générale was unable to take any action.[77] Moreover, the subversive threats were both internal and external in nature—indigenous Communist activists in Lebanon and those who instigated them from outside often moved across borders throughout the Middle East.

To better understand the nature of the threat posed by international Communism and how to tackle it, Emir Chehab worked closely with Lebanon's neighbors, such as Jordan and Iraq, which faced similar problems. These intelligence liaisons were often arranged on an ad hoc basis. An "anti-Communist triangle" was founded in 1952 on the basis of the personal ties between Emir Chehab; Bahjat Beg Attiyah, the director of the Iraqi CID; and Col. Sir Patrick Coghill, the director of the Jordanian CID. They considered involving the Syrians in this liaison arrangement but decided that the Syrians "were far too unreliable."[78] This security liaison consisted of intelligence sharing not only about Communist activities in Lebanon, Iraq, and Jordan but also about subversive activities elsewhere, most of which were instigated by Egypt. This cooperation was later extended to accommodate their Iranian and Turkish counterparts.[79] The arrangements were nevertheless short-lived owing to the volatile politics of the Middle East in the period. Sir Patrick Coghill left Jordan following the dismissal of Sir John Bagot Glubb ("Glubb Pasha") from the Arab Legion in 1956. The Iranian officer was dismissed from his post the following year, then Bahjat Attiyah was hanged as a result of the Iraqi revolution in 1958, the same year that Emir Chehab left the Sûreté.[80]

Emir Chehab also contributed to the coordination of anti-Communist measures with neighboring Arab states by establishing closer liaison between the Arab security services under the Arab League. This regional coordination became known in 1954 as the foundation for a covert cooperation effort in "the fight against communism and Zionism."[81] The official history of the Sûreté notes that the fear of Communism was the "prevailing threat" in this agreement.[82] Emir Chehab met his Iraqi, Jordanian, Syrian, and Egyptian counterparts to discuss their measures to contain and eliminate these threats and exchange intelligence, including watch lists, assessments of Communist espionage and subversion methods, and intelligence reports.[83] This regional cooperation nevertheless ended abruptly in 1955 when Nasser suspended and subsequently ended anti-Communist measures by the Arab League. According to one account, despite this setback, the Sûreté Générale kept up its surveillance and monitoring and "watched over communist movements not only in Lebanon, but also in Syria, Iraq, and Jordan, including Palestine leftist and communist organizations operating in these countries." Later, this surveillance spread to cover "a number of communist groups in the Arabian Gulf area."[84]

Emir Chehab also maintained contact with his counterparts in Britain and the United States. He had been in contact with his British counterpart before his appointment as chief of the Sûreté Générale in 1948 and received training in counterespionage and anti-Communist measures in Britain.[85] He remained in personal contact with his Western counterparts, such as Sir Maurice Oldfield, Anthony Cavendish, William Donovan, Kermit Roosevelt, and Miles Copeland, even after his resignation from the Sûreté in 1958.[86] He worked alongside the Western powers in supporting a militant opposition group's attempt to overthrow the leftist Syrian government in 1957.[87]

Relationship with Policy Makers

Emir Chehab was nominated for his appointment in 1948 as the director of the Sûreté Générale by the inner circle of the cabinet; the minister for the interior, Camille Chamoun; and the prime minister, Riad El-Solh. Ultimately, however, the appointment was decided by President Bechara El-Khoury (1943–52) himself, and his continuation in his post was based on Emir Chehab's personal connection with President El-Khoury and, subsequently, President Camille Chamoun (1952–58).[88] Both presidents regularly read his intelligence reports and listened to his views. Owing to this close relationship with the presidents, combined with his web of clandestine sources, he was feared by many politicians, even those in the cabinet.[89]

The Lebanese political system was devised by the French and resembled that of the French high commissioners under the mandate. It granted the president ultimate authority, including great powers over the executive and legislature. Presidents El-Khoury and Chamoun, both of whom were Maronite Christians, made full use of their presidential powers. The postwar period in Lebanon, especially under the Chamoun presidency, has been characterized as one of presidential authoritarianism.[90] The role of the Sûreté was to implement government policy. In addition to supervising the administration, public bodies, the activities of political parties, and the arrival and departure of foreigners, and monitoring applicants for political asylum, the Sûreté also advised the government on actions it deemed necessary to internal security.[91] In relation to countersubversion and counterespionage, the Lebanese army had similar functions, but conflict was mostly avoided during Emir Chehab's tenure as chief owing to his good relationship with his cousin, General Fuad Chehab.[92] Nevertheless, like the other Arab intelligence and security services of the time, the Sûreté Générale acted more to maintain the security of the regime than that of the state.[93] It maintained the security of the president, and Emir Chehab was his main source of information.[94]

As chief of the Sûreté, Emir Chehab was able to monitor all political activities in the country. The official history of the Sûreté notes that all politicians, both supporters and opponents of the president, were targets of wiretapping. Emir Chehab was the only person to have a full picture of the internal political affairs in the country. He monitored the activities of all suspects—including local politicians and even cabinet ministers who were in contact with members of the Communist Party, the Syrians, or the Egyptians—looking for subversive activities.[95] The wiretapping materials were delivered personally by a trusted officer to his desk. He then selected certain materials to be distributed to the president, prime minister, minister for the interior, or other relevant persons or authorities, but Emir Chehab redacted the information and concealed the source of the information before distribution. The information was delivered at his discretion; his decision was sensitive and entirely political. The wiretapping materials sometimes included personal insults about him—Chehab kept such materials in his private archives for use after his career in the Sûreté.[96]

Despite his personal connection with the president, the El-Khoury administration was an uneasy period for Emir Chehab. The roles and responsibilities of the Sûreté were still undeveloped, and the organization was under the control of the Ministry of the Interior. A series of decrees successively redefined the remit of the Sûreté—its power was weakened and restricted in 1950, while the powers of the police were increased at the expense of those of the Sûreté.[97] The position of director-general of the Sûreté was downgraded.[98] Its staff was cut in half, from two hundred to one hundred.[99] Another reason for his unease during the El-Khoury presidency was Emir Chehab's bad relationship with the president's brother, Salim El-Khoury, nicknamed "the Sultan," who "nakedly exploited his brother's position as head of state for his own political and financial gain."[100] At "Sultan" Salim El-Khoury's insistence, the president curtailed the power of the Sûreté.[101] Salim even had his own agent within the Sûreté who tapped Emir Chehab's official telephone line.[102]

As chief, Emir Chehab also acted as a personal emissary of the president. As part of the government's efforts to normalize Lebanon's relationship with Syria, he frequently crossed the border with Syria in 1949 to meet Syrian president Husni al-Za'im, whom Emir Chehab had known as a fellow inmate when he had been imprisoned under the French mandate.[103] Emir Chehab also supervised the extradition of Antoun Saadeh, founder of the SSNP, who was executed after a secret trial in Lebanon in July 1949.[104] The official history of the Sûreté notes that Emir Chehab retained bitter memories both of the extradition and secret trial and of the subsequent assassination of Prime Minister Riad El-Solh in 1951. Despite the revolt by Antoun Saadeh in 1949 against the El-Khoury presidency, Emir Chehab considered the SSNP a negligible threat to the independence of Lebanon. For him, Communist activities and underground movements in the country were far more serious. At the very least, Emir Chehab believed that Antoun Saadeh did not deserve the death sentence.[105] President El-Khoury did not listen either to Chehab's protests or to his advice on Communist matters, and also disregarded Prime Minister Riad El-Solh's opinion that Antoun Saadeh should not be executed. The president overreacted and decided to execute Antoun Saddeh in a secret trial.[106]

Throughout his tenure as chief, Emir Chehab was consistently frustrated by the ineffective policies and lax attitudes of Middle Eastern governments toward the Communist activities within their borders.[107] He lamented to Keith Wheeler:

> The governments of the Middle East are not fighting communism. They have no real policy against communism; they have no regional politick to unite them against communism. Some don't care. And some think a little communism is a good thing to punish you (the West and particularly America). They

will tell you they are fighting communism, but it is only because they think it will please you to hear that. If it was just a question of punishing you (the West) I wouldn't care. But, something they do not realize but I do, it is more than that; we (the Arabs) can lose and are losing our own lands to communism.[108]

Emir Chehab frequently found little support from Lebanese ministers. They did not take action, even when he reported that someone in the government was "working for the Russians." Emir Chehab was also unable to rely on the ordinary police to implement anti-Communist measures because it had been penetrated by Communist sympathizers.[109] This frustration continued throughout his entire tenure.

Consequently, Emir Chehab's allegiance to the regime was not unconditional. In the late 1940s and early 1950s, he submitted ultimatums and resignation letters to El-Khoury numerous times following quarrels over the remit of the Sûreté and government policy, including the execution of Antoun Saadeh, but the president always refused to accept his resignation.[110] Nevertheless, President El-Khoury restored the Sûreté's powers before leaving office as a result of the tragic assassination of Riad El-Solh in June 1951, which the Sûreté had been unable to prevent or even predict.[111] Emir Chehab remained in the position of chief, and the Sûreté gradually recovered its standing in the years that followed. By the time of Camille Chamoun's presidency, the agency operated more as the security body of the president than as a security apparatus under ministerial control.[112] Serving under such strong presidencies, Emir Chehab subsequently formed his view that until Lebanon became a truly democratic society, the role of the Sûreté was to remain the "eyes and ears" of the government in the interests of political stability, "so that unwelcome surprises would be avoided."[113]

Chehab's Resignation and Afterward

Using all his available sources of intelligence, including wiretapping, official reports, his private agents, and liaison with his regional counterparts, Emir Chehab foresaw the 1958 crisis in Lebanon. From early 1958 he appealed to President Chamoun to adopt more lenient policies in view of local sectarian sensitivities and to try to reach an understanding with the opposition to curtail their cooperation with Gamal Abdel Nasser.[114] Nevertheless, Camille Chamoun chose not to listen. During the crisis, in the face of mounting atrocities and terrorism by local politicians and politically motivated activists, Emir Chehab powerlessly observed the first civil war by wiretapping materials that included transcripts of both sides of telephone conversations. He could then hear the sound of gunfire and explosions close to the headquarters of the Sûreté.[115]

While maintaining his service to the state, Emir Chehab was able to separate the private and public parts of his life. He had a clear idea about just how far he could go in his service to the state and was aware of where his professional responsibilities should end and where his duties to family and friends began.[116] After narrowly escaping three assassination attempts, Emir Chehab eventually decided to step down from his position in September 1958.[117]

Camille Chamoun was replaced as president by Gen. Fuad Chehab (1958–64).[118] President Fuad Chehab appointed his fellow army officer, Toufic Jalbout, as director-general of the Sûreté Générale (1958–64), but the president later made the army's Deuxième Bureau responsible for internal security in response to the failed coup attempt by the SSNP in December 1961.[119] Emir Chehab stayed in the civil service and asked for a transfer to the foreign service. Using his considerable language skills and his natural ability as a socialite, he took on various ambassadorial positions in Ghana, Nigeria, Cameroon, Tunisia, and Cyprus before retiring in 1969.[120] Intriguingly, however, Emir Chehab's interest in Lebanon's internal security did not end with his resignation, nor did his influence in the Sûreté. It is evident from his private papers at St. Antony's College, Oxford, that he continued receiving high-level intelligence until the 1970s.[121] How and why he received such intelligence after his resignation is unclear.[122]

In the Soviet government newspaper *Izvestia* on October 1, 1971, Emir Chehab was named as a "British agent." This was a direct retaliation by the Soviet Union to the mass expulsion of Soviet intelligence officers from the United Kingdom by the British government in 1971. *Izvestia* published a list of the British intelligence officers and agents; Kim Philby, the legendary KGB spy who stayed in Beirut from 1956 until his escape to Moscow in January 1963, collaborated with the newspaper in publishing it.[123] Emir Chehab never trusted Philby and did not like his working as a journalist in Beirut and maintaining connections with British intelligence officers.[124] Despite Chehab's suspicions about him, the British Foreign Office insisted that Philby had not been a Soviet agent and had no connection with the Soviets.[125] After Philby's escape in 1963, Emir Chehab was puzzled by the behavior of his British colleagues and could not understand how Philby had been allowed to escape. He commented to Richard Beeston, a *Daily Telegraph* correspondent, that the Sûreté "could so easily have arranged a small accident" to arrest Philby.[126] Together with three other Lebanese named as "British agents," Emir Chehab sued TASS, the official Soviet news agency, for libel and won his case in

1972.[127] His victory in his lawsuit against the Soviet government was widely publicized in the Western media. Emir Chehab was congratulated by many of his old friends from his time as chief of the Sûreté.[128]

Conclusion

Emir Chehab played a formative role in establishing the Sûreté Générale as the principal security service in Lebanon during its critical period of postwar independence. He served the state diligently and fought for Lebanon's independence from Communist and radical Arab nationalist movements. During his tenure as chief, the Sûreté Générale was reorganized and played a crucial role in safeguarding the internal security of postwar Lebanon. His ideas, rules, and professionalism became the foundation of the Sûreté and underpinned the professionalism of its officers. Owing to Lebanon's religious sectarianism and policy of nonalignment, Emir Chehab encountered great difficulties in maintaining the country's security; Guy Liddell noted that these made his job "almost impossible." Nevertheless, Emir Chehab gave good service to the state, even though, owing to Lebanon's political system, he and the Sûreté Générale necessarily served the regime more than the state. Once the civil war erupted in 1958, Emir Chehab found the Sûreté had little role to play in politics. Youmna Asseily, his daughter, once asked her father how he made it through his time at the Sûreté. He responded, "I tried to go to sleep every evening with the feeling I had done my best during the day."[129] Emir Chehab is still remembered as the father of the Sûreté Générale today.

Notes

I would like to acknowledge the support I received from Youmna Asseily and Ahmad Asfahani in undertaking my research on Emir Farid Chehab.

1. Quoted from Youmna Asseily and Ahmad Asfahani, eds., *A Face in the Crowd: The Secret Papers of Emir Farid Chehab, 1942–1972* (London: Stacey International, 2007), xi.

2. There are several birth certificates for him from that period. See ibid., 8.

3. Personal conversation with Youmna Asseily.

4. Nicolas Nassif, *Ser Aldawlah: fousol fe tarekh ala'men ala'am, 1945–1977* [State secret: Chapters in the history of the Sûreté Générale in Lebanon, 1945–1977] (Lebanon: General Security, 2013), 54.

5. Personal conversation with Youmna Asseily.

6. The Center for Arab and Middle Eastern Studies (hereafter, CAMES), the American University of Beirut, transcript of an audio interview (in Arabic), "The Emir Farid

Chehab," accessed March 4, 2015, http://ddc.aub.edu.lb/projects/cames/interviews /farid_chehab/.

7. Nassif, *State Secret*, 57.

8. Ibid., 56; and Asseily and Asfahani, *Face in the Crowd*, 8–9.

9. CAMES, transcript that records Emir Chehab's account: "Actually a lot of people admired Hitler because Arabs in general love power and Hitler was known as a powerful person. . . . One night, I went out with the director [of the Sûreté Générale]. . . . We were both single . . . met some French army officers who were very envious and tried to kick us out of our jobs many times. . . . [One of them] had a fight with the director . . . [later Emir Chehab] found that the French officer was pointing his gun at the director and about to kill him. I took the gun by force from him and put it away. . . . The next day I was arrested." Also see Asseily and Asfahani, *Face in the Crowd*, 193–203.

10. See John Munro's chapter in Asseily and Asfahani, *Face in the Crowd*, 202–3.

11. Asseily and Asfahani, *Face in the Crowd*, 8–10. He was the second director-general. His predecessor was Edward Abu Jaoude (1945–48).

12. John Munro in Asseily and Asfahani, *Face in the Crowd*, 198–99; and Nassif, *State Secret*, 52, 59.

13. "Before I Forget," Private Papers of Lieutenant-Colonel Sir Patrick Coghill, London: Imperial War Museum (IWM), 2:117.

14. Nassif, *State Secret*, 60.

15. CAMES, transcript of an audio interview (in Arabic) with Emir Farid Chehab.

16. Nassif, *State Secret*, 56.

17. Asseily and Asfahani, *Face in the Crowd*, viii.

18. Nassif, *State Secret*, 54–55.

19. Ibid., 170.

20. Personal conversation with Youmna Asseily.

21. John Munro in Asseily and Asfahani, *Face in the Crowd*, 188.

22. Personal conversation with Youmna Asseily.

23. John Munro in Asseily and Asfahani, *Face in the Crowd*, 188.

24. Ibid., 191.

25. This was mostly so until the 1970s, when the civil war occurred.

26. Private Papers of Emir Farid Chehab in the possession of the family of Emir Farid Chehab [hereafter, Chehab Papers "F"], report by Keith Wheeler [*sic*], Middle East correspondent of *Time*, "Subject: Communism in the Middle East," November 13, 1954, designated "4Q."

27. Yaacov Caroz, *The Arab Secret Services* (London: Corgi, 1978), 17.

28. The National Archives (TNA), London: PRO CAB134/3: AC (O) (50) 18: report (annex) by JIC, "Communist Influence in the Middle East," April 21, 1950.

29. See Said K. Aburish, *Beirut Spy: The St George Hotel Bar* (London: Bloomsbury, 1989).

30. For an account of Antoun Saadeh's in Lebanon and Syria, see Patrick Seale, *The Struggle for Arab Independence: Riad El-Solh and the Makers of the Modern Middle East* (Cambridge: Cambridge University Press, 2010), 687–730.

31. Fawwaz Traboulsi, *A History of Modern Lebanon,* 2nd ed. (London: Pluto Press, 2012), 112–13. See also Patrick Seale, *The Struggle for Syria: A Study of Post-War Arab Politics, 1945–1958* (Oxford: Oxford University Press, 1965).

32. See Asseily and Asfahani, *Face in the Crowd.* Also see the Middle East Centre Archive (MECA), St. Antony's College, Oxford: Private Papers of Emir Farid Chehab: GB165-0384 for further details.

33. Chehab Papers "F," handwritten note by Farid on Communism, dated November 26, 1954, designated "5Q."

34. Nassif, *State Secret,* 95.

35. East Sussex Record Office (ESRO), The Keep, Brighton: Papers of Baron Chelwood, ME, DL (formerly Sir Tufton Beamish MP): Political and family papers 1850–1984: CLW1/4/3, the Middle East, 1949, "Record of a conversation with Emir Farid Shehab, Chief of the Political Police of the Lebanon."

36. See TNA: PRO KV4/470, the Liddell Diaries, December 29, 1948; Document of 16/9/34 in Asseily and Asfahani, *Face in the Crowd,* 84–85. See also Chikara Hashimoto, "Fighting the Cold War or Post-Colonialism? Britain in the Middle East from 1945 to 1958: Looking through the Records of the British Security Service," *International History Review* 36 (2014): 32.

37. The nature and scale can be seen from his private papers at the MECA. Also see Asseily and Asfahani, *Face in the Crowd,* 68–70.

38. Nassif, *State Secret,* 94.

39. ESRO, Papers of Baron Chelwood, "Record of a conversation with Emir Farid Shehab, Chief of the Political Police of the Lebanon."

40. Asseily and Asfahani, *Face in the Crowd,* 68.

41. Nassif, *State Secret,* 170.

42. Ibid., 159–60, 165–69.

43. TNA: PRO FO371/133792: V10316/1: minute "Egyptian subversive activity in the Middle East," July 19, 1957. For a discussion of the Egyptians' subversive activities, see Caroz, *Arab Secret Services,* 63–86; and Keith Wheelock, *Nasser's New Egypt: A Critical Analysis* (London: Atlantic Books, 1960), 251–52.

44. Chehab Papers "F," report by Keith Wheeler, "Subject: Communism in the Middle East," November 13, 1954, designated "4Q."

45. Nassif, *State Secret,* 70.

46. Ibid., 96–97.

47. Ibid., 88. Also see Aburish, *Beirut Spy,* 192; and Asseily and Asfahani, *Face in the Crowd,* 182–85.

48. Nassif, *State Secret,* 94.

49. Ibid., 90.

50. See Asseily and Asfahani, *Face in the Crowd,* chap. 3.

51. Nassif, *State Secret,* 91.

52. See Kermit Roosevelt, *Countercoup: The Struggle for the Control of Iran* (New York: McGraw-Hill, 1979), 137–38; and Wilbur Crane Eveland, *Ropes of Sand: America's Failure in the Middle East* (London: W. W. Norton, 1980), 177, 198. Also see Tom Bower, *The Perfect English Spy* (London: Heinemann, 1995), 232–34; and Stephen

Dorril, *MI6: Inside the Covert World of Her Majesty's Secret Intelligence Service* (London: Free Press, 2000), 665.

53. On the organization of French intelligence, see Douglas Porch, *The French Secret Services* (New York: Farrar, Straus and Girous, 1995).

54. See Stephen Longrigg, *Syria and Lebanon under French Mandate* (Oxford: Oxford University Press, 1958), 138.

55. Nassif, *State Secret*, 51. See also Seale, *Struggle for Arab Independence*, 622.

56. Asseily and Asfahani, *Face in the Crowd*, 203.

57. Nassif, *State Secret*, 62–64.

58. TNA: PRO FO371/75319: E8783/G, report by D. Beaumont-Nesbitt to Head Office [MI5] (B1) and SIME (B), June 27, 1949.

59. Nassif, *State Secret*, 81. For Emir Chehab's connection with the British, see Chikara Hashimoto, "British Security Liaison in the Middle East: The Introduction of Police/Security Advisers and the Lebanon-Iraq-Jordan 'Anti-Communist Triangle' from 1949 to 1958," *Intelligence and National Security* 27, no. 6 (2012): 848–74.

60. TNA: PRO KV4/473, the Guy Liddell Diaries, June 25, 1951.

61. Helena Cobban, *The Making of Modern Lebanon* (London: Hutchinson, 1985), 77.

62. Nassif, *State Secret*, 171.

63. "The director [Emir Chehab] has told me that the latest petty annoyance with which he has to contend is the fact that his official telephone line in the Sûreté is tapped by agents of the president's brother. The mechanics of this preposterous operation, if true, are, as one may imagine, highly complex and there are the usual wheels within wheels, the agents concerned being simultaneously employed by various organisations." Quoted from TNA: PRO FO371/75319: E8783/G, report by D. Beaumont-Nesbitt to Head Office [MI5] (B1) and SIME (B), June 27, 1949.

64. Guy Liddell of MI5 noted in his diary when he met Emir Chehab in his office that "out of the 100 [officers] there were barely 5% upon whom he could positively rely. If he could ever bring this up to 10% he would feel that he had achieved a good deal, but in fact such a possibility only appeared extremely dimly over the horizon." Quoted from TNA: PRO KV4/473, the Guy Liddell Diaries, June 25, 1951.

65. Nassif, *State Secret*, 66–68.

66. Ibid.

67. Ibid., 73.

68. Ibid., 62.

69. Ibid., 91.

70. Ibid., 60–62.

71. Ibid., 75.

72. Ibid., 86.

73. Ibid., 60–62.

74. Chehab Papers "F," a draft speech designated "7S."

75. TNA: PRO FO371/128002: VL1017/1: letter from Sir George Middleton, the British ambassador in Beirut, to Selwyn Lloyd, Foreign Secretary, March 18, 1957.

76. TNA: PRO FO371/75131: a report by the (probable) representative of MI5 in

Baghdad, Philip Bicknell Ray, "The Iraqi Communist Party": "XII. Russian Links with the Party," 55–58, March 1949.

77. TNA: PRO FO371/128002: VL1017/1: letter from Middleton to Lloyd, March 18, 1957.

78. IWM: Private Papers of Sir Patrick Coghill, 2:118.

79. See Hashimoto, "British Security Liaison in the Middle East," *INS* 27, no. 6 (2012): 848–74; and Nassif, *State Secret*, 92.

80. IWM: Private Papers of Sir Patrick Coghill, 2:119.

81. Hashimoto, "British Security Liaison in the Middle East," *INS* 27, no. 6 (2012): 867.

82. Nassif, *State Secret*, 92.

83. Ibid.

84. Asseily and Asfahani, *Face in the Crowd*, 8, 68.

85. See Hashimoto, "British Security Liaison in the Middle East," *INS* 27, no. 6 (2012): 854–59.

86. Richard Deacon, *"C": A Biography of Sir Maurice Oldfield* (London: Futura, 1984), 52. See also Chehab Papers "F": letter designated "14M" from Julian Amery and dated October 23, 1969; letter designated "17N" from Oldfield and dated July 17, 1975; letter designated "26N" from Anthony Cavendish (formerly of SIS) and dated March 1, 1977; letters designated "L14" from William Donovan and dated March 2, 1954, and February 1, 1955; letter designated "L39" from Miles Copeland and dated August 11, 1958; and letters designated "9N" from Kim Roosevelt dated between July 17 and August 2, 1972.

87. For Emir Chehab's involvement see Eveland, *Rope of Sand*, 247. See also Nassif, *State Secret*, 86.

88. Nassif, *State Secret*, 16, 52, 59.

89. Ibid., 90.

90. Traboulsi, *History of Modern Lebanon*, 130.

91. Nassif, *State Secret*, 16.

92. Ibid., 90.

93. See the general overview of Arab intelligence and security services in Caroz, *Arab Secret Services*, 2–19.

94. Nassif, *State Secret*, 90.

95. Ibid., 98, 100.

96. Ibid., 97–98.

97. Ibid., 62–66.

98. Ibid., 142.

99. TNA: PRO KV4/473, the Liddell Diaries, June 25, 1951.

100. Quoted from Seale, *Struggle for Arab Independence*, 588.

101. Nassif, *State Secret*, 140.

102. TNA: PRO FO371/75319: E8783/G, report by D. Beaumont-Nesbitt to Head Office [MI5] (B1) and SIME (B), June 27, 1949.

103. Asseily and Asfahani, *Face in the Crowd*, 9.

104. Nassif, *State Secret*, 128–37.

105. Nassif, *State Secret*, 129–30, 35–37.

106. Seale, *Struggle for Arab Independence*, 685.

107. That was apart from the Iraqi government, which at that time had fairly strong attitudes and a firm policy on Communist activities.

108. Chehab Papers "F," report by Keith Wheeler, "Subject: Communism in the Middle East," November 13, 1954, designated "4Q."

109. TNA: PRO KV4/473, the Liddell Diaries, June 25, 1951.

110. Nassif, *State Secret*, 138–39.

111. Ibid., 142.

112. Ibid., 71–74, 91, 138–42.

113. Asseily and Asfahani, *Face in the Crowd*, 189.

114. Nassif, *State Secret*, 150.

115. Ibid., 165–71.

116. Asseily and Asfahani, *Face in the Crowd*, 190.

117. Nassif, *State Secret*, 165–71.

118. Ibid., 171.

119. Ibid., 190–290.

120. Asseily and Asfahani, *Face in the Crowd*, 8–10; CAMES, the transcript of an audio interview (in Arabic) with Emir Farid Chehab.

121. See Asseily and Asfahani, *Face in the Crowd*.

122. Ibid., 179.

123. Christopher Andrew and Vasili Mitrokhin, *The Mitrokhin Archive* (London: Allen Lane / Penguin Press, 1999), 544–45.

124. Richard Beeston, *Looking for Trouble: The Life and Times of a Foreign Correspondent* (London: Tauris Parke, 2006), 34.

125. Personal conversation with Youmna Asseily.

126. Beeston, *Looking for Trouble*, 34.

127. Andrew and Mitrokhin, *Mitrokhin Archive*, 544–45. "TASS" stood for "Telegraph Agency of the Soviet Union."

128. Letter dated March 28, 1972, in the possession of Youmna Asseily.

129. Asseily and Asfahani, *Face in the Crowd*, xii.

10 Egypt's Spy Chiefs

Servants or Leaders?

Dina Rezk ▬▬▬▬▬▬▬▬▬▬▬▬▬▬▬▬▬▬▬▬▬▬▬▬▬

In 2014 the Egyptian General Intelligence Service (GIS) celebrated its sixtieth anniversary since its official founding by nationalist president Gamal Abdel Nasser.[1] With a reputation as the most effective intelligence agency in the Arab world, it is a notoriously secretive institution. It should perhaps come as little surprise that the election of Egypt's latest pharaoh, Abdel Fattah al-Sisi, in May 2014 brought a former spy chief to the helm of the state. Sisi's presidency serves as a stark reminder of the powerful role this institution has played in the country's history and politics.

This chapter examines the influence and leadership of Egypt's three most important and powerful spy chiefs and the way they contributed to shaping the nation's republican history. The literature on Egypt's intelligence community and its various leaders is predictably sparse.[2] We know little about the men who have headed this secretive bulwark of Egypt's recent past. As in other chapters of this book, we explore patterns in their mentalities and approaches to intelligence and security. The chapter asks, How has intelligence been conceptualized and practiced over the years? How well have these leaders served the regime? How have Egypt's internal security policies changed under the leadership of these spy chiefs?

Some obvious problems present themselves in such an investigation. The power and controversy surrounding intelligence institutions in Egypt render access to Egyptian archival source material difficult, if not impossible. The scant secondary literature that has been written on this subject has been forced to rely on memoirs and interviews with surviving participants, complemented by the occasional smattering of Anglo-American archival resources that mention these men. Political memoirs offer perhaps the richest source base available to historians, although they are, like all memoirs, problematic in nature. Memoirs tend to be written by spy chiefs to justify actions or failures that occurred under their command, to highlight successes, or to settle political scores with their enemies. Interestingly, all the memoirs of Egypt's spy chiefs highlight their reluctance to abandon secrecy. They claim to be overwhelmed, however, by a patriotic duty to convey to their fellow country-men the importance and courage of their security services.[3]

This investigation also raises important issues about intelligence scholarship and the positivist approaches that dominate the field. The main question that the book as a whole seeks to answer is, what makes a good spy chief? Posing such a question implies normative assumptions about "success" and "failure" that might lead us to ignore more important complex and critical questions about the nature of security.[4] Is it even possible to determine what makes a "good" spy chief? The answer to such an inquiry will surely depend on how notions of "good" in relation to security are construed. "Security," much like the notions of "success" and "failure," does not have a generally accepted meaning.

The findings of this chapter therefore constitute a preliminary investigation that will no doubt require further development with the benefit of additional research devoted to consideration of these critical perspectives. Notwith-standing the limitations of sources that currently exist, it appears clear that intelligence in Egypt has been a fundamentally domestic endeavor, designed above all else to secure the regime from its immediate internal enemies. Intel-ligence leaders under Nasser regarded propaganda and covert action abroad as a fundamental means of achieving security for the regime. Domestically, rival spy chiefs led an internal war between the military and civilian sectors of the security apparatus. Under Mubarak, eliminating the threat from polit-ical Islam gained greater prominence, a trend that continued and intensified in the aftermath of the dramatic deposal of President Morsi, the leader of the Muslim Brotherhood, in July 2013. This chapter argues that security has been conceived by all three spy chiefs in fairly narrow, personal terms; spy bosses have worked both to cultivate and assuage the fears of their political masters. While today the Egyptian intelligence services present themselves as servants of the nation, the chapter suggests that in fact these spy chiefs were quite clearly servants of the regime and indeed, at times, of factions within it, accruing for themselves considerable power along the way. Examining Egypt's intelligence community in this way challenges fallacious notions of a cohe-sive polity, illuminating the fragmentation and competition contained within authoritarian rule.

Nasser's Egypt: The Foundations of a "State within a State"

On June 5, 1967, Egypt was attacked by Israel in a lightning preemptive strike. Egypt was defeated so quickly and completely that the conflict came to be

known in the West as the "Six-Day War." Israel absorbed three times its former territory, and Egypt, Syria, and Jordan were forced to turn their attention
to regaining both their land and their honor over the coming decades. On
March 3, 1968, Nasser publicly blamed the intelligence services for Egypt's
humiliating setback, arguing that security officers had transformed the nation
into a "Mukhabarat state." According to Nasser, the security services had
failed in their basic function to protect Egypt from foreign machinations,
spending too much time spying on ordinary Egyptian citizens. He promised
the Egyptian people that he would dismantle the security establishment and
rein in the security services' power.[5]

Nasser's speech was partly correct: the 1967 war was easy to classify as
an intelligence failure of the greatest magnitude. The defense establishment
evidently thought that it could defeat Israel in the months leading up to the
attack; defense chiefs asserted this repeatedly in private and in public. In February 1968, Defense Minister Shams Badran testified at his trial for conspiracy,
"We were confident that our army was ready and that Israel could not attack
because intelligence estimates pointed to the fact that we were superior in
armored weapons, artillery and air power. It was calculated that Israel would
not walk into an open grave."[6] In retrospect, it is clear that these intelligence
assessments grossly overestimated Egypt's military strength. Moreover, they
indicated that Egypt's intelligence services had taken their eye off the ball.
American analysts reported one prominent Egyptian complaining in the aftermath of the 1967 defeat that "our intelligence service is the most ignorant in
the world. Whereas the Israelis knew the name of every Egyptian on relief,
and his wife's name too, we didn't even know where Moshe Dayan's house
was!"[7]

However, it was disingenuous of Nasser to suggest that blame for the
disaster did not lie at his door as well. A fact-finding committee after the war
attributed the defeat to the political leadership's "loss of control over the military and security agencies, which behaved as autonomous, unsupervised and
self-sufficient organizations."[8] In fact, the reality was even more serious. By
1967 Egypt's security services had become embroiled in an internal conflict
between the military and the presidency in a civilian-military rivalry that
would survive well into the following century.

Founder of the Egyptian republic, Gamal Abdel Nasser was an avid con-
sumer of intelligence. His conspiratorial background opposing the British
occupation combined with a more intrinsic "passion for information" to fuel
his intelligence appetite.[9] Nasser's founding spy chief was an infantry officer
called Zakaria Muhi al-Din. As director of the Military Intelligence Department (MID), Zakaria was instrumental in directing the agency toward internal
functions (namely, monitoring dissidents and "coup proofing") alongside its

official role in spying on foreign militaries.[10] In January and March 1954, Nasser faced mutinies in the military that heightened his fears of this internal threat.

The officer corps was subordinate to the chief of staff of Egypt's army and defense minister, Field Marshal Abdel Hakim Amer. Amer was a friend and comrade of Nasser's, but the two men had a tumultuous and competitive relationship. Amer controlled the security agencies of the armed forces, above all the MID, and was able to expand his power dramatically when his protégé, spy chief Salah Nasr, took charge of the civilian GIS in 1957. Amer built up support for himself within the officer corps by means of financial incentives, benefits, and promotions.[11] Spy chief Salah Nasr was undoubtedly well rewarded for his loyalty to Amer.

The first sign of tensions between Nasser and Amer emerged with the tripartite British-French-Israeli attack on Suez in 1956. According to Egyptian accounts, Amer had wanted to surrender in the face of the Anglo-French fighting force. Nasser allegedly replied to Amer's hysteria with the retort that "your behavior is unmanly; the first shots have hardly been fired." Nasser insisted that "not only must I take direct command of the army, but I also don't want you issuing any orders. . . . If you can't do better than mope around like an old hag then you will be court martialed."[12] This marked the beginning of a brewing mistrust between Nasser and Amer, which intensified in the years leading up to the 1967 war. During this period, Amer's protégé Nasr thrived as head of the GIS, Egypt's first civilian intelligence agency, and Egypt's security services were divided between those serving Amer and those others reporting to Nasser.

The GIS was tasked with conducting covert action and the collection and assessment of political and economic intelligence. According to the secret testimony of then GIS chief Omar Suleiman in 2011 at the trial of deposed president Hosni Mubarak, today the organization "is responsible for gathering political, economic, and military information from abroad which enables the political leadership to take political, economic, and military decisions." He suggested that the domestic remit was restricted, describing a "body" within the GIS that "coordinates with the rest of the security establishment in gathering information. This agency is responsible for protecting foreigners, counter-intelligence, and protecting confidential information. The agents therein gather intelligence on people present in Egyptian society." However, Suleiman claimed that the GIS "is an information-gathering service and it does not take measures."[13] More forthright Egyptian accounts indicate that the GIS was modeled on the United States' Central Intelligence Agency (CIA) in its capacity as the supervisor and coordinator of the Egyptian intelligence community and that its responsibilities also include that for covert action.[14]

Salah Nasr

Salah Nasr is perhaps Egypt's most hated spy chief. Nobel Prize laureate Naguib Mahfouz popularized him in the Egyptian collective memory as a corrupt and ruthless figure in his famous book *Karnak*, a controversial exposé of the excesses of Nasser's police state. Such was Nasr's consternation at how he was depicted in the novel and its cinematic adaptation that he unsuccessfully brought a lawsuit against both Mahfouz and the film's producer in the 1970s in a vain bid to restore his reputation.[15]

Like other free officers, Nasr was a graduate of the military academy and claimed that he was quite ignorant of intelligence matters before taking the post as head of the GIS. Exploiting the GIS library, he investigated a number of foreign intelligence services before settling on the CIA as the most suitable model. Nasr was rare among Egypt's spy chiefs as something of an intellectual, publishing a number of works on intelligence and psychological warfare. In 1967, while in prison, he published an autobiography and a two-volume work in Arabic titled *Al-Harb Al-Nafsiyah: Maraka Al-Kalimah wal Moutaqad* (Psychological Warfare: The Battle of Words and Perceptions).[16]

Nasr's writings give us a good sense of how he conceived intelligence and the purpose it served. He describes a Hobbesian state of nature in which "governments these days live in a world resembling a jungle full of beasts," where the "law of the jungle governs international relations: live to eat or be eaten."[17] This graphic imagery may go some way toward explaining the priority that Nasr gave to covert action in the regional sphere. The conservative monarchies of Jordan, Iraq, Yemen, Saudi Arabia, and Libya were all targeted by the GIS under Nasr's leadership in what came to be known as the "Arab Cold War."[18] Covert action in these countries deployed a combination of hard and soft power, encompassing a range of activities from propaganda to assassination and arming rebels. In contrast, Nasr seems to have regarded intelligence analysis as a secondary, quasi-academic activity that he compared to the work of a publishing house, collating and synthesizing information to turn into intelligence products.[19]

Propaganda constituted the primary element of the regime's strategy to export the revolution. Under Nasr's direction, the GIS quickly recognized the importance of soft power in spreading Nasser's revolutionary message. Thus the organization played a key role in developing a sophisticated propaganda arm known throughout the world as Voice of the Arabs. This was instrumental in extending nationalist revolutionary fervor throughout North Africa and the Middle East. Voice of the Arabs and Radio Cairo called for the overthrow of monarchies in Iraq and Jordan, fueled the Algerian rebellion against France, and nurtured Egypt's dramatic though short-lived union with Syria in 1958.[20]

At the time, foreign observers regarded this psychological warfare as uniquely effective. In 1958 the British Joint Intelligence Committee assessed the ability of Egyptian radio propaganda to persuade the Arab masses to overthrow their governments. The "insidious techniques" of Egypt's radio propaganda included "graphic reporting of imaginary disturbances and acts of violence which is intended as a signal for the audience to translate these imaginary events into reality." Another technique was "to exaggerate harmless demonstrations in order to stimulate more serious disorder." The committee reported to Whitehall that "the constant reiteration of the hypnotic theme of 'kill' and 'blood' has a dramatic effect, particularly when directed at the mob psychology of the Arab listening public."[21] Notwithstanding the evident Orientalism of this analysis, the use of propaganda under Nasr was evidently regarded by British intelligence as a highly effective means of subversion and contributed to a sense that Nasser's revolutionary fervor was spreading throughout the region.[22]

On the significance of soft power, Nasser and Nasr could agree. This had clear domestic implications for what could be expressed within Egypt. Nasr was reportedly quick to crack down on any challenge to the regime's authority, however insignificant. According to one account, he was convinced that the US embassy in Cairo was behind a collection of jokes going around about Nasser. Apparently the directorate "assigned dozens of offices throughout Egypt to collect the jokes and study their meaning. These were written up and sent as regular reports to the president's office."[23]

However, evidence of solidarity between Nasr and Nasser appears quite rarely in the secondary literature. A close reading of these sources indicates clearly that more than the other spy chiefs analyzed in this chapter, Nasr was not simply a servant of the regime. Indeed, he seems to have accrued for himself considerable autonomy. According to one scholar, Nasr was one of an "unholy trio who ran a government within the government in Egypt."[24] This substantiates suspicions that "in many autocratic systems, the gatekeepers to the boss often become important power centres in their own right."[25] Under Nasr's leadership, the GIS became allied with the military and Nasr became well known as Field Marshal Amer's right-hand man.

The rivalry between Nasser and Amer is well documented in Egyptian sources.[26] It was a love-hate relationship: Nasser would refer to Amer as his brother, and the two men were indeed related by marriage. Nasser's successor as president, Anwar al Sadat, recalls Nasser telling him that Egypt was "run by a gang . . . I am responsible as president, but it is Amer that rules."[27] It is not surprising then that Amer's principal ally, Nasr, feared Nasser's attempts to challenge his authority during his leadership of the GIS. He often complained that the Arab Socialist Union (an organization set up by Nasser in 1962 to substitute for outlawed political parties and mobilize the masses) and the rival intelligence agency, the Presidential Bureau of Information (PBI), led by Sami Sharaf, were spying on his own intelligence men.[28] In addition, Nasser appointed several confidants to high positions in the GIS to keep an eye on his powerful spy chief. The memoirs of Nasser's primary confidant, Mohamed Hassanein Heikal, contain numerous examples of confrontations between Nasr and the president.[29]

The spy chief's rivalry with Nasser reached its apogee with the 1967 war when Nasr was blamed for the devastating defeat. According to Heikal, in the immediate aftermath of the Israeli attack Nasr went to visit Nasser to warn that changes to the general staff might prompt a crisis in the military.[30] Nasser replied that he would hold Nasr responsible for any such crisis. Within days of the Israeli attack on Egypt, the spy chief transferred his political master Amer to an intelligence safe house in Cairo, where he implored him to carry out a coup against Nasser. Nasr came up with a simple plot. He planned that commando units would escort Amer to an air base on the outskirts of Cairo; he would then be flown to the west bank of the Suez Canal, where the army was concentrated.[31] Declassified records suggest that Nasr even turned to the CIA for help in carrying out his plan to overthrow Nasser. The spy chief made the case to American diplomats that if US support was forthcoming, Egypt would recognize Israel and liberalize the economy.[32] The State Department warned against such a move, seemingly unable to believe that the Egyptian president's position could be challenged in this manner. Rather, they suspected that Nasr's anti–Nasser stance was "designed for its effect on the US. We have only his word that he has a group—including 'Amir [sic] and Zakariya Muhi al-Din—behind him." The State Department appears to have had total faith in Nasser's authority, struggling to conceive that a mere spy chief could seriously challenge the president. It presciently noted the limits of Nasr's loyalty, however, suggesting that he gave "the impression of being mainly concerned with the preservation of his own position."[33]

Ultimately Nasr's plan to overthrow Nasser failed. Amer was hesitant about the spy chief's daring plan and decided instead to meet Nasser to settle their dispute peacefully, believing that Nasser would "give in as he had always done."[34] The president's other security chiefs got wind of Nasr's plan, launching a counterattack designed to eliminate Amer's power once and for all. In August 1967 Amer and Nasr were arrested together with eighteen intelligence officers. Amer was kept in custody and the following month either committed suicide or was murdered. Nasr was charged with false arrests, use of torture to extract confessions, blackmail, and embezzlement, for which he was imprisoned.[35]

Nasr's leadership of the GIS not only failed to serve the nation, leading Egypt to a spectacular defeat in 1967, but through service to a faction in the regime ultimately brought destruction upon it. With his fall from grace came a decline in the army's influence and the beginning of a concerted attempt to curb its power. In public, Nasser called for the dismantling of the intelligence state, describing it as "one of the most important negative aspects which we dispensed with in our bid to purge public life in Egypt."[36] Scapegoating the unpopular spy chief thus served two functions for the regime: signifying a public break with the police state of the past and undermining the power of a rival faction within the security services that had come to threaten Nasser's authority.

Sami Sharaf

In whom did Nasser really confide? Since the president could not trust the head of the GIS, he was forced to place his faith and security in the hands of an alternative spy chief. His choice was a potbellied man with a drooping mustache by the name of Sami Sharaf, who served as the head of the civilian PBI from 1955 to 1971. The PBI was an office specifically designed to serve only the president. Under Sharaf's leadership, the PBI thrived not only on Nasser's "pathologically suspicious" character but also on Sharaf's skill at playing "Iago to the president's paranoid Othello."[37] American diplomat John Badeau described Sharaf as a "serpentine personality."[38]

Despite his distinctly upper-middle-class origins, Sharaf had a reputation as an enthusiast for the Soviet Union. His relations with it were so good that some suspect that Soviet intelligence actually recruited him, though this is an allegation he has always denied. The Soviet agent allegedly tasked with penetrating Nasser's entourage in Cairo, Vadim Kirpichenko, insisted in his memoir that Sami Sharaf "was never our agent and I did not even know him."[39] Sharaf himself has spoken scathingly about the Communists in retrospective interviews.[40] Whatever the truth of his connection with the Soviet Union, he was certainly regarded as sitting on the left of Egyptian politics.

In contrast to Nasr, Sharaf appears to have enjoyed the complete trust of the president. A recent article about the spy chief in the Egyptian daily *Al Ahram* describes his office as "virtually the nerve centre" of Nasser's regime. It served as a filter through which "every piece of information relevant to the state passed" before reaching the president. Officially, "Sharaf's job entailed poring over all the information gathered and presenting it in a concise form to the president. . . . [He] acted as Nasser's eyes and ears: he reported everything of consequence, often twice or thrice a day."[41] This included extensive human and electronic surveillance of ministers and army officers. Sharaf recalls that Nasser's enthusiasm for intelligence meant unrestricted access to the president: "We could phone him at any time, even well past midnight, to relay an important message."[42]

In turn, Sharaf's personal and political loyalty to Nasser went unquestioned. Research by Hamada Hosni highlights the degree to which Sharaf was prepared to sacrifice personal relationships to give service to his political master.[43] In an interrogation after Nasser's death, Sharaf claims, "I never did anything except follow the orders of the president and uphold moral principles, even if this raised personal conflicts. For example, despite my presence in this workplace, I myself reported two of my brothers." Sharaf goes on to describe that

> one of them was a police officer and belonged to the Muslim Brotherhood, so I reported that he was a dangerous member of the Brotherhood, and he was transferred to the provinces. The other one was an officer in the armed forces, and I reported him to the president himself, saying that he had undertaken communications with other officers, and that these communications were considered to be damaging to the safety and security of the country. This second brother was arrested and remained in detention until President Gamal Abdel Nasser ordered his release without my knowledge.[44]

The period after the Six-Day War saw a further increase in Sharaf's commitment to Nasser. According to one Egyptian actor who interviewed Sharaf in 2006 when preparing to play his role in a new television series, "during this significant era, his life concerns changed. . . . He became a 24/7 working machine. He used to sleep in his office for a maximum of three hours, a brief respite before he had to wake up the following day and delve into the almost-deafening clamor of work." Sharaf recalled, "I never had a fixed time at which I went home, I never knew which of my children was in which school and in which grade; I never knew how they were brought up."[45] According to his own memoir, Sharaf was working in this period to depoliticize the military and refocus intelligence efforts on foreign targets.[46]

But in reality Sharaf's primary concern had always been to protect his political master from the machinations of Amer and the military faction he led. As Sharaf himself put it in his memoir, "we suffered an imbalance, the weight of the military was growing beyond control."[47] There were two notable occasions when Sharaf proved his worth to Nasser in this regard. In 1961 Amer was humiliatingly sent back to Cairo from Syria after an anti-Egyptian coup dissolved the short-lived union between Syria and Egypt that had led to Amer being appointed commander in chief of the two countries' joint military command. Amer resigned as the Egyptian army's chief of staff; Nasser accepted his resignation with relief. However, in January 1962, Sharaf uncovered a military plot to reinstate Amer and dismiss the president if he resisted.[48] Nasser attempted to confront Amer but, fearing a military coup, eventually yielded. The second occasion was the more successful attempt in 1967 to eliminate the threat from Amer and his spy chief Nasr for good. Sharaf was instrumental in formulating the plan to lure Amer to a safehouse where he was arrested and allegedly committed suicide.

Notwithstanding Sharaf's noble professions and obvious worth to Nasser, it seems clear that he also sought to consolidate his own power. Reducing the military's power enhanced Sharaf's already impressive standing as Nasser's most trusted spy chief. Sharaf, Interior Minister Sha'rawi Gomaa, and head of the Arab Socialist Union Ali Sabri became known as Egypt's "hidden government."[49] After Nasser's death, Sharaf appeared intoxicated with the power that the role of spy chief held: "Sami Sharaf thought he could become the strongest man in the country."[50] Under his new political master, Anwar al Sadat, however, Sharaf suffered as a result of Sadat's de-Nasserization program, which became known as the "Corrective Revolution." He was imprisoned in May 1971 for being a KGB asset and only released ten years later. Decades on, Sharaf has vociferously defended his absolute and total devotion to Nasser.[51]

Reflecting on the similarities and differences between Nasser's two spy chiefs, it seems clear that both regarded the day-to-day business of intelligence as serving highly personal purposes. Although Nasr was committed to covert action and propaganda as a means of exporting the revolution, many of his efforts as spy chief were directed toward empowering his political master Abdel Hakim Amer. Sharaf had an equally factional concept of intelligence; his main aim was to protect his political master Gamal Abdel Nasser. It is indicative of the power and reach of these two men that the latest scholarship on the civilian-military rivalry in Egypt concludes that "the real players in this struggle were neither Nasser nor Amer, but rather their security associates."[52]

Omar Suleiman

Omar Suleiman was Egypt's longest-serving spy chief, occupying the office of director of the GIS from 1993 to 2011. He is also probably the intelligence leader about whom we know the most, though his sudden death in 2012 remains shrouded in mystery.[53] In many ways, we know much about this man because he was considerably more than a spy chief. Moreover, his achievements have been publicly celebrated in recent years. His appointment as vice president on January 29, 2011, by President Hosni Mubarak (Mubarak resigned as president less than a fortnight later) indicates just how much power the spy chief was able to acquire for himself during his service to the regime.

Describing Suleiman's personality as "charming and urbane," one senior British diplomat who met him often recalls that he was "a bit grand but very friendly, both a big picture and a detail man."[54] The former US ambassador to Egypt described him as "very bright, very realistic . . . [and] not squeamish by the way."[55] Suleiman was fluent in English, which served him well in his liaison with the US intelligence community. Under his guidance, the Egyptian security services worked as close partners of the CIA in its most unsavory counterterrorism programs. Like Egypt's other spy chiefs, however, domestic concerns took precedence for him. When Suleiman was chosen to be director of the GIS in 1993, Egypt was in the throes of an insurgency waged by the Islamist groups al-Gama'a al-Islamiyya and al-Gihad against prominent tourist sites and parts of Egypt's critical infrastructure. It was not just Islamist extremists that gripped Suleiman's attention. While the Muslim Brotherhood tried to position itself as the moderate Islamist alternative, the regime portrayed it as colluding with violent Islamists. Government repression of the Brotherhood continued even after the insurgency was defeated in 1997; its leaders were periodically arrested and tried.

Suleiman thus built his career and reputation on a ruthless campaign against Mubarak's Islamist opponents. In particular, he earned international fame in 1995 for insisting that Mubarak's armored Mercedes be flown to Ethiopia for a state visit, a move that saved the president's life during an assassination attempt the next day.[56] The individuals involved included Osama bin Laden and Ayman al-Zawahiri, who were making their transition to a global jihad. Suleiman was evidently keen to honor the legacy of previous spy chiefs by focusing on domestic, rather than external, threats. As one Egyptian journalist put it, "I think his [Suleiman's] most important impact" was "his change of [the organization's] creed; change of dogma to perceive that the Islamists are the most critical threat, not any other entity, whether Israel or the Mossad."[57]

This fit well with Egypt's geopolitical priorities. Since Egypt's signing of a peace treaty with Israel in 1979, the United States emerged as the country's principal ally and provided unprecedented quantities of military and economic aid. It also provided intelligence assistance; according to a CIA report, one of the primary objectives of the president of the United States' Counterterrorism Initiative in 1995 was to "provide critical assistance in determining who was responsible for the assassination attempt on Egyptian President

Hosni Mubarak in Addis Ababa."[58] The United States made some attempt to maintain an even hand in the internal battle that was raging between Islamists and the Egyptian government, but this approach was abandoned as the threat to the United States from al Qaeda increased.

It was a symbiotic relationship; the Egyptians had much to give in return. While Suleiman's "concern was very much the Egyptian interest," he "worked hard at his relations with key Western and other partners."[59] Particularly after al Qaeda's attacks on the United States on September 11, 2001, the Egyptian spy chief became a key ally of the British and American intelligence services in their "war against terror."[60] Like Salah Nasr, he enjoyed a reputation for ruthlessness, notably owing to his participation in the CIA's extraordinary rendition program. One victim published his memoir and described his brutal interrogation at Suleiman's own hands; in 2005 investigative journalist Dana Priest published the first exposé in the media of Egyptian-born Australian citizen Mamdouh Habib's torture.[61] Suleiman was also implicated in the more high-profile torture of Ibn al-Shaykh al-Libi. Director of Central Intelligence George Tenet's memoir reveals that evidence from al-Libi's confession was presented to the United Nations (UN) by Secretary of State Colin Powell to make the case for an al Qaeda connection with Iraqi president Saddam Hussein in order to justify the 2003 invasion of Iraq.[62]

Perhaps because of his close links with the West, Suleiman enjoyed complete and total access to the president. According to Stephen Grey, Suleiman was "the main channel to President Hosni Mubarak himself, even on matters far removed from intelligence and security."[63] The extent to which Mubarak trusted his spy chief is indicated by the multiple roles that he occupied, many of which lay in the public sphere. As one interviewee put it, his "writ clearly extended further than that of earlier holders of his office."[64]

The most important and public of these responsibilities was his diplomatic role as Mubarak's personal emissary. Consequently, from about 2001 Suleiman's name and picture began to appear on the government daily newspaper *Al Ahram* and was even known to occupy Mubarak's space on the front page. Suleiman was renowned for his involvement in Palestinian-Israeli negotiations (particularly mediating between the terrorist organizations Hamas and Fatah) and also for his intervention in several regional crises in the 1990s, such as Sudan's civil wars. He attempted to reconcile Saudi Arabia's King Abdullah and Libyan leader Muammar el-Qaddafi after alleged Saudi attempts to assassinate the latter; he also put pressure on Syria to resolve tensions with Lebanon and distance itself from Iran.[65] On the diplomatic matters of greatest concern to Egypt he was "a, if not the, key interlocutor."[66]

This public involvement in politics made Suleiman a natural candidate for Egypt's vice presidency. A strikingly prescient Wikileaks cable in May 2007 speculated on the spy chief's future, noting that in past years Suleiman was "often cited as likely to be named to the long-vacant vice-presidential post." It was significant that Suleiman had "stepped out of the shadows, and allowed himself to be photographed, and his meetings with foreign leaders reported. Many of our contacts believe that Soliman [*sic*], because of his military background, would at least have to figure in any succession scenario."[67] One British diplomat reflected that "he must have judged that he had a chance of reaching the highest office but you didn't get the sense of driving ambition; he had already arrived, and overshadowed ministers and generals who technically outranked him."[68]

In retrospect, the extent of Suleiman's political ambitions is clear. Western diplomats observed that his "interest and dedication to national service is obvious" and asserted that his "loyalty to Mubarak seems rock solid." But they also noted that Mubarak's quest to groom his son for the presidency had caused a rift in their relationship. It was "an idea that Suleiman apparently detested." Moreover, he was "deeply personally hurt" by the fact that Mubarak promised to appoint him vice president but then reneged.[69] His candidacy for the presidency after Mubarak's resignation from the position also made clear just how far Suleiman was willing to go in his quest for political power. After he threatened to unleash classified information from his "black-box," the GIS had to release its first ever public statement: a reminder of "Law Number 100 of the Intelligence Service," which bans political involvement on the part of its members and the release of classified information.[70]

Although this part of the story is more murky, it is clear enough that Suleiman played a role in the civilian-military rivalry that has plagued the Egyptian republic since its inception. Sources from within the US intelligence community suggest that "Suleiman spent 80% of his time devoted to monitoring Egypt's generals and colonels, the officers who could order the tanks to seize the presidential palace. Suleiman no doubt had every one of their phones tapped, knew who was in debt and who wasn't, who left the country and who didn't. He knew exactly who took which bribes and for how much—a weapon for keeping them in line."[71] Some Egyptian sources take a more defensive view of the spy chief. According to one National Democratic Party member, Mohamed Kamal, "Is Omar Suleiman powerful? Yes he is. Does he have a strong say in politics? Yes, but any talk about Omar Suleiman drafting domestic policy or competing for power is pure exaggeration and fiction."[72] It is notable, however, that Suleiman was excluded from the Supreme Council of the Armed Forces that took power after Mubarak resigned the presidency. "He belonged to a faction within the ruling establishment that believed that Hosni Mubarak should survive at any cost. . . . This faction did not get its way." It is particularly significant that Sisi's Military Intelligence Department was "reportedly" granted some of the GIS's "responsibilities and extra-judicial powers."[73]

Notwithstanding Suleiman's contribution to the long-standing civilian-military rivalry, there has been a remarkable coherence to the story that is being put out by the security agencies and the regime in the face of the popular protests that challenged both the security and military factions in 2011. The court transcript of Suleiman's testimony in Mubarak's trial is particularly revealing in this regard. Suleiman claimed that from 2005 "foreign operations began cooperating with NGOs [nongovernmental organizations] based in Egypt to stir the emotions of the people against the regime." In August 2010 the GIS picked up "communications between the opposition movements and abroad" specifying "directives to receive training in mass mobilization, protests, and police confrontations" in Poland and Cairo. Suleiman went on to say that the GIS assessed the situation as "highly unstable" and that the "assessment was proved correct when people . . . began clashing with police and setting fire to various buildings and objects. Crime rings and felons began to storm police stations." Advancing an explanation that has been accepted as conventional wisdom in Egyptian circles, Suleiman testified that by January 28, 2011, "Hamas and Hezbollah had succeeded in freeing their comrades from prison" ("their comrades" was an allusion to the Muslim Brotherhood). Linking the Brotherhood to Hamas and Hezbollah reflected the widespread belief that these groups represent a homogeneous terrorist threat to the Egyptian polity.[74]

A more public statement by Suleiman in an interview with ABC News in 2011 endorsed the position of the Foreign Ministry that the revolutionary protests were "backed by foreign powers." The interview provided a telling insight into the patriarchal mentality of the spy chief. When asked how the protestors would be dispersed, he said that violence would not be used, but they would be "asked to leave." If they refused to leave, he would "call their parents to ask them to leave," drawing on yet another official narrative of the protestors as infantile troublemakers. When politely reminded by the interviewer that parents were also among the crowds he said that in that case, "we will call their grandparents."[75] These depictions of protestors as well-intentioned but ultimately foolish subjects who had been manipulated by foreign powers (including the United States, Hamas, and Hezbollah) are today accepted as conventional wisdom in Egypt. Similarly, the idea that the Muslim Brotherhood was working in collusion with terrorist organizations such as Hamas and Hezbollah to destroy Egypt now goes unchallenged in Egyptian public life. Egyptian courts recently sentenced the Brotherhood leader Mohamed Morsi to life imprisonment for espionage and collusion with Hamas, Hezbollah, and Qatar against the national interest. Dissenters are at best dismissed as ignorant and naive and at worst depicted as traitors complicit in this global conspiracy.

Far from hiding in the shadows, spy chief Omar Suleiman played a key role in rescripting Egypt's revolution in an attempt to ensure that the people never again sought to challenge the regime.

In conclusion, there appear to have been three defining features about Suleiman's apparent success as spy chief. First, like his predecessors, he prioritized domestic concerns over foreign threats, focusing on Islamist opposition within Egypt. Second, this made him a crucial ally of the CIA, consolidating an important geopolitical relationship between Egypt and the West. Third, Suleiman's success in these two fields allowed him to occupy multiple roles within the Egyptian government that extended his responsibilities far beyond those of a spy chief. His importance to the regime enabled him to develop a standing with the public like that of no other spy chief before him and to shape public narratives about threats to Egypt's national security.

Conclusion

This examination of Egypt's three most important spy chiefs reveals much about the way in which intelligence and security work has been conducted in the country's recent history. The domestic focus of these spy chiefs is perhaps the strongest theme that emerges from the investigation. It also seems clear that the job description of spy chief in Egypt encompasses a much larger remit than comparable posts in the West. Moreover, any "success," at least in the short term, was almost entirely dependent on the personal relationships that these men cultivated with their political masters and perhaps also with their geopolitical allies. While they all aspired to the status of leader and attempted to build up power fiefdoms of their own, they have ultimately been servants of the regime or factions within it. A final observation is that important intelligence "failures" or "successes" in the service of their political masters made or broke their careers. Nasr was imprisoned after Egypt's defeat in the Six-Day War, whereas the fact that Suleiman's prudence saved Mubarak's life in 1995 earned him the president's trust.

Although he has the worst reputation among Egyptians today, Salah Nasr was a thoughtful man. He had a clear sense of what "soft power" could achieve, deploying propaganda to considerable effect in the quest to export nationalist revolutionary fervor to the Arab world in the post–World War II era. The overriding characteristic of his leadership of the GIS, however, was the fuel it provided to the rivalry between his nominal political master President Nasser and his actual military master Field Marshal Amer. This civilian-military rivalry endured for decades thereafter. It also ended Nasr's career. After Amer's death in 1967, he was thrown into prison and the dustbin of history as a repressive and corrupt spy boss who had failed to save the nation from the most humiliating defeat in Egypt's modern history.

Sami Sharaf is less controversial. Above all, he is known for his unbounded loyalty to Nasser. He seems to have protected Nasser from the machinations of Field Marshal Amer and his spy chief Salah Nasr. In turn, Sharaf enjoyed the full trust of the president and consequently had much wider responsi-bility than that of simply spy chief. Awarded titles as broad as "Presidential Adviser" and "Minister of Information," his reputation as the eyes and ears of the president foreshadowed the close relationship that Omar Suleiman had with President Hosni Mubarak. This closeness served as a double-edged sword, however: while it gave them power for the duration of their time as spy chiefs, the fate and legacy of both men was ultimately subject to the fortunes of their political masters.

Omar Suleiman's legacy is in some ways the most interesting. Despite once having a reputation as Egypt's "Torturer in Chief," today, as Mubarak's rule is rehabilitated in public memory, he has been posthumously portrayed as a worthy servant of the nation. Alongside the dubious status that Suleiman earned in bringing about Egypt's geopolitical alignment with the West in the global "war on terror," Suleiman is credited with the adoption of the repres-sive policies toward the Muslim Brotherhood that the new military regime is pursuing with a vengeance in Egypt today. Moreover, his view that protestors and opponents of the regime were either foreign agitators or members of the Brotherhood has survived his death in 2012.

With an unprecedented public profile for an Egyptian spy chief, Sulei-man began a trend of making the intelligence service, the Mukhabarat, a palatable word in the Egyptian lexicon. Intelligence can now be discussed in the public sphere with a sense of pride rather than shame or terror. This was perhaps Suleiman's greatest contribution to the regime he served. Today Egyptian television is overrun with commemorations of the intelligence ser-vices, reminding compatriots that "the Eye of Egyptian Intelligence Does Not Sleep."[76] This glorification of the security state is unprecedented in Egypt's history and points to an uneasy future for those who seek to challenge the powers that be.

Notes

1. In Arabic the Gihaz al-Mukhabarat al-Amma (GIS) is often shortened to Mukhabarat.

2. Exceptions include Owen Sirrs, *A History of the Egyptian Intelligence Service: A History of the Mukhabarat, 1910–2009* (New York: Routledge, 2010); and Hazem Kandil, *Soldiers, Spies and Statesmen: Egypt's Road to Revolt* (London: Verso, 2012).

3. Joseph Sasson, *Anatomy of Authoritarianism in the Arab Republics* (Cambridge: Cambridge University Press), 24.

4. For an excellent recent study along these lines, see Stuart Croft, *Securitizing Islam: Identity and the Search for Security* (Cambridge: Cambridge University Press, 2012).

5. Kandil, *Soldiers, Spies and Statesmen*, 43.

6. Shams Badran cited in Laura James, "Nasser and His Enemies: Foreign Policy Decision Making in Egypt on the Eve of the Six-Day War," *Middle East Review of International Affairs* 9, no. 2 (June 2005), accessed April 1, 2016, http://www.mafhoum.com/press8/244P541.htm.

7. Intelligence Information Cable, "Views of Deputy UAR Prime Minister Zakariyah Muhiy Al Din on His Power Status within the UAR," July 31, 1967, *Declassified Documents Referencing System*.

8. Amin Huwaidi, *Khamsin 'Am Min Al-'Awasif: Ma Ra'ituh Qultuh* [Fifty stormy years: I told what I saw] (Cairo: Markaz Al-Ahram lel-Targama wa-Nashr, 2002), 190–91.

9. Khaled Muhi al-Din, *Memories of a Revolution: Egypt 1952* (Cairo: Al Ahram, 1995), 240.

10. Abd al-Fattah Abu Al Fadl, *Kunt Naiban Le Rais Al-Mukhabarat* [I was deputy director of the Mukhabarat] (Cairo: Dar El Shorook, 2008), 87.

11. Roger Owen, *The Rise and Fall of Arab Presidents for Life: With a New Afterword* (Cambridge, MA: Harvard University Press, 2014), 20.

12. Said K. Aburish, *Nasser: The Last Arab* (New York: St. Martin's Press, 2004), 119.

13. Testimony of Omar Suleiman, Session 9/14/2011, transcript translated and made available by *Rebel Economy*, accessed April 1, 2016, http://rebeleconomy.com/economy/voice-from-the-grave-omar-suleimans-testimony/.

14. Nasr and Abd Allah Imam, *Al Thawrah, Al Naksah, Al Mukhabarat* [The revolution, the setback of June 1967 and the intelligence services] (Cairo: Dar al Khayyal, 1999), 59.

15. Benjamin Geer, "Prophets and Priests of the Nation: Naguib Mahfouz's Karnak Café and the 1967 Crisis in Egypt," *International Journal of Middle East Studies* 41, no. 4 (November 2009): 660.

16. Youssef Aboul-Enein, "Spymaster: Former Egyptian Intelligence Chief Discusses Psychological Warfare," *The Free Library*, July 1, 2006, accessed April 1, 2016, http://www.thefreelibrary.com/Spymaster:%20former%20Egyptian%20intelligence%20chief%20discusses%20psychological . . . -a0155736031.

17. Nasr cited in Sirrs, *History of the Egyptian Intelligence Service*, 61.

18. Malcolm H. Kerr, *The Arab Cold War: Gamal 'Abd al-Nasir and His Rivals, 1958–1970* (Oxford: Oxford University Press, 1971).

19. Sirrs, *History of the Egyptian Intelligence Service*, 61.

20. James P. Jankowski, *Nasser's Egypt, Arab Nationalism and the United Arab Republic* (Boulder, CO: Lynne Rienner, 2002), 55.

21. JIC memorandum (58) 83, "Lebanon and Jordan—infiltration and subversion

by the United Arab Republic," August 8, 1958, The National Archives (TNA), CAB 158/33.

22. Edward Said, *Orientalism* (London: Penguin, 2003).

23. Alaa Al Aswany, "Egypt's Ancient Snark," *New York Times*, March 13, 2014, accessed April 1, 2016, http://www.nytimes.com/2014/03/14/opinion/aswany -egypts-jokers-wont-be-gagged.html?_r=0.

24. Said K. Aburish, *Nasser: The Last Arab* (New York: St. Martin's Press, 2004), 267.

25. Sirrs, *History of the Egyptian Intelligence Service*, 64.

26. Mohamed Abdel Ghani El-Gamasy, *The October War: Memoirs of Field Marshal Al Gamasy of Egypt* (Cairo: American University of Cairo Press, 1993), 41.

27. Anwar al Sadat, *Al-Bahth'an al-zat* [In search of identity] (Cairo: al-Maktab al-Misri al-Hadith, 1978), 220.

28. Mohamed Hassanein Heikal, *1967: Al-Infigar* [1967: The explosion] (Cairo: Markaz Al-Ahram lel-Targama wa-Nashr, 1990), 401.

29. Heikal, *1967*, 875–86.

30. Ibid.

31. Gamal Hammad, *Asrar Thawrat 23 Yunyu* [Secrets of the July 23 revolution], vols. 1 and 2 (Cairo: Dar Al-'Ulum 2010), 1345.

32. Sirrs, *History of the Egyptian Intelligence Service*, 105.

33. Memorandum from the Director of the Bureau of Intelligence and Research (Hughes) to Secretary of State Rusk, July 3, 1967, *Foreign Relations of the United States* [FRUS], *1964–1968*, vol. XIX, no. 339.

34. Kandil, *Soldiers, Spies and Statesmen*, 88.

35. Sirrs, *History of the Egyptian Intelligence Service*, 105.

36. Ibid., 106.

37. Ibid., 63–64.

38. John Badeau, *The Middle East Remembered* (Washington, DC: Middle East Institute, 1983), 229.

39. Vadim Kirpichenko cited in Christopher Andrew and Vasili Mitrokhin, *The Mitrokin Archive II: The KGB and the World* (London: Penguin, 2005), 147.

40. Gamal Nkrumah, "Sami Sharaf: Shadows of the Revolution," *Al-Ahram Weekly Online*, August 2001, accessed April 1, 2016, http://weekly.ahram.org.eg/Archive /2001/546/profile.htm.

41. Ibid.

42. Ibid.

43. Mamdouh Al Sheikh, "Egyptian Author Names Nasser Spies in New Book," *Al Arabiya News*, November 26, 2007, accessed April 1, 2016, https://www.alarabiya.net /articles/2007/11/26/42161.html.

44. Belal Fadl, "Egypt: The Nation of Snitches Makes a Comeback," *Mada Masr*, November 9, 2014, accessed April 1, 2016, http://www.madamasr.com/en/2014/11/09 /opinion/u/egypt-the-nation-of-snitches-makes-a-comeback/.

45. Mohamed Ghoneim, "Reliving a Piece of History," *Daily News Egypt*,

September 22, 2006, accessed April 1, 2016, http://www.dailynewsegypt.com/2006 /09/22/reliving-a-piece-of-history/.

46. Samy Sharaf, *Abd al-Nasser: Keif Hakam Masr?* [Abd al-Nasser: How did he rule Egypt?] (Cairo: Madbouli al-Saghir, 1996), 175.

47. Ibid., 228.

48. Kandil, *Soldiers, Spies and Statesmen*, 53.

49. Gamal Hammad, *Al-Hukuma al-Khafiya Fei 'ahd Abd Al-Nasser wa Asrar Masra' Almushir Amer* [The invisible government during the reign of Nasser and the secrets of Field Marshal Amer's death] (Cairo: Al-Shareka Al-Mutaheda lel-Teba'a wel-Nashr wel Tawzee, 2008), 1.

50. Kandil, *Soldiers, Spies and Statesmen*, 110.

51. Gamal Nkrumah, "Sami Sharaf: Shadows of the Revolution," *Al-Ahram Weekly Online*, August 2001, accessed April 1, 2016, http://weekly.ahram.org.eg/Archive /2001/546/profile.htm.

52. Kandil, *Soldiers, Spies and Statesmen*, 55.

53. Heba Afify, "Sunday's Papers: Omar Suleiman, Mysterious in Death as well as Life," *Egypt Independent*, July 22, 2012, accessed April 1, 2016, http://www.egyptindependent .com/news/sunday-s-papers-omar-suleiman-mysterious-death-well-life.

54. Email correspondence with senior British diplomat, February 18, 2015.

55. Jane Mayer, *The Dark Side: The Inside Story of How the War on Terror Turned into a War on American Ideals* (New York: Random House, 2008), 131.

56. Steven Cook, *The Struggle for Egypt: From Nasser to Tahrir Square* (New York: Oxford University Press, 2011), 204.

57. Kristen Chick, "Omar Suleiman, Mubarak Intel Chief, Dies as Quietly as He Worked," *Christian Science Monitor*, July 19, 2012, accessed April 1, 2016, http://www .csmonitor.com/World/Middle-East/2012/0719/Omar-Suleiman-Mubarak-intel -chief-dies-as-quietly-as-he-worked.

58. CIA Annual Report on Intelligence Community Activities, January 1, 1997, provided by Nate Jones, "Document Friday: Mubarak, al-Bashir, al-Zawahiri, and bin Laden. The 1995 Assassination Attempt in Addis Ababa," *UNREDACTED*, February 4, 2011, accessed April 1, 2016, https://nsarchive.wordpress.com/2011/02/04/document -friday-mubarak-al-bashir-al-zawahiriand-bin-laden-the-1995-assassination-atempt -in-addis-ababa/.

59. Email correspondence with senior British diplomat, February 18, 2015.

60. Matthew Aid, *Intel Wars: The Secret History of the Fight against Terror* (New York: Bloomsbury, 2012), 194.

61. Mamdouh Habib, *My Story: The Tale of a Terrorist Who Wasn't* (Melbourne: Scribe: 2008).

62. Lisa Hajjar, "Suleiman: The CIA's Man in Cairo," *Al Jazeera*, February 7, 2011, accessed April 1, 2016, http://www.aljazeera.com/indepth/opinion/2011/02 /20112711482738265.html.

63. Stephen Grey, *Ghost Plane: The Untold Story of the CIA's Torture Programme* (New York: St. Martin's Press 2007), 142.

64. Email correspondence with senior British diplomat, February 18, 2015.

65. Hossam Hamalawy, "Powerful Egyptian Spy Chief No Longer behind the Scenes," *Los Angeles Times*, February 8, 2005, accessed April 1, 2016, http://articles.latimes.com/2005/feb/08/world/fg-omar8.

66. Email correspondence with senior British diplomat, February 18, 2015.

67. Hajjar, "Suleiman: The CIA's Man in Cairo."

68. Email correspondence with senior British diplomat, February 18, 2015.

69. Jake Tapper, "WikiLeaks Cables Shed Light on Egypt's New VP," ABC News, January 29, 2011, accessed April 1, 2016, http://blogs.abcnews.com/politicalpunch/2011/01/wikileaks-cables-shed-light-on-egypts-new-vp-.html.

70. Omar Ashour, "Death of Suleiman: Egypt's Revolution Outlives Its Torturers," *Al Jazeera*, July 21, 2012, accessed April 1, 2016, http://www.aljazeera.com/indepth/opinion/2012/07/2012720132344865981.html.

71. Robert Baer, "The One Person Who May Know What Egypt's Generals Will Do," *Time*, January 30, 2011, accessed April 1, 2016, http://content.time.com/time/world/article/0,8599,2045174,00.html.

72. Mohamed Kamal cited in Joshua Stacher, *Adaptable Autocrats: Regime Power in Egypt and Syria* (Stanford, CA: Stanford University Press, 2012), 145.

73. Ashour, "Death of Suleiman."

74. Testimony of Omar Suleiman, Session 9/14/2011, transcript translated and made available by *Rebel Economy*, accessed April 1, 2016, http://rebeleconomy.com/economy/voice-from-the-grave-omar-suleimans-testimony/.

75. Omar Suleiman, interview by Christiane Amanpour, ABC News, February 3, 2011, accessed April 1, 2016, http://abcnews.go.com/International/egypt-abc-news-christiane-amanpour-exclusive-interview-vice/story?id=12836594.

76. Aya Batrawy, "Egypt Intelligence Agency in Image Makeover Drive," *Arab News*, July 19, 2012, accessed April 1, 2016, http://www.arabnews.com/egypt-intelligence-agency-image-makeover-drive.

Conclusion

Government Men

Paul Maddrell

Chapter 1 of this book developed principles of good organizational leadership derived from the study of business management, the closest parallel to leadership of a government agency. The aim of this conclusion is to establish how and how well the intelligence leaders discussed in this collection did their job. In each case it is clear that the character of the leadership they provided was influenced by the culture of their organization and of the government of which it formed a part. The name by which officials of the FBI became popularly known in the 1930s—"government men (G-men)"—suits them well.

The preliminary point needs to be made—one entirely consistent with the findings of scholars who have researched into business leadership— that the organization is more important than the leader. This book underlines the fact that intelligence agencies are more important than their directors. It contains striking examples of agencies and leaders that managed to survive radical political changes. Nazi Germany's Gen. Reinhard Gehlen, for example, managed after the Second World War to reestablish his military intelligence unit Fremde Heere Ost (FHO: Foreign Armies East) under American control as the "Gehlen Organization." As during the war, it collected intelligence on the Soviet armed forces in Eastern Germany and Eastern Europe. Without Gehlen's guile, a German foreign intelligence organization would not have emerged so quickly after the war. Nevertheless, however much cunning he displayed in persuading the US Army's Counter-Intelligence Corps to allow him to reestablish his service, he survived because his service was regarded as important rather than the other way round.

The chapters by Ioanna Iordanou and Emrah Safa Gürkan on the intelligence-collection system of the great trading city of Venice show how early in European history the gathering of information was conducted in an organized way. It is no accident that this occurred in a relatively small polity, a city, with a strong civic culture derived from its guilds; good organization was easier for such a polity to achieve than it was for the ruler of a large territory. Venice developed a culture of obsessive concern for secrecy: state secrets were to be kept and public security was to be further enhanced by calling on the general public to report troubling matters. Venice made great efforts to ensure that information flowed strongly to a small group of secretive old men. Iordanou shows how the political leadership provided to Venice by the Council of Ten was of the "transactional" and "transformational" types that the modern academic literature on leadership has identified. One of the great objectives of the council's leadership was to obtain information to guide the government of the city. The three channels of information it exploited—diplomats, merchants, and the general public—are, of course, still in use today. Gürkan demonstrates that, by contrast, as intelligence collectors Venice's baili in Istanbul were entrepreneurs who were left by their masters to gather intelligence as they thought best.

The history of Venice shows the importance of organized intelligence collection. This raises the question: How important are leaders to the performance of their agencies? This book contains examples of leaders who enhanced their organizations' performance.

Such was the importance attributed by Communist regimes to domestic repression and intelligence collection, both at home and abroad, that very able men could and did achieve the position of leader of the security or foreign intelligence service. Feliks Dzerzhinsky and Markus Wolf are examples. Significantly, both were appointed early in the lifetime of their respective services; Dzerzhinsky was the first chairman of the Cheka, Wolf the second chief of foreign intelligence. Both were young men when they were appointed (Dzerzhinsky was forty, Wolf twenty-nine) and were not regarded as posing any threat to the party leader.

Feliks Dzerzhinsky was an outstanding political policeman. Indeed, as Iain Lauchlan demonstrates in his chapter, he was one of the most important Communist leaders in the history of the Soviet regime. In the first place, that fragile regime owed its survival, in the terrible years of the Russian Civil War and the ensuing crisis of the Russian Empire, to him and men like Leon Trotsky, who shared his energy, intelligence, and fanaticism. Dzerzhinsky had a much more long-lasting, and even more harmful, influence on the lives of those who lived—and died—under Communist rule than that: he played a key role in the process by which the Communist leadership of the Soviet Union came to delude itself about popular dissatisfaction with its misrule. Since Lenin and his followers insisted that their ideology, Marxism-Leninism, was correct, they were forced to regard popular dissatisfaction as a hostile conspiracy arising from class resistance. Dzerzhinsky was Lenin's most faithful disciple and incorporated this gross distortion of reality into the daily practice of the political police. On the instructions of the party leader, whether it was Lenin or Stalin or any of their successors, the political police came to see conspiracy everywhere and encouraged their leaders to be more paranoid than they would otherwise have been. Each encouraged the delusions and cruelties of the other. By means of the Cheka and its leader, Lenin turned himself into the Soviet peoples' persecutor—for seventy-four years. The civil war that Dzerzhinsky declared on the Soviet peoples, in the name of revolution, prevented any possibility that the regime's rule might come to rest on popular consent. The regime, and at its core its political police, existed to coerce the people. As Lauchlan rightly says, Dzerzhinsky became the regime's "holy executioner."

Lauchlan shows that Dzerzhinsky and the political police he created prompted key steps in the development of the Communist regime and of its vicious repression of society. The evidence indicates that it was Dzerzhinsky, rather than Lenin, who first proposed late in 1917 that a political police agency be founded. Lauchlan demonstrates that it was Dzerzhinsky, together with Viacheslav Molotov, who in 1921, in the wake of the civil war, first proposed the theory later taken up by Stalin that class struggle would intensify as class enemies grew weaker. It was Dzerzhinsky who suggested to Lenin in 1921 that the first show trials (of Socialist revolutionaries) be held; his reason was the very ideological one of blaming the regime's crisis on opponents. Fanatical Communist that he was, Dzerzhinsky turned his service into the Communist Party's Inquisition—ideologically correct, completely loyal to the leader, and utterly vicious. In the 1920s the Communist Party leadership came increasingly to trust the political police's intelligence reports precisely because they were so distorted by ideology. This deluded and alarmist reporting was, according to Molotov, one of the reasons why Stalin and his acolytes carried out their campaign of mass murder that Western historians know as the "Great Terror." Stalin's political police chief, Nikolai Yezhov, was merely his boss's agent in supervising this terrible purge of imaginary enemies; in this, as Lauchlan shows, he followed the example of obedience to the Communist Party's leader set by Dzerzhinsky. Stalin exploited Yezhov to the full before he had him executed, deflecting on to his underling much of the responsibility for the mass killings that Russians remember as the "Yezhovshchina" ("time of Yezhov").

Lauchlan argues that Dzerzhinsky belongs to the "Great Man" type of leader. This is open to question; rather, the Dzerzhinsky myth, carefully cultivated by first the Soviet and now the Russian security service, presents him as such a leader. That myth is the outstanding example of an intelligence agency trying to strengthen its culture and morale by claiming for its officials virtues attributed to a past leader.

Because in the last decade and a half of his life Markus Wolf sought publicity, a great deal is known about his leadership of the GDR's principal foreign
intelligence service, the Stasi's Main Intelligence Directorate (Hauptverwaltung Aufklärung, HVA). He even wrote an autobiography—something very
rare for a Communist spy chief. He was a very good director of the HVA. His
achievements speak for themselves: during his time as chief (1952–86) the
service created a very large network of agents in its main target, the Federal
Republic of Germany. This network consisted of approximately 6,000 spies;
other departments of the Stasi recruited and ran another 6,000 in the same
period. This total number of 12,000 spies was supported by about 40,000
East German couriers and instructors. The entire network gathered a wealth
of high-grade political, military, scientific and technological, and counterintelligence information for the GDR and the Soviet Union.[1]

In truth, Wolf was both a success and a failure. His careful, calm, methodical, intelligent approach to espionage was an important reason for his service's success. Wolf was a highly intelligent man, and his intellectual brand of
Marxism-Leninism made him very cynical in his dealings with others (particularly his spies): he regarded them as means to his end—the triumph of
Marxism-Leninism. He had a very careful, systematic way of thinking, one
encouraged by his study of aeronautical engineering as a young man (for the
rest of his life he was a keen reader of aviation magazines). These are ideal
qualities in a spy chief. Under his leadership, the HVA was both very concerned with security and supremely successful in recruiting promising agents
and infiltrating them into its targets.[2] Of course, it had the great advantage that
the Cold War lasted a long time: it had decades in which to become proficient
in infiltrating its targets. The division of Germany, mass migration from East
to West, and proliferation of contacts between East and West Germans that
the HVA could exploit greatly facilitated his task. Nevertheless, similar opportunities were available to West Germany's intelligence agencies, which did not
exploit them nearly as well. Wolf was an ambitious and demanding man who
set high standards of achievement for his service; he consistently pressed his
subordinates to obtain high-quality intelligence.[3]

Since obtaining information from spies was his work, he saw the importance of building good relationships with people; his vanity helped him here,
for he was keen to impress others.[4] Very unusually for a foreign intelligence
chief, he always ran a few agents himself. One of his top sources in the BND,
Gabriele Gast, was one of them. She writes in her memoir that the two of them
became friends and that he planned every meeting with her carefully and
intelligently. However, his vanity and self-importance always shone through.[5]

Wolf's cynicism served him both well and ill. It caused him to regard others as means to his ends. It lay behind his spectacularly successful "Romeo"

operations—the use of male agents, usually supplied with false identities, to obtain intelligence over long periods from lonely, middle-aged West German women, usually working as secretaries in ministries or intelligence agencies in the Federal Republic. This was an intelligent development of the KGB's long-standing technique of blackmail following sexual entrapment. It was so successful that the KGB itself made use of the method—it is a rare case of the KGB adopting an operational technique from a satellite service.[6] However, his cynicism was visible to others and may have led to his downfall. Gabriele Gast, herself seduced by a "Romeo" sent by Wolf, was bitterly disappointed at the cynicism with which he tried to justify deceiving lonely women with false expressions of love into betraying classified information.[7] He treated his wives just as badly. He was unfaithful to his first wife. His divorce from his second wife was acrimonious and turned him into a security risk for the Stasi because the BND tried to recruit his ex-wife. It is uncertain whether Wolf retired from the HVA in 1986 at his own request or whether he was forced out because of the security concerns arising from his divorce. Gast, who found him depressed at their last meeting a few weeks before he retired, believes that he was forced out of his job. In his memoir Wolf presents himself as having sought early retirement because he wanted to finish a film script left incomplete by his late brother. In fact, Mielke had given him a lot of time to do this while remaining in post as HVA chief.[8]

Wolf had shortcomings as a foreign intelligence chief that put limits on his success. His main failing, like Dzerzhinsky's, was his orthodox Marxism-Leninism. Since the Marxist-Leninist social system was doomed to fail, so was Wolf's intelligence service. As HVA chief, he contributed to the GDR's downfall. The SED regime was overthrown because the party leaders greatly overestimated its stability; Wolf, in his intelligence reporting, encouraged them to believe that its rule was stable and that popular opposition was stirred up by a hostile Western reactionary conspiracy. His intelligence reporting was not good enough.

The intelligence analysts of Western states today regard their task as to tell their political masters what they do not want to hear. Orthodox Stalinist that he was, Wolf knew he could not do this: he never argued before the party leaders that the intelligence his service had so skillfully obtained was correct. His intelligence assessors (who prepared their reports under his direction) did not analyze intelligence; they did not try to reach any view of their own. Instead, they summarized the information available to them. Their reports were accordingly very factual in character. They were sent on to the party leaders. They pointed to numerous failings, particularly economic and political ones, which West German leaders saw the GDR as having.[9] Being very factual reports on information collected in the West, in the party leaders' eyes they were very similar to Western press reports that they read about in summaries of information in the Western press; the leaders were very used to dismissing such reports. Consequently, according to Wolf's successor as HVA chief Werner Großmann, they were very skeptical of his service's reports.[10] The intelligence so arduously collected made little impression on them; despite having an excellent foreign intelligence service, the Socialist Unity Party leadership was ill-informed. Neither Wolf nor Großmann stood his ground and argued that the information contained in their reports was correct. Wolf claims that, in the last years of his time as chief of the HVA, he realized that Western criticisms of the Soviet Bloc's growing economic backwardness and military decline were well-founded, but he did not voice this view. Party discipline was too strict.[11] Another failing in the HVA's reporting is that it collected intelligence only on subjects on which the party wanted information, which further hindered it from showing the leadership the real state of affairs. Not that it wanted to show the party how matters really stood: the HVA officers were as committed to Marxism-Leninism as their leaders.

Wolf's vanity was another shortcoming. No one was more impressed by him than Wolf himself.[12] He was also very impressed by his family, which he regarded as a special one—intellectually minded, culturally gifted, and a bright light of the German Communist movement. His interest in other people was small and largely prompted by his work. Some were impressed by him, but others had more insight and were not. However, unlike Gehlen, Wolf was able to keep his vanity in check; it did not interfere with his work. It is a tribute to Wolf's commitment to secrecy that he acquired the nickname "the man without a face."

However, his vanity became apparent when, like Gehlen's, his reputation came under attack. It prompted him—after the collapse of the SED regime, the GDR, and the Soviet Union and his own forced return from exile in Russia to criminal prosecution in the reunited Germany—to seek the limelight. He published several books and gave numerous interviews to television companies and the press. His aim throughout was to present himself as a humanitarian reform Communist who bore little responsibility for the Stasi's crimes and infringements of human rights. His claim that, by the early 1980s at the latest, he had realized that the GDR's "actually existing socialism" was a failure and needed to be radically reformed, has been dismissed by both Werner Großmann and Gabriele Gast as a lie.[13]

While able men could rise to the top of the Communist political police and foreign intelligence services, there was a strong tendency among Communist regimes to put the former, the more important of these, in the hands of men of mediocre ability: such men were less likely to pose a political threat to the leader. Brutal, narrow-minded, suspicious, of very ordinary intelligence, sycophantic toward his political masters and a bully toward his subordinates, Erich Mielke was an archetypal Communist political policeman of the Cold War era and a mediocre minister for state security. His career shows how important an influence on leadership the cultural (including political) influences on a leader are. He continued the tradition established by Dzerzhinsky of subordinating his ministry completely to his political masters. However, as the chief of the security service of a Soviet satellite, he had two masters: the leadership of the Socialist Unity Party and the KGB. He codirected his ministry with them. Mielke's longevity in office is explained by his seniority and standing among East German security officials, the backing of the general secretaries he served (to whom he groveled), and the support of the Russians (to whom he also groveled). He retained his position for so long because he did what his masters told him to do. Only one GDR state security minister, Ernst Wollweber (1953–57), seems to have done his job ably. His predecessor, Wilhelm Zaisser (1950–53), failed in the position.

Nevertheless, Mielke's long reign had benefits for the Stasi. It was not affected, as the KGB was, by political clientelism; its leading officials were not clients of leading politicians. This was a reflection of the East German political system, which was less patrimonial than the Soviet. Stasi officers also tended to be professional policemen rather than party officials who had been transferred to the security service. From the very start of the Stasi's existence, its leading officers were chosen by Mielke, the ministry's deputy chief from its creation in 1950 and the minister from 1957. This is one reason why Mielke was an authoritative minister and lasted so long in the position (thirty-two years).[14]

Like the Soviet security service, the Stasi took on the flaws of the regime it served. However, Soviet influence over the Stasi and over the Socialist Unity Party's leaders themselves made it harder for the party's general secretaries to take control of it; it did not become a weapon in their struggles for power (as the KGB and its predecessors did). Though Erich Mielke was very much Walter Ulbricht's man, Ulbricht was unable to use the Stasi against his rivals. When he became party leader, Erich Honecker did not even try to replace Mielke. One reason for this was probably that he regarded Mielke as held in high esteem by the Russians.[15]

Markus Wolf's West German counterpart, Reinhard Gehlen, was also vain; he too sought fame. He made contact with the West German press in the early 1950s, purportedly to defend his service, the "Gehlen Organization," from Communist disinformation, but evidently also to enhance his own reputation at the expense of his rivals in the nascent West German intelligence community.[16] His photograph first appeared on the front cover of *Der Spiegel*, the leading West German news magazine, in 1954. His unreliable memoir, *Der Dienst* (*The Service*), published in 1971, has been rightly described by Dieter

Krüger as "less an assessment than a justification of his life's work";[17] it was clearly intended to maintain his service's reputation and play down its failures while extoling the work of Fremde Heere Ost, the military intelligence unit on the eastern front that Gehlen had led from 1942 to 1945.[18]

He also sought to wield political influence. Bodo Hechelhammer's chapter on Gehlen's special card file continues the trend among historians to show how much Gehlen curried favor with Konrad Adenauer and the powerful state secretary of the federal chancellery, Hans Maria Globke; Gehlen was West Germany's counterpart to J. Edgar Hoover. He sought contact with the federal chancellor as soon as Adenauer achieved that position in October 1949, even though Gehlen's organization was firmly subordinated to the United States' CIA. Financed and directed by the federal chancellery, the Gehlen Organization (which from its incorporation into the federal government in 1956 was known as the Bundesnachrichtendienst) placed West Germany's political elite under surveillance into the 1960s. This reflects how extraordinarily divided the new, fragile Federal Republic was—how great the tension was between the conservative right and the Socialist left and how much the conservative government feared Communist infiltration. Gehlen's fear of such infiltration seems, from Hechelhammer's account, to have reached absurd proportions. That said, his political masters shared many of his fears. One reason Adenauer was so willing to allow Gehlen to collect intelligence domestically was that he did not trust the Federal Republic's security service, the Bundesamt für Verfassungsschutz (BfV, Federal Office for the Protection of the Constitution). The BfV's president, Otto John, had not only been the United Kingdom's candidate for the position—Adenauer had a considerable mistrust of the British—but also defected to the GDR in 1954.

Gehlen tried to wield political influence not just on his own behalf but also in favor of the conservative, nationalist politics of the German army he had joined as a teenager. Gehlen sought to continue a tradition—that of the Prussian general staff and its military intelligence service—by heavy recruitment into his organization of former Wehrmacht and SS officers. While his collection of damaging information on West German political figures was not illegal, it served Gehlen's purposes and those of his political masters rather than the cause of West Germany's defense. He tried to profit from the Federal Republic's early insecurity.[19]

Gehlen's efforts to wield political influence were, over time, unsuccessful. West German politics drifted in the 1960s ever further to the left, and the BND was extensively reformed by the Social Democratic–Free Democratic government after Gehlen's retirement. His role in the "Spiegel Affair" of 1962 is still obscure—it resulted in the resignation of West Germany's defense minister, Franz Josef Strauß, who was then an enemy of Gehlen's—but his involvement damaged Gehlen's reputation. All Gehlen achieved by his investigation of the pasts of the Federal Republic's political elite was to win the favor of Adenauer and Globke.

Even more important, Gehlen's BND lost its espionage struggle with the GDR's Stasi; the Stasi did its agent network serious damage in its "Big Operations" (*Großaktionen*) of the years 1953–55, when Western agents were arrested in large numbers. The BND's success against the GDR declined from then on. It reconstructed its network in the late 1950s, but in the 1960s, in the wake of the Berlin Wall's construction, the Stasi was able very largely to dissolve the network.[20] Gehlen's poor judgment of people contributed to his service's decline, the best example of this being the trust he long showed in his apparently successful Soviet counterintelligence chief, Heinz Felfe. Felfe was exposed in 1961 as a traitor in the pay of the KGB. Gehlen retired in April 1968 a failed man. He should have stepped down a decade earlier.

In his introduction to a book on the Gehlen Organization by two journalists for *Der Spiegel*, Oxford professor (and officer of Britain's Security Service in the Second World War) Hugh Trevor-Roper pointed out that foreign intelligence agencies have a more difficult job than security agencies and therefore need better leadership: "Espionage is always at a disadvantage compared with counter-espionage, for the former depends on individual skill in hostile surroundings, while the latter operates on home ground, supported by the ample resources of the state. Successful espionage therefore requires continual regeneration: fresh thought, constant vigilance, continuous adaptation to changing circumstances."[21]

As Trevor-Roper observes, Gehlen used the secrecy his service enjoyed to cover up its failures. His poor judgment was an important reason for them: not only did he trust traitors like Felfe (and others) and see Communist infiltration where none existed, he did not show the same concern for strict security and the collection of high-grade intelligence that his more successful counterparts, such as Markus Wolf, did. He selected his staff in the late 1940s for political reasons: they came from the Wehrmacht, and he wanted them to form the core of a new German army. Such men proved incapable of building an intelligence service to match the Stasi. Gehlen cultivated his political masters well: it is clear from Hechelhammer's chapter that Adenauer and Globke were willing to defend him because they valued the information they had received from him. However, Gehlen devoted too much attention to pursuing his own political ambitions and too little to ensuring the skill and security of his service.

While Gehlen was able to conceal his failures, the Federal Republic's democratic system prevented him from running amok. The lesson to be drawn from Paul McGarr's chapter on the three Indian intelligence chiefs—

T. G. Sanjeevi Pillai, B. N. Mullik, and R. N. Kao—is what a triumphant success Indian democracy has been: the chapter shows that all three men were wholly obedient to political authority. Kao had such good relations with Jawaharlal Nehru and Indira Gandhi and such skill at foreign liaison that he sounds like an Indian Dick White. India's democracy has kept Indian intelligence within the Western tradition of intelligence leadership.

By contrast, Chikara Hashimoto's chapter on Emir Farid Chehab, the director-general of the principal Lebanese security service, the Sûreté Générale, from 1948 to 1958, shows what a failure Lebanon's sectarianism has made that artificial state. Hashimoto demonstrates that, as in most of the other Arab states, the security service's task was chiefly to protect the regime rather than the state. Since Lebanon was riven by sectarian tensions between Maronite Christians (of whom Chehab was one) and Sunni and Shia Muslims, this task was an impossible one, and Chehab resigned when the country fell into political crisis in 1958.

The chapter by Dina Rezk on Egypt's notorious intelligence chiefs Salah Nasr, Sami Sharaf, and Omar Suleiman shows that their primary job was to protect an unstable military dictatorship from overthrow, whether by a popular uprising or by a coup organized by the armed forces or the security services themselves. The regimes they served also had a great fear of Western, particularly American, spying and subversion. The force that created the Egyptian police state was the profound suspiciousness of Egypt's rulers since 1952: Gamal Abdel Nasser, Anwar Sadat, and Hosni Mubarak. In the view of United Nations secretary-general Dag Hammarskjöld, Nasser was "pathologically suspicious."[22] He placed even his closest colleagues under covert surveillance, using informers, bugs, and cameras, and his meetings with them were recorded on microphone and camera. Egypt's intelligence chiefs have been the creations of the regimes they have served.

The suspiciousness and insecurity of Egypt's rulers has led to extensive surveillance of society; several security agencies have looked for any sign of disloyalty. The main security agencies since 1952 have been the General Investigations Directorate (GID), a civilian security service subordinate to the Ministry of the Interior, which was established in 1952; the Military Intelligence Department, the intelligence branch of the armed forces that is subordinate to the Defense Ministry; and the General Intelligence Service (GIS), the foreign intelligence service established at Nasser's behest in 1954 and subordinated to the president. Though modeled on the CIA, the GIS also collects counterintelligence within Egypt and conducts covert action abroad. It was (and remains) the leading intelligence agency, to which Nasser gave the task of coordinating all Egypt's intelligence services.[23]

Egypt's intelligence chiefs have been crucial props of the regime, feared and hated by the presidents' critics and the population at large. They were doomed to hatred and notoriety as soon as they assumed their positions. However, like their Communist counterparts, Nasser, Sadat, and Mubarak also took a fateful step in appointing them; dependent, as they were, on their intelligence chiefs, they were the victims just as they were the beneficiaries of the wide-ranging intelligence collection they had ordered. Some, at least, of the information they received gave them a distorted picture of reality. Sami Sharaf was very sympathetic to the Soviet Union and Communism and was believed by the US embassy in Cairo to have passed to Nasser false intelligence received from the KGB about CIA plots to assassinate him and overthrow his regime. It has even been alleged that Sharaf was a KGB agent who was given the code name "Asad" ("Lion"). Nasser's willingness to believe these reports harmed US-Egyptian relations.[24]

While Nasser used his security agencies in his attempts to export his revolution to the rest of the Arab world, their key task has been to keep tabs on one another. Like the Ba'athist regimes in Iraq and Syria, Egypt's leaders have tried to secure their rule by having several security agencies report to them. Nasr was chief of the General Intelligence Service. Sharaf, his rival, was head of the president's own intelligence service, the Presidential Bureau of Information. Nasser and Sharaf made common cause in 1967 to overthrow their respective rivals—Field Marshal Abdel Hakim Amer, the chief of staff of Egypt's army, and Salah Nasr. Amer was either murdered or committed suicide, preferring suicide to trial and execution. Nasr was imprisoned.[25] Under President Sadat, Egypt's General Intelligence Service gravitated toward cooperation with the CIA as part of Sadat's reorientation of Egyptian policy regarding the Middle East and the superpowers. Sadat's assassination at the hands of Islamists in 1981 naturally increased the regime's fear of Islamism. The last Egyptian intelligence chief Rezk examines, Omar Suleiman, the director of GIS from 1993 to 2011, turned the service into a key element in the CIA's global anti-Islamist intelligence alliance. Such was the regime's dependence on the United States that his closeness to the CIA much increased Suleiman's influence. President Mubarak's confidence in him enabled Suleiman to become an important actor in foreign policy, particularly in connection with Israeli-Palestinian relations.[26] However important he may have been, he, like the other intelligence leaders studied in this book, was merely an agent of his government, and as an agent, he took on the government's character.

This book, like the first volume of *Spy Chiefs*, has presented intelligence chiefs as leaders of organizations whose success needs to be measured according to their ability to improve their organizations' performance. They are chief executive officers who, like business leaders, have the job of directing organizations, motivating subordinates, and solving problems. However, there are key differences between the two types of leader, all of which cause intelligence chiefs to identify very closely with the regime they serve and to seek a close relationship with their political masters. All the men analyzed in this book did so. In the first place, an intelligence chief has less autonomy than the business leader: policy makers determine the mission of the intelligence or security agency. Success is measured not by profit but by the assistance the information obtained by the agency gives to policy making. The second difference is that the intelligence chief contends with enemies, not mere competitors; failure on the part of his or her agency may lead to severe harm being caused to the state or regime. Third, the organization's successes have to be kept secret and so cannot be used to motivate subordinates or to influence the organization's culture. Consequently, an intelligence agency's esprit de corps depends heavily on the idea of public service and thus on patriotism. Its officers are inspired by carefully cultivated legends surrounding *past* leaders, spies, and successes. The purpose of these legends is to make them obedient, loyal, and effective in their work. All intelligence and security agencies discussed in this book were core parts of the governments they served; their officers, including their leaders, were dedicated agents of government—"government men."

Notes

1. Georg Herbstritt, *Bundesbürger im Dienst der DDR-Spionage: Eine analytische Studie* [Citizens of the Federal Republic in the service of GDR espionage: An analytical study] (Göttingen: Vandenhoeck and Ruprecht, 2007), 84; and Jens Gieseke, *Der Mielke-Konzern: Die Geschichte der Stasi, 1945–1990* [The Mielke business: The history of the Stasi, 1945–1990] (Munich: Deutsche Verlags-Anstalt, 2006), 213–32.

2. Paul Maddrell, "Cooperation between the HVA and the KGB, 1951–1989," in *Bulletin of German Historical Institute*, suppl. 9 (2014): *The Stasi at Home and Abroad: Domestic Order and Foreign Intelligence*, ed. Uwe Spiekermann, 182–83; and Peter Siebenmorgen, *"Staatssicherheit" der DDR. Der Westen im Fadenkreuz der Stasi* ["State Security" of the GDR: The West in the Stasi's sights] (Bonn: Bouvier Verlag, 1993), 130–31.

3. Interview with Klaus Eichner, formerly of the HVA's Department IX/C, April 16, 2003.

4. Markus Wolf, *Man without a Face* (London: Jonathan Cape, 1997), 131, 185, 187, 207.

5. Gabriele Gast, *Kundschafterin des Friedens: 17 Jahre Topspionin der DDR beim BND* [A scout for peace: 17 years as a top GDR spy in the BND] (Frankfurt/Main: Eichborn, 1999), 188–213.

6. Christopher Andrew and Vasili Mitrokhin, *The Mitrokhin Archive: The KGB in Europe and the West* (London: Allen Lane / Penguin Press, 1999), 581–88.

7. Gast, *Kundschafterin des Friedens*, 65–66, 75–76.

8. Markus Wolf, *Spionagechef im geheimen Krieg: Erinnerungen* [Spy chief in the secret war: Memoirs] (Munich: List Verlag, 1997), 425–26; and Gast, *Kundschafterin des Friedens*, 292–95.

9. See Paul Maddrell, "The Economic Dimension of Cold War Intelligence-Gathering: The West's Spies in the GDR's Economy," *Journal of Cold War Studies* 15, no. 3 (2013): 76–107.

10. Werner Großmann, *Bonn im Blick: Die DDR-Aufklärung aus der Sicht ihres letzten Chefs* [Bonn in view: The GDR Foreign Intelligence Service from the perspective of its last head] (Berlin: Das Neue Berlin, 2001), 117–18.

11. Wolf, *Man without a Face*, 317.

12. See David Childs and Richard Popplewell, *The Stasi: The East German Intelligence and Security Service* (London: Macmillan, 1996), 121–22.

13. Wolf, *Spionagechef im geheimen Krieg*, 423–39; Gast, *Kundschafterin des Friedens*, 296–97; and Werner Großmann, interview with the author, August 6, 2007.

14. Markus Wolf, *In Eigenem Auftrag*, 73–74.

15. Reinhold Andert and Wolfgang Herzberg, *Der Sturz: Erich Honecker im Kreuzverhör* [The fall: Erich Honecker cross-examined] (Berlin: Aufbau-Verlag, 1990), 376.

16. On Communist propaganda directed against Gehlen and his organization, see Paul Maddrell, "What We Have Discovered about the Cold War Is What We Already Knew: Julius Mader and the Western Secret Services during the Cold War," *Cold War History* 5, no. 2 (2005): 235–58.

17. Dieter Krüger, "Reinhard Gehlen (1902–1979). Der BND-Chef als Schattenmann der Ära Adenauer," in *Konspiration als Beruf: Deutsche Geheimdienstchefs im Kalten Krieg* [Secrecy as an occupation: German secret service chiefs in the Cold War], ed. Dieter Krüger and Armin Wagner (Berlin: Christoph Links, 2003), 333. In the original German quote, Krüger states *"weniger Bilanz als Rechtfertigung seines Lebenswerkes."*

18. Reinhard Gehlen, *Der Dienst. Erinnerungen, 1942–1971* [The service: Memoirs, 1942–1971] (Mainz: von Hase and Koehler, 1971).

19. Krüger, "Reinhard Gehlen (1902–1979)," 218–36.

20. Paul Maddrell, *Spying on Science: Western Intelligence in Divided Germany, 1945–1961* (Oxford, UK: Oxford University Press, 2006), 260–62.

21. H. R. Trevor-Roper, introduction to Heinz Höhne and Hermann Zolling, *Network: The Truth about General Gehlen and His Spy Ring* (London: Secker and Warburg, 1972), xv.

22. Quoted in Owen L. Sirrs, *A History of the Egyptian Intelligence Service: A History of the Mukhabarat, 1910–2009* (Abingdon: Routledge, 2010), 63.

23. Ibid., 30–34, 44.

24. Ibid., 51, 64, 88–93.

25. Ibid., 105–6.

26. Ibid., 169–71, 173–76, 183–86.

CONTRIBUTORS

Sir Richard Dearlove, KCMG, OBE served as chief (known as "C") of the British Secret Intelligence Service (SIS) from August 1999 until his retirement in July 2004. For the preceding five years he was director of operations, and from 1998 he was assistant chief. As director of finance, administration, and personnel he also oversaw the move of SIS into its headquarters building at Vauxhall Cross in 1994. He is a career intelligence officer of thirty-eight years' standing and has served in Nairobi, Prague, Paris, Geneva, and Washington as well as in a number of key London-based posts.

Emrah Safa Gürkan is currently working at Istanbul 29 Mayis University. He is a historian of the early modern Mediterranean, focusing on the Ottoman Empire. His research interests include piracy, espionage, conversion, vernacular diplomacy, slavery, frontiers, political factions, and power-broking. He completed his PhD thesis, titled "Espionage in the 16th Century Mediterranean: Secret Diplomacy, Mediterranean Go-betweens and the Ottoman-Habsburg Rivalry," in 2012 at Georgetown University. In addition to a monograph in Turkish, titled *Sultan'ın Casusları: 16. Yüzyılda İstihbarat, Sabotaj ve Rüşvet Ağları*, he has published several articles in journals such as the *Journal of Early Modern History*, the *Turkish Historical Review*, the *Journal of Ottoman History*, and *Acta Orientalia Scientiarum Hungaricum*; he has also published chapters in edited books.

The late **Chikara Hashimoto** was, at the time of his untimely death in September 2016 at the age of forty, an assistant professor of international relations at the University of Sharjah in the United Arab Emirates and assistant editor of the journal *Intelligence and National Security*. He took BSc, MSc, and PhD degrees at Aberystwyth University, United Kingdom; in 2014 his PhD thesis won the Leigh Douglas Memorial Prize of the British Society for Middle Eastern Studies. His PhD research led to his book *The Twilight of the British Empire: British Intelligence and Counter-Subversion in the Middle East,*

1948–1963, which was published by Edinburgh University Press in 2017. He published articles in English in the *International History Review, Intelligence and National Security*, and *Middle Eastern Studies*. He also published many articles in Japanese in *Japan Military Review* and the journal of *The Japan Society for Strategic Studies*.

Bodo V. Hechelhammer is chief historian of the German Federal Intelligence Service (BND). He completed his PhD thesis in 2000 and worked thereafter as a research assistant at the Technical University, Darmstadt. Since 2002 he has worked for the BND, and in 2010 he became head of the research group responsible for the history of the service. He has also been a doctoral research fellow of the graduate college Mittelalterliche und Neuzeitliche Staatlichkeit at the Justus Liebig University, Gießen. Intelligence history is his main research interest. In addition to publications of his own, he is also chief editor of the BND publication *Mitteilungen der Forschungs- und Arbeitsgruppe Geschichte des BND*. He is currently working on a biography of the traitor Heinz Felfe.

Ioanna Iordanou is a senior lecturer in human resources management at Oxford Brookes University, United Kingdom, and an associate fellow of the Centre for the Study of the Renaissance, Warwick University, United Kingdom. She has published her research in the *Economic History Review* and *Intelligence and National Security*. She is the coeditor of the two volumes of *Spy Chiefs* (Georgetown University Press, 2017) and the author of the forthcoming monograph *Venice's Secret Service: Intelligence Organisation in the Renaissance* (to be published by Oxford University Press in 2018).

Iain Lauchlan is a senior lecturer in modern history at the University of Edinburgh, United Kingdom. He is the author of *Russian Hide-and-Seek: The Tsarist Secret Police in St. Petersburg* (Helsinki: SKS, 2002) and numerous journal articles on the tsarist and Soviet security services. He is currently working on a biography of Feliks Dzerzhinsky.

Kristie Macrakis is a professor in the School of History and Sociology at Georgia Tech, Atlanta, Georgia. She is the author or editor of five books, including *Seduced by Secrets: Inside the Stasi's Spy Tech World* (New York: Cambridge University Press, 2008); *Prisoners, Lovers and Spies: The Story of Invisible Ink from Herodotus to Al-Qaeda* (New Haven: Yale University Press, 2014); and *East German Foreign Intelligence: Myth, Reality and Controversy* (London: Routledge, 2009). Her books have been translated into German, Italian, Czech, Slovak, Estonian, and Chinese. See www.kristiemacrakis.com.

Paul Maddrell is a lecturer in modern German history at Loughborough University, United Kingdom. He is a fellow of the United Kingdom's Royal Historical Society and of the Higher Education Academy and a member of the editorial board of the *International Journal of Intelligence and CounterIntelligence*. His principal publications are his single-authored monograph *Spying on Science: Western Intelligence in Divided Germany, 1945–1961* (Oxford University Press, 2006) and his edited book *The Image of the Enemy: Intelligence Analysis of Adversaries since 1945* (Georgetown University Press, 2015). He has also published many journal articles and book chapters on the history of intelligence, Germany, and the Cold War. His research has been funded by, among other bodies, the United Kingdom's Arts and Humanities Research Council, the British Academy, and the German Academic Exchange Service.

Paul M. McGarr is an assistant professor in US foreign policy at the University of Nottingham. He is the author of *The Cold War in South Asia: Britain, the United States and the Indian Subcontinent, 1945–1965* (Cambridge University Press, 2013). He has published on Anglo-American relations with postindependence South Asia in *Diplomatic History*, the *International History Review*, *Modern Asian Studies*, *Diplomacy & Statecraft*, the *Journal of Imperial and Commonwealth History*, and *History*. His research has been funded by the Arts and Humanities Research Council; the Mellon Foundation; the Rothermere American Institute, Oxford University; the British Library's Eccles Centre for American Studies; the John F. Kennedy Presidential Library, Boston; and the Centre for Policy Studies, New Delhi. He is currently completing a second monograph for Cambridge University Press that examines connections between US intelligence operations and American diplomacy in South Asia, a nexus of the ongoing "war on terror."

Dina Rezk is a lecturer in Middle Eastern History at the University of Reading. She received her PhD from Cambridge University in 2013 and subsequently spent two years at the Politics and International Studies Department of Warwick University as a Teaching Fellow in Intelligence and Security. Her monograph *Western Intelligence and the Arab World: Analysing the Middle East* will be published in 2017. She is currently working on a major collaborative project, funded by the United Kingdom's Arts and Humanities Research Council, exploring popular culture and politics in Egypt since the overthrow of President Hosni Mubarak in 2011.

INDEX